PHENOMENOLOGY AND SOCIAL REALITY

ALFRED SCHUTZ (1899-1959)

PHENOMENOLOGY AND SOCIAL REALITY

Essays in Memory of Alfred Schutz

Edited by

MAURICE NATANSON

MARTINUS NIJHOFF / THE HAGUE / 1970

TABLE OF CONTENTS

ACKNOWLEDGMENTS

A number of people have helped in various ways in bringing this volume to appropriate completion. Valuable suggestions and advice have come from many of the contributors. In addition, I wish to thank Drs. Carl Mayer, Herbert Spiegelberg, and Helmut Wagner for bibliographical information. I am especially grateful to Mrs. Ilse Schutz for biographical and bibliographical material and for the photograph which appears as the frontispiece. Other assistance came from Mrs. Joan Hodgson of the Library of the University of California at Santa Cruz and Mrs. Phyllis Halpin and Mrs. Charlotte Cassidy of the Cowell College Steno Pool at UCSC. Lois Natanson has helped me solve some problems of language and style. Dr. H. J. H. Hartgerink of Martinus Nijhoff has been patient and understanding in his treatment of this work.

The paper by Adolph Lowe is reprinted with the permission of Prentice-Hall, Inc., and the paper by Maurice Natanson is reprinted with the permission of *Social Research*.

It was my hope that Dr. Albert Salomon would be part of this venture, but he died before my letter of invitation reached him. I would like, however, to record his name here. And, alas, Dr. Philip Merlan did not live to see the publication of his essay.

The kindness and cooperation of colleagues, friends, and assistants have enhanced this tribute to Alfred Schutz, but responsibility for the volume rests solely with the editor.

INTRODUCTION

Alfred Schutz was born in Vienna on April 13, 1899, and died in New York City on May 20, 1959. The year 1969, then, marks the seventieth anniversary of his birth and the tenth year of his death. The essays which follow are offered not only as a tribute to an irreplaceable friend, colleague, and teacher, but as evidence of the contributors' conviction of the eminence of his work. No special pleading is needed here to support that claim, for it is widely acknowledged that his ideas have had a significant impact on present-day philosophy and phenomenology of the social sciences. In place of either argument or evaluation, I choose to restrict myself to some biographical information and a fragmentary memoir.*

The only child of Johanna and Otto Schutz (an executive in a private bank in Vienna), Alfred attended the Esterhazy Gymnasium in Vienna, an academic high school whose curriculum included eight years of Latin and Greek. He graduated at seventeen – in time to spend one year of service in the Austrian army in the First World War. For bravery at the front on the battlefield in Italy, he was decorated by his country. After the war ended, he entered the University of Vienna, completing a four year curriculum in only two and one half years and receiving his doctorate in Law. Upon obtaining his degree, he became secretary to an association of banks in Vienna. After a few years, he joined a private banking firm in Vienna with international interests. His work involved legal contracts, agreements, and tax matters. In 1938, the Nazi occupation of Austria compelled Schutz and his wife and two children to emigrate. After a stay in Paris, they came to New York City in 1939 and settled there. From 1943 on, he taught at the Graduate Faculty of the New School for Social Research as a lecturer and professor of philosophy and sociology, offering such courses as the Methodology of the Social Sciences, Theory of Social Role, Sociology of Lan-

* This is not intended to be a history of Schutz's career. For further information see Professor Van Breda's Preface to the first volume of Schutz's Collected Papers.

guage, and Self and Society. For most of his life, Schutz continued to work full time as – in his own words – a businessman. His philosophical-academic career was an additional labor, carried on at the expense of an enormous and precious effort. Husserl once called him "a banker by day and a phenomenologist by night." The union of the businessman and the philosopher seemed to me not only understandable but even necessary – as remarkable yet as natural as the combination of insurance and poetry in the life of Wallace Stevens. That Schutz chose to be a teacher as well, however, was a supreme and priceless gift.

Now I turn to the memoir, recognizing how paradoxical it is to ask a reader who did not know Schutz to remember him with me. Still, I insist on addressing those who never knew him. Those who did have no need of this report. The paradox is that to grasp the essential meaning of the description you need to have known the man, at least to have had some direct impression of him. Bergson made the point when he wrote of the artist who is passing through Paris and who makes a series of sketches:

> Now beneath all the sketches he has made at Paris the visitor will probably by way of memento, write the word "Paris". And as he has really seen Paris, he will be able, with the help of the original intuition he had of the whole, to place his sketches therein, and so join them together. But there is no way of performing the inverse operation; it is impossible, even with an infinite number of accurate sketches, and even with the word "Paris" which indicates that they must be combined together, to get back to an intuition that one has never had, and to give oneself an impression of what Paris is like if one has never seen it.

Of course, the reader can "typify" the description given. He can appreciate the qualities of what some might call Schutz's "old world charm" or "Viennese manner." Yet such characterizations tend to avoid as well as obscure the truth. In trying to suggest the semblance of a fugitive intuition, I prefer to approach the past more obliquely, starting with some physical description.

Schutz was slight. His face was profoundly lined, and although his eyes were penetrating and searching, his gaze was never demeaning or scathing. The expression was intense without any sense of strain. It was the face of a man capable of extraordinary discernment. The first time he looked at me, I thought that the ventricles of my brain were exposed. Yet his appraisal was reassuring, not surgical. He spoke of "common work," and I left him challenged to intellectual candor and my best effort. In class, Schutz demanded a great deal of himself. His courses were thoroughly prepared, and he was painstaking in developing a new course (for example, he spent years collecting and organizing material in preparation for a course on the sociology of invention and technical progress). Notes for his classes filled large loose-leaf books. While lecturing, he would turn their pages with long-fingered hands – hands which were often in movement, playing with a cigarette lighter as he talked or holding a cigarette in a way which could be fully described and accounted for only by one who had a subtle grasp of the last one hundred years of European civilization. Schutz was a teacher by instinct – the only dramatic and unrehearsable way. The warmth and wit which gave ballast to his lectures and discussions were the joy of those he taught. Very often after class, he would go to a cafetaria or coffee house with a band of students interested in continuing the analysis, pursuing other questions, or just delighting in a man whose manifold concerns included them as it did so many others and so many realms: the worlds of children and music, philosophy and social science, business and poetry.

Presupposed in this souvenir is a philosophical conversation which must remain unstated and unexamined. Yet looking back eighteen years to the time I first met him, I find it difficult to separate in Schutz the philosopher and the person. In my copy of his *Der sinnhafte Aufbau der sozialen Welt*, he inscribed a favorite quotation from Hume: "Be a philosopher; but amid all your philosophy, be still a man." Alfred Schutz was both.

M. N.

Santa Cruz, California
1969

VALUES AND THE SCOPE OF SCIENTIFIC INQUIRY

by

MARVIN FARBER

> *"One of our chief problems will be to find out how it is possible that the life-world of all of us can be made an object of theoretical contemplation and that the outcome of this contemplation can be used within the world of working."* – Alfred Schutz [*]

I. THE QUESTION OF PHILOSOPHY AS A SCIENCE

Whether philosophy may be regarded as a science is still a disputed question. The historical functions of philosophy have been diversified, with religious, political, socioeconomic, and individual motives playing a role, in addition to the influence of the sciences upon philosophic thought. The view that philosophy is the most fundamental and rigorous science has coexisted with attempts to subordinate it to institutions representing vested interests.

Early in the modern period philosophy was conceived by the great rationalists as a universal deductive structure, in keeping with the growth of mathematics and physical science. This conception could only remain an unfulfilled ideal program which was to become more meaningful in later centuries. The speculative excesses of philosophy in the recent past, especially after Kant, at times brought philosophy into disrepute among scientists. Philosophers have often been on the side of scientists in the prolonged warfare between religion and science; but it is also true that philosophers have made adjustment to religious interests, and have advanced elaborate theories to reconcile the conflicting views. This is conspicuously seen in the treatment of values, supposedly excluded from the domain of scientific inquiry. They have been popularly derived from the religious traditions, and supported by the dominant interests of the social system. It is not always easy to discover the nature of the adjustment made by philosophers, who may become in effect supporters or apologists for the existing order of society. Modes of adjustment are illustrated, historically and in the present, by dualistic philosophers (Descartes, Kant, Spencer), authoritarianism (the medieval tradition, and politically derived forms), and various types of

[*] Alfred Schutz, *Collected Papers*, Vol. I, *The Problem of Social Reality*, ed. by Maurice Natanson, The Hague, Martinus Nijhoff, 1962.

fideism (as illustrated by James and the "will to believe"). Philosophical idealism and subjectivism in its various forms have frequently been prime modes of accommodation. This may even be said to be the case if a writer is not adequately aware of his motivation, which often happens. Thus the feeling of hostility toward a science-oriented philosophy, which is so prevalent in many parts of the world of philosophy, usually has strands of connection with social and religious interests.

Even the ideal of portraying philosophy as a science must be considered carefully. For it may combine rigor in a specialized region of questions with renunciation of the existing social world. Preoccupation with subjective processes and essential structures may readily go along with neglect of the pressing problems of human existence. A critical and well-balanced conception of the methods of inquiry can help to avoid such one-sidedness. Narrowness must be avoided in the conception of science; for scientific knowledge ranges all the way from descriptive findings in natural experience to formal and purely reflective results of inquiry. The domain of science is enlarged, not restricted, by additions to the methods of establishing knowledge. No one limited model should be allowed to be dominant, in view of the nature of experience and of man as a finite, fallible being. Although these considerations also apply to ontology and the theory of knowledge, it is in the philosophy of human values that they come into bold relief.

II. ON SCIENCE AND VALUES

Let us now turn to the much discussed question of the relationship of science and values, in order to bring to the fore the issue of the scope of scientific inquiry. Much has been written and said about the theme of science and values by philosophers seeking to determine limits to scientific inquiry, and to assign values to another region.

The interest in restricting the scope of scientific inquiry seemed to gain support from the excesses and abuses to which technological advances were subjected. Uppermost in the minds of many were the facts of the destructive powers unleashed by scientific inquiry. The use of scientific devices in the gas chambers of the Third Reich could only add notoriously to the case for linking science with human values. For it seemed evident that a "value-free" conception of science, allowing free play to inquiry, was bound to incur dangerous consequences. Everything depends, however, upon the conception of values that is introduced. It would hardly be helpful to state that it must be values of the right kind. For the late dictator of Italy, to live dangerously was to pursue the right course; and the ethical ideas of the late *Fuehrer* implied and condoned genocide. They were not scientifically instated or justified ideals, and they could not be; for the principle of objective science, with unlimited validity for all thinking beings, was repudiated in the interest of a national (or "political") conception of science.

One need not go to such extremes for illustrations, although it is precisely such extremes that most clearly call attention to what is at issue. If value principles are brought in from the outside – whether that be from one of the various cultural traditions, or from the dominant preferences of the existing social system – science will be guided, used, and judged in the light of those principles. Science in that case is the name for an organization of knowledge and techniques, which may be judged to be good and useful, or bad and useless – from the point of view that is imposed or accepted. But the question of the justification of the point of view must be answered, unless reason is renounced.

If it can be said that science in its long history has carried on an offensive against a precarious cosmos, and a difficult human world, it can also be said that there was a never-absent counteroffensive against science. This has taken the form of an attack, or criticism, of the philosophy inspired by the scientific advances of a given period. Efforts were made repeatedly and in different ways to "contain" the sciences, to delimit their scope, so that long-cherished ideals and values would not be affected by disillusioning progress. Frequently such efforts were made by philosophers. Sometimes the efforts were made covertly and were not recognized as such. That has recently been the case with existentialist or subjectivist writers. According to one of the favored lines of criticism, a limited model or conception of science cannot be extended to entire regions of experience. The historical background of this argument goes back to Descartes: the physical universe was amenable to mathematical treatment and causal determination; but the realm of mind, or inner experience, was free. The assumptions concerning the physical and the mental realms predetermined the outcome.

Kant circumscribed the area of scientific thought by means of a profound dualism, which allowed for an unknowable realm. But he was careful to allow science unlimited scope so far as space and time are concerned. Nevertheless, the region accessible to the human knower was compared to an island surrounded by an inaccessible sea – which could not even be identified as a sea. Spencer's dualism, a century later in the evolutionary period, although it had a similar outcome, was more confused, especially when he sought to justify his conception of an unknowable realm. The restriction of science to the knowable was softened by the evolutionist

Thomas Huxley, who was impressed by the need for caution in making claims for scientific knowledge as such. In his view the "act of faith" which leads us to take the experience of the past as a guide for the present and future was justified by results. The question of the validity and cogency of scientific prediction was involved.

It was also urged repeatedly – and never more vociferously than in the American counteroffensive against evolutionism and naturalism – that whole regions of questions were not open to scientific inquiry, at least as represented by the science of the time. The question of the scope of science and scientific inquiry is raised therewith. Is science to be regarded as a limited, circumscribed area of human interest; or is it unlimited, and co-extensive with all inquiry concerned with the answering of questions or the solving of problems? If science is regarded as limited in its scope, values can be introduced from another source, with conflicts of values the frequent outcome. But if the scope of scientific inquiry is held to be unlimited, all questions that are meaningful in terms of human experience are viewed as belonging to special systems of knowledge, subject to the requirements of the logic of science. There are to be sure incomplete systems. In fact, most systems of knowledge are unavoidably incomplete, but may nevertheless be as valuable as they may be said to be scientific. Their incompleteness and openness act as a spur to the activity of inquiry. At times a scientific investigator may prefer to work in a more restricted or definite area, as though to have respite from the endless complexity of an "open" system.

The point is, that every meaningful question must be assignable to a logically organized system of knowledge. Some systems are in an early stage of organization, and others are relatively advanced. New systems are always being developed. It is also true that apparently disparate systems are found to be related, and may be united into one system.

If the term science were used narrowly, the never-ending series of nascent and developing systems would not be said to be scientific throughout, and some systems would be regarded as nonscientific. But it is not necessary to construe science narrowly. In its broadest meaning, all logically organized and validly obtained knowledge may be said to be scientific, and the phrase "scientific inquiry" applies to all logically acceptable procedures, or ways of answering questions and solving problems. The burden is then placed upon the conception of what is logical – and, fortunately, there is sufficient lore and argument under that heading to bear the burden well. Logic must be broadly conceived as a universal methodology, or, as Dewey expressed it, as inquiry concerning inquiry. Never is a limit to be set to inquiry, or to the modes of inquiry. If questions are not to be restricted, or to be predicted and frozen into permanent molds, there will always be an endless set of questions and problems, making necessary, with the progress of knowledge, the organization of ever new systems and new procedures. That happens in the development of formal, mathematical sciences, as well as in the sciences dealing with the physical and cultural world. This pluralistic view is required by the nature of things, by the complexity of the world, and because of man's limited place in the world.

In his status as a knowing being, man had to become a problem-solver in order to sustain and advance himself in the world. Science as the most carefully controlled knowledge developed early in response to practical motivation. Hence there is always a pragmatic aspect of science, which is judged by its results, by its successes, and by its satisfaction of human needs and interests. To say that science is intrinsically valuable as a pursuit would not add anything to the conception of the valuable as that which satisfies human needs or interests, the conception that is being favored here. One could indeed use other definitions. But this conception appears to be especially useful for many questions about human activities; and it has been proved to be fruitful. "Valuable" means, then, "valuable" with respect to human interests. What is called an intrinsic value is really an abbreviated mode of expression, meaning that a complex value-situation has been compressed into a limiting case.

Thus, it is said that it is intrinsically valuable to understand a mathematical proof, or a logical demonstration of any kind. That understanding is intrinsically valuable as such may be taken to mean that there is an interest in understanding, and that the satisfaction of that interest is good or valuable. It would follow that the answer to any question, regardless of practical utility, would be a value – even the answer to an admittedly personal question with no apparent interest for others; thus a scholar may succeed in establishing results that interest no one except himself. But in spite of such extreme cases freedom of inquiry may not be restricted to what is known to be practical – for practical as well as purely intellectual reasons. For it cannot be decided with finality, whether a seemingly nonpractical study will never have an application to reality in the future. Apart from the possible practical value for human beings, one must consider the nature of needs and interests, which include an interest in understanding in abstract, imaginative, and theoretical fields. The overzealous confidence of the nineteenth-century prophet of a cult of science, Auguste Comte, remains a warning. Mill's indignant rejection of Comte's proposal to eliminate all species of animals and plants not useful to man did not go far enough; for usefulness to man is not the final justification for a right to exist. Once man has safeguarded himself against threats to his own welfare, he can afford to be magnanimous toward other forms of existence, plant and animal. But the human organism is no more central in his cosmic status than thought in any form can be really central for ontology.

The dangers resulting from attempts to control scientific inquiry in some countries is well known. It can be said that the interests of society are best served by an open program for research of all kinds. That does not in the least preclude sufficient attention to immediate, concrete problems. It can be said in this case that it is more profoundly practical to set considerations of practice aside. What is involved is the contrast between a broad and a narrow conception of practice. In the larger sense of the term, all intellectual activities are also practical, for they are instances of the process of living experience. Theory is in short a select and often an excellent mode of practice.

III. THE HUMAN SUBJECT

Some recent philosophical writers have sought to reestablish man "existentially" as the fulcrum if not the fountainhead of inquiry, both philosophical and scientific. The so-called human subject (a name for man as a knower and inquirer, and also as a moral agent) has been given special ontological standing, as an omnipresent factor in experience and knowing. The term ontological may be used in an acceptable sense, meaningful in terms of actual experience. But it has also been misused for purposes other than those of science or a logical philosophy, to refer to something more fundamental than anything controlled inquiry could establish. In its good sense, it refers to basic truths about existence, always considered in connection with the facts established by the sciences. The human subject, meaning the human being as a knower and as an active being, is surely always involved in experience. It could not be otherwise. But the world and a culture system are also involved. In the great tradition of philosophy, the human subject was at times out of place, and the true place of man in the cosmos was forgotten, if it was ever known. To look to the nature and the structure of the mind for clues to the nature of existence may be to forget the simple fact that minds do not occur without human beings, and that human beings are relatively recent emergents in an indefinitely long process of natural development. Some writers have regarded the finitude of man, and his limited access to an infinite world, as a predicament. It is an eternal predicament, so far as man is concerned, for a finite knower cannot hope to encompass the whole of an infinite field for inquiry – whether it be infinite in temporal and spatial expansiveness, or in complexity; and any finite situation is endlessly analyzable. But it is also an opportunity, for there are no limits that can be set beyond which human thought could not penetrate. There is no assignable limit to human ingenuity, as seen in experimental devices, and in the use of fictions and patterns of explanation. There are endless difficulties, but not fateful, insuperable obstacles of the kind some philosophers have supposed.

On the other hand, the factor of infinite complexity can be overdrawn. That nature, and anything in nature, are always capable of further analysis does not mean that decisive answers to questions cannot be given. The process of the descriptive analysis of all circumstances bearing upon a steel-workers' strike, for example, might well go on endlessly. But it proves to be possible to determine the effective causes resulting in social conflict. The question of the cause or causes of such events can be answered with practical success; and that is the important point. If we had to wait for the conclusion of an endless process of inquiry to meet such problems, the strike in question, our culture system, and the earth itself might well yield their transient existence to other stages of the cosmic process. In short, the insight into the infinite complexity of reality should not interfere with one's grasp of questions and problems that can be handled from the human perspective.

Despite the acknowledgment of the potential powers of reason, which has been indicated, it must be conceded that there are innumerable questions never to be answered. There are surely quantitative limits for human inquiry. Apart from the infinite horizons of time, space, and complexity, there are more questions than we are likely to be aware of within the immediate field of experience that are likely to remain unanswered – and many of them will leave us undisturbed. It seems that only when a cherished hope is involved, the failure to supply an answer to a question becomes intolerable (as seen in the argument about the alleged necessity of assuming a first cause). In practice, there are always open questions. Probably we shall never know much more about Arnold of Brescia, the follower of Abelard and one of the martyrs to the cause of reason. Many questions about recent events are sure to remain unanswered as well – say concerning the origins of the Russian revolution, and many other events on the earth, within the earth, and beyond this planet.

Only a being comprising all reality would have no unanswered questions. To be sure, such a being would have no questions at all. The entire scientific and philosophical enterprise is for limited beings. From the finitude of the human knower there follows the fallibility on principle of all his devices.

No statement can be asserted to hold unconditionally, once and for all time. Every statement admitted to the body of scientific knowledge in any realm – real, formal, or purely subjective – has at most tentative standing. It is forever subject to possible future modification or cancellation.

This is not to cast a shadow over the worth of scientific knowledge, including philosophical knowledge. It is merely to warn against the danger of dogmatism, and to emphasize the dependence upon evidence for all claims to knowledge. The criticism exemplified in all logically controlled inquiry must be carried over to the appraisal of knowledge claims as such, to the examination of the conditions affecting our knowledge of the future, as well as the present or the past. That includes the question of the continued validity of a given statement. The question is not whether a given statement S (say a geometrical theorem, or a chemical equation, or a statement about the cause or causes of a given disease, or a given war) will stand the test of time. It is rather whether the statement will continue to be borne out by the relevant facts. Our confidence is understandably greatest in the area of formal thought, and it is most qualified in the area of human conflicts, where self-interest and partisanship introduce further obstacles to inquiry.

The human subject so-called (or man the inquirer) is not a being set apart from and exempt from inquiry. Man too is a subject for investigation; and his problems fall within the scope of scientific inquiry. Even the much-talked-of subjective realm of "private" experience must be open to rigorous methods of inquiry. Whether such methods are called scientific is a minor question, so long as they are regarded as logical procedures, subject to the principles of methodology. It would however be desirable usage to call all such procedures scientific in the larger sense of that term.

Does this point of view sacrifice anything of the dignity of man; or does it fail to do justice to the nature of man and his knowing? That would not be the case, for there is no implied restriction as to methods of inquiry; and there is no suggestion of a restricted type of scientific explanation, whether mechanistic or organic, for example. All methods and devices that can lead to the solution of problems are to be admitted, so long as they are logically acceptable. Thus there will be no place for mysterious or obscure processes purporting to probe beyond the limits of possible experience. The criticism of narrow conceptions of scientific inquiry (e.g., whether mechanistic or behavioristic) may continue, but that will be done in the light of a more complete conception of method. Narrow, inadequate conceptions of scientific inquiry are corrected by means of broader and more adequate conceptions.

But what about the question of the ethical dignity of the human subject, it has been asked by writers reluctant to accept so broad a conception of science. Man is regarded as being somehow incommensurable with the rest of existence, as belonging to another order of reality. Hence his values appear to be something *sui generis*, as some kind of intrusion into the course of natural existence from another source. Various philosophical expressions and arguments have been advanced to support this view. The resulting turgid atmosphere permits little light to enter. The unwary reader or listener is treated to a show of words involving a virtual nest of unclarified assumptions. Science is supposedly delimited in the course of the barrage; and insight into something inexpressibly deeper is the presumed reward. There is talk of subjective (inner) freedom, which would mean deliverance from the inexorable limits and conditions of nature; and there is talk of transcendence beyond nature, which might mean a locus for the fulfillment of ultimate human aspirations, the definition of which varies with different persons. As a rule, such aspirations require more than can be assured by scientific knowledge and ordinary experience, and hence the talk of transcendence.

IV. ETHICS AND THE PRIMACY OF FACTS

It is a long time since the attempt was first made to divide man up among the various sciences. In the recent past, the soul, the mind, the will, and purpose were the objects of critical scrutiny. The denial of the existence of consciousness by William James was a kind of concluding phase of a long process of reduction and elimination of transnatural entities and structures. There was a danger of oversimplification, especially at the hands of writers who generalized hastily from the scientific literature. This danger was in part met by philosophers who knew how to learn from the findings of science. Thus a more balanced and complete view of man could result. It is important to do full justice to the complications introduced by experience and knowing, to the idealizations and constructive activities of thought processes.

So far as human values were concerned, nothing was lost by the elaborate process of so-called naturalistic "reduction." Value, defined in terms of the fulfillment of human interests, is descriptively founded in the biological and cultural interests of individuals and groups of people. A large amount of scientific knowledge is implied by this view, with many special sciences providing relevant knowledge. The construction of a theory of values on that basis is an important function of philosophy. The task is synthetic to begin with, in that numerous facts must be organized with respect to questions concerning values and lines of conduct; and it is logical, in that basic definitions and premises must be clearly formulated, and examined for their soundness and adequacy. Such a logical formulation of a system of ethical knowledge may be termed scientific, in accordance with the broad conception of science as logically organized knowledge. It shares features of formal science as well as empirical science. Its questions are distinctive, and involve the formulation of norms, of standards and goals of conduct. Norms must be transformed into factual or theoretical propositions, if they are to be acceptable.[1] They must be justified by their consequences for human life, ultimately in terms of real desires and interests. There is a final element of preference, and that depends upon the thinking and wishing of the majority of the people. It is possible to demonstrate to what extent values may be achieved, if a given program is carried through. That may be an objective demonstration, as valid as any other scientific demonstration. But in the field of values, the conscious decision of a sufficiently large number is necessary for the realization of a program. There are degrees of realization, and the maximum remains an ideal. The element of a conscious decision of preference, or of commitment, is a point at which ethics differs from other types of science. It is nevertheless still a science; and it will be borne in mind that the other sciences also differ from one another in type, structure, or principle.

The question of the relationship of ethics to the factual sciences was obscured by much discussion of the possibility (or impossibility) of deriving normative from descriptive statements of fact (or deriving what ought to be from what is the case). It seemed evident that there was an unbridgeable gap between the order of facts ("the is") and the order of what should be, the normative order ("the ought"). How then could there be a science of values? If these two realms of discourse are defined in such a way that the one may never be derived from the other, the issue is predetermined – assumptively, it must be noted. Similarly, an "ought" could be defined as rooted in a transcendent realm, or as ordained by some transcendent source. There is nothing to prevent such conceptions. In each case of that kind, it would clearly be impossible to derive statements of what should be (in the sense in question) from statements of fact. What occurs, however, is merely an artificially induced obstacle, which can be removed by the construction of a value philosophy within the descriptive field of human existence.

---

[1] On the question of the transformation of normative into theoretical propositions, cf. M. Farber, *The Foundation of Phenomenology,* Third Edition, Albany, State University of New York Press, 1967, pp. 157 ff.

V. THE STATUS OF ESSENCES AND IDEALITIES

In addition to assumptively conceived norms, essences and idealities have been regarded as providing an impasse to scientific methods. The concept of essence, which is of central importance for phenomenology, is also widely used in appropriate versions by objective investigators; and the same holds for idealities, without which no logical procedure would be possible. It is necessary to clarify them reflectively, and with respect to all phases of knowledge and experience.

Essences and essential structures are supposedly lifted out of time and change, even though they are associated with things that change. An essence is defined by those features of a thing or event, without which the thing or event could not exist. One can speak of the essence of a diamond as soon as it is known to exist. In that case the essence is an object of thought that makes it possible to know and characterize the diamond as a concrete thing. The features determining the essence exist only in the thing. An essence should not be said to exist or to be real independently for it is a cognitive instrumentality, a feature of experience as widespread as the "synthesis of identification" exhibited everywhere in experience.

Essences presuppose ideal identification cognitively, along with an ontological principle of conservation, which provides stability. No preferred or privileged form of insight can guarantee the conservation of essences, which belong rather to the order of hypothetical knowledge, and are sterile without the empirical world. An individual event exhibits or embodies a structure, which can be regarded as an ideal individual essence. The natural order of events can thus be treated in ideal terms for the purposes of reflective analysis and knowledge.

This is not to suggest, however, that the exploration of alternative definitions and assumptions be abandoned. There is a place for alternative systems of thought that are concerned with human values. They are to be treated as hypothetical systems, with bearing upon the facts and problems of conduct. The choice of a value system will then depend upon its usefulness in enabling us to set up organized programs of conduct for the fulfillment of human interests, and for the realization of well-defined ideals. The ultimate ideal is the greatest possible degree of fulfillment of interests of all the people, on a world scale.

VI. HUMAN EXISTENCE AND THE SCALE OF VALUES

That a scale of human values can be determined in a number of ways is evident in the literature of the philosophy of values. If a scale of values is to attract most people, or is to be at all convincing, it must be capable of making application to human needs. General requirements to be met include definitions of the lowest and the highest levels of value, with reference to goodness or positive fulfillment and evil or frustration. There must be a set of premises, whether explicit or implicit, in order to provide norms of conduct. But if norms are to make application to human conduct, they must be based upon the facts of human behavior.

The formalistic and intuitionistic approaches to ethics, self-realization theories, and phenomenological theories must be judged according to their success in making effective contact with the facts of human life. In general, an abstract treatment of values that is not based directly upon the facts of human existence cannot be expected to deal effectively with its problems. One can speak of goodness, justice, and benevolence on an abstract level, and fail to reach the problems of conduct requiring critical evaluation. There is, however, an important place for the abstract treatment of the philosophy of values, so long as it is undertaken on the basis of actual human existence. Any "suspension of beliefs" (epoché) introduced for the purposes of reflective analysis is merely a methodological device; it is ancillary in character, and is subject at all times to reconsideration. The realm of reflection, including radical reflection, is not necessarily exempt from error or immune from change.

In addition to approaching a philosophy of values abstractly and externally, it is necessary to do so with reference to actual human situations and problems. The real basis of human values comprises the needs, interests, and desires, the conflicts and the aims, of living beings. That may never be lost sight of even when resorting to the purely abstract level for the purposes of a rational theory; for an abstract theory is a moral as well as a logical device, which presupposes the social and natural world and must always be guided by the facts. As a matter of fact, an examination of a philosophy of values will not fail to show connections with the existing social system and with a cultural tradition. This relationship must be explicitly recognized as the source and the goal of all value theory. With the social attachment adequately acknowledged, the greatest possible degree of critical detachment is required for analysis. In actual practice, there are degrees and styles of detachment, which is always partial and selective. Total detachment is not what is wanted, unless the aim is to turn away from the real world and to deal exclusively with an ideal realm. What is needed is the degree or kind of detachment that makes objective analysis possible.

The problem of achieving objectivity in analysis should not be underestimated, for even a reflective philosophy aiming at the greatest possible freedom from presuppositions may leave factors conditioning individual and class interests unexamined. It is necessary to consider property relations and historical conditions in order to understand ethical concepts. For the institution of private property must have been developed before the formulation of principles intended to prevent or resolve conflicts of property interests. This also applies to all talk of a "just" settlement of an industrial conflict, or of arrangements to satisfy the demands of any group or class for equality. One can no more disregard such concrete realities than he can discard his body.

If the subject matter of the philosophy of values is made up of human beings in their social relationships, any exaggeration of detachment is pointless. The problems that arise for concrete objective inquiry must allow for two dimensions of influence: (1) the influence of needs and interests as constituting the very substance of value realization and value conflicts; and (2) the influence of private, class, or traditional interests on a person making value judgments, as well as on the philosopher of values who is supposed to reflect objectively upon all human activities. The question of the influence of needs and interests is a theme for description for a number of sciences, whereas the question of the influences bearing upon value judgments and value philosophers presents the problem of the attainment of objective truth. It, too, is a theme for descriptive inquiry, requiring emancipation from standpoint narrowness in turn if it is to be successful.

VII. PHILOSOPHY AND THE SCIENTIFIC ENTERPRISE

The scientific enterprise, which knows no distinctions of race, color, or class, is a powerful organization for the achievement of ethical values. For it is concerned with problems and questions in all contexts – in the understanding and control of nature, in the understanding and guidance of human beings, and in the progressive realization of a scientifically constructed philosophy of values. Whatever the various cultural traditions have contributed toward that end may be reformulated in the setting of this nonpersonal, objective system of ethical knowledge. The content is sure to be familiar to all in many of its principles. But the form of statement and of instatement are different. Neither is there any semblance of sectarianism or nationalism. With the assimilation of the knowledge of values to science (which means also, with the extension of the scope of science to include the knowledge of values), no value principle or precept is exempt from the requirements of scientific knowledge generally. They include the need to justify all moral rules and practical policies, for which reasons may be justly demanded. This challenging requirement may itself be formulated as an ethical precept, for it is to be justified finally in terms of its satisfactory consequences for human beings. If observed, it adds to human values, i.e., to fulfillments of human interests.

Not only is it pertinent to note the logical and ethical aspects of the scientific enterprise; the social and political, or the cultural aspects should be considered as well. One important requirement must be freedom from interference by any nonscientific persons or sources. The assurance of non-interference must be sufficiently implemented to be effective; but the means to realize that ideal are still inadequate. On the other hand, critical reactions on the part of all specialists, in the area that may be in question, constitute only one group of reactions to be welcomed. They constitute the primary group. But there are others who may react as well – as critics or evaluators – in the spirit of free inquiry. No one should be ruled out, except insofar as his arguments are untenable. So far as a possible decision by experts is concerned, on controversial or problematical issues particularly, there are warnings to be borne in mind. It is often necessary to go against the stream of accepted ideas, as shown by Georg Cantor, Frege, Russell, Veblen, and many others. How thinkers like Feuerbach fared at the hands of official scholars may be illustrated at will. The nature of experts and the way in which they respond to prevailing influences is a pertinent theme, involving logical and social-historical clarification. On notable occasions, a minority of one has proved to be right. In philosophy proper, and especially in the philosophy of values, the going may be much rougher than in some other fields; for long strands of connection reach out from traditional or vested interests to members of that learned profession. Even those that aspire to make of philosophy a rigorous science must make sure that there are no hidden strands of connection of that kind remaining unexamined.

The fact that some philosophers have made a special plea for a philosophy that could qualify as a rigorous science, if not as the most rigorous of all sciences, bespeaks the prestige of science for our era. But although its prestige is great, it is not unqualified. The evils attendant upon extreme specialization were pointed out long ago. Preoccupation with a narrow speciality was seen to be an obstacle in the way of understanding the major problems confronting society and the sciences. But specialization does not necessarily preclude broader cultural interests. That has been sufficiently shown in eminent cases. The philosophical perspective, representing as it does the function of synthesis and the broad conception of a general methodology, as well as the function of establishing value principles, may provide an important part of the answer to this criticism. Only it must be a sound perspective, answerable at all times to logical standards, and to all the available evidence. Knowledge at its best is to be found in the sciences, and the technical requirements for its understanding, not to speak of adding to it, are very great. The genuine scientist enjoys a well-deserved prestige, so long as he fulfills the exacting requirements of his science. But there is nothing "charismatic" about his prestige, except in the minds of the ignorant or naive; and such people are ever ready, in any case, to succumb to the allure of passing irrationalistic doctrines. The matter of appropriate recognition or valuation is finally an educational problem.

The designation "being a scientist" should not be jealously guarded by partisans of any type of discipline. In more than one sense, all science can be conceived to be one; there is unity. But it is not an undifferentiated kind of unity. An equally strong case can be made out for the diversity of systems or types of science, comprising real and formal sciences, pure and applied sciences, factual and normative sciences. Despite the far-reaching differences, there is always a possible frame of unity. Thus, the sciences may be regarded as unitable in a collective system of knowledge, in which all the special sciences are subsystems and with physics occupying the fundamental position among the sciences of reality. They are also unitable with reference to human interests and their fulfillments. For all scientific pursuits, including the interest of a pure mathematician in proving a theorem, or of a biologist or social scientist in their types of inquiry, or of a value philosopher in systematizing questions of human ideals and their organization in concrete programs – all of these activities are related to human interests. There are thus at least two conspicuous frames of unity (only two will be mentioned here), both of which make allowance for the endless diversity of special systems of knowledge. The so-called unity of science turns out to be highly complex; and all unity is seen to be partial and selective.

What holds for the sciences and their relationships also holds for their methods. No type of method is monopolized by any one discipline. Ideally every science may make use of deductive procedures. The same may be said of methods of experimentation, which are in greater use in some areas of inquiry than in others, especially in the natural sciences; and also of explanatory devices. No closure is possible with respect to questions and problems; and neither can there be any final list of methods of procedure. The method of pure phenomenology, which may be called pure or radically reflective analysis, should not be opposed to other methods because they presuppose the realm of natural existence. Exponents of the method of pure reflective analysis must also acknowledge the pre-existence of that realm. That method is to be used in cooperation with the other types of method, and it is to be judged with respect to its success in solving the problems for which it was devised, as well as from the perspective of the special sciences and ordinary experience.[2] In its best examples, it adds to the scope of scientific inquiry.

"Nature loves to hide," said the ancient philosopher Heraclitus. Bringing nature, physical and human, to evidence in all its aspects and forms, is an ideal goal of scientific inquiry. The interest in the progressive understanding and control of nature and man in all his conditions, relations, and aspirations is for the sciences the perpetual motivater of inquiry. That is at once the highest logical and ethical concern of mankind.

[2] Cf. M. Farber, *Basic Issues of Philosophy,* New York, Harper & Row, 1968.

THE PHENOMENOLOGY OF EPISTEMIC CLAIMS:
AND ITS BEARING ON THE ESSENCE OF PHILOSOPHY

by

R<small>ICHARD</small> M. Z<small>ANER</small>

I

Every claim to knowledge is contextual in a double sense. On the one hand, every such claim occurs within a specific situation of action, belief, or inquiry – i.e. within a particular sphere of concern or finite province of meaning,[1] or in terms of the prevailing stock of knowledge at hand.[2] As such, no claim can be properly understood or analyzed except in light of the specific context (which may be designated as the "outer" context) within which it occurs. Thus the claim, "This is red," differs in important respects depending upon whether it occurs in the context of an inquiry into color perception, a driving test, a mother's warning to her child concerning objects which burn, a hearing concerning subversive activity, and so on.

On the other hand, every epistemic claim sets up, within this outer context, another: the claim is expressed in some linguistic form (which can and does vary widely) and asserts something about affairs other than itself. In this sense, the epistemic claim not only occurs within an outer context, but establishes its own specific "inner" context of concern.[3] It itself "bears on" or points to some particular state-of-affairs and thereby establishes a context in terms of which these and those specific "things" (in a maximally broad sense) are focused thematically at the center of attention, while others are relegated by the claim to the "margin" of interest.[4] The articula-

---

[1] Cf. Alfred Schutz, "On Multiple Realities," in: Alfred Schutz, *Collected Papers*, Volume I, *Phaenomenologica* 11, Martinus Nijhoff (The Hague, 1962), pp. 207–259.

[2] Cf. *Ibid.*, "Common-Sense and Scientific Interpretation of Human Action," pp. 3–47.

[3] As the term "context" (whether inner or outer) is here used, it is quite parallel with the Husserlian notion of "horizon"; cf. E. Husserl, *Ideen* I, Max Niemeyer (Halle a. d. S., 1913), section 82, and Husserl, *Cartesianische Meditationen und Pariser Vorträge*, *Husserliana* Bd. I, Martinus Nijhoff (The Hague, 1950), esp. section 19.

[4] For the fully developed conception of "contextuality" (as the principle of the organization of consciousness into "thematic center" and "marginal field"), cf. Aron Gur-

tion of a claim sets up zones of relevance and irrelevance, it focuses attention on certain affairs and not others, and it thus has its own inner structures as well as outer ones. Hence, while the understanding of a claim requires that one understand its outer setting, such placement does not exhaust its nature. The claim has as well its own (inner) setting; it is itself a context, one may say, which is highly complex and stratified. To concern oneself with epistemic claims *as claims* is to focus on their contextuality.

Accordingly, whatever may be the modality of certainty or uncertainty with which a particular claim is asserted, and whatever one may say as regards its clarity, adequacy, or truth-value, it is doubly contextual. Precisely to that extent, any claim is problematic. This is not to say that it is questionable or dubious (in the manner of skepticism), but rather that the epistemic claim *as claim* is essentially *open to inquiry*. It opens up questions bearing on its inner and outer contexts.

In order to have a manageable problem, the present essay will be restricted to the inner context of epistemic claims. Before turning to this analysis, several more general observations seem in order. First, insofar as a claim alleges that some state-of-affairs is thus-and-so, the claim is essentially open to questions in respect of *whether* or not the state-of-affairs is indeed as alleged (or, whether there is any such state-of-affairs at all). But these questions, it should be stressed, and the inquiries they necessitate, are strictly a function of the specific outer context at hand. Thus, for instance, if a claim is made in the (outer) context of physical science, determining whether the affairs are as alleged is a matter of further inquiry in the physical sciences themselves. However, the claim may not only be examined in respect of what is allegedly known, but also in respect of its being a *claim*, i.e. as regards what this or any claim necessarily presupposes in order to be a claim of knowledge. The latter inquiry, unlike the former, is not a function of the specific outer context within which the claim occurs, but rather of the inner context of the claim as claim – i.e. its structure as an epistemic claim. This is so universally: every such claim presupposes the conditions of the very possibility of its being asserted as a claim of knowledge (whatever may be its particular level or type of knowledge asserted). Precisely because this is the case, epistemic claims as such necessitate an epistemic inquiry, i.e. epistemology.

This brings up a second general observation. Epistemological inquiry is one among many concerns of philosophy, it is sometimes held. But this discipline is more fundamental than such a view implies. Philosophers

witsch, *Théorie du champ de la conscience,* Desclée de Brouwer (Paris, 1957); also published in English by Duquesne University Press (1964).

make, of course, a great many epistemic claims – metaphysical, axiological, logical, and others. To this extent (i.e. to the extent that there are particular philosophical outer contexts, or finite provinces of meaning), these claims are no different from any other. They, too, establish complex inner contexts and hence are essentially open to epistemological inquiry bearing on their epistemic character. In this respect, philosophy may be designated universally, in its epistemological discipline, as the critique of epistemic claims as such, including its own. But such analysis itself involves the making of epistemic claims (such as those being made here concerning epistemic claims), and these are no more exempt from inquiry than are any others. Hence, the philosophical critique of epistemic claims as claims must at every point be a critique of the claims made in that very critique, it must elucidate the conditions for the possibility of that very critique itself: philosophy in this respect is not only a critical, but an essentially self-critical, discipline, and it is in this sense that we understand the present study to be a phenomenology of epistemic claims. More generally, in every philosophical inquiry the nature and significance of this act itself is in its very unfolding an inevitable issue. In another connection, Aron Gurwitsch has expressed the point succinctly:

Every philosophical system is subject to the obligation of accounting for its own possibility; it must at least be able to give such an account in its own terms. Less radically expressed, there must be no incompatibility between the doctrinal content of a philosophical theory, that which is maintained and asserted in it, on the one hand, and, on the other, the mere fact of the formulation of the theory in question. An incompatibility of such a kind would provide the basis for a decisive argument against the theory beset by that incompatibility.[5]

Hence, the critical and self-critical examination of epistemic claims as claims – the "accounting" for philosophy's own possibility – constitutes the fundamental dimension of philosophy. It is therefore reasonable to expect that the effort to delineate the eidetic structures of epistemic claims – which is here conceived as a major direction of phenomenological inquiry – will provide at the same time at least some insights into the nature and significance of philosophy itself. In order to draw out these implications more fully, it is necessary now to turn to this delineation.

II

We begin by noting that epistemic claims have a certain complexity. In

[5] Aron Gurwitsch, "An Apparent Paradox in Leibnizianism," *Social Research*, Spring, 1966 (Vol. 33, No. 1), p. 47.

rough terms, this complexity may be described as follows: the claim, for instance, "immediate experience is transparent," is a linguistically expressed judgment which alleges something to be the case ("transparence") about something else ("immediate experience"). The epistemic claim, then, is an affair expressed in some language (leaving open the question concerning how widely "language" and "linguistic expression" should be interpreted), and has the characteristic of asserting (alleging, supposing) something about some state-of-affairs other than the judgment itself. This claim, thus, is an assertion about that state-of-affairs called "immediate experience" in respect of what is taken to be decisive about it, that it is "transparent". It is not the case that this claim merely looks like it asserts something about experience, but "really" is a way of saying how the *term* "immediate experience" (and the other terms) are to be properly used. Determining how a term is "properly" used, after all, depends upon whether or not immediate experience is the way it is asserted to be – i.e. the epistemic claim alleges to be *about that experience* and not about the way terms are to be used.

Furthermore, as Dorion Cairns has shown,[6] there are at least five distinguishable components inherent in any verbal expression. Using the example, "My hat is grey," he distinguishes: (1) something psychic or mental which is manifested (i.e. the psychic activity of actually ongoing judging), (2) some sense or meaning which is articulated (i.e. the judgment or proposition), (3) the expression of this sense (i.e. the sentence, which is formulated in some actual language), (4) something physical, which embodies the expression manifesting the psychic activity of expressing the sense or judgment (i.e. the physical sounds or marks produced), and (5) some supposed or alleged object or objects which the expressed and embodied sense is about (i.e. my hat in respect of its color).

Thus, my actually ongoing psychic process of judging produces a judgment. That these are not identical is readily seen from the circumstance that while the judging may vary, the judgment remains identically the same (I may judge the same judgment time and again, where the judging is temporally individuated and hence non-repeatable, but the judgment is identically the same and hence is what is repeated in the several judgings). Similar systematic variation ("free variation")[7] shows that the sense or judgment

---

[6] Dorion Cairns, "The Ideality of Verbal Expressions," *Philosophy and Phenomenological Research*, Vol. I, No. 1 (1940–41), pp. 453–62. See also Husserl, *Formale und transzendentale Logik*, Max Niemeyer Verlag (Halle, 1929), sections 1–4.

[7] The analogy to the empirico-scientific method of experimentation is worth mentioning. As Max Black points out, scientific experimentation, as a method, consists fundamentally in this "systematic variation" to determine functional dependency-

is not identical with the expression or sentence: the judgment remains identically the same even though the sentence can vary (as when it is expressed in other languages than English, in cryptograms, codes, etc.).

Again, the sentence is not identical with its physical embodiment: the sentence may be embodied in actual sounds or in actual marks (both of which may obviously vary), or in phantasy-sounds or phantasy-marks (which, again, may both vary, as when I "say silently" or "picture to myself" in various manners). Finally, the same procedure shows that the things the judgment claims to be about are distinct from all the foregoing: neither the judging, the judgment, the sentence, nor the physical embodiments are identical with my actual grey hat – which, unlike any of these, I place on my head or on the shelf.

This brief explication makes another feature of the complexity stand out: the psychic activity of judging produces, not the hat or its color, nor the sentence, nor its physical embodiments. It rather produces the judgment. That this is so may be seen from the circumstance that it is always possible to say that a particular sentence (or, its words, phrases, and the like) does not adequately or exactly express the judgment. While, as it is sometimes said, the judgment may be true or false, the sentence is only more or less adequate and/or exact; and conversely, the linguistic expression's exactness and/or adequacy are not characteristics of the judgment. Similarly, the particular physical marks or sounds may be said to be illegible; but the

relations between events and their concomitant conditions (both temporally past and simultaneous conditions). Similarly, what is called for in the present effort is systematic variation to determine dependency-relations. But, inasmuch as the issues here concern, not empirical states-of-affairs but necessary or essential ones, the kind of "relations" in question also vary. Rather than speak of functional dependencies, Husserl speaks of "founding-founded" ones; and rather than speak of "experimentation" he speaks of the method of "free-variation". Hence, what constitutes the analogue here is not that philosophy is empirical, or science essential (concerned with essences): both empirical science and "strict" philosophy are, as sciences, subject to certain identical criteria, one of which is method. We are not suggesting, then, a simplistic identification of philosophy, nor a reduction of one to the other. It is rather argued that, granted a reasonable broadening of the notion of "science", one can see many parallels between such a broadly conceived science and what Husserl conceives phenomenology to be insofar as it is, ideally, a "rigorous science".

See, for the above discussion, Max Black, *Critical Thinking: An Introduction to Logic and Scientific Method*, Prentice-Hall (New York, 2nd Ed., 1952), Chaps. 16–18; Husserl, *Ideen* I, *op. cit.*, sections 69–71, and his "Philosophy as a Strict Science," published in *Phenomenology and the Crisis of Philosophy* (trans. and ed. by Quentin Lauer), Harper Torchbooks (New York, 1965). Other philosophers have noted the same points: see, for instance, Felix Kaufmann, *Methodology of the Social Sciences,* Oxford University Press (New York, 1944); and Alfred Schutz, *Collected Papers,* esp. volumes 1 and 3, *op. cit.* and his *The Phenomenology of the Social World,* Northwestern University Press (Evanston, 1967).

judgment could hardly be similarly criticized, any more than physical marks or sounds could be called true or false. Accordingly, such characteristics are clearly distinguishable. This, however, in no way argues for them as separable or separate: they are distinguishable but inseparable features of epistemic claims.

In light of this, it is necessary to recognize that there may be judgments which a particular language, or a particular natural language, is simply not capable of adequately or exactly expressing (or, perhaps, incapable of expressing at all). There may be judgments, moreover, which are expressible only by indirect means (as in metaphor, irony, satire, and the like). It is probably also necessary to say that there is a profoundly reciprocal relationship between judgments and expressions (such that the expression of a judgment could well disclose unexpected features of the judgment, or such that the effort to express the judgment could reveal unexpected ways of being expressed). Finally, these distinctions make it clear that not all judgments are necessarily capable of being expressed in any natural language. It may be, in other words, that some judgments are capable of being expressed physiognomically, or in musical tones and themes, in forms of wood, paint, stone, and so on (such phrases as "musical statements" may not be merely metaphorical ways of talking). In any case, such possibilities cannot be ruled out *a priori* or by simple fiat.

Furthermore, the immediate product of the judging activity being the judgment, it is clear (1) that the judgment is not an inherent component of the judging process, not a part of the stream of mental activity producing the judgment (it is not itself an activity); and (2) that the judgment bears a peculiar relation to the things judged about, one which neither the judging, the sentence, nor the physical embodiments have to these things. It is the second point which will concern us, for it is in this relationship (more accurately, in the judgment insofar as it asserts this "peculiar" relationship) that we find the epistemic claim *as claim*.

For terminological clarity, we shall say: (1) the judging articulates (or produces) the judgment, while the judgment is what is articulated as a claim; (2) insofar as the judgment is the articulated claim, it may be designated synonymously as the "*supposed state-of-affairs as supposed*," or what is claimed *as claimed* (in Husserl's expression, it is the *Vermeinter Sachverhalt*, or the *vermeinte Gegenstandlichkeit als solche*[8]); (3) the sentence is the linguistic expression of the articulated claim; (4) the physical marks or sounds are the embodiments of the expression, and thus also of the

---

[8] Following Husserl, *Formale und transzendentale Logik, op. cit.*, pp. 108–12.

articulated claim and ultimately of the psychic activity of articulating;[9] (5) finally, as distinguished from what the judgment *supposes* (claims, alleges) to be the case, there are the "things" which the judgment claims to be about, and which may therefore be designated as the "state-of-affairs itself, pure and simple" (the *Sachverhalt schlechthin,* or *Gegenstandlichkeit schlechthin*[10]).

Being concerned here strictly with the epistemic claims as such (the judgment, articulated claim, or supposed state-of-affairs as supposed) it is necessary to take up the other distinguishable components only as they bear on the claim itself. It was necessary to explicate them, if only briefly, in order to bring the specific issues into focus. This done, we may now return momentarily to the beginning of this explication and pick out another aspect of the mentioned complexity.

The judgment, for example, "immediate experience is transparent," is an articulated claim which is linguistically expressed in the English language and embodied in the physical marks appropriate to that language. Precisely because the articulated claim is given linguistic expression, however, there occur a series of essential *suppositions* which, as implicit conditions for the *claim as claim,* may properly be designated as *pre-suppositions.* In effect, to focus upon one of these, it is pre-supposed by the claim that the specific expression (including the phrases, words, and other linguistic affairs) are *intelligible,* that the expression is formulated in conformity with at least the minimum standards of linguistic usage prevailing in the language community in question. Whether or not the judgment *must* be expressed, in other words, *if* it is, it implicitly and essentially makes this pre-supposition concerning the language used, that it is intelligible in that language-community. Hence, it is pre-supposed that the linguistic expression is understandable by anyone who either *in fact* shares or who could *in principle* share that language-context.

Put simply, any proposition which is expressed in some language not only asserts some claim about "things" but as well supposes that the language used is shared or shareable by others and thus is intelligible to them.[11] This makes clear that there is another pre-supposition essentially

---

[9] It seems to me that there is a strict parallel between the embodiment of consciousness by a specific animate organism (my own) and the embodiment of a linguistic expression by specific physical marks or sounds. Gibson Winter has argued for an even further parallel, in his book, *Elements for a Social Ethic,* Macmillan (New York, 1966), esp. pp. 135–39, where he argues that "mind/body" embodiment is the basic analogue for understanding the relations between the consciousness of the social world and the structures of the social world.

[10] Husserl, *op. cit., ibid.*

[11] A purely or strictly private language, in these terms, is either no language at all,

connected to this one. Specifically, to say that the claim *as articulated* (whether or not it receives some linguistic expression) is *able to be expressed* in some fashion. Every judgment is if expressed pre-supposed as intelligible; but every judgment as well inherently pre-supposes qua judgment that some expression in some form is in principle possible. Indeed, it is solely in view of this pre-supposition that it is at all possible to say that a particular expression is or is not adequate, complete, or exact as regards the judgment. That we seek terms, phrases, words, by which to express a judgment shows not only that the expression and the judgment are different affairs but also that the judgment qua judgment (the claim as claim) involves the supposition (the pre-supposition) of expressibility.[12]

The relationship, then, between judgments and expressions is essentially *a reciprocal or mutual one*: the judgment is pre-supposed as expressible and the expression as intelligible. Hence, as Husserl has shown,[13] several regions of inquiry are opened up: that concerned with delineating and explicating the steps by means of which a judgment becomes articulated (the stratification of the articulated claim *as articulated*), and that concerned with the modes of expression of such claims. While obviously important, these problems will not concern us here.

Thus far, then, we have found it necessary to recognize that a judgment in respect of its being an articulated claim, involves at least the two pre-suppositions mentioned. Precisely because of these implicit and essential pre-suppositions, we may now say, certain types of critical inquiries and questions become necessary and relevant. In other words, the "relevance" of certain critical questions concerning the inner context of epistemic claims is established by the essential characteristics of the claims themselves: inasmuch as a linguistically expressed articulated claim itself essentially makes the pre-suppositions of intelligibility and expressibility, critical questions bearing on these are both relevant and necessary for the understanding of the claims, much less for the discussion of them.

The claim that "immediate experience is transparent," is a case in point. It is pre-supposed that these terms, and the whole expression, are intelligi-

---

or else a limiting case of language. The point at issue here is that to the extent that a judgment receives (or could receive) linguistic expression, the language in which it receives this is minimally shareable by others, and therefore the language used is pre-supposed to be intelligible by others.

[12] It is precisely this specific relationship, between the articulated claim as articulated (as expressible) and the expression, which is at issue in such cases as, in class logic, attempting to determine the asserted connection between subject-terms and predicate-terms (inclusion, sub-inclusion, contrareity, and the like).

[13] Husserl, *op. cit.;* see also his *Erfahrung und Urteil: Untersuchungen zur Genealogie der Logik,* red. und heraus. von L. Landgrebe, Classen Verlag (Hamburg, 1954).

ble. It is pre-supposed that, for instance, we understand (or can come to understand) what is meant by "immediate"; sometimes, of course, the philosopher will himself seek to make this clear, by definition, example, standard cases, and the like. In any event, it is always relevant and necessary to raise critical questions concerning the expression and its components, since all other criticisms presuppose that one is clear about what is asserted. However, not only is it presupposed that the expression is intelligible, but also that the judgment has been exactly and adequately enough formulated or articulated as to be intelligibly expressible in some language. In these terms, we may well critically wonder whether it is at all sufficiently exact (and/or adequate) to characterize "experience" as "immediate", or to predicate "transparency" of "experience" of any sort: transparence may very well express, for instance, the properties of window-glass, but does it express immediacy of experience as well? We are not, of course, concerned here to take this claim to task, but only to illustrate the grounds for a certain type of critical question which is made possible and necessary for the understanding of such claims: grounds which are found in the pre-suppositional structure of the claims themselves.

Hence, what may be viewed as the philosopher's "obligation" to discuss his position and statements becomes clarified and grounded – in the things themselves, i.e. in the pre-suppositions implicit in the claims. To be sure, a philosopher may refuse to discuss his claims; but in so doing, it might be reasonable to ask whether he deserves the title of philosopher – an *ad hominem* may be in order. But we can now say more firmly, if the philosopher refuses to discuss his pre-suppositions (as thus far explicated), either he simply has not recognized that these are indeed essential to his claims (in which case he can well be charged with naivety), or his statements are not intended as claims at all (but merely have the guise of claims), or the statements have been modified from their apparent status as claims to that of mere dogma, prejudice, or manifestations of private feeling. The point here is that the ground for the "obligation to discuss" is *not in the man, but in the nature of the claims he articulates and linguistically expresses.* What opens up and makes necessary such criticisms is the pre-suppositional structure of the claims themselves.

III

The explication thus far has concerned only what may be called the internal pre-suppositional character of claims (in respect of their "inner context") and their correlative critical questions. Claims are not only articulated and linguistically expressed, but are claims: *every claim supposes something about affairs other than itself*, and in this respect we encounter the more fundamental features of epistemic claims.

Thus, as regards the claim we have used as an example, it pre-supposes not only the expressibility and intelligibility of the judgment, "immediate experience is tranparent," but also *that there is* "experience" *which is* "immediate" and *that it is as supposed,* i.e., "transparent". Whether or not there is such an affair as immediate experience and whether or not it is transparent, are separate issues which can be determined only after the full implicit structures of the claim as claim have been brought out. Maintaining our neutrality (epoché) regarding these issues, we must turn to the structures themselves.

The articulated claim (supposed state-of-affairs as supposed) asserts *that there are* the things the claim alleges to be about, and it asserts *that these things are the way alleged*. In other words, the *epistemic claim is ontological* in character: [14] it asserts the being of the affairs in question. This is still somewhat ambiguous, however. What the claim supposes, more accurately, is the *"being-that"* and the *"being-thus-and-so"* of the affairs it claims to be about.

Although the obvious *clue* to this ontological characteristic is the linguistic expression, these should not be identified nor reduced to one another. The linguistic expression, that such and such "is" thus and so, in other words, is clearly only a clue to the ontological characteristic of the epistemic claim. The latter is not "merely" a "linguistic" affair, nor is the assertion of the being-that and the being-thus-and-so identical to its linguistic expression. Our reflections have already established the in principle difference between the articulated claim and its linguistic expression, and we have already taken note of the circumstance that it is the judgment which asserts the claim, not the sentence. The sentence only expresses (well or badly) the judgment, and hence does not in itself have the ontological-assertive character of the judgment.

The epistemic claim, in respect of its ontological bearing (its "supposal" of being-that and being-thus-and-so), shows a further complexity. Just as the claim as articulated and expressed could be critically inspected as regards the adequacy and exactness of the expression and its intelligibility, so, too, the articulated claim as claim is essentially open to criticism regarding the sufficiency and accuracy of its "supposal". It can always be asked, i.e.,

---

[14] Cf. Frederick Ferré, *Language, Logic and God*, Harper (New York, 1961), pp. 162–65.

whether or not the affairs the claim is allegedly about have been sufficiently and/or accurately "supposed".

More technically, the ontological claim inherent in the judgment is complex, revealing at least two pre-suppositions, distinctively different from those of adequacy and exactness regarding the expressibility and intelligibility of the judgment. There, it is a question of the expression of the intended sense, the claim, and the extent to which the expression expresses that sense. It would not at all be proper to ask whether the expression is either a sufficient or a true expression of the intended sense, but only how well and how completely it is expressed. But when it is a question of the relationship between the articulated *claim as claim* (the *Vermeinter Sachverhalt*) and the things about which the claim is made (the *Sachverhalt schlechthin*), it is indeed necessary to look into the sufficiency and truth of the claim.

The claim asserts the being-that and the being-thus-and-so of the affairs in question; insofar, the claim pre-supposes implicitly its own sufficiency as regards these things and its being true of them (to one degree or another, ranging from the modality of uncertainty to that of complete apodicticity). What further distinguishes these two pre-suppositions from those already discussed is that the former are founded on another pre-supposition which has its locus in and points to an *underlying level of experience* (in a broad sense) which has as its 'objects' the things themselves simpliciter. This feature calls for further explanation.

We have noted that the judging articulates the judgment, not the things being judged about. Yet, although the judgment claims to be about these things (about the things other than the judgment itself, of whatever kind they may be), it is not itself an activity, an experience of these things. The judgment points beyond itself, not as an awareness, but in the sense of being a claim about these things. It asserts something to be the case about the things, thus asserting *that* they are, and that they are *as* claimed.

What are these "things"? Precisely those which are the "objects" of an experience other than and underlying the judging. Which specific type of experiencing is involved will, of course, vary, depending upon which "things" the judgment claims to be about. Thus, if I judge, "My hat is grey," the presupposition in question here is that the things simpliciter (the *Sachverhalt schlechthin*), the hat and its color, are perceptually experienced states-of-affairs. In these terms, the "things" to which the judgment points (in the sense of being a "supposing" concerning them) are not the objects of the judging, nor are they identical with the judgment. They are the objects of that specific kind of experiencing called sense perception, and

it is *this* perceptual awareness/object-of-perception complex which underlies the judging/judgment complex. In short, *the judgment is not simply
about "things" divorced from the mode of experience through which these
"things" appear; rather, it is about the things-as-perceived.* The judgment
alleges or supposes that the *things-as-seen* (the hat in respect of its color)
are as the judgment supposes them to be.

To characterize the situation more loosely, the judgment claims to be
sufficient and true (to one degree or another) about these perceptually
experienced states-of-affairs, the hat and its color. To take a different
example, if I judge, "All right triangles conform to the Pythagorean theorem," the pre-supposition in question here is that the judgment claims to
be sufficient and true about the mathematico-cognitively apprehended
states-of-affairs, the right triangle and the Pythagorean theorem. To speak
of things themselves simpliciter, in other words, about which a claim is
made, is *not* to smuggle in a concealed naive realism, or another metaphysical judgment concerning the reality or nature of the objects in question.
It is the epistemic claim which asserts the being-that and the being-thus-
and-so of the "things" and not the epistemologist investigating the claim.
What we thus note is the experiential structures which underlie every judg-
ing-judgment complex; to speak of "things themselves" is to speak of the
things which the judgment in question asserts to be and to be thus-and-so.

The relationship between the latter complex (judging/judgment) and the
underlying experiential one (which may itself, of course, be another judg-
ing/judgment complex, as when I judge *that* another judgment is, say,
false) is, therefore, what Husserl calls "Fundierung" (foundedness), or
between what is founded and what is founding: the experiential complex
(which has its own subjective-objective structure) is the founding stratum
for the judging/judgment complex (which has its own subjective-objective
structure).

The ontological character of epistemic claims, then, shows the structural
complexity of implicit and essential pre-suppositions of sufficiency and
truth, and these are founded on the underlying level of experience indicated. But the articulated claim as claim is complex in still another way,
one which turns out to be fundamental.

It is essential to perceptual awarenesses (to take this as merely an illustration), Aron Gurwitsch shows clearly,[15] that the act of perceiving is
strictly correlative to something perceived, and vice versa. Moreover, what

[15] Aron Gurwitsch, *Théorie du champ de la conscience, op. cit.,* Part IV. And his
Studies in Psychology and Phenomenology, Northwestern University Press (Evanston,
1966).

is perceived (the "perceptual noema") in the act of perceiving (the "perceptual noesis") is implicitly posited (intended or experienced) as *not* itself an immanent component of the perceiving activity, the stream of experience, but rather, precisely as "objective correlate" of that stream.[16] As such, the perceived object (*as perceived*, from a particular point of view) is experienced as "able to be perceived again and again," i.e. as an object of future possible perceptions. Of course, *whether or not* the object either does become experienced again is up to the further course of experience. Without entering into the detailed explication of this feature of perceptual noemata (found in other experiences as well), it is necessary only to note here that what pertains to the perceptual experiences also pertains to the higher, founded, stratum of judgment.

When one judges, not only is there the implicit complexity of pre-suppositions already brought out, but as well the further pre-supposition that the things judged about can be judged-about again and again, and in different ways (one may judge a table as useful, and also as brown, in the corner, and so on, where each time it is the same table about which judgments are being made; or, one may judge an event as thus-and-so at one time, and later on revise one's claim, where in both cases it is the same event which is being judged). Neither the judging nor the judgment produces the "things" but rather alleges to be about them (*as* perceived, remembered, expected, valued, and so on). The things are not, so to speak, exhaustively enclosed in a single act of judging (nor in any number of judgings). In this sense, founded on an indefinite number of acts of experiencing the things in question, an indefinite number of acts of judging may be articulated. The judgment is repeatable because the things judged-about can be repeatedly experienced, in some manner or other.[17]

[16] As opposed to what Brentano had advocated. Husserl and, following him, Gurwitsch, reject Brentano's advocacy of the medieval notion of "intentional inexistence" of the objects of psychic processes, which Brentano interpreted as "immanent objectivity" – an interpretation which results in an untenable duplication of objects, the physical and the psychical objects. Cf. Franz Brentano, *Psychologie vom empirischen Standpunkt*, Erster Band, Felix Meiner (Hamburg, 1955), pp. 124–25. The ambiguity here can be found also in Bergson's early works, especially in his *Matière et Mémoire* (cf. the first chapter's discussion of the "object" and the notion of "image"). W. Köhler had also maintained this duplication theory, and had the same difficulties of trying to relate the two; cf. his *Gestalt Psychology*, Liveright (New York, 1929), pp. 228–29. Cf. also Gurwitsch's excellent discussion of this, *Théorie du champ . . ., op. cit.*, Part II.

[17] Even so-called "unique," non-repeatable, affairs, can be repeatedly judged-about – further judgments being founded on, however, a memorial consciousness of the unique affair, or perchance on a phantasy-consciousness of it. The point is not only that judgments can be articulated indefinitely, but that each articulation of a judgment is founded on such a sub-stratum of experience.

Nor is this all, for to articulate a claim about things is not only to pre-suppose that the person judging can repeatedly judge them, but also that *others can do so* (which is not to say either that others must judge them, nor that they will do so, but only that they can, in principle). And, in such an event, there is an essential pre-supposition, that *the things being judged-about are accessible by others independent of the judger's claim and its linguistic expression.* Thus, when one asserts the claim about immediate experience, whether or not it falls within an argument, one essentially pre-supposes that others (who either read or listen to it) are able to gain access to the sphere of immediate experience independent of the linguistically expressed claim. Indeed, it is only on that condition that the claim can ultimately be at all understood, much less affirmed or disputed.

It is therefore clear that this pre-supposition of independent accessibility is an *implicit appeal to others* (neither "everyone" nor a particular "some-one" but precisely *anyone* who is both willing and able to do so) *to "go and see for themselves" whether the things are as they are asserted to be* (or, in-deed, whether there are any such things at all). This crucial presupposition may be designated as the *co-subjective accessibility of the things judged-about.*[18]

The latter point indicates a final crucial complexity. Just as we found implicit in the ontological character of the epistemic claim the pre-supposi-tion concerning the experiential stratum underlying the predication, so, too, here we find a fundamental pre-supposition, one which connects that con-cerning the ontological with the co-subjective accessibility. The pre-suppo-sition that others will be able to find what is claimed to be the case (suffi-ciently and truly), and the implicit appeal to them to "go and see for themselves" *is at the same time the claim that "going and seeing"* (co-subjective accessibility) *is a matter of actualizing the relevant type of ex-perience underlying the epistemic claim itself.* In other words, the pre-supposition referring to the relevant experience is an implicit *pre-supposi-tion of evidence,* specifically that kind of evidence which, it is pre-supposed by the claim, legitimates its pre-suppositions of sufficiency and truth. And, the pre-supposition of co-subjective accessibility is now clearly the *very same pre-supposition of evidence*: others will be able, it is pre-supposed,

---

[18] This term was suggested by Sherman M. Stanage as more descriptive than "ob-jectivity," a term which has become too closely associated with empirical science for it to serve our purposes here. Additionally, what we point to is the ground for "objectivi-ty" as understood in science – i.e. the supposal, not only that the affairs judged-about are repeatable but also that systematic observings by an indefinite number of qualified observers is inherently possible and necessary. The stress on "observ*ings*" is the ration-ale for the use of the term "co-subjective". Cf. also above, footnote 7.

to find what the claim asserts to be the case (being-that and being-thus-and-so), if they "check-it-out," i.e. if they "do-what-I-did," if they actualize the relevant type of experience which underlies the claim itself. In simple terms, inasmuch as the claim alleges, e.g. that "my hat is grey," it includes the pre-supposition that these "things" are accessible by others, and, if they "look" at the "things," they will find them to be as I allege in my judgment viz., "hat" and "mine" and "grey").[19] In a similar way, the judgment concerning the Pythagorean theorem asserts that there are "right triangles," and that, if others do what is necessary (i.e. actualize the relevant type of experience through which such affairs are presented – think in that specific cognitive manner which results in geometry), they will also find that right triangles conform to the Pythagorean theorem.

Evidence, therefore, as that which would legitimate or justify the claim in question, is *not* in the first instance a matter of argument. It is rather a matter of relevant experience (in the broadest sense of the term); it is, Husserl says, *Erfahrung*.[20] To consider the claim concerning immediate experience: one implicitly supposes that one has in some sense experienced or encountered this affair, such that one is able to assert, in the first place, that it is "transparent". It is also pre-supposed that the relevant mode of experiencing in this case is one which is freely available to others (although it may well be a difficult one to actualize), and that when these others do actualize it they will find out *that there is* such an affair as "immediate experience", and that it is *as* the claim alleges – all of this over and above the other pre-suppositions delineated at the beginning of this analysis.

Only on the grounds of such an actualizing of the relevant mode of experience, finally, can the claim be criticized, discussed, argued, verified, disverified – in short, found to be evident and to what degree, if any. Since, apparently, the mode of access to immediate experience is not itself immediate experience, it is apparently through some other mode, possibly that of reflection. Hence, if this is so, to check-out the claim (which it not only invites but makes possible and necessary) would mean to actualize a reflection which would focus on "immediate experience," and then to determine the sufficiency and truth of (i.e. the evidence for) the claim ar-

[19] It is *not* the case, of course, here any more than in other disciplines (e.g. the physical sciences), that these others must "have *my* experienc*ings*." That makes no sense, since my experiencings, my observings, are strictly my own. But this is not what is pre-supposed in any case: rather, what is pre-supposed is that others will be able to find the *things-experienced* and will be able to verify (find evidence for) the claim (whatever the "things" may be). Thus, when I ask, "Do you see what I see?" what I am pre-supposing is that you can see what I see, not that you can have my seeing.

[20] Cf. Husserl, *op. cit.*, sections 84–86; and his *Cartesian Meditations*, Martinus Nijhoff (The Hague, 1960), Meditation I.

ticulated. All of this "checking-out," of course, can come only if it is first of all clear what is being alleged; that is, only after what we have called the internal criticism of the inner context of epistemic claims has been conducted.

Other types of epistemic claims are obviously possible: we claim to know numbers, relations, principles, physical things, past affairs, values, and so on. Accordingly, the claims and pre-suppositions will vary, as will the specific type of relevant experiences (evidences) relative to them. Similarly, the modality of claims can and does vary; i.e. not all claims are asserted as apodictic or as probable, but have different modalities (probably true, doubtful, certain, uncertain, and the like). But, regardless of these variations, the fundamental structure of epistemic claims is quite invariant, i.e. essential. It is not essential that a claim be asserted as apodictic or probable for it to be epistemic, nor is it essential that a claim be asserted only about the sense-perceivable world for it to be epistemic. It is essential that it be asserted with some modality, that it be asserted about some state-of-affairs or other, and that it have at least the pre-suppositions thus far brought out.

When it is said, then, that every philosopher has the "obligation" to discuss his statements, we have now made explicit the grounds for this. Over and above what has already been said on this, we may say as well that just because these statements are epistemic claims (or insofar as statements involve such claims), with the complex pre-suppositional structure delineated, they invite the critical scrutiny of others. Indeed, for them to be *epistemic, they make such critical inspection necessary, since every claim to knowledge, we have argued, must always be critical, i.e. open to and subject to criticism.*

Insofar as these others do engage in making (critical) claims, these too invite and necessitate even further discussion, and so on indefinitely or open-endedly. This open-ended structure which is essential to articulated claims, is grounded in the nature of the claims themselves. Hence, we may now say, inasmuch as *philosophizing is precisely such critical articulation and criticism,* that is to say *dialogue, it has its grounds in epistemic activity.* Philosophizing, therefore, is *self-grounding,* percisely because it is the critical inspection or critique of all epistemic claims, including its own.

IV

The final issue which remains is that with which we began: what is it, to philosophize? We have already indicated the bearing of our inquiry on this question, but this needs to be brought out more explicitly.

Philosophy cannot tolerate what is hidden, unexamined, ulterior, and taken-for-granted without question. What our inquiry has shown, in part, is that this is a fundamental and essential feature of philosophy. As a "quest for knowledge" and ultimately for "wisdom," it is an activity which results in epistemic claims of a variety of orders. But beyond this (which, after all, characterizes much of what is not philosophy), philosophy is that specific reflective activity which seeks to make explicit and to criticize what is hidden, pre-supposed or implicit – *universally*, i.e. it concerns itself with the pre-supposed in every dimension of human life, action, and thought. In this sense, as Natanson has remarked, philosophy "is the critique of man's experience through a persistent effort to explore its foundational presuppositions, its claims to truth, its dreams of justice, and its moments of transcendence."[21] Expressed in different terms, it is just the kind of effort in which we have been involved: the systematic explication of epistemic claims as such – an inquiry which is not the whole of philosophy, obviously, but which is philosophical in the sense in question. *Philosophy is the systematic critique of foundations of every sort.*

But it is not only the critique of these; it is also the *search* for them. That is, philosophers not only criticize, they also engage in making epistemic claims about quite a variety of affairs. These claims, as we have seen, are essentially invitations to criticisms, and in this sense they are of necessity critical in character. To say this is to say that philosophical claims must be *responsible*: responsive to the criticisms of others and to one's own continued critical reflections, and therefore open to discussion at every point – whatever may be the modality of certainty with which they are asserted (not even claims asserted as apodictic are exempt from further discussion, as Descartes knew very well and clearly expresses in his *Meditations*). In brief, our inquiry has disclosed what seems to be one fundamental feature of philosophy itself (over and above what it has disclosed regarding epistemic claims): *philosophy is critical dialogue*, and precisely because of this it is always and essentially *open-ended*.

This points to another unique characteristic of philosophy as dialogue. Collingwood remarks that, "Philosophy . . . has this peculiarity, that reflection upon it is part of itself . . . the theory of philosophy is itself a problem

---

[21] Maurice Natanson, "Philosophy and the Social Sciences," in: M. Natanson *Literature, Philosophy and the Social Sciences*, Martinus Nijhoff (The Hague, 1962), pp. 165–66.

for philosophy; and not only a possible problem, but an inevitable one."[22] This is not the case for other regions of human activity and thought: the theory of poetry is not a part of poetry, but of philosophy; that of science is not a part of science, but of philosophy; that of rhetoric is not a part of rhetoric, but of philosophy; and so on. In a similar vein, Husserl emphasized that if philosophy is to be at all rigorous, it must constantly and persistently make explicit and seek to justify all presuppositions – *the philosopher's own most of all.*[23] It is in this sense alone that he wrote of the necessity for a "presuppositionless philosophy" – the philosopher must at all times seek to ground his own claims and pre-suppositions or else, as James once said, make an explicit "act of faith" to the effect that certain assumptions are made, "I know not why," remaining open at all times to all possible evidence pro and con. *Philosophy, thus, is the science of pre-suppositions: of beginnings, or origins, of foundations – including its own.* Similarly, Merleau-Ponty speaks of the philosopher as "un commençant perpétuel."[24] And Natanson makes the same fundamental point in another connection, stressing that philosophizing about philosophy (metaphilosophy) is but one dimension of philosophy itself – that dimension which is most significant and essential.[25]

It is, then, always incumbent on the philosopher to ground his own claims first and foremost, as well as to seek the foundations of everything else. And it is this reflexive character of philosophical dialogue which uniquely distinguishes its dialectical movement. To the extent that reflexivity is constitutive of human being,[26] philosophy represents the fundamental expression of that being.

---

[22] R. G. Collingwood, *An Essay on Philosophical Method,* Oxford University Press (London, 1933), pp. 1–2.

[23] Husserl, "Philosophy as a Rigorous Science," *op. cit.,* pp. 88–91, 110–122, and 142–47.

[24] Maurice Merleau-Ponty, *Phénoménologie de la perception,* Librairie Gallimard (Paris, 1945), p. ix.

[25] M. Natanson, "Foreword," *Philosophy of the Social Sciences: A Reader,* Random House (New York, 1963), p. 6.

[26] Cf. R. Zaner, "An Approach to Philosophical Anthropology," *Philosophy and Phenomenological Research,* Vol. XXVII, No. 1 (September, 1966), pp. 55–68, esp. 65–68.

PROBLEMS OF THE LIFE-WORLD

by

ARON GURWITSCH

INTRODUCTION

As early as 1913, Husserl in *Ideen zu einer reinen Phänomenologie und phänomenologischen Philosophie* designated a descriptive and analytical study of the world of common experience or – as it has come to be denoted in the terminology of his later writings – the life-world (*Lebenswelt*) as an urgent desideratum. What is meant is the world as encountered in everyday life and given in direct and immediate experience, especially perceptual experience and its derivatives like memory, expectation, and the like, independently of and prior to scientific interpretation. At every moment of our life, we find ourselves in the world of common everyday experience; with this world we have a certain familiarity not derived from what science might teach us; within that world we pursue all our goals and carry on all our activities, including scientific ones. As the universal scene of our life, the soil, so to speak, upon which all human activities, productions, and creations take place, the world of common experience proves the foundation of the latter as well as of whatever might result from them. As far as the construction of the scientific universe as well as the elaboration of a science in the specific modern, "Galilean", style is concerned, the perceptual world underlies it and is presupposed by it in a still further sense, in that it serves as a point both of departure and of reference for that construction which is to provide an explanation in mathematical terms of events and occurrences in the world of perceptual experience. Accordingly, Husserl postulated an all-encompassing description of that world, pursuing it in all its dimensions and considering it under the totality of its aspects, as a scientific task of the first order of importance, a task which at the time of Husserl's writing (1913) had hardly been embarked upon nor even seen as a task.[1] It must be noted that the term "scientific", as used in the pre-

---

[1] E. Husserl, *Ideen zu einer reinen Phänomenologie und phänomenologischen Phi-*

ceding sentence, has to be construed in the broad sense of its German equivalent *wissenschaftlich,* that is to say, it is not restricted to natural science
nor does it have technological connotations.

In the more than fifty years that have passed since the publication of
Ideen I, what Husserl had denoted as a desideratum has found at least
partial fulfilment. Husserl himself, in his later writings, especially in his
last work *Die Krisis der Europäischen Wissenschaften und die transzendentale Phänomenologie,*[2] but also in *Phänomenologische Psychologie,*
University lectures delivered in the years 1925, 1926/27, and 1928,[3] went
far beyond the first general delineations of the world of everyday experience
which he had presented in *Ideen* I.[4] What in *Krisis* Husserl came to denote
as the life-world has also been dealt with by writers, both German and
French, whom it has become customary to classify as "existentialists":
Heidegger,[5] Sartre,[6] and Merleau-Ponty,[7] and it stands in the center of interest of these philosophers. Finally, we have to mention the work of Schutz,
his endeavors to lay down the philosophical foundations of the social sciences and to provide a clarification, by means of phenomenological analysis, of their basic notions.[8] It is Schutz who has seen the life-world as
primarily a social world and who has done more than anybody else to advance its study and elucidation from the point of view of its social aspect,
which obviously is of primordial importance.

In present day philosophical discussions, outside the several trends of
what is summarily called "analytical philosophy", the life-world occupies a

---

losophie (republished in *Husserliana* III, 1950), p. 52. We refer to the pagination of the
original edition which is indicated on the margin of the *Husserliana* edition. Hereafter
the work is referred to as *Ideen* I.

[2] Husserl, *Die Krisis der Europäischen Wissenschaften und die transzendentale Phänomenologie, Husserliana* VI, 1954 (hereafter referred to as *Krisis*). Cf. our report "The
last Work of Edmund Husserl," *Philosophy and Phenomenological Research* XVI, 1956
and XVII, 1957 (reprinted in our *Studies in Phenomenology and Psychology,* 1966).

[3] Husserl, *Phänomenologische Psychologie, Husserliana* IX, 1962; cf. our report
"Edmund Husserl's Conception of Phenomenological Psychology" *The Review of
Metaphysics* XIX, 1966.

[4] Husserl, *Ideen* I, §§ 27 ff.

[5] M. Heidegger, *Sein und Zeit,* 1927 (trans. by J. Macquarrie and E. Robinson: *Being
and Time,* 1962).

[5] J. P. Sartre, *L'Être et le néant,* 1943 (trans. by H. E. Barnes: *Being and Nothingness,* 1956).

[7] M. Merleau-Ponty, *Phénoménologie de la Perception,* 1945 (trans. by C. Smith:
Phenomenology of Perception, 1962).

[8] A. Schutz, *Collected Papers,* especially vols. I and III, *Phaenomenologica* 11, 1962
and 22, 1966. See also his earlier book *Der sinnhafte Aufbau der sozialen Welt,* 1932
and 1960 (trans. by G. Walsh and F. Lehnert: *The Phenomenology of the Social World,*
1967).

central and focal position. Its discovery must be reckoned among the most momentous accomplishments of contemporary philosophical thought, an accomplishment and acquisition, we submit, of enduring value which will prove to be of significant consequence for the future development of philosophy.

Still, certain problems arise with respect to the very notion of the life-world, and the time seems to have come to formulate these problems. To do so appears particularly urgent in view of the fact that the main writings of the existentialist thinkers are, on account of the extant translations, better known in the English-speaking world or, at least, are more easily accessible than the works of Husserl, of which only very few have thus far been adequately translated. Among the problems we have in mind, we mention in the first place that of the methodological significance of the notion of the life-world, of the role it is to play, and of the function it is destined to fulfill within the systematic context of philosophical, especially phenomenological theory. Closely related thereto is the question of whether with the discovery of the life-world philosophy has found its definitive field and domain of work, its permanent resting place, so to speak. Is philosophy from now on to be nothing other than a complete, all-encompassing, and systematic exploration of the life-world? Or is it perhaps the case that with the discovery of the life-world, notwithstanding the paramount importance of that discovery, the ultimate philosophical dimension has not yet been reached? If such should prove to be the case, one might ask further whether the importance of the discovery in question does not consist, among other things, in its being a phase of the journey toward the ultimate philosophical dimension.

We propose to discuss these two problems in terms of principle, i.e., in general terms, since it is impossible to enter into details within the compass of this essay.

I. EXISTENTIAL PHILOSOPHY AND PHILOSOPHICAL ANTHROPOLOGY

For our purpose it is opportune to take a glance at the intentions of the existentialist writers, as their intentions have found realization in their actual work. It appears that in dealing with the life-world they do not so much concern themselves with the *world of common experience, the world of daily life,* but rather with *man and his existence, his ways of existing in the life-world.* This distinction is more than merely a matter of emphasis. It defines the line of demarcation which separates Husserl's work from that of the existentialists of every persuasion.

Husserl, to be sure, embarks upon the world as directly and immediately given in human experience in contradistinction to the universe of science which is not experienced in direct immediacy but constructed for purposes of explanation.[9] The world of common experience, as it is given prior not only to specific scientific interpretation but also to logical operations of all sorts which might be performed upon the several items it contains, undoubtedly has human significance. From the outset Husserl has stressed that among the things and objects encountered in the world of common experience, there are those essentially characterized by human significance in a pre-eminent sense, as, e.g. tools, instruments, utensils of every description, works of art, literary documents, objects of cultural value, and the like.[10] By their very sense, such objects refer to their having been produced and their being destined to be used by human beings. In his account of the life-world Husserl sets himself the task of providing a complete and systematic description of such objects and other ones, not man-made, as they are directly experienced, and of analyzing the different ways in which they present themselves in experience. Concerning the life-world as a whole, he endeavors – as we shall see later – to lay bare its general style in its several specifications along various dimensions. Man is encountered within the life-world and as inserted into it. Each one of us is aware both of himself and of his fellow-men, the likes of him, as mundane existents among other mundane existents, the sense of mundanity being defined by the above-mentioned insertion. Man, to be sure, is characterized by distinctive features. Hence problems of a particular and highly specific nature arise with respect to man and human existence. Along the lines of Husserlian phenomenology, man and human existence would have to be considered within the frame, and against the background, of the life-world, as, so to speak, a secondary theme to be treated with reference to the primary one. We have used the grammatical form of the conditional because, as a matter of fact, Husserl has not dealt with the specific problems of human existence, except for a few occasional remarks, which are not very significant and are rather in the nature of promissary notes.[11] He has concerned himself with the problem of the constitution of the cultural world, a world made by men in the various forms of their mutual cooperation, and upon whose objects sense and meaning is bestowed by virtue of intellectual and mental functions. As we shall see later, he conceives of the cultural world, or rather worlds, as arising on the basis of the "natural world" – "natural" now to be

---

[9] Husserl, *Krisis,* § 34 d.

[10] Husserl, *Ideen* I, p. 50.

[11] Cf., e.g., Husserl, *Cartesianische Meditationen* (*Husserliana* I, 1963) p. 169 (trans. by D. Cairns: *Cartesian Meditations,* 1960, p. 142).

construed as not man-made, but still as given in direct perceptual experience. Just because they deal with what is accomplished by man and with the conditions of its being accomplished, these investigations pertain to a philosophy of culture rather than of human existence, as that term has later come to be understood.

The preceding remarks should suffice to dissipate the erroneous opinion, all too often encountered, of Husserl as a forerunner of existentialism in the sense that the main value of his work had consisted in preparing the way for existentialist philosophy and had been superseded by the advent of the latter. Certainly, existentialist philosophers have learned a great deal from Husserl; they have availed themselves of a great many results arrived at in his analyses of consciousness, and most of them have not failed to acknowledge their indebtedness to him. Still, they have not espoused his guiding radical philosophical intentions, about which we shall say more in the subsequent section.

Our initial statement that existentialist philosophy is concerned with human existence in the world requires some greater precision. First of all, *that man exists in the world means that he is involved in it.* Such involvement and the various modes and forms it assumes are of central interest in existential philosophy in which man is considered with regard to his conduct in his environment and the different ways in which he comes or tries to come to terms with it, especially with his fellow-men, and as confronted with certain situations of vital importance in which he has to make decisions, to assume responsibilities, and to enter into commitments. Man is viewed as planning his future and as living towards it in his multifarious endeavors to realize his projects. In a word, man is seen as fashioning his ambiance as the scene of his committed life. It is needless to stress that inter-human relations of all kinds hold a preeminent place in considerations of this sort.

Thus to approach the study of man means considering him in the full concreteness of his existence. This point has been underlined by the existentialist writers as well as by their commentators. Consequently, the emphasis can no longer be mainly, and certainly not exclusively, on man's mental and conscious life, on his intellectual functions, and on what is accomplished and produced by them. Taken in full concreteness, man proves to be a psycho-somatic unity. Each one of us has his body or – as one often finds it expressed – each one *is* his body. It is perfectly in keeping with the logic of the existentialist orientation that both Sartre and Merleau-Ponty, though not Heidegger, have devoted their attention to the somatic aspects of human existence of which they have presented extensive and fruitful analyses.[12] In speaking of the body, of course, they do not have in view that which is described and studied in anatomy, physiology, and the other biological sciences, which take the standpoint of a detached onlooking observer, but, on the contrary, the somatic body as it is experienced and "lived" by us in our very involvement with it.

Human existence taken in full concreteness furthermore comprises a socio-historical aspect. Man is born into a certain cultural group whose language he speaks and whose interpretation of and outlook upon the world has been conveyed to him, and is accepted by him as a matter of course. He lives in a certain society at a given period of its history. In this society he occupies a certain place, either assigned to him by birth, as in a class-society of rigid social stratification, or defined by his profession, his function, his wealth, influence, etc. Once again, what is in question are not social and historical facts and the connections between them as they are or may be ascertained and formulated by an impartial observer, but as they appear to and enter the consciousness (in whatever mode) of those whose historical and social conditions they define and determine, and who are involved in that situation, again to the point of saying that they *are* their situation. Hence the Hegelian strain which may be discerned in all existential philosophers and, in the case of French existentialists and writers influenced by them, the interest in and the preoccupation with the thought of Marx, especially the early Marx. Sartre's relinquishment of his earlier existentialist philosophy and his espousal of Marxism[13] appear as the logical outcome of this earlier existentialism.

However superficial, the preceding sketchy survey makes it clear that existentialism is not so much an exploration of the life-world as a *philosophical anthropology* whose theoretical procedures have to a considerable extent been borrowed from Husserlian phenomenology. This characterization also holds for the work of Heidegger, his strong protestations to the contrary notwithstanding.[14] The term "anthropology" is not to be construed in the technical sense as synonymous with "ethnology", but must be given the broader meaning of a general preoccupation with man and his existence.

We are far from challenging the legitimacy of a philosophical anthropology and equally far from denying the fruitfulness of the insights into the

[12] Sartre, *L'Être et le néant,* Part III, chap. II; Merleau-Ponty, *La Structure du comportement,* 1942 (trans. by A. L. Fisher: *The Structure of Behavior* 1963). Cf. also the exposition of their views by R. M. Zaner, *The Problem of Embodiment* (*Phaenomenologica* 17, 1964), Part II, chap. II and Part III, chap. II.

[13] Sartre, *Critique de la raison dialectique,* 1960.

[14] Heidegger, *Sein und Zeit,* § 10.

forms and modes of human involvement, the somatic and social aspects of human existence that have resulted from the existentialist enterprise which, as we readily grant, holds out the promise of still further valuable insights to be attained. Nor do we overlook the many fruitful applications which, understandingly enough, the existentialist approach to man and existential thought has found in the contemporary psychological sciences, especially psychiatry. Since, as already mentioned, the existentialist philosophers have made ample use of Husserl's results and ideas, the latter have penetrated, at least by way of mediation, into the work of contemporary psychologists and psychiatrists, some of whom, incidentally, have derived consequential stimulation from immediate contact and direct acquaintance with Husserl's work. It is most gratifying to see that phenomenological theory has proved valuable and fruitful in fields of research other than that in which it was originally developed.

Still, we must not permit ourselves to become fascinated by the fruits which the tree of phenomenology has borne to the point of neglecting its roots so as to jeopardize, perhaps, the growth of further fruits which the tree might yield in the future, were its roots cultivated with the utmost care. Apart from such "pragmatic" considerations, we have to face the question of whether to accept the transformation of philosophy into anthropology, its dissolution into psychology, however widely the latter be conceived. Granting the legitimacy of philosophical anthropology, granting even, for the sake of the discussion, the correctness of whatever results have been achieved thus far, does it follow that the ultimately radical philosophical dimension has been reached?

II. THE PRIMACY OF CONSCIOUSNESS

From the Husserlian point of view we now have to raise the problem of access. Whether we concern ourselves with the universe as constructed and interpreted in the sciences of modern style or, for that matter, of any style, or with the life-world as directly experienced, or with whatever else, it is through acts of consciousness and through such acts alone that what we deal with is given and presented to us and thus becomes accessible to us. In the case of the life-world and whatever it comprises, the acts in question pertain to perceptual consciousness in both its originary and derivative modes.[15] As regards the scientific universe, allowance must be made not only for perceptual experience but also for specific acts of conceptualization, idealization, and formalization which presuppose perceptual experi-

15 Husserl, *Ideen* I, § 99.

ence, because they are founded upon it in a way we shall discuss in the last
section.

In raising the problem of access to "reality" – in whatever sense the term
is understood – we come to discern the preeminent role played by perceptual consciousness. On the one hand, it is required as an avenue of access
to reality; it is in fact the only avenue. On the other hand, by its very nature,
perceptual consciousness does yield that access. Existential philosophy is
often credited with having accounted for the immediacy of our contact with
the world and mundane existence, for our being "at" the world. Such immediacy of contact, however – as we have shown elsewhere [16] – follows from
Husserl's theory of the intentionality of consciousness, especially perceptual
intentionality.[17] The novelty which is original with existentialism consists in
the emphasis on involvement and commitment. However, for involvement
in any of its forms and modes to be a possible topic of discussion and even
to be experienced or "lived" acts of consciousness are required through
which the involved subject becomes aware of his being involved and of the
specific form and sense which his involvement assumes in a particular
situation.[18]

Correspondingly the same holds for the socio-historical aspect of human
existence. Even if a social or historical situation is taken as an objective
fact, i.e., as it is ascertained by an historian or a social scientist, it refers to,
and in that sense, presupposes acts of consciousness on the part of the objective observer through which he gains access to the subject-matter of his
studies. In existentialism and philosophical anthropology, however, socio-
historical situations, as previously mentioned, are not considered as they are
seen by a detached and impartial observer, but rather as to what they mean

[16] A. Gurwitsch, "Husserl's Theory of Intentionality of Consciousness in Historical
Perspective" II, in *Phenomenology and Existentialism* (ed. by E. N. Lee and M. Mandel-
baum), 1967.

[17] G. Funke, *Phänomenologie – Metaphysik oder Methode?*", 1966, p. 44 maintains
that already for Descartes consciousness is always consciousness of objects (*Objekt-
bewusstsein*) such that there is no gulf separating and isolating man as a self-sufficient
subject from a world of equally self-sufficient objects. In our article (quoted in the
preceding footnote) I b, we have dealt with that Cartesian problem, but have come to a
somewhat different interpretation.

[18] H. L. Dreyfus, "Why Computers Must Have Bodies in Order to be Intelligent,"
The Review of Metaphysics XXI, 1967, p. 15 f maintains that transcendental phenomenology is based on the "assumption" that "everything can be understood from the point
of view of a detached objective thinker". Against this "assumption" he emphasizes "the
crucial role of human involvement" which – as following Merleau-Ponty he points out
(p. 19 f) – can only be understood in terms of "the body which confers the meanings
discovered by Husserl". At this point we ask whether involvement as experienced does
not refer to consciousness experiencing it. Presently we shall raise the same question
with respect to somatic experience.

to the subjects concerned and involved. Obviously, we are again referred to acts of consciousness (different, of course, from those of the scientific observer) through which the socio-historical subjects and agents conceive of and interpret the society in which they live and their respective social roles, functions, situations, and positions.

In principle, the case is not different with regard to the somatic aspect of human existence. Undoubtedly, it is a great merit of the existentialist philosophers to have called attention to the body with which we live and as we live it. Again the problem of access arises. We could not speak of somatic existence in the sense in question, if it were not for acts of consciousness through which we become aware both of our being embodied in general and of particular postures, motions, motory tendencies, and the like. To be sure, the acts of consciousness which yield access to our embodied or somatic existence are of a specific nature. Their very specificity proves them to be acts of consciousness just the same.[19]

Whether we concern ourselves with the life-world along the lines of Husserl's orientation or, following the direction of existentialism and philosophical anthropology, deal with human existence within the life-world, in raising the problem of access we are led to considering consciousness and its acts: acts through which the life-world presents itself to us and is interpreted in the sense it has for the socio-historical group to which we belong (the life-world, as we shall show in the subsequent section, is essentially a cultural world), further acts through which we conceive of ourselves as mundane existents,[20] as human beings in a sense which is congruous with that in which we interpret our life-world. Acts of consciousness are in play in all our conduct, in all our doings, involvements, commitments, hopes, fears, actions and projects.

This is not the place to enter into a description of those acts and the generic differences between them, nor to analyse their systematic groupings and concatenations of a sometimes high degree of complexity, nor, finally, to study the relations of foundation in which certain acts may stand to others. What alone matters in the present context is the *reference to consciousness as the universal and only medium of access*. Granting as we did

---

[19] Cf. A. Gurwitsch, *The Field of Consciousness* (1964) p. 303 ff and R. M. Zaner, *The Problem of Embodiment*, Part III, chap. III 2 a.

[20] Husserl, "Phänomenologie und Anthropologie", *Philosophy and Phenomenological Research* II, 1941 p. 8: "Sich als Mensch nehmen, das ist schon die Weltgeltung voraussetzen"; cf. also p. 9 f. This article, which reproduces a lecture given in Berlin, June 10, 1931, is Husserl's reply to the anthropological tendencies of Heidegger, whose name, however, is not mentioned. See also "Nachwort", *Ideen* III (*Husserliana* V, 1952), p. 138 ff.

at the outset, the significance of the disclosure of the life-world as an ac-complishment of permanent value, we must not overlook or forget another no less definitive accomplishment which philosophy achieved more than 300 years ago: the discovery in the second of his *Meditations on First Philosophy* which Descartes made of the privilege and primacy of con-sciousness not only on account of its indubitability but also as the universal medium of access to whatever we might be dealing with.

When consciousness is considered under that perspective, it must not be taken, as it was by Descartes, for a partial mundane domain, a series or set of mundane events alongside other mundane events with which the former are intervowen and to which they stand in multifarious relations of causal or functional dependency. Such an approach would be beset by the absur-dity of regarding the medium of access as forming part of that to which it yields access. Hence a special methodological device is required by means of which consciousness is stripped of the sense of mundanity or, it may also be put, which permits us to consider consciousness exclusively under the aspect of its presentational or presentifying function, that is to say, as opening up access to objects and entities of every kind, including those which pertain to the life-world. This device is the phenomenological or transcendental reduction. It is not possible to consider it here.[21]

Recognizing its legitimacy does not mean granting that philosophical anthropology is autochthonous in the sense of being in no need of radical clarification and justification. It does not mean that philosophical anthro-pology stands on its own legs in the sense of having no presuppositions. In inquiring into its foundations by raising the problem of access, we discovered consciousness as required for our apprehension of ourselves as mundane human beings, hence as a presupposition of philosophical anthropology, a presupposition most often taken for granted and, therefore, overlooked. By this token, *the life-world and all that it comprises, man as a mundane exis-tent, all his modes of existing and conducting himself in the life-world reveal themselves as correlates of acts and operations of consciousness and of multifarious concatenations, syntheses, and systematic organizations of those acts and operations.* With respect to the life-world as well as with regard to any domain of being, the task arises of setting forth and analyzing the corresponding and correlated "equivalent of consciousness" (*Bewusst-*

---

[21] The transcendental and phenomenological reductions are treated by Husserl in almost all of his writings since *Ideen* I. The second part of *Erste Philosophy* (*Husserl-iana* VIII, 1959) is entirely devoted to that topic.

seinsäquivalent), an expression which might well serve as a succinct formulation of the program of Husserl's constitutive phenomenology.[22]

Recently the idea of the correlation between that which is given to consciousness and the consciousness of it has been stressed by Funke quite generally and with special reference to the life-world.[23] Funke goes still further. In his thoroughgoing critical discussion of Heidegger's philosophy and also of the attempts made in Germany in the twenties at a "revival" of metaphysics, Funke insists upon the profound difference between *simply existing* and *formulating a philosophy of existence*. For the latter, acts of a specific kind of reflection, i.e., specific acts and operations of consciousness are required by means of which mere existing is articulated and rendered explicit, hence, in a sense, transcended.[24] Heidegger's "fundamental ontology" (*Fundamentalontologie*), to mention a particularly striking point, deals with the facticity of Existence (*Dasein*) as such, not with a particular factual existent, with the fact of *this* Ego, *this* man; he does not write "*eine Biographie dieses und nur dieses besonderen Lebens*".[25] Rather the factual particular existence is seen under the aspect and as an exemplar of facticity, i.e., from a certain point of view. This requires specific acts of ideation and conceptualization. Philosophy, existentialist and other, must be recognized as a mental product and accomplishment and must be referred to the processes and operations of consciousness in which it orginates. Differently expressed, every philosophy – constitutive phenomenology being no exception – stands under the obligation of accounting in its own terms for its very possibility.

This amounts to nothing less than a reassertion of the supreme law under which philosophy stands, a law which Plato formulated in the expression λόγον διδόναι, rendering accounts, and which Husserl has in view when he repeatedly speaks of radicality as the task of philosophy and of the intellectual responsibility and self-responsibility of the philosopher. Throughout his book Funke, with whom we find ourselves in agreement on a great many points, lays stress on philosophy as having the essential and even only function of providing grounds and foundations (*Begründungen* and *Begründungszusammenhänge*). Adopting and appropriating the supreme law of philosophy, we are led to consciousness as the ultimate ground of all our awareness and knowledge, of all validation and invalidation, of all founding and grounding.

[22] Husserl, *Ideen* I, § 152; in *Krisis* §§ 46 and 48 Husserl speaks of "universales Korrelationsapriori" and "Korrelationssystem".
[23] G. Funke, *Phänomenologie – Metaphysik oder Methode?* pp. 99, 139 ff, 168 ff.
[24] Funke, *loc. cit.*, pp. 30, 41 ff, 67 f, 174 f, 234 ff.
[25] Funke, *loc. cit.*, p. 236.

As a result of our discussion, the discovery of the life-world cannot be considered as the disclosure of the ultimate philosophical dimension but, at the most, as a stepping-stone on the way towards that disclosure. We may say that with the discovery of the life-world the penultimate but not the ultimate philosophical dimension is reached, the ultimate one being consciousness under the aspect of its transcendental function. This view is borne out by the literary organization of *Krisis*, which very significantly, like two other books by Husserl, bears the sub-title "An Introduction to Phenomenological Philosophy".[26] After having rehabilitated the life-world by an analysis of the origin and the presuppositions of modern physics, physics of the Galilean style (in the subsequent section we shall briefly deal with that analysis), Husserl embarks upon the treatment of the life-world with a view to opening up an avenue of approach to transcendental phenomenology.[27] We point this out in order to dissipate some misunderstandings. In some quarters *Krisis* is considered as Husserl's most important book to the disregard of his work in logic or rather philosophy of logic; moreover, its importance is seen to consist in his having broken with his past, having somehow relinquished the idea of constitutive phenomenology, and having moved in the direction of existentialist philosophy.[28] A close and thorough study of *Krisis* does not justify the distinction, in the sense of an opposition, between the philosophy of the late and that of the early Husserl. Rather it makes clear the intrinsic connection between the last work of Husserl and his earlier writings and testifies to the remarkable continuity in the development of his thought.[29]

In concluding our discussion of the idea and program of existentialist philosophy and philosophical anthropology, we wish to note that our criticism does not apply, at least not without qualification, to the work of Schutz, whose significance for the elucidation of the social aspect of the life-world was mentioned at the beginning. Throughout all his writings, Schutz deliberately abided by the "natural" as contrasted with the transcendental attitude, the latter being contingent upon the performance of the phenomenological reduction. His analyses fall under the purview of mun-

[26] The two other books are *Ideen* I and *Cartesianische Meditationen*.

[27] Husserl, *Krisis,* Part III A whose heading reads: "Der Weg in die phänomenologische Transzendentalphilosophie in der Rückfrage von der vorgegebenen Lebenswelt aus".

[28] Cf. Funke, *Phänomenologie – Metaphysik oder Methode*? p. 156 f. Even S. Bachelard, *La Logique de Husserl*, 1957, p. 216 note 1, believes that in *Krisis* Husserl has not remained faithful to himself but has made concessions "au goût du jour, aux philosophies de l'existence". See also *infra* p. 54 note 54.

[29] This view is also maintained by J. M. Broekman, *Phänomenologie und Egologie* (*Phaenomenologica* 12, 1963), pp. 5 f and 27.

dane phenomenological psychology rather than transcendental phenomenology; they may be said to be parts and fragments of a philosophical anthropology which he had planned to write, but which it was not given to him to work out.[30] In proceeding in this manner, Schutz has made use of the right of every scholar and of which, as he has pointed out himself,[31] no scholar can fail to avail himself, namely the right to define his field of inquiry and to indicate lines of demarcation which he does not intend to transcend in his research. Such a circumscription of a delineated field is at the same time a recognition of a domain extending beyond the lines of demarcation. With respect to Schutz' work this means that by deliberately confining his analyses within the limits of phenomenological psychology he has taken notice of the transcendental problematic, a recognition of which numerous explicit formulations appear in his several writings. He never claimed philosophical finality for his theories but was well aware of their being capable of receiving a transcendental-phenomenological underpinning, though he himself did not enter into the transcendental dimension. It is in this light that our discussion of his article "On Multiple Realities" must be understood.[32]

III. THE LIFE-WORLD AS A CULTURAL WORLD

To approach the life-world from a different angle, we recall that Husserl was led to its discovery by an analysis of Galilean physics and the disclosure of its presuppositions.[33] By Galilean physics Husserl does not mean the work of the historical Galileo, but rather the science inaugurated by Galileo, the science of physics of the specific modern style. The universe, as it has come to be conceived in the course of the history of modern science (a conception entertained at every period of that history), is a construction, a system of constructs resulting from, and being the correlates of, conceptualizations of a specific sort, namely idealizations, mathematizations, algebraizations, formalizations. Such processes which, of course, are mental in nature, require materials upon which to operate. Those materials, which

---

[30] Cf. Schutz' programmatic statement in "Husserl's Importance for the Social Sciences", *Collected Papers* I, p. 149; see also M. Natanson's Introduction to that volume, p. XLVI f.

[31] Schutz, "On Multiple Realities", *Collected Papers* I, p. 249 f.

[32] Schutz, *Collected Papers* I, p. 207 ff; A. Gurwitsch, *The Field of Consciousness,* Part VI 4 b; cf. also M. Natanson's remarks in his very sympathetic and appreciative review of the French version of our book in *The Philosophical Review* LXVIII, 1959, p. 538.

[33] Husserl, *Krisis,* § 9.

must be pre-given, can be nothing other than the objects of everyday common experience. The life-world is defined as comprising all items and objects which present themselves in pre-scientific experience, and as they present themselves prior to their scientific interpretation in the specific modern sense. As thus understood, the life-world proves to be a most essential presupposition or "foundation of sense" (*Sinnesfundament*) of the science of physics, insofar as the scientific universe is constructed on the basis of the multiple experiences of the life-world.

However, this foundation of sense has become obscured, obfuscated, and forgotten. Since the beginning of the modern development, the life-world has been concealed under a "tissue of ideas" (*Ideenkleid*) which has been cast upon it like a disguise, the ideas in question pertaining to mathematics and mathematical natural science. What in truth is a method, more precisely, the result and product of a method has come to be taken for "true being" (*wahres Sein*),[34] while the life-world which for us is the only truly real world has been relegated to the inferior status of a merely subjective phenomenon. On account of our historical situation as heirs to the modern scientific tradition, the world presents itself to us, including those of us who are not professional scientists or are even ignorant of the details of scientific theories, with reference to and in the light of its possible mathematical idealization.[35] It is apprehended as indicating and pointing to an "objective reality", i.e., a reality once and for all determined in itself and hence the same for everybody. The task of the scientist is the disclosure of that objective reality which is hidden beneath the varying subjective appearances. We may likewise say that his task consists of specifying in detail the general scheme of our comprehension and interpretation of the world as it has historically developed.

For the sake of clarifying the presuppositions and the sense of modern natural science, we have to turn to the life-world, as given in direct experience, though, according to Husserl,[36] the life-world may and must be made a topic of investigation in its own right and independently of the foundational problems of modern science. To restore the life-world in its original form, the sediment of sense which has accrued to it in the course of and due to the development of modern science, must be removed. More is required than no longer basing oneself on starting from, accepting, or even no longer taking notice of, particular scientific interpretations of the world, like the physics of Newton, that of Einstein, contemporary quantum

[34] Husserl, *Krisis*, p. 52.
[35] Husserl, *Erfahrung und Urteil*, § 10.
[36] Husserl, *Krisis*, §§ 33 and 34 f.

physics, etc. *What is in question is the very sense of objectivity which belongs to our comprehension of the world.* Reinstating the life-world in its original and authentic shape requires not merely turning away from every specific scientific interpretation, relinquishing the idea of the universe as already scientifically determined, as already disclosed as to what it is in itself, but also and above all *removing and eliminating the very sense of scientific explicability as such and at large. To find access to the life-world, our experience of the world must be stripped of the reference to possible scientific explanation, of the component of sense by virtue of which the world is apperceived and apprehended as lending itself to scientific interpretation,* whatever that interpretation might be in detail. Another way of expressing it is to say that the reference to an ideal mathematical order must be eliminated from our experience of the world and that the latter must no longer be seen under the perspective of that order.

What are we left with, after this subtractive operation has been performed? Perceptual experience is reinstated in its right. The yellow color of the chair over there is considered as a property of the thing itself and is not taken for a subjective sensation provoked by processes describable in mathematico-physical terms, which impinge upon our sense organs. The same holds for all "secondary" qualities, while the "primary" ones have to be taken as they present themselves in perceptual experience, without reference to geometrical idealization.

However, the things encountered in the life-world are not adequately and certainly not completely characterized, when they are described in terms only of their primary and secondary qualities. The chair has not only a certain shape and color, but is also perceived as something to sit in. Things present themselves as suitable and serviceable for certain purposes, as to be manipulated and handled in certain ways, as instruments and utensils, in a word with reference to actions to be performed, or performable, upon them.[37] They appear in the light of schemes of apperception and apprehension which belong to what Schutz calls the "stock of knowledge at hand". That stock comprises, among other things, a set of more or less loosely

[37] Heidegger's notions of "equipment" (*Zeug*) and "readiness-to-hand" (*Zuhandenheit*) are applicable here; cf. *Sein und Zeit*, p. 68 ff (*Being and Time* p. 98 ff). On other grounds and in an entirely different context, already Bergson, *Matière et Mémoire* (transl. by N. M. Paul and W. S. Palmer: *Matter and Memory*), chap. I, insisted upon the intrinsic connection between perception and action. Challenging the traditional "postulate" that "la perception a un intérêt tout spéculatif; elle est connaissance pure" (p. 14; trans. p. 17), Bergson maintains that, on the contrary, "Les objets qui entourent mon corps réfléchissent l'action possible de mon corps sur eux" (p. 6; trans. p. 6 f). "La perception ... mesure notre action possible sur les choses et par là, inversement, l'action possible des choses sur nous" (p. 48; trans. p. 57).

connected rules and maxims of behavior in typical situations, recipes for handling things of certain types so as to attain typical results.[38] The elements composing the "stock of knowledge at hand" are socially approved and socially derived.[39] Social approval does not mean explicit promulgation, nor any kind of legal of formal sanction, but rather the fact that in a given society certain modes of conduct are tacitly and as a matter of course accepted and taken for granted as behavior appropriate and in this sense, "natural" in typical situations. The "stock of knowledge at hand" is socially derived because only a comparatively small part of it originates in the personal experience of the individual, the bulk being transmitted to him by his parents, teachers, other persons in authority, and also by all kinds of associates.

Going beyond Schutz, who has not dealt with this problem, it must be stressed that the perception of a thing under the perspective of the "stock of knowledge at hand" is not to be understood as though a sense or meaning were superveniently bestowed or imposed upon a mere corporeal object which, prior to that imposition, was devoid of all sense and was to be described in terms of both primary and secondary qualities, but in those terms alone.[40] On the contrary, *the schemes of apperception and apprehension* play a determining role in and for perception; they *contribute essentially toward making the things encountered such as they appear in perceptual experience*. As a result of the elimination of the reference to scientific explicability and an ideal mathematical order, we are not reduced to perceptual experience in its pristine purity, that is to say, yielding primary and secondary qualities only. Rather *the things perceived present themselves* as defined by the purpose they serve, the use that can be made of them, the manner in which they are to be handled, and so on, briefly as *determined by schemes of apprehension*. Accordingly, the life-world, to which we gain access by the subtractive procedure in question, does not consist of mere corporeal objects in the sense just mentioned. On the contrary, it is a world interpreted, apperceived, and apprehended in a specific way; in a word, it is a *cultural world*, more precisely the cultural world of a certain socio-historical group, that of our society at the present moment of its history.

Husserl[41] emphasizes that the cultural sense of an instrument, a utensil, a machine, but also of a garden, a building, a work of art, a literary document, etc., is not externally attached to or associated with a mere corporeal

    [38] Schutz, "Some Structures of the Life-World", *Collected Papers* III, p. 120 f.

    [39] Schutz, "The Stranger" and "The Well-Informed Citizen", *Collected Papers* II (*Phaenomenologica* 15, 1964) p. 95 f. and 133.

    [40] Cf. Heidegger, *Sein und Zeit*, p. 71 (*Being and Time* p. 101).

    [41] Husserl, *Phänomenologische Psychologie*, § 16.

thing. Rather its sense is incorporated and impressed (*eingedrückt*) in the cultural object and thus proves to be a character proper to that object. To be sure, all cultural objects as defined by the sense embodied and embedded in them refer to mental life, to the plans, projects, designs, intentions, and the like of makers and users.[42] However, the cultural sense must not, because of that reference, be mistaken for a psychological event of a special kind, a misconception which would entail the interpretation of a cultural object in terms of the perception of a mere corporeal thing accompanied by a special psychological occurrence.

Although a cultural object exhibits its sense as a property pertaining to it and essentially determining and defining it, an abstraction is possible by means of which cultural senses come to be disregarded. By virtue of this abstraction, cultural objects are reduced to mere corporeal things (*pure dingliche Realitäten*) and, accordingly, the life-world, originally a cultural world, becomes a world of mere things (*Dingwelt*).[43] Though it is attained by an abstraction, the thing-world has, according to Husserl, priority with respect to the cultural world.[44] That is to say, the cultural world presupposes the thing-world as a substratum. It arises by virtue of specific acts of a "higher order" which are founded upon acts of "pure" perceptual experience (yielding mere corporeal things in the sense just referred to) and whose intentional or noematic correlates are the several cultural senses impressed in the corporeal things, whereby the latter are transformed into cultural objects exhibiting their cultural senses as properties of their own.[45] In other

---

[42] In this connection we refer to the very important distinction between the "subjective" and the "objective" sense of artifacts, but also actions, judgments, etc. which Schutz has established in *Der sinnhafte Aufbau der sozialen Welt* § 27.

[43] Husserl, *Phänomenologische Psychologie* § 17. This abstraction still leaves intact human beings and animals as psycho-somatic entities. A further abstraction is required for the disclosure of "Natur im prägnanten Sinne der physischen Natur" that is to say, which leads to corporeal things, merely defined by spatio-temporal extendedness, between which relations of physical causality obtain. In passing we note that in *Phänomenologische Psychologie* no mention is made of the mathematization of nature, i.e., the reference to an ideal mathematical order, which plays a preeminent role in *Krisis* (§§ 8 ff).

[44] Husserl, *Phänomenologische Psychologie* p. 119: "Offenbar ist diese Dingwelt gegenüber der Kulturwelt das an sich Frühere". He even considers the result of the second abstraction (see the preceding note) as "eine universale und offenbar rein in sich geschlossene Kernstruktur der Welt", though he does not wish to imply that "reine Physis je für sich existiere und existieren könne; als ob eine Welt als reine Natur denkbar wäre.

[45] Similarly Schutz, "Symbol, Reality, and Society", *Collected Papers* I, p. 328, refers to "appresentational functions ... which *transform* things into cultural objects, human bodies into fellow-men, their bodily movements into actions or significant gestures, waves of sound into speech, etc." (Italics ours). The term "transform" seems to imply

words, the phenomenological account of cultural objects takes its departure from the thing-world and traverses the same path as the abstraction just indicated, but in the opposite direction. This view is in line with Husserl's account of intersubjectivity on the basis of the perceptual experience of corporeal things, allowance being made, of course, for the specific experience everyone has of his somatic body.[46]

It is not possible to enter here into a systematic presentation and critical discussion of Husserl's theory of the constitution of the cultural world, urgent though this task seems to us to be. Suffice it to point out that while the transition, by means of the abstraction referred to, from the cultural object to the corporeal thing appears intelligible, it is hard to see how the cultural object can be reconstructed or constituted on the basis of and starting from the corporeal thing. We confine ourselves to stating the following thesis which, of course, requires more substantiation than we are able to present here: As the result of the removal or elimination of the historically accrued sediment of sense owing to which the world appears under the perspective of an ideal mathematical order, hence as determined in itself and amenable to scientific explanation of the specific modern style, we are not confronted with a world of mere corporeal things as given in "pristinely pure" perceptual experience. In other words, we do not encounter *the* "perceptual world",[47] the same for all human beings and all socio-historical groups, on the basis of which the several cultural worlds arise subsequently by means of acts of apprehension, apperception, and interpretation. Rather we are confronted with *our* cultural world which is *our* life-world, a world apperceived, apprehended, and interpreted in a specific way. To corroborate our thesis we refer to the conclusion at which Piaget[48] arrives in the course of his studies of the intellectual development of the human child, namely, that on no level of the development is there "direct experience either of the self or of the external environment. There only exist 'interpreted' experiences". What holds for the development of the individual is certainly true with regard to different socio-historical groups.

that prior to the operations of the "appresentational functions" the items mentioned are "things", i.e., "outer objects, facts, and events".

[46] Husserl, *Cartesianische Meditationen* V. In the present context § 58 is of particular interest. A very penetrating critical analysis of Husserl's theory of intersubjectivity has been presented by Schutz: "The Problem of Transcendental Intersubjectivity in Husserl", *Collected Papers* III.

[47] In *Phänomenologische Psychologie* Husserl uses this term in preference to the expression "life-world".

[48] J. Piaget, *La Naissance de l'intelligence chez l'enfant*, 1936, p. 143 (trans. by M. Cook: *The Origins of Intelligence in Children*, 1952, p. 136).

IV. SOCIO-HISTORICAL RELATIVISM

Historical reflections strip any cultural world of the matter of course character which it has for those who simply live in it.[49] In the light of such reflections, our cultural world appears as one among a great many others, for instance the world of the ancient Egyptians, that of the ancient Mesopotamians, the numerous cultural worlds corresponding to the numerous socio-historical groups that have existed in the course of history or are still in existence. Funke[50] goes as far as maintaining that the notion of the life-world has meaning and especially unity only with regard to the scientific universe and the specific experiences of which that universe is the correlate. Prior to the constitution of that universe and apart from it, there are only the innumerable experiences of the individual subjects, their "topico-doxic apprehensions" and positions which hardly have anything in common but all of which differ from and in a sense are opposed to the scientific universe. According to Funke, the concept of the life-world is a counterconcept with respect to that of the scientific universe and hence presupposes the latter. It seems to us that in establishing his thesis Funke has failed to make due allowance for the social dimension. Every socio-historical group has its cultural world which, to be sure, appears to each member of the group from his point of view and under a special perspective related to that point of view. The latter is to be understood in both the spatial and figurative senses, in such a way that each member takes it for granted that the world in which he finds himself is the same for him as for his fellow-men whom he encounters, and that they apprehend it, as a matter of course, in the way he does, as one and the same for all.[51]

In view of our exposition, in section II, of the correlation between that which is given to consciousness and the consciousness of it, there arises the task of setting forth in detail the specific form which this correlation assumes in the case, to state it in Funke's terminology, of a special "topico-doxic position" with respect to what he calls the corresponding "Bewusst-seinslage".[52] In terms of the thesis here maintained, the problem can be formulated as follows: given a certain cultural world as the life-world of a socio-historical group, the task is to find and to lay bare the acts of consciousness which in their systematic concatenation and intertexture make

---

[49] Funke, "*Phänomenologie – Metaphysik oder Methode?*" p. 48 f.

[50] Funke, *loc. cit.,* pp. 153 ff. and 178 ff.

[51] Cf. on this point the detailed analysis of Schutz, "Common-Sense and Scientific Interpretation of Human Action", II 2, *Collected Papers* I.

[52] In addition to the passages quoted on p. 45, note 23, cf. also pp. 50 ff, 146, 157.

this specific world possible as their correlate. Answering this question for a particular cultural world amounts to understanding that world from within by referring it to the mental life in which it originates. Inasmuch as cultural worlds evolve in historical continuity with one another, investigations of this kind lead to a study of consciousness itself in its historical development. Along such lines it is possible to realize some of the profound intentions of Dilthey.

In granting the legitimacy and stressing the significance of historical studies along the lines just mentioned, we have to face the *problem of relativism* which arises at this point. Not only are we confronted with a multiplicity of different cultural worlds or life-worlds, but all of them are on a par with one another. *From a historical point of view, there is no right to assign a privilege to any particular life-world, e.g., our own.* However, this statement can be made only on the level of a historical reflection, that is to say, it presupposes relinquishing the attitude of simply living in the life-world and taking it for granted. It requires adopting a point of view outside of or beyond our own life-world, from which we may look at the latter as well as at other life-worlds. In any event *one cannot avoid the question of whether the main and perhaps only task of philosophy consists in understanding and accounting for the multiple cultural worlds which have made their appearance in history.* Just as in consequence of existentialist trends philosophy is in danger of being transformed into anthropology or psychology, so it is now threatened with being dissolved into a series of historical studies which, however legitimate, and significant in themselves, cannot but lead to socio-historical relativism.

In his early discussion with Dilthey, Husserl dealt with historical relativism.[53] Against the historical relativization of philosophical systems Husserl upheld the idea of philosophy as a rigorous science (*strenge Wissenschaft*), "objectively" valid, i.e., valid for everybody, because built on unassailable foundations and proceeding in a cogent manner.[54] This idea found an incipient realization in Husserl's transcendental or constitutive phenomenology, which is a universal theory of consciousness considered under the aspect of

---

[53] Husserl. "Philosophie als strenge Wissenschaft", *Logos* I, 1911, pp. 323 ff. (trans. by Q. Lauer: *Phenomenology and the Crisis of Philosophy*, 1965, pp. 122 ff.).

[54] Husserl's phrase in *Krisis* p. 508 "der Traum ist ausgeträumt" is often misinterpreted to mean that in his late period Husserl had abandoned the idea of philosophy as a rigorous science. As H. Spiegelberg, *The Phenomenological Movement* (*Phaenomenologica* 5, second ed. 1965) Vol. I, p. 77, has shown, referring both to the context of the phrase in question and to further corroborating evidence, it must be understood as a characterization of the intellectual climate of the time, and not as an expression of Husserl's own position.

the correlation (expounded in section II) between objects of any kind whatever and the acts of consciousness through which those objects present themselves. On the basis of this general correlation the relativism is overcome. Whatever differences might obtain between the several cultural worlds and, correspondingly, between the several particular forms of conscious life in which the cultural worlds originate and of which they are the correlates, the general reference of every such world to the corresponding consciousness, which underlies all relativities, is not relative itself.[55] The task arises of setting forth and elucidating the universal structures of consciousness which make possible *any* cultural world as the life-world of a socio-historical group. Only on the basis of a general theory of consciousness as developed by Husserl in his several writings under the heading of intentionality, can the aforementioned program of understanding the various cultural worlds by referring each one of them to the corresponding mental life be realized and carried out, since all particularizations of consciousness here in question are variations within an invariant framework as delineated and defined by the essential and universal structure of consciousness.

V. THE PERCEPTUAL WORLD AND ITS METHODOLOGICAL SIGNIFICANCE FOR A PHENOMENOLOGICAL THEORY OF THE NATURAL SCIENCES

There remains the question of whether relativism cannot be overcome in still another way. Husserl has formulated the problem of relativism as it arises in connection with the diversity of cultural worlds.[56] While living in our life-world, we hold certain truths which we share with our fellow-men who belong to the same socio-historical group, that is to say, we share with them a certain cultural world common to all of us, in whatever way such agreement might have been brought about. When we come to another socio-historical group, e.g., to Chinese peasants or to Negroes in the Congo, we find that their truths are not the same as ours. Is it possible – asks Husserl – to establish a body of truths valid for all subjects, truths about which normal Westerners, normal Hindus, normal Chinese can agree, all relativities and divergencies notwithstanding? Differently expressed, the question concerns a stratum or core common to all life-worlds and truths holding for that core. The truths sought for are to refer to the life-world or to what has just been called a stratum of it, not to the scientific universe of

---

[55] Cf. Funke, *Phänomenologie – Metaphysik oder Methode?"* p. 102 ff.
[56] Husserl, *Krisis,* § 36.

objective science in the specific modern sense. As mentioned before, the
scientific universe is an ideal mathematical construction superseding, and
substituted for, the life-world. Presently we shall see that a radical philosophical account of the very possibility of the construction and constitution
of the scientific universe is contingent upon providing an answer to the
question raised.

To that end, Husserl points to the universal invariant structure exhibited
by every life-world. However they are interpreted and apprehended, things
encountered in the life-world – any life-world – have spatial shapes. Trees,
for instance, have a cylindrical shape. Of course, they are not cylinders in
the strict geometrical sense; rather their shape is of a cylindrical type or, as
we may say, they present a cylindrical physiognomy. Spatial shapes must be
taken as they are given in perceptual experience, without referring them to
ideal geometrical figures, even without conceiving of them as approxima-
ting the latter. In perceptual experience, the spatial shapes of things are
determined only as to type, which is to say that a margin of latitude is left
for variations, deviations, and fluctuations.[57] Things endure in time, whether changing or remaining unchanged. Change may be faster or slower, as
in the case of motion. Fastness and slowness of motion must again be understood in conformity with the nature of perceptual experience, and not in
terms of velocity and acceleration as defined mathematically.

None of the things encountered in any life-world presents itself in isolation. The house in front of which we happen to stand is surrounded by a
garden; it lies on a street; the street leads to other parts of the city, and so
on. Every thing is encountered within a perceptual environment or, as
Husserl calls it, an "outer horizon" (*Aussenhorizont*) which is not delimited
by fixed boundaries but continues indefinitely in both space and time.[58]
This all-encompassing spatio-temporal horizon – all-encompassing because
every thing and event has its place within it – *defines the universal form of
the perceptual world, an invariant structure of every life-world or cultural
world* whose unity is founded upon the unity of space and of time. Deliberately we have spoken of the outer horizon as continuing indefinitely and
not infinitely in order to eschew all mathematical connotations. With regard
to the space of the perceptual world, the question of whether it is Euclidean
or non-Euclidean cannot be meaningfully raised since it is *perceptual* space
and not the idealized, still less formalized, space of geometry.

[57] Husserl, *Krisis,* p. 22.
[58] Husserl, *Krisis,* p. 165 and § 37; *Phänomenologische Psychologie,* p. 62 and § 11;
the most detailed description and analysis is to be found in *Ideen* I, § 27 and *Erfahrung
und Urteil,* § 8. We may refer also to our article "Edmund Husserl's Conception of
Phenomenological Psychology," section II, *loc. cit.,* and *The Field of Consciousness,*
Part VI 2a.

Things pertaining to the life-world are subject to changes which, however, do not take place in a haphazard manner but with a certain regularity. In particular, changes of a certain kind are concomitant with other events which occur either in the changing thing itself (as when a glass falls down and breaks) or in its environment (e.g., a piece of ice melts when brought into a warm room). Things have their "habits" of regularly behaving in typical ways under typical circumstances. Regularities of the kind in question are also exhibited by the world as a whole, as exemplified by the alternation of day and night, the sequence of the seasons, and the like. Differently expressed, causal connections and regularities of a certain style and type prevail in the behavior of particular things as well as in the behavior of the life-world as a whole.[59] On this account, inductions and predictions are possible whose importance for practical conduct and the orientation in the life-world – any life-world – is too obvious to need further comment. Again it must be stressed that the regularities of the causal connections here in question are determined merely as to style and type, i.e., they admit of fluctuations and variations within certain limits not precisely defined. They are not relations of functional dependency capable of being expressed in the form of mathematical equations.

In addition to the invariant structures of every life-world as such, which Husserl has set forth, we may mention the fact that every such world is apprehended and interpreted in some way or other. Though the interpretations vary as to their content from one socio-historical group to another and, therefore, are relative to those groups, *all these relative apprehensions are diverse specifications of interpretedness at large*, which itself is not relative, but the invariant ground upon which, or the invariant framework within which all relative specifications arise. By virtue of its being apprehended and interpreted in a certain way, a life-world is a socio-cultural world of a given historical group. Schutz has pointed out invariant structures and features of every social world of any description whatever.[60] According to him, these invariant structures of social existence in a cultural world have their roots in the human condition; therefore, their ultimate clarification calls for a philosophical anthropology.

At this point it is possible to formulate the theoretical motivation for the aforementioned abstraction by means of which cultural objects are reduced to mere corporeal things. In the face of the multiplicity and diversity of cultural worlds, the problem arises of whether there is not a "world" com-

---

[59] Husserl, *Krisis*, p. 28 f; *Phänomenologische Psychologie*, pp. 68 f, 101 f, 133 ff.

[60] Schutz, "Equality and the Meaning Structure of the Social World", *Collected Papers* II, p. 229 ff; Some of these structures have been mentioned above p. 49 f.

mon to all socio-historical groups, the same for all of them, a universal human life-world, so to speak. To arrive at it, all acts of apprehension and interpretation are disregarded and their contributions discarded, which means stripping cultural objects of their cultural sense and human significance.[61] What remains is a perceptual world, that is to say, a world given in – as we have expressed it before – pristinely pure perceptual experience. It is not a mathematized world, nor is it conceived under the perspective of its possible mathematization, nor does it have the sense of being amenable to objective scientific explanation of the specific modern variety. Finally, the objects encountered in it are perceptual things retaining what are called their secondary qualities. Still, it is attained by means of an abstraction. It might, therefore, seem advisable to introduce a terminological distinction between the perceptual world and the life-world, though Husserl has not made that distinction, at least not explicitly.

In the spatiality of perceptual things, the indefinite spatio-temporal extendedness of the perceptual world, the specific causality prevailing in it, the invariant *categorial structure* or *constitution of the perceptual world* becomes manifest. The categories which pertain to the life-world or, as we should prefer to say, perceptual world are denoted by the same names as those which underlie the elaboration of the objectively valid scientific universe.[62] However, the former categories are not to be understood in the light of subsequent theoretical idealizations, formalizations, and constructions of geometry and physics, but on the contrary, in the sense of typicality and conformity to style as prevailing in the perceptual world. Hence Husserl establishes a distinction between the a priori pertaining to the perceptual world (*lebensweltliches Apriori*) and the logico-objective a priori of the exact sciences. If, as it must be, the former is made the theme of special investigations, there arises the idea of an "ontology of the life-world", *an a priori science of the universal structures of the perceptual world*, a science whose objective is the *systematic description of the categorial constitution* of that world, the explicit articulation of the "notion of the natural world" (*natürlicher Weltbegriff*).[63] Husserl conceives of a "transcendental aesthetics" in a sense different from that which Kant gave to the term, though not totally unrelated to it.[64] Transcendental aesthetics in Husserl's sense concerns itself with the "eidetische Problem einer möglichen Welt überhaupt

---

[61] Husserl, *Phänomenologische Psychologie*, p. 121.
[62] Husserl, *Krisis*, p. 142 f.
[63] Husserl, *Krisis*, § 51; *Phänomenologische Psychologie*, § 8; concerning the term "natürlicher Weltbegriff" cf. *ibid.*, pp. 62 and 93 f.
[64] Husserl, *Formale und transzendentale Logik*, 1929, p. 256 f.

als *Welt 'reiner Erfahrung'*". It is to provide "eine eidetische Deskription des universalen Apriori, ohne welches in blosser Erfahrung . . . einheitlich Objekte nicht erscheinen und so überhaupt Einheit einer Natur, einer Welt sich . . . nicht konstituieren könnte". Its task consists in disengaging the "Logos" of the perceptual world, the logicality which prevails in it. Of course, logicality as here meant must not be understood in the sense of fully conceptualized, still less formalized, logic, but rather in the same sense in which Husserl understands the a priori and the categories of the perceptual world, namely, determinateness as to style and type, but absence of exactness. Since the logicality in question proves to be the germ out of which logic in the proper and formal sense develops, it seems appropriate to denote it as "proto-logic".[65] In fact, for the transition from proto-logic to logic proper (understood in the widest sense so as to include all mathematization, algebraization, and formalization) specific idealizing operations are required which, of course, are working on the proto-logical structures as underlying pregiven materials.[66] Future phenomenological research will have, first, to complete Husserl's work in exhaustively setting forth the proto-logical structures and, then, to account for the acts and operations of consciousness which are involved in the transition to the logical level in the wider sense.

This is not the place to embark upon those problems. We only wish to illustrate the transition in question by one of Husserl's examples. As a rule, the perceptual process related to a certain material thing develops harmoniously, that is to say later phases of the process confirm earlier ones, all of them being in agreement and conformity with one another: throughout the perceptual process the thing perceived proves to be what it had appeared to be at first. Occasionally the harmonious development of the perceptual process is broken. Discrepancies and conflicts arise, as when what we see in a display-window appears to be a living person and, a few moments later, a clothed dummy.[67] Such discrepancies have always been

---

[65] For the term "proto-logic", the author is endebted to his student, Mr. L. Embree. We prefer that term to the Husserlian "pre-predicative experience", because it indicates the logicality inherent in "pre-predicative experience".

[66] Husserl, *Krisis*, p. 143 f: "Eine gewisse idealisierende Leistung ist es, welche die höherstufige Sinnbildung und Seinsgeltung des mathematischen und jedes objektiven Apriori zustande bringt, aufgrund des lebensweltlichen Apriori"; cf. also p. 398 where he speaks of "Logifizierung der vorwissenschaftlichen Erkenntnis oder korrelativ . . . Idealisierung des lebensweltlichen Seins (des relativen) in ein ideal identisches . . ."

[67] Husserl, *Erfahrung und Urteil*, p. 99 f. For a criticism of Husserl's account of this phenomenon in terms of unvarying sense-data and alternating perceptual apprehensions (*Wahrnehmungsauffassungen*) cf. A. Gurwitsch, *The Field of Consciousness*, Part IV, chap. II, 6.

resolved in the course of perceptual experience, so that its coherence and inner consistency have been reestablished by means of revisions and corrections. Perceptual experience carries with it the horizonal presumption (*Horizont-Präsumtion*) that further experience will come into play by virtue of which all horizons will be explored, all conflicts reconciled, and the world disclosed as intrinsically concordant (*einstimmig*).[68] The idealization of this horizonal presumption, which pertains to the universal style of perceptual experience and the perceptual world, yields the notion of the world as it is in itself, as in its true reality it exists behind and beneath all mere appearances and deceptions.[69] Obviously, this idea of the world as determined in itself is decisive for the objective sciences, especially the natural sciences, in their endeavor to disclose the true constitution of the real world.

At the beginning of section III we pointed out the difference between the scientific universe and the life-world. Now we have come to see that the scientific universe as well as its construction is rooted in the life-world out of which it arises by the mediation of what here has been called the perceptual world. In a very important, though perhaps not the only aspect, *the methodological significance of the notion of the life-world lies in the fact that this notion provides the basis for a phenomenological theory of the sciences, especially the exact sciences.* To that end, a phenomenological account of the constitution of mathematics along the suggested lines is required.[70] Substantially the same question arises with respect to formal logic, both traditional and modern, in the narrower technical sense. Its philosophical foundation and justification, the elucidation of its sense cannot be given except on the basis of a theory of pre-predicative experience.[71] We can here do no more than refer to *Erfahrung und Urteil* with its significant subtitle "Untersuchungen zur Genealogie der Logik". In that work Husserl attempts to trace the phenomenological origin of the logical categories to the proto-logical categories of pre-predicative experience.

In recent decades the theory of the sciences has not received sufficient attention in phenomenological literature.[72] Thus the impression could arise

[68] Husserl, *Phänomenologische Psychologie*, p. 63 f.
[69] Husserl, *Phänomenologische Psychologie*, p. 63 f.
[70] As to geometry, cf. Husserl, *Krisis*, Beilage III. This text, which was already published by E. Fink in *Revue Internationale de Philosophie* I, 1939, has been carefully analyzed by D. Cairns, *Philosophy and Phenomenological Research* I, 1940, p. 98 ff.
[71] Husserl, *Formale und tranzendentale Logik*, § 86.
[72] Among the exceptions are S. Bachelard, *La Logique de Husserl* and *La Conscience de rationalité,* 1958; J. J. Compton, "Understanding Science", *Dialectica*, XVI, 1963 and "Natural Science and the Experience of Nature", *Phenomenology in America* (ed. by J. M. Edie), 1967; J. Kockelmans, *Phenomenology and Physical Science*, 1966.

that phenomenology did not have much to say in that field of research, had withdrawn from it altogether to leave it to those contemporary philosophical trends, such as logical positivism, which call themselves "scientific". Since the necessary preparatory work was done in Husserl's later writings, the time seems to have come for phenomenology to reclaim possession of the field from which it took its departure in Husserl's earliest writings.

CONCLUSION

Let us take a brief glance at the preceding discussion. As far as the role of consciousness is concerned, we have come to the same result as in our earlier discussion of existentialism and philosophical anthropology. As a cultural world the life-world refers to acts of apprehension and interpretation The same holds for the perceptual world which is attained by an abstraction. Mental operations of a specific kind are involved in the elaboration and construction of the scientific universe. The notion of the life-world is of central importance because of its location at the junction of a great many roads. Along each one of them, the problem of access is bound to arise, to remind us of the privilege and priority of consciousness.

We also refer to our articles "Présuppositions philosophiques de la logique", *Revue de Métaphysique et de Morale* LVI, 1951 (reprinted in *Phénoménologie – Existence*, 1953), "Sur une racine perceptive de l'abstraction", *Proceedings of the XIth International Congress of Philosophy* II (1953), "Sur la pensée conceptuelle" *Phaenomenologica* IV, 1959; all of them are now available in English translation in *Studies in Phenomenology and Psychology*, cf. also "Comments on H. Marcuse, On Science and Phenomenology", *Boston Studies in the Philosophy of Science* II, 1965.

THE LIFE-WORLD AND THE PARTICULAR SUB-WORLDS

by

WERNER MARX

I

In his paper "On Multiple Realities" (*Collected Papers*, Vol. I, p. 207) Alfred Schutz develops a "typology" (p. 234) of sub-universes of reality which he prefers to call "finite provinces of meaning" (p. 230). He points out the "cognitive style" of these worlds through general characterizations of the various ways in which consciousness in experience relates to each of them (pp. 229ff.) and through an exposition of the differing basic features of the diverse worlds themselves. The particular sub-universe of "working" (which to a certain extent he equates with that of the "natural attitude") stands out as paramount over against the many other sub-universes of reality (p. 226). All other sub-universes such as the ones produced by the imagination, the worlds experienced in dreams and the worlds of the sciences (especially those of the social sciences) are considered to be modifications of it (p. 232). The main topic of Schutz's paper was the question of how such a modification is brought about by the unified life of consciousness and how, specifically, the transition from one particular sub-universe to another is effected by withdrawing or bestowing (respectively) "the accent of reality" (pp. 233ff.).

Now it seems that for Schutz a stream of experience involved with the particular sub-universe of working (the arche-type of all other sub-universes) or with the world investigated by a scientific discipline must at the same time comport itself to that "world" which for Husserl represented the *Lebenswelt* (life-world). Witness p. 247, where we read that: "The whole universe of life, that which Husserl calls the *Lebenswelt*, is pre-given to both the man in the world of working and to the theoretical thinker."

Within the scope of his paper Alfred Schutz did not ask the question of how in general the particular sub-universes which are intended in a consciousness directed specifically at them relate to that pre-given life-world.[1]

---

[1] A. Gurwitsch takes up this question in his book *The Field of Consciousness* (Pitts-

However, in the footnote to the sentence just quoted, he refers to parts I and II of Husserl's treatise *Die Krisis der europäischen Wissenschaften und die transzendentale Phaenomenologie*, which later appeared together with the previously unpublished parts IIA and IIB and a number of relevant supplementary texts in Vol. VI of the *Husserliana*. In this work, Husserl takes as his topic, the relationship of the life-world to the experience of the specific "objectivity" of a world which has been constituted in the scientific attitude of the mathematical natural sciences. This "world" is rather the construct of a world which for the scientist represents the universe in all its regions but which for Husserl has only the meaning of a sub-universe, since the attitude of the natural scientist is guided by the one specific purpose of finding a truth which is unconditionally and universally valid.

II

Upon an examination of Husserl's work * as a whole, one comes to the conclusion that the problem of the relationship of the world, as accepted by experience (*wie sie gilt für das Erfahren*), to sub-universes, as accepted by specific experiences, was treated very late only with respect to sub-universes constituted by goals and ends which, for this reason alone, were called *"Sonderwelten"*.** Why is this the case?

In the first volume of *Ideen* a "real world" (pp. 58, 390), in so far as it constitutes the "natural surrounding world" (*Umwelt* – pp. 57ff.) for wakeful consciousness in the manifold changing spontaneity of its actual and possible experiences, is articulated, on the basis of its "changing components", into a "world of things, a world of values, a world of goods, a practical world" (p. 59). Since these different kinds of components are experienced as making up "one and the same" surrounding real world in all its regions and since all of them represent certain goals and ends, the question

* Page-references to Husserl refer in all cases to the German text, when available to the *Husserliana*.

** In this paper, *"Sonderwelten"* has been translated into "particular sub-worlds".

burgh, Pa., 1964) pp. 382 ff. He conceives of the life-world (p. 386) as perceptual world only, as the "one, real, objective, spatio-temporal world" (pp. 383, 387, 405). (Gurwitsch has since enlarged this conception.) The life-world is for him the whole within which various spheres of life and activity are distinguished (p. 383). Gurwitsch specifically mentions the spheres of professional activity, family life and other "orders of existence" of a similar sort (*ibid.*). He conceives of the incorporation of these special worlds into the real world as a whole as being determined as regards form – here following Husserl – by their location in objective time (cf. p. 387, also footnote 14), and as regards their content by specific "relevancy-principles" of a certain kind (p. 394).

of the relationship of this real surrounding world – as accepted by experience – to "particular worlds", i.e., to worlds, constituted in turn by certain
goals and ends, could not have arisen.

The second volume of *Ideen* (p. 193) shows that consciousness in a
personal-spiritual attitude accepts its personal-spiritual surrounding world
– constituted intersubjectively – likewise as "one and the same" world
whose different types of content or meanings are all equally expressive of
community purposes and goals. Thus, also here, the question of the relationship of the surrounding world to "particular sub-worlds" could not have
come up.[2]

Only in the later works, was the question posed: what makes up the
concrete content (*die volle Konkretion*) of world as the correlate of the
"natural attitude"; the "phenomenological reduction", as it was developed
in *Ideen I,* only made it evident that world as accepted by experience is
such a correlate in regard to its various modes of "to be". The phenomenologist now turns to that correlate as a noema of quite a specific kind and
recognizes it as an intersubjectively constituted universal field forming the
foundation for every experience and being the horizon of all real or possible
praxis as well as cognitive activity (cf. *Krisis,* pp. 136, 145; *Erfahrung und
Urteil*, p. 52).[3] This world as accepted by everyday prescientific experience
is called the life-world.

For our particular problem it is important to note that the world now
designated as the life-world is no longer understood as being directed toward certain proposed goals and ends as was the case for the surrounding
world both in *Ideen I* and *Ideen II*. On the contrary, this world, within
which our everyday life unfolds, is experienced as "always and in each case
passively pre-given" to us (*E & U,* pp. 26, 74, 171). It is the field which is
"already there" for cognition and practical activity "without any accessory
activity of direction of the apperceptive gaze (toward the world as object), without the awakening of any interest" (*E & U,* p. 24). It "stands

[2] In the Appendix to the second volume of *Ideen* (p. 354) the question is discussed
of how "the" world appears as the "same" – despite changes in the appearance of the
subjectively perceived surrounding world and changes in the very substance of the
various culture-worlds in the course of history. However, the problems involved here
are not directly related to the question of the relationship of the surrounding world to
whatever particular sub-world happens to be present.

[3] The question of how the life-world qua "world for us all" constitutes itself through
all realities and modes of appearance of the surrounding world, as a unity such as "each
of us has" before him, does not affect the problem treated here. Equally our question
has nothing to do with that of how the absolute subject in constitutive transcendental
phenomenology "contains the real universe and all possible worlds in itself" (*Ideen I,*
p. 73). Finally our problem is not in what sense the world is "unique" (*Ideen II,* p. 195).

there for us on the basis of previous experience" (*E & U*, p. 75). This world, in its historical genesis, is "well known to us in advance as regards its typology" (*E & U*, p. 32) so that we move in it with "typological familiarity" (*E & U*, p. 39), i.e., with familiarity with the general types of objects which we might encounter. It is, in this sense, the "field of well-proven certainties" (*Krisis*, p. 441), of "truths relative to the situation" (*Situationswahrheiten*) (*Krisis*, p. 135) and of mere opinions, of doxa (*E & U*, p. 24). Only after the surrounding world has thus been recognized as one which is accepted by everyday experience as pre-given without any specific purpose, then and only then, could the question have arisen in what relation the experience of this world stands to the experience of "particular worlds", i.e., of worlds constituted by goals and ends.

From this development of Husserl's conception of the world, which we briefly traced and which he himself nowhere makes explicit, we can now understand why this question came up so very late. Once it did come up, however, one would have expected that it would have been treated as an important and pressing question of phenomenology. But, as has already been remarked, the *Krisis* treats extensively only the relationship of the life-world to that one "particular world" which is constituted in the scientific attitude of the mathematical-natural sciences and which it accepts as the unconditional and universally valid truth. The general problem of the relationship of the life-world as experienced in everyday attitude to "particular sub-worlds" as experienced in varying specific attitudes has been taken up generally only in an appendix to the *Krisis*. Up to now, this Appendix XVII has not been discussed in the literature.

III

How is a particular sub-world constituted from a "vocation" or from other "common goals", i.e., of individuals or of communities, and how are particular sub-worlds constituted from the tasks of scientists and philosophers? According to the appendix, particular sub-worlds come into existence precisely through these definite ends, through that which is "to be attained". The constitution of a "world horizon" occurs which "is closed in upon itself" (*Krisis*, p. 459). A "horizon of interest" encompasses the "life devoted to these special interests", and the latter's whole "work world" as well as its products.

How is the relationship of the experience of these particular sub-worlds to the experience of the life-world characterized in the appendix? Because of their "closed horizon," the subject experiencing such a particular sub-world "has eyes for nothing except the aims and work-horizons of his particular sub-world" (*ibid.*, p. 462). However, although experience moves wide awake and *thematically* in the particular sub-world, it is at the same time non-thematically conscious of the life-world as a horizon. Experience comports itself "within the constantly and self-evidently existing world, the life-world in its full, universal sense" (*ibid.*, p. 459). In this *non-thematic* way, the life-world is "continually pre-given, constantly accepted beforehand as existing" (*ibid.*, p. 461).

For our question of the relationship of the experience of the particular sub-worlds to the experience of the life-world, this noetic side is less important to consider than the following noematic one. The meaning of the life-world is said to be determined by its "radical difference" vis-à-vis the particular sub-worlds: the difference is the one already discussed by us, namely, that the life-world is precisely not "accepted for some purpose" (*Krisis*, p. 461), but rather always exist "of itself" (*ibid.*). The decisive aspect of the meaning of the life-world lies in the fact that it is not a "teleologic construct" (*Krisis*, p. 462). Consequently, the relationship of the particular worlds which by definition are all of a teleological nature to that non-teleological life-world, is seen in the following: the life-world is the "foundation for all designs, ends and end-horizons at any given time, and for work-horizons of ends of a higher degree" (*Krisis*, p. 462). It is as such a foundation that precedes all experience of particular sub-worlds. However, the appendix defines the relationship of the experience of particular sub-worlds to the experience of the life-world noematically yet in different ways, and it is these noematic characteristics which will stand in the center of interest of our further discussion.

First of all, to the life-world is ascribed "full, universal being" (*Krisis*, p. 462, line 33). As such it is explicitly designated as the "Weltall" (*ibid.*, p. 460, 462). Of this *Weltall* (emphasis of this word and the following by me) it is now said that it "*absorbs eo ipso* all human teleologic constructs", that it *absorbs* all products originating from the particular sub-worlds "*ex post facto*". It is said that to the "Weltall" "*belong* people just as we meet them and become acquainted with them without further ado, with all their designs, and all the products which have come into being through them". And not only do the particular sub-worlds constituted by ends belong to the Weltall, but also "all men and human communities and their human goals, both individual and communal goals with their corresponding products", and equally those "worlds" outlined in a scientific discipline as the object of that profession, for instance, the "world" of science, the "world" of mathematics, and those "worlds" sketched by philosophers in the traditional manner. "All these totalities", Husserl writers, "*fit*" into the "Weltall" which *embraces* all that exists and all existing totalities as well as their purposes and themes and races of men which are their ends".

IV

As its first step the "new science of the life-world" is given "the great task of a pure theory of essences" (*Krisis*, p. 144); it is to uncover the "general structure of the life-world" (*ibid.*, p. 142), "the invariant typology of its essences" (*ibid.*, p. 229) and, thereby make visible the "universal a priori of the life-world" (*ibid.*, p. 143). This is, however, not to come about in the manner of the traditional ontologies which asked their questions on the "natural ground" (*Boden*) of the factual world. Rather, a transcendental epoché and phenomenological reduction must already have been carried out, since it is a question of uncovering how the "function of being such a ground" belongs to the life-world. A "standpoint above and beyond the pre-givenness of the world" (*ibid.*, p. 153) must already have been won and the "binding tie to the pregivenness of the world" must have been given up. Now, the phenomenologist has in view the stream of consciousness, the cogitations and – as constituted by it intersubjectively – the cogitatum, the world as the correlate of these cogitations. In the reflexive attitude he now inquires as to *how* this correlate, the world qua life-world, is accepted and tries to answer this question by first uncovering it in its essential structure. Though Husserl does not say so explicitly in the *Krisis* itself, the method he follows for this purpose is that of an "ideation" (cf., e.g., p. 28). In Appendix III (p. 383) to the *Krisis* he demands specifically that "by free variation and running through all conceivable possibilities within the life-world, something by its very essence general and enduring be found, which remains constant through all the variants".

But what is the subject matter to be varied in the given case? To answer this question, we should first briefly set forth our understanding of the rather controversial issue of Husserl's method of ideation as set forth in *Phänomenologische Psychologie* (*Husserliana* IX, pp. 72ff.) and in *Erfahrung und Urteil* (pp. 409ff.). Through the phenomenological reduction, the subject matter has ceased to be a "factum", it has attained the status of a "cogitatum" and, through the eidetic reduction, it has been raised to that of a "pure possibility".[4] In this mode it serves as a "model" (*Vorbild*) for the process of variation by means of which the phenomenologist "freely"

---

[4] With reference to the difficult problem of the relation of the eidetic reduction to the phenomenologic, cf. *Cartesianische Meditationen, Husserliana I*, p. 103.

imagines "copies" (*Nachbilder*), and runs through them with the purpose of bringing to the fore those structures which remain invariant in this process and which define the *eidos* of that subject matter in question. It is in this way that the "a priori" rules governing the actual life-world are "constituted"[5] as the "same", i.e., as the very ones which remain invariant throughout all these variations.

It is of the greatest importance for our evaluation of those invariant determinants which Husserl has submitted in the appendix that he has conceived of ideation in such a way that "the subject matter" – in the mode of a "pure possibility" and a "model" – limits the "freedom" of variation by establishing the "domain" within which alone it can be carried out. Thus, e.g., the free way of varying the "perception of a table" is limited by that very subject matter; it has established the domain which can be varied and from which alone the invariant structures can eventually result. This implies that a phenomenologist who would submit as invariant determinants of the "perception of a table", e.g., those of the "remembering of a wardrobe" or of something else other than the perception of a thing, would not have remained within the domain prescribed by that subject matter with the consequence that the invariants submitted would have to be evaluated as "illegitimate" invariants.

Which "model" would guide and, at the same time, limit the process of variation of the subject matter which is here in question: the relationship of the life-world as it is accepted in everyday experience to the particular worlds as they are accepted in specific experiences? It seems to us that this "model" cannot be anything else but the everyday life-world – not taken as a factum but as a cogitatum and, moreover, raised to the status of a "pure possibility". And this means it is the "inexplicit" typicality in which the life-world is accepted by everyday experience in its relationship to the "inexplicit typicality" of particular sub-worlds as accepted by specific experience. This "inexplicit typicality" is the domain within which the phenomenologist can freely vary and which also has set the limits within which this process of variation may only take place and from which alone invariant structures can eventually result.

---

[5] Ideation as conceived by Husserl is actually not genuine "constitution" of an eidos through the process of variation but rather its explication insofar as that "pure possibility" which serves as the "model" setting the limits for the free variation is really nothing else but the eidos. Ideation must therefore only be considered as the means of articulating the a priori rules as they govern factual experiences. To personal conversations with A. Gurwitsch I owe the clarification of my view that the "inexplicit typicality" of the life-world is the "model" and for the variation taking place in this instance.

V

The question with which we are confronted is therefore the following: Is it feasible that the domain of the "inexplicit typicality" of everyday experience of the life-world in its relation to the specific experiences of particular worlds could have resulted in invariant structures that – as we saw – ascribe to the life-world "full universal being" and designate it as a "Weltall" which "absorbs" all human teleological constructs and all products originating from the particular sub-worlds *ex post facto* and to which "belong" people and all their products as well as all persons and communal goals and specifically all sub-worlds constituted with such goals? Could the variation of the "inexplicit typicality" of the life-world as accepted by everyday experience have yielded as its invariant a "Weltall" of which it can be said that it "embraces" these sub-worlds as well as other existants, and that all these sub-worlds "fit" into it? We have to start from the fact that the appendix *expressis verbis* designates the life-world as a "Weltall" (p. 462). Is this only meant to determine the "form" of the life-world in its spatial and temporal ways?

In *Ideen I,* the "Weltall" as a "real one" (pp. 72ff.) was the name for precisely that "totality of entities" which the phenomenological epoché was to deprive of validity (cf. pp. 13, 73). In *Ideen II,* "Weltall" was a term for nature, both material nature – the "sphere of mere things" (*ibid.,* p. 24) – and animate nature (*ibid.,* pp. 1, 27) as constituted in the natural-naturalistic attitude in "real apperception". Nature manifests itself under the forms of an "extended" space and time, likewise extended, insofar as it is a duration of movable, corporal things. Husserl himself in the Appendices to *Ideen II* no longer calls nature "Weltall", but speaks of the "universal nature" (*die Allnatur,* pp. 361, 392) or of the "totality of realities" (pp. 361, 374) in which is grounded the common personal-spiritual surrounding world, there specifically not called "Weltall" but "mere nature" (cf. pp. 379, 378, 392). In the posthumous work, *Erfahrung und Urteil,* the manner in which nature "grounds" this spiritual layer and that of the life-world is conceived so that everything in the world, "human and animal subjects, cultural artifacts, commodities, works of art" have an "existence-in" the spatio-temporal sphere of nature (*E & U,* p. 29). But this "pure universal nature", which is here also called "the spatio-temporal universal nature" (*Allnatur, E & U,* pp. 157, 159) is expressly conceived only as the universe of "corporal substrates" such as are the objects of simple, sensuous perception resulting in experience. All "grounded" modes of experiencing the world as "always and in each case pre-given as a whole in passive doxa" and its substrates, all such modes which imply "comprehension of expression" are differentiated from such a nature. We thus come to the conclusion that the designation "Weltall" as used in the appendix cannot mean the spatio-temporal aspect of the life-world. It cannot mean its form. Could it mean its "contents"?

The life-world in all his other publications is understood by Husserl strictly as the "human" world, i.e., as a sphere characterized by its specific spiritual and cultural character; it is the human world of human experience as interpreted by man which is continuously in the process of becoming in the course of history. If this defines the "contents" of the life-world, why does Husserl then ascribe to this human "region" expressively "full universal being"? To "be" fully and universally can only be an invariant way of a universe comprising the non-human regions as well as the human ones. It seems obvious that this invariant can never have been arrived at by an ideation of the inexplicit typicality of the life-world as accepted by everyday experience. And what about those other invariants defining the relationship of the "Weltall" to the particular sub-worlds? All of them have this in common: they reflect an active power. It takes power to "absorb" all human teleological constructs *eo ipso* and all the works produced in the workworld, of all the particular worlds. Power must be exerted to "embrace" all beings and all purposes of men and of mankind and of all sub-worlds. It certainly takes active power to so gather all particular sub-worlds to itself so that it can be said of them that they "belong" and moreover "fit" into it as if it were a framework. We can safely assert that a phenomenologist who varies everyday experience of the life-world in its relation to the experience of particular sub-worlds would within that range established by that inexplicit typicality never have come across "pure possible modes" revealing such an active power. It must, therefore, be concluded that Husserl must have gone beyond that range so that all the above invariants must be considered to have been arrived at in violation of the method of ideation and not to be "legitimate" from the point of view of phenomenology. They all appear to be invariants which could only have been arrived at by an ideation of the Cosmos itself; provided, of course, that this were feasible.

A corroboration of this result might be seen in the fact that the determinants as stated in the appendix cannot be reconciled with the ways in which Husserl – in different contexts – has termed the thetic character of the life-world as a "unity", as a "whole", and as a "horizon" for everyday experience.

The life-world is experienced as a "unity", as the corollate-idea to the "idea of experiences" to be brought to coherence with one another in a never ending "infinite" way (cf. *C.M.*, pp. 97, 115 and *Krisis,* p. 148). Unity has therefore only the meaning of a coherence of experiences going on in a never ending way – despite all corrections and historical changes. Similarly, the sense of the "whole" of the life-world does not mean a "closed whole" but, as Husserl has expressly stated (*Krisis*, p. 29), an "infinite" whole, i.e., one that is essentially held open for new experiences to enter. This sense of an essential openness for every new experience is also one of the significances connected with the term "horizon" which Husserl has introduced to designate "how" the cogitatum life-world is typically being experienced (*E & U*, p. 33).

None of these determinants are expressive of the power of the Cosmos relating to its particular sub-worlds.[6]

<h1 style="text-align:center">VI</h1>

In general, one could say the deeper Husserl penetrated into the complex of problems presented by the life-world, the more enigmatic it became for him. He felt the "groundlessness" of all philosophizing up to now exactly in view of the "seemingly so paradoxical, all-encompassing mode of the being of the life-world" (*Krisis*, p. 134). The question of its "universal concretion" (*ibid.*) began to disturb him fundamentally. He did see clearly that "the difference in mode of being between an object in the world and the world itself dictates fundamentally different modes of correlative consciousness" (*Krisis*, p. 146). Yet, "world" remained for him a topic – as far as its concrete content is concerned – only insofar as it is accepted by the experience of singular, innerworldly substrates (in which connection primarily the experience of perception was paradigmatic), and the life-world, specifically, remained for him a topic only insofar as it was experienced in the natural, everyday attitude.

It seems to us very noteworthy that Husserl overstepped the limitations governing the process of ideation precisely where the question was no longer the determination of a world for the experience of individual, innerworldly substrates but rather the determination of the relationship of

---

[6] In this paper we shall not try to develop how the relationship between the life-world – experienced in the non-thematic way – to the particular sub-world – experienced thematically – could be resolved. It seems to us that A. Gurwitsch's reference to noematic time, which is in line with Husserl's exposition in *Erfahrung und Urteil*, p. 189 ff., only provides a formal answer. Reference to Husserl's conception of the relationship of the "whole" to its "parts" (Stücke) would not yield any results: anyway, it only applies to individual substrata and not to the relationship of the "world" to particular "worlds".

"world" to its "sub-worlds" and where aspects of the "world" became relevant that could never be fathomed in an everyday, natural attitude.

It is impossible to say whether Husserl voluntarily transgressed the limits of his own method of ideation or whether the "subject-matter itself" forced him into this transgression. It might be a "legitimate need of contemporary philosophy" to try to determine the Cosmos or the universe comprising the non-human as well as human world and to attempt to bring to the fore its concrete and actual power, and it might be an equally "legitimate need of contemporary philosophy" to attempt to do so for an experience not restricted to that of everyday life. Husserl's restriction of the "world" to the "world of man" – a restriction first introduced by his contemporary Dilthey to overcome the Hegelian conception of world as a form (Gestalt) of "absolute spirit" – and the further restriction of that "world of man" to that of mere "everydayness" does not seem to satisfy that need. Husserl's conception of the "life-world", at the outset, suffers from it in that "life" comprises more than everyday occurrences; it also comprises – as Dilthey had seen (cf. *Gesammelte Werke*, pp. 291, 256) – many other events pertaining to the "facticity of history" and to "historical man"; it comprises the contingent, essentially inexplicable and "irrational" that can only be articulated by a philosophy that conceives of itself as a "self-reflection of life", i.e., of a way "in which life itself grasps life" (*ibid.*, VII, p. 136), and restricts itself to "interpreting" life in a "circular way" as if it were "a text". Husserl's phenomenology, which through "phenomenological reduction" and "transcendental epoché" tries to gain a position "beyond" the world and have it as its theme only from the point of view of a disinterested observer and which, as a "transcendental" phenomenology, only aims at displaying in a universal and "apodictically evident way" how meanings are constituted by acts (*Leistungen*) of consciousness, cannot possibly assume such a task. For the same reasons it cannot arrive at cosmological determinants, which spell out the power of the Cosmos, comprising also the non-human regions in it, and which are not accessible from the standpoint of an everyday attitude.

We have seen that the determinations in the appendix are statements about the Cosmos. Within the context of Husserl's "science of the life-world", specifically its method of ideation, they must be considered as "illegitimate". But from a different vantage point, they might yet be considered "relevant" statements, though they certainly do not have the kind of "apodictic evidence" required by phenomenology. Thus in the passage interpreted, the boundaries of that domain for which the methods of the "strict science" of phenomenology are valid become visible and it becomes clear that there are domains for which this is not the case.

ON THE BOUNDARIES OF THE SOCIAL WORLD

by

THOMAS LUCKMANN

I. INTRODUCTION

It may seem less than reasonable to reexamine an issue on which there is widespread agreement. What is more evident than the boundary that separates the social from the non-social? Common sense permits no doubt that social reality is composed of human affairs. This certitude of common sense informs our ordinary actions as well as our most elevated sentiments. Nor is the exclusively human nature of social reality seriously questioned in the main traditions of Western philosophy. The coincidence of the social order with the pattern of relations between human beings is taken for granted. One can hardly blame the social scientist for failing to investigate the origin and the significance of this division of reality with as much detached interest as he would devote to the study of more obviously "culture-bound" assumptions of common sense.

There are however excellent reasons for reopening the issue. First, more than a purely theoretical dispute is involved. The boundary between the social and the non-social separates that which is directly pertinent to our moral sense from that which is only loosely connected to it. Second, the coincidence of the social and the human which is evident to us is by no means universally perceived. Historical and ethnographic accounts include descriptions of human attitudes that clearly testify to lines of demarcation different from those which are drawn by our common sense. It is remarkable, moreover, that children are not born with an automatical appreciation of the divisions in reality that we take for granted as adults. It is from us that they learn where the social begins and where it ends.

What is the origin of our habitual division of reality? Is the prevailing contemporary understanding of what is social and what is not a faithful reflection, in the human mind, of preestablished partitions in reality? Are all other lines of demarcation deviations from what is normal and reasonable? Or is perhaps the line drawn by our common sense neither more nor less compelling than the boundaries that have been observed at different times and places? Were we to admit this second possibility we should want to know to what common source divergent conceptions of the social world could be traced.

The choice before us is thus between two main possibilities. First, the division of reality into a social and a non-social part is based on a substantive ontological principle. The human mind is capable of apprehending that principle. This results in the identification of the social with the human. Specific circumstances may however result in a distorted apprehension of that principle – leading to such peculiar conceptions as animism or totemism. Second, the boundaries of the social world are determined in human interpretations of a reality that is not rigidly predetermined in its division of the social and the non-social. The contours of the social world are to be attributed to complex patterns of social and cultural circumstance, to the historical context in which such interpretations originate. This does not preclude the possibility that there is a common element in the formal structure of such interpretations.

It may be useful to explore some implications of the two alternatives. Psychological theory, especially as represented by Gestalt psychology, and phenomenological psychology agrees in one point that is directly pertinent to our present discussion: in the recognition of invariant structures in the processes of human consciousness. Starting with any concrete experience it is possible to distinguish specific, biographically and historically variable components from "formal" structures without which that and similar experiences are unthinkable.[1] In other words, it should be possible to separate those strata of human experience in the concrete socio-historical world which belong to what Max Scheler called the relative-natural view of the world from the underlying essential structures of the life-world. The program was concisely articulated by Edmund Husserl: ". . . daß doch diese Lebenswelt in allen ihren Relativitäten ihre a l l g e m e i n e S t r u k t u r hat. Diese allgemeine Struktur, an die alles relativ Seiende gebunden ist, ist nicht selbst relativ. Wir können sie in ihrer Allgemeinheit beachten und mit entsprechen-

---

[1] It is obvious that this carries important implications not only for the problem discussed here but also more generally for the logical foundation and the methodology of the social sciences. It is one of the great merits of the work of Alfred Schutz to have shown that the method of phenomenological psychology and its findings provide a firmer footing than arbitrary "naturalist" constructions for the social scientist eager to avoid the pitfalls of naive ethnocentrism. Cf. Alfred Schutz, *Collected Papers*, I, II, III, The Hague, 1962, 1964, 1966.

der Vorsicht ein für allemal und für jedermann gleich zugänglich feststel-
len." [2]

Among the most obvious illustrations of such underlying structures are
the categories of subjective orientation in space, such as above and below,
before me and behind me, and the articulation of inner time in "flying
stretches" and "resting places" as described by William James. Less obvious
but nonetheless convincing illustrations were provided by Schutz's analysis
of the structuring of social relations according to degrees of immediacy,
intimacy and anonymity. In all these instances it is possible to show the
necessary relation of the socio-cultural, linguistically articulated and often
institutionalized categories of space, time and social interaction to the underlying structures of subjective orientation in the life world. As to the historically and biographically variable strata of experience, the supply of illustrations is nearly inexhaustible. Confrontation of categories of conduct and
thought common in one society – where their invariant status is normally
taken for granted – with categories that prevailed at other times and in other
places clearly shows the "relativity" of such categories. They range from
notions of everyday-life etiquette that prohibit joking in front of mothers-
in-law to complex cultural edifices such as monotheism.

It hardly needs to be pointed out that any concrete experience may be
either "reduced" to its invariant formal properties or analyzed as a complex
socio-cultural phenomenon. Perceiving a red suface I may be led to the
underlying structures of surface-perception and the necessary relation of
color-perception to surface-perception. On the other hand I may simply
assume that some such "essential" structures are presupposed in the concrete experience under scrutiny and analyze the processes by which "objective" but culturally "relative" categories, the segmentation of the semantic
"field" of color in a given language, for instance, come to influence that
experience. Similarly, the analysis of the temporal dimension of habitual
conduct in everyday life will show, on the one hand, invariant forms of the
articulation of inner time and, on the other hand, institutionally determined
categories of time-keeping and the calendar.

II. INTERSUBJECTIVITY IN HISTORICAL LIFE-WORLDS

What status is to be accorded the boundary of the social world? May one
legitimately regard a fixed boundary of the social as an essential structure
of the life-world? I shall try to show that this is not the case. Assigning any

---

[2] E. Husserl, *Die Krisis der Europäischen Wissenschaften und die transzendentale
Phänomenologie,* The Hague, 1954, p. 142.

fixed boundary – as for instance one that identifies the social with the human – a status comparable to that of the articulations of the *durée* or of the universal structuring of the face-to-face situation, leads to insuperable difficulties. The acceptance of such status is not justified by the results of an analysis of the structures of the life-world. It is based on an illegitimate "empirical" generalization from a particular life-world.

It is interesting to note that Husserl did not explicitly deal with the problem of the boundaries of the social world in his program for a description of the life-world. In the closely related context of his discussion of intersubjectivity, however, the terms of his argument carry the subscript "human".[3] Thus the problem under discussion here is bypassed: the alter ego is constituted as a human alter ego. We may perhaps leave aside here the question whether Husserl's egological conception of consciousness – on which his resolution of the problem of intersubjectivity is based – is tenable.[4] We may also disregard the difficulty involved in the assumption that an "apperceptive transfer" from my own living body (*Leib*), which "stands out" in my primordial perceptual field in a unique manner, should bestow the sense "living body" on other bodies which appear in my perceptual field in a radically different manner.[5] Directly pertinent here is the implication in Husserl's argument that for a human alter ego to be constituted, the ego in whose consciousness the alter ego is constituted should itself be human. Husserl does not seem to perceive that this implication cannot be justified on the premises on which his argument rests. The transcendental reduction carried out by Husserl results in "der Ausschaltung der natürlichen Welt mit ihren Dingen, Animalien, Menschen" and entails the bracketing of all "durch wertende und praktische Bewußtseinsfunktionen sich konstituierenden individuellen Gegenständlichkeiten."[6] The empirical and worldly ego is therefore placed within the brackets of the transcendental reduction. What remains is the transcendental "pure ego". Now it is obvious that "humanness" as a perceived quality is a consequence of historically specific social processes. There is no justification for excluding the humanness of the empirical ego from the operation of the transcendental reduc-

---

[3] Cf. especially his *Cartesianische Meditationen*, (1950) V and *Die Krisis . . .* (1962), Par. 53.

[4] Cf. Jean-Paul Sartre, "La Transcendance de l'ego", *Recherches Philosophiques,* VI (1936–37), pp. 85–123 and Aron Gurwitsch, "A Non-egological Conception of Consciousness", *Philosophy and Phenomenological Research,* I (September 1940–June 1941).

[5] Cf. Alfred Schutz, "Das Problem der transzendentalen Intersubjektivität bei Husserl", *Philosophische Rundschau,* V (1957), pp. 81–107; English translation in Schutz, *Collected Papers,* III (1966, pp. 51–91, esp. p. 63 f. of the English translation).

[6] *Ideen,* I, 1950, p. 136.

tion. In Husserl's analysis, however, the transcendental ego, within whose consciousness the whole world, the alter ego included, is constituted, surreptitiously retains its human quality. On this basis only is it possible for Husserl to imply that the alter ego, constituted in the consciousness of the transcendental ego, is human. For similar reasons neither the procedure by which Husserl constructs a "regional typology" of the life-world nor the results to which he is lead by it can be accepted. For Husserl it seems indubitable that the meaning "animal" is a modification of the primary sense "human being": "Unter den animalischen Dingen sind ausgezeichnet die Menschen, und so sehr, daß erst von ihnen her die b l o s s e n (italics mine) Tiere als ihre Abwandlung Seinssinn haben".[7] And again: "Die Tiere finden wir in unserer Welt vor durch Einfühlung, die eine assimilierende Abwandlung der mitmenschlichen Einfühlung ist".[8] Obviously these assertions ultimately rest on the assumption that the transcendental ego is somehow human.[9] If this assumption is shown to be untenable it can no longer be argued that there is a primary sense "human being" of which the sense "animal" is a modification.

Even were we to retain Husserl's egological conception of consciousness and his notion of the "pure ego", we should have to remove from the latter every trace of its "human" quality. The basis for the assumption, that the alter ego that is constituted in the consciousness of the "pure ego" is human, collapses. There remains no reason to prejudge the problem of intersubjectivity by positing it in exclusively human terms. The acceptance of any concrete boundary of the social world as a constitutive element of the life-world *tout court* is therefore unsound. Correspondingly, the "regional typology" of the life-world proposed by Husserl must be carefully reviewed. In the following, I shall reverse Husserl's argument on this matter by suggesting that the sense "human being" is a modification of the primary sense "living body".

We begin by following Husserl's account of the constitution of the alter ego *but* with a transcendental ego divested of all material traces of "humanness". We need not retrace all the steps in his account, from the description

---

[7] *Die Krisis . . .*, p. 230.

[8] Mss. transcript C 11, III, pp. 15–16, Husserl Archives, Louvain, cited after René Toulemont, *L'Essence de la société selon Husserl*, Paris, 1962, p. 79.

[9] The assumption is explicitly stated in the following passage: "Im Bezug auf das Tier ist der Mensch, konstitutiv gesprochen, der Normalfall, wie ich selbst konstitutiv die Urnorm bin für alle Menschen; Tiere sind wesensmäßig konstituiert für mich als anomale A b w a n d l u n g e n meiner Menschlichkeit . . .". *C.M.*, p. 154. It is clear from the context that the *ich selbst* is the transcendental ego. Why this ego should be human is a question that remains unanswered.

of the passive syntheses of pairing to the separation, within the transcendentally reduced sphere, of the primordial sphere containing only what is properly of the ego (*Eigentlichkeitssphäre*).[10] We enter the account at the point that is crucial for the resolution of our problem. According to Husserl, bodies that stand out in my primordial sphere and that are similar to my own living body receive, as a result of an apperceptive transfer of meaning, the sense "living body".[11] We must ask now what constitutes similarity. As an empirical and worldly ego I "know" of course that I am human and "I know" how my body looks (I have learned to recognize myself in the mirror, for example, a feat of which no other animal seems to be capable) and I "know" therefore what is similar to my body. For the transcendental ego however, whose knowledge of its humanness as well as its knowledge of the "*objective*" appearance of its own body must be placed within the brackets of the transcendental reduction, the apperceptive transfer must originally bestow the sense "*living body*" on everything that stands out in its primordial sphere. The distinction between inanimate bodies (*Körpern*) and living bodies (*Leibern*) is not, as Husserl suggests, a basic and irreducible distinction in the primordial sphere of the transcendental ego. Rather, it is a distinction that emerges from synthetic activities of consciousness in which the "original" *universal* apperceptive transfer is confirmed, modified or canceled. Husserl's remark on the constitution of the objective world in general applies here: "Dasein hat sie vermöge einstimmiger Bewährung der einmal gelungenen apperzeptiven Konstitution durch Fortgang des erfahrenden Lebens in konsequenter, eventuell durch Korrekturen hindurch sich immer wieder herstellender Einstimmigkeit. Die Einstimmigkeit erhält sich nun auch vermöge einer Umbildung der Apperzeption durch Unterscheidung von Normalität und Anomalitäten als ihre intentionale Modifikation bzw. der Konstitution neuer Einheiten im Wechsel dieser Anomalitäten."[12] We may disregard here the somewhat problematic – or, at least, awkward – notion of normalcy and turn to our present concern. Typologies of objects in the life-world are formed by means of original apperceptive transfers of sense which are confirmed by later consonant experiences or modified by later dissonant experiences. New typologies may be formed on the basis of formerly established types which had to be seriously modified or abandoned in the course of later experience. Since humanness is not

---

[10] Cf. *C.M.*, V.

[11] "Tritt nun ein Körper in meiner primordialen Sphäre abgehoben auf, der dem meinen ä h n l i c h ist, d.h. so beschaffen ist, daß er mit dem meinen eine phänomenale Paarung eingehen muß, so erscheint nun ohne weiteres klar, daß er in der Sinnüberschiebung alsbald den Sinn Leib von dem meinen her übernehmen muß." (*C.M.*, p. 143).

[12] Cf. *C.M.*, p. 145.

"somehow" a constitutive trait of the transcendental ego, "human being" is a typification of certain objects in the life-world – a typification, further- more, that may arise from "revisions" of prior typifications. The sense "human being" is established in a manner that is analogous to the formation of other typifications of the life-world. It is *not* the constitutive basis for the formation of "regional typologies" of the life-world.

Several difficult questions must be raised at this point. How precisely does an originally "successful apperceptive constitution" (Husserl's *einmal gelungene apperzeptive Konstitution*) come about? What is it in the course of later experience that proves to be consonant (*einstimmig*) with the original transfer of sense and thus serves as its confirmation (*Bewährung*)?

As to the first question, Husserl's account of the constitution of the alter ego offers no satisfactory answer. It is an open matter, to say the least, what bodies in the primordial sphere of the transcendental ego *must* enter into phenomenal pairing with the ego. The assumption that the sense "living body" (like mine) is originally transferred only to the bodies of fellow human beings is untenable. It is based on the faulty premise that humanness is constitutive of the transcendental ego. More specifically, the restriction of the transfer of the sense "living body" to members of the species *homo sapiens* presupposes something that must be placed within the brackets of the transcendental reduction: "knowledge" of what "human beings" look like – in which case it would be a typification that already presupposes inter- subjectivity – or "knowledge" on the part of the transcendental ego how its body looks from the *outside* – which also presupposes intersubjectivity. The sense "living body" that serves as the basis of the apperceptive sense- transfer cannot be identical with the meaning that my own body may have for me as an object. Taking up the argument developed earlier I suggest therefore that the *original* transfer of the sense "living body" has the char- acter of a "universal projection". It is at first limited by nothing but the requirement that the object which enters into "pairing" with the living body of the ego be a body that stands out in ego's phenomenal field.

Thus we avoid the *impasse* into which must be led any analysis of the boundaries of the social world that follows Husserl's attempt to resolve the problem of intersubjectivity. Within the primordial sphere of the tran- scendental ego one finds only a "universal" transfer of the sense "living body". Any restrictions of this sense-transfer belong already to historical life-worlds and should be investigated by the methods of "phenomenologi- cal psychology". It is the empirical and worldly ego that may "become" human. Its humanness is constituted rather than constitutive. It is founded on the humanness of the alter ego and not *vice-versa*. To put it differently, the sense "human being" is a modification of the sense "living body".[13]

It must be admitted that in avoiding one *impasse* we transpose the problem to a different level on which we encounter new difficulties. If we agree that the *original* transfer of the sense "living body" is not as restricted as Husserl assumes, we must seek to account for those qualities of bodies appearing in the phenomenal field of the ego that are likely to induce *subsequent* modifications and restrictions of the original "universal" sense-transfer. The processes of confirmation, modification and cancellation of apperceptive sense-transfers belong to historical life-worlds. In other words, they are thoroughly "contaminated" by the subjective sedimentations of socially transmitted categories that are objectivated in a given historical culture, most pervasively in the matrix of a language. It is of course extraordinarily difficult to separate the "pure" qualities, appearing in the primordial sphere of the transcendental ego, from the culturally determined categories which are first acquired by the empirical ego in social processes and then recede into "secondary passivity" and thus guide its habitual experiences. If we wish to account for the varying boundaries of the social universe in historical life-worlds, this difficulty must not deter us. We must try to arrive at a tentative identification, at least, of those qualities of bodies, appearing in the phenomenal fields of the inhabitants of *any* life world, that may induce restrictions of the "universal" transfer of the sense "living body" in *historical* life-worlds. I shall return to this task in a later part of the essay.

The argument developed in the preceding pages leads to the following conclusion: A "regional typology" of the life world is not constituted by the transcendental ego – unless we restrict the meaning of that expression to refer to the distinction, in the primordial sphere, between what is properly of the ego and what is not. "Regional typologies" are inter-subjective structures of historical life-worlds. They are constituted as follows: 1) The alter ego that is constituted in the consciousness of the *transcendental* ego is not originally a "human being" but any body appearing in its primordial sphere. The apperceptive transfer of the sense "living body" is a universal projec-

---

[13] This means, as was already indicated, that the typification "human being" has a status and an origin comparable to other typifications in the "regional typologies" of the life world. One difficulty inherent in Husserl's account and pointed out by Schutz is therefore removed: ". . . the concept of the Other also embraces, in at least one of its significations, other 'ego-like living beings', as, e.g. animals. If we apply to these Husserl's theory of representative sense-transference from my organism it proves impossible to explain how it happens that this and that body appearing in my primordial sphere comes to be construed as the body of a fish or as the body of a bird, i.e., as belonging to an 'ego-like being' living 'in' it." – Schutz, *op. cit.,* p. 64.

tion. 2) Subsequent restrictions of this projection are founded on certain qualities of bodies appearing in the primordial sphere of the transcendental ego. But the motive to "discover" such qualities and to base on them a "regional typology" can only be attributed to the intersubjective relevance structures of the worldly ego. 3) The restrictions of the "universal" projection are objectivated in social processes. In these they are "sedimented" into a more or less coherent cultural system of typifications: a regional typology of a historical life-world. The qualities of the bodies that may induce restrictions of the "universal" sense-transfer are therefore no more but a phenomenal substratum of an intersubjectively constituted system of interpretations of the universe. 4) The regional typology of a historical life-world is acquired by the *worldly* ego in the process of socialization. It determines its habitual perceptions of what is social and what is not. The "reality" and plausibility of such perceptions depends as much on the coherence of the regional typology as a cultural system of interpretations, as on the "rediscovery" of the phenomenal substratum of such interpretations by the worldly ego.

III. ANIMISM AND TOTEMISM

Before proceeding it will be useful to look at our problems from a different perspective. Over the generations, ethnologists and students of comparative religion collected information on the customs and beliefs of primitive societies.[14] Despite disagreements on how to define and to interpret them, certain kinds of beliefs were catalogued under the labels of "animism", "shamanism" and "totemism", occasionally also of "fetishism". It became clear that the identification of the social with the human could not be considered universal and that the neat separation between nature and society had not been evident to all men at all times. If the modern way was but one among many ways of dividing the universe into a social and a non-social part, the social sciences were confronting a problem. Ethnology, in particular, had to look for an explanation for the variability of such a central dimension of culture. It is not surprising, of course, that the identity of the social with the human in one's own culture was at first taken as a standard by which the deviations from what seemed so eminently reasonable were to be measured. The problem of the boundaries of the social world was thus prejudged. Conceptions of the universe that were obviously other than nor-

---

[14] Cf. that classical inventory, Sir James George Frazer's *"The Golden Bough"*, originally published in 1890 and now available in a revised and abridged edition, by Theodor H. Gaster: *The New Golden Bough*, New York 1959, esp. pp. 72–87.

mal had to be explained by special psychological and sociological factors. For a time the view was popular that primitive man was deceived as it were, by the metaphorical character of language and its personification of nature and natural events. Slightly more sophisticated were explanations of totemism that saw a causal relation between the economic dependence of primitive hunters on certain species and their "identification" with them.

Under the influence of functionalism and structural functionalism more persuasive theoretical accounts of the relationship of such systems of classification with social institutions were given. Nevertheless, the premise on which the traditional view of animism and totemism rested, was not critically re-examined. When "ethnocentrism" came to be regarded as a serious, if not the most serious methodological problem of cultural anthropology, the debate did not extend to such a central notion of culture as is the delineation of the boundaries of the social world. And yet, compared to the consequences of "ethnocentric bias" for a Western scholar's ability to grasp divisions of the social and the non-social that differ from his own, the "ethnocentric" selectivity of observation and distortion of judgment concerning, for example, primitive sexual customs would seem almost trivial.

One must insist that there are neither empirical nor theoretical reasons that justify setting up the identification of the social with the human as a standard of normalcy. All boundaries of the social world, including our own, originate in human thought and are rooted in forms of consciousness that are universally human. For the social scientist the cultural objectivations that emerge from this basis in social processes have "equal status". The identification of the social with the human is, therefore, just as much a "problem" for cultural anthropology as, for example, animism.

It seems plausible today to find a direction in historical processes which leads from an undifferentiated social universe to a view of the world in which the social is coextensive with the human, and clearly distinct from that which is "mere" nature. The social scientist, however, is bound to treat with caution something that is merely plausible. In order to accept something as a genuine line of "cultural evolution" he needs more than the hind-sight of the common-sense of his period. He must verify it by careful comparative and historical studies. On this particular problem such studies are sorely lacking.

Claims of superiority for one culture, a cultural system of classification, a language, etc., are met with scepticism in cultural anthropology today.[15]

---

[15] "Il est probable que le nombre, la nature, et la 'qualité' de ces axes logiques ne sont pas les mêmes selon les cultures, et qu'on pourrait classer celles-ci en plus riches et en plus pauvres, d'après les propriétés formelles des systèmes de référence auxquelles

A similar attitude on the boundaries of the social world, as an important element of culture, is slow to emerge, however, perhaps because the "correctness" of one's own culture is so obvious in this regard that no explicit claims need be made for its superiority. Nevertheless, the position I develop in this essay is not based on a new insight. It would serve no useful purpose here to trace in detail the background for various departures from the traditional views on animism and totemism in cultural anthropology.[16] Nevertheless, I should like to link my own position to certain concepts of other scholars which are related to the present problem. Lévy-Bruhl occupies a position midway between the traditional view and the perspective introduced in this essay. He explicitly rejected the attribution, to the mythologies of primitive societies of what may be termed metaphorical anthropomorphism. Many fertile insights in his work rest on his taking *au serieux* the experiences and interpretations of nature that characterize such societies. His attempt to discover the internal logic of the world views of primitive societies, however, ended in failure. The main reason for this is to be found in his reduction of such world views to what he supposed to be characteristically "primitive" mental functions for which he coined the unfortunate term "prelogical mentality".[17] Lévi-Strauss tries to develop a systematic analysis of the elementary structures of classificatory systems in different types of societies. Like others before him, he distinguishes between magic and scientific modes of thought, but he insists, against the traditional view, that both originate in comparable kinds of mental operations. The former cannot be explained as an "infantile" phase or a pathological regression of the latter. To the traditional view in which totemism appears as an institutional "inventory" of classifications that distort, for specific psychological, social or economic reasons, an underlying natural taxonomy, Lévi-Strauss opposes the argument that totemism is a mode of thought which functions as a guiding principle in a unitary classification of the world as a social universe.[18] This view provides an excellent starting point for our own consider-

---

elles font appel, pour édifier leurs structures de classification. Mais, même les moins douées sous ce rapport opèrent avec des logiques à plusieurs dimensions, dont l'inventaire, l'analyse et l'interprétation exigeraient une richesse d'informations ethnographiques et générales qui font trop souvent défaut." (Claude Lévi-Strauss, *La Pensée sauvage*, Paris 1962, p. 85 f.).

[16] For excellent review and critique cf. Claude Lévi-Strauss, *Le Totémisme aujourd'hui*, Paris 1962.

[17] Cf. Lucien Lévy-Bruhl, *Les Fonctions mentales dans les sociétés inférieures*, Paris 1922; *L'Âme primitive*, Paris 1930; *La Mentalité primitive*, Paris 1959; *La Mythologie primitive*, Paris 1963².

[18] "L'erreur des ethnologues classiques a été de vouloir réifier cette forme, de la lier à un contenu déterminé, alors qu'elle se présente a l'observateur comme une méthode pour assimiler toute espèce de contenu. Loin d'être une institution autonome,

ations. We shall try to show that there are levels of restriction of the "universal projection" which serve as guiding principles in the construction of comprehensive "taxonomies". We need not go here into Lévi-Strauss' analyses of the relation of classificatory systems, including totemism, to the social structure. We may add, however, that he shows clearly that totemism, like any other systems of classification, is multi-dimensional and that it may be based on various combinations of perceptual similarity, functional similarity, contiguity, etc.

Another scholar whose theories are pertinent to our problem is Arnold Gehlen. In a book,[19] whose content he describes as a philosophy of institutions, he analyzes the origin, the structure and function of institutions in archaic cultures. According to Gehlen the animation of the external world is a primary category of experience which is stabilized in the languages and the institutions of archaic cultures. Later, non-animistic, conceptions of the world are the result of complex historical transformations of such institutions; in a manner of speaking, the universe is de-socialized. Again, we need not enter into the details of Gehlen's theory. Apart from his acceptance of a universal "animation" of the world, we consider his insistence on the institutional stabilization of this mode of thought of particular importance to our argument.

Finally, we should like to mention Tenbruck. In an interesting attempt to integrate different typologies of social structure and culture into a systematic theory that revolves around changes in the modes of relationship between individual and society, he introduces a notion of "empathy" that is basically not restricted to human partners.[20] It is this original universality of "empathy" that is pertinent to the present discussion.

With Lévi-Strauss, Gehlen and Tenbruck we recognize that the "primitive" view of the world represents a consistent structure of interpretations whose logic originates in "normal" mental faculties. These authors proceed to investigate the formal properties of that logic, its institutional stabilization and its functions for socialization. The foundation of that logic and its origin in the activities of consciousness, however, are of subordinate interest to them. Gehlen suggests that the animation of the world is based on the perception of "objective" *Gestalt* qualities in natural phenomena (as an

définissable par des caractères intrinsèques, le totémisme ou prétendu tel correspond à certaines modalités arbitrairement isolées d'un système formel, dont la fonction est de garantir la convertibilité idéale des différents niveaux de la réalité sociale." – *op. cit.* p. 101.

[19] *Urmensch und Spätkultur,* Frankfurt and Bonn 1964² (Bonn 1956¹).

[20] Cf. Friedrich Tenbruck, *Geschichte und Gesellschaft (Habilitationsschrift,* University of Freiburg, to be published shortly).

example he repeats Koehler's reference to the threatening expression of mountains), on dream experience and the "willful" resistance of physical objects. There is something to these suggestions – but they leave unresolved the question why *Gestalt* qualities should be personified and why the resistance of objects should be perceived as willful. Nor is Tenbruck's notion of "empathy" – although it serves a useful purpose in his theory – anything but a label for processes that need to be described with precision.

The questions that are understandably of subordinate importance to these authors are, of course, in the center of our interest. Taking over Husserl's concept of the apperceptive transfer of sense, I tried to describe, in the preceding section of this essay, the activities of consciousness that lead to a universal animation of the world. It should be noted that an important step in this account was anticipated by Wundt. Before the turn of the century Wundt wrote of a function of the mind which he called the "personifying apperception":[21] ". . . auf deren verschiedenartiger Betätigung alle mythologischen Vorstellungen beruhen".[22] It is significant that he considers the "personifying apperception" a general and basic function: ". . . eine eigentümliche, dem naiven Bewußtsein überall zukommende Art der Apperzeption."[23] Unfortunately, Wundt did not specify the exact character of this apperception, beyond saying that the apperceived objects are determined by the nature of the perceiving subject.[24] Two additional observations are, however, suggestive for our further discussion. According to Wundt the "personifying apperception" is entirely normal and thus to be found in all children. Its operation is modified, restricted or repressed by the adult environment of the child in advanced societies or reinforced by the mythologies of primitive societies.[25] Wundt also indicates that, while the personifying apperception" may result in the animation of the entire world, additional distinctions are often made between immobile and moving things, between mere animation and activity.[26]

While traditional ethnology failed to place the problem in the proper perspective, traditional philosophy ignored it entirely with few exceptions.[27] It is remarkable, however, that two outstanding representatives of modern philosophical anthropology not only saw the problem but anticipated, in the essential point, its solution. Max Scheler insists, *en passant,* as it were,

---

[21] The general notion of "personification", however, was used long before Wundt.
[22] Wilhelm Wundt, *Grundriss der Psychologie,* Leipzig 1896, p. 355 f.
[23] *ibid.*
[25] Cf. *op. cit.,* p. 357.
[26] Cf. *op. cit.,* p. 356.
[27] Cf. C. Lévi-Strauss' reference to certain ideas of Rousseau and Bergson, Lévi-Strauss, *Le Totémisme aujourd'hui,* pp. 133–147.

on the ontogenetic and philogenetic priority of an animated universe.[28]

Kurt Riezler, also without delving further into the matter, makes a similar point.[29]

The solution to the problem of the boundaries of the social world that I present in this essay, although in opposition to the traditional views on animism and totemism in 19th century ethnology, may be thus taken as an elaboration of a concept introduced by an eminent 19th century ethnologist and psychologist. This solution, as I have shown, can be also linked to certain ideas of modern philosophical anthropology, cultural anthropology and sociology.

IV. DE-SOCIALIZATION OF THE UNIVERSE

We viewed the boundaries of the social world in two different perspectives, as a problem in the phenomenology of the life-world and as a controversial issue in ethnological and sociological theory. We saw that these boundaries are constituted in historical life-worlds, but also that their constitution is founded on an apperceptive transfer of sense (the "universal projection") that is an elementary process in the experience of the life-world *tout court*. Viewed as elements in a cultural system of classification, these boundaries were seen to originate in a basic mental function (the "personifying apperception"). Both lines of analysis converge in the question: What are the qualities of bodies, appearing in the phenomenal fields of the inhabitants of any life-world (of the members of any culture) that may induce such restrictions of the "universal projection" (the "personifying apperception") as are to be found, in fact, in the life-worlds of different societies?

[28] Cf. Max Scheler, *Wesen und Formen der Sympathie*, Frankfurt 1948[5] (Halle 1913[1]) pp. 257/58: "Primär ist alles überhaupt Gegebene "Ausdruck", und das, was wir Entwicklung durch "Lernen" nennen, ist nicht eine nachträgliche Hinzufügung von psychischen Komponenten zu einer vorher schon gegebenen 'toten', dinglich gegliederten Körperwelt, sondern eine fortgesetzte Enttäuschung darüber, daß sich nur einige sinnliche Erscheinungen als Darstellungsfunktionen von Ausdruck bewähren – andere aber nicht. 'Lernen' ist in diesem Sinne zunehmende Entseelung – nicht aber *Be*-seelung. Man darf weder dem Kinde, noch darf man dem Primitiven das Weltbild des Erwachsenen und Zivilisierten unter- und einlegen, um dann reale Prozesse anzunehmen, die dieses Weltbild zu dem des Kindes und des Primitiven erst umzugestalten hätten."

[29] Cf. Kurt Riezler, *Man: Mutable and Immutable*, Chicago 1950, p. 60: "Many an interpreter of the 'animism' of primitive religion seems to pressuppose that the thing, born as a dead thing, has been subjectified, humanized, and endowed with a kind of living soul in the course of a religious interpretation. It is, however, far more probable that this evolution took the opposite course. The it – as the other thing confronting us – had been endowed with a kind of soul before it became a thing, and has later been deprived of its soul, depersonalized and objectified ..."

In trying to answer this question I shall observe certain limitations that should be immediately noted. First, I shall do no more than indicate those qualities which are most likely to resist the transfer of the sense "living body" to bodies that have such qualities – assuming, of course, that the perception of these qualities is not automatically cancelled or modified by an interpretational system of a historical life-world that is internalized by the perceiving ego. This means that I shall not offer an account of that complex interdependence of perceptual syntheses, appresentative schemes and relevance structures which determines when and in what manner such qualities of objects in the phenomenal field become thematic for the world-ly ego.

A second limitation concerns the sociological dimension of the analysis. I shall not describe in detail the social processes by which subjectively plausible restrictions of the "universal projection" are socially objectivated nor analyze the institutions that may stabilize the boundaries of the social world as cultural norms, nor discuss the incorporation of the latter in overarching religious schemes of legitimation.[30]

The "universal projection" is an elementary component of the experience of the world. All things encountered in the life-world are experienced in a synthesis of their perceived qualities with the appresented sense "living body". This sense refers to something that has a *durée,* not merely a location; an inside is appresented to the perceptible outside.

The animation of the entire life-world presupposes that the elementary transfer of the sense "living body" is not canceled in specific instances by the qualities of some bodies to which this meaning is appresented. Is this presupposition justified? After all, sense transfers are tentative. They are confirmed, modified or canceled by the *relevant* qualities of the things to which some meaning is transferred. Thus, for example, the sense "loud", which is constituted in my present experience of a sound and which is automatically transferred to the next phase of that experience, will be confirmed by the loudness of the sound perceived in that phase or canceled by subsequent silence. Confirmations, modifications and frustrations of elementary sense-transfers are sedimented in the subjective stock of knowledge and form patterns of expectation. One learns to expect automatically that the murmuring of a brook will continue and that a fog-horn will be blown at regular intervals. Does it not seem likely, therefore, that the "universal projection", too, will be necessarily confirmed in the case of certain bodies

---

[30] For a general treatment of these problems cf. Peter Berger and Thomas Luckmann, *The Social Construction of Reality,* Garden City, N.Y. 1966.

and *just as necessarily* refuted by such qualities of other bodies as resist that sense-transfer?

The "universal projection" differs from other elementary sense-transfers in one important regard. The evidence which serves to confirm, modify or cancel the transfer of the sense "living body" is of a special kind. I do not directly experience the "inside" of the thing to which the meaning "living body" is transferred. The evidence for any stream of consciousness but my own is circumstantial. The "universal projection" is not *directly* affected by the perception of objective qualities. Only an interpretation of such qualities, either as symptoms of a *durée* or as indications of its absence, leads to the confirmation, modification or cancellation of specific apperceptive transfers of the sense "living body". As all other interpretations, such interpretations, too, are actualized in the context of an interpretational scheme. Restrictions of the "universal projection" are therefore determined for the empirical ego by socially derived systems of relevance in which interpretational schemes have their origin.[31]

Since the "universal projection" is not necessarily restricted by qualities of things that must be inevitably perceived by the inhabitants of any life-world, it is conceivable that the unmodified results of this general sense-transfer should determine basic dimensions of the world view of a historical life-world. In other words, the "universal projection", an automatic apperceptive transfer of sense, may be transformed in communicative processes into an objective social system of classification and stabilized by social institutions. Such a world view defines all relations between an individual and his world as socially significant and all his actions as morally relevant. The social world is not a subdivision of the life-world but coextensive with it.

A world view that is based entirely on the unrestricted operation of the "universal projection" is, of course, an ideal typical construct that will be only approximated but not fully exemplified by historical world views. World views originate in the shared systems of relevance of historical societies. These systems of relevance are determined by various conditions: the topography of a territory, the ecology of a habitat, dependence on certain plants and animal species, the differentiation of roles in a kinship system, the distribution of power and authority, the level of technology, etc. In combination, these factors represent the "functional requirements" of a social structure and form the matrix within which originate shared systems of relevance. The latter, in turn, influence the social objectivation of classifi-

---

[31] My view of relevance is based on the theory of topical, interpretational and motivational relevance developed by Schutz in a manuscript (working title: *Das große Relevanzmanuskript*) which is being prepared for publication by Richard Zaner.

cation systems. In the evolution of a world view the differentiations of importance, familiarity, subordination and super-ordination, etc., that spring from social *interaction* will thus significantly influence the *taxonomy* of socially relevant relations. In a world view in which the social world is coextensive with the universe, degrees or kinds of sociality will be distinguished. The typical form taken by such distinctions is the division of the social world into fellow beings encountered in everyday experience and beings on a different plane, endowed with extraordinary qualities or powers [32] and encountered only in special, ritualized relations.[33] I shall return to this point later.

While the "functional requirements" of a society modify the social objectivation of the "universal projection" in a world view, it would be wrong to assume that the resulting taxonomy would be closer to a classification of nature and society that seems reasonable to modern man. The relevance structures of a tribe of hunters and gatherers or of a community based on slash-and-burn agriculture differ from one another; they are radically different from those of a complex society based on a developed technology, functionally rational institutions and bureaucratized organizational systems. The classification system of a society has a logic of its own that is not easily comprehensible to an outsider. "Classificatory totemism" found among Australian tribes, for example, takes the unity of man and nature for granted. Man and all relevant natural phenomena are grouped in *one* system and subdivided according to a pervasive clan or moiety principle that cuts across or, rather, ignores the distinction between human beings, animals, plants and physical objects.[34]

Once a world view is socially objectivated it presents the individual with an obligatory system of interpretations. The system is internalized by the individual and has for him the objectivity of a cultural norm, shared by everybody in his right mind, as well as the inevitability of a subjective category

[32] Cf. G. van der Leeuw, *Religion in Essence and Manifestation,* London 1938, pp. 23–64.

[33] Cf. Jean Cazeneuve, *Les Rites et la condition humaine,* Paris 1958.

[34] "Thus, in the Port Mackay district, Queensland, where each tribe is divided into two moieties, the impression made on one who knew them was that the moiety division of nature was fundamental, and that man naturally was subject to it; as he also says: 'The Blacks seem to have an idea that these classes (moieties and sections) are a universal law of nature, so they divide everything between them.' It is often difficult for us to see the principle of division, but the native can usually say straight off to which moiety or other group kangaroo, bamboo, particular trees, grasses, or stones belong, just as readily as he knows the moiety or clan or section of his fellow tribesmen. The division or classification implies a relationship between the human beings and natural species and phenomena which are grouped together." A. P. Elkin, *The Australian Aborigines,* Garden City, N.Y. 1964[4] (Sidney-London, 1938[1]), p. 207 f.

of cognition. In the case of a world view that approximates the ideal type described above, this means that the "universal projection" will receive continuous social support. Potential, subjectively perceptible restrictions of that sense-transfer will be implausible. Those qualities of things that are interpreted as refutations of the "universal projection" in another society are habitually ignored.

If the results of the subjective operation of the "universal projection" are not socially objectivated and institutionally stabilized (or if the plausibility of a world view of the first type breaks down), a potentially significant difference among the things to which the sense "living body" was transferred is likely to claim attention. Some of these things do and some do not change their expression. A rock, for example, is at first experienced as an agent in an intersubjective context of action. I stumble over a rock: the rock hurt my toe. The outside of the rock is experienced as the embodiment of a *durée*. But, in addition – in consequence of specific apperceptive transfers of sense that are founded on the "universal projection" – a particular state of the outside is apprehended as an expression of a particular internal state of the rock, e.g. anger. If I regard the same rock after some time has elapsed, I notice, however, that its expression did not change. Comparing the rock with other bodies in my experience – whatever the motivation for such comparison – I am struck by the constancy of its expression. The expressions of many bodies encountered in the life-world change and these changes are experienced as symptoms of a transformation of the "inside" of these bodies. As for rocks, no such transformation can be read off a comparable external change.

Generally speaking, the sense "living body", which is originally transferred to all things in the life-world, receives additional and specific support whenever perceptible transformations of the outside of the object are directly and consistently apprehended as changes of expression. Whenever specific synchronizations between ego's stream of consciousness and the *durée* of some body are not successful, the "universal projection" rests exclusively on the ("empirically" irrefutable) elementary sense transfer. The "universal projection" is less plausible in these instances, unless specific, socially derived and institutionally supported interpretations "explain away" the physiognomic immobility of certain objects in the life-world. In other words, while physiognomic mobility subjectively reinforces the transfer of the sense "living body" to some parts of the life-world, physiognomic immobility has the opposite effect, except where it can be explicated in terms of the overall scheme of a world view in which the unrestricted operation of the "universal projection" has the status of a cultural norm.

Physiognomic immobility is therefore the weakest element in the plausibility structure of historical world views that approximate the ideal type described above. If the relevance systems that support the continuity of such world views change [35] and if the plausibility structure of the world views changes accordingly, the subjective perceptions of physiognomic immobility have a chance to be socially objectivated. Physiognomic immobility may thus become a decisive criterion in the classification of the boundaries of the social world. Transformations of a world view of the first type then result in the institutional stabilization of a world view in which the objects in the life world that are characterized by physiognomic immobility are "de-socialized".

It should be noted that this is again an ideal-typical construction from which historical world views deviate to a greater or lesser extent. An interesting example is the culture of Dobu, an island in the Western Pacific.[36] It agrees with the ideal type inasmuch as human beings (the natives) and certain plants (the yam, which is extremely important in Dobu agriculture) are grouped together and refered to by one word (*tomot*), while objects characterized by physiognomic immobility are not part of the social world. It deviates significantly from the ideal type inasmuch as the "universal projection" is partially restricted by additional criteria. The social world does not include all plants nor animals and, even more remarkably, the term *tomot* is not used to refer to white men. Yams, however, are experienced as personal beings that may be typified by sex and age, as capable of emotion,[37] sensory perception,[38] locomotion [39] and speech.[40] Certain qualities of the yams, the fact that they can be never seen to walk, for example, are interpreted in such a manner that the elementary sense-transfer is not threatened. As was said earlier, once the "universal projection" is socially objectivated and institutionally stabilized at a given level of restriction, qualities of objects that might weaken the plausibility structure of the world view are either habitually ignored or explained so as to fit the scheme.[41]

[35] For a general discussion of the structural and cultural conditions for the transformation of world views cf. Berger and Luckmann, *op. cit.*, esp. pp. 96–118.

[36] Cf. R. F. Fortune, *Sorcerers of Dobu*, London 1963 (rev. ed.), 1932[1].

[37] A Dobuan, speaking of a yam plant: "O he is angry and he shoot up strongly" – *op. cit.*, p. 109.

[38] "The yams see it (smoke). They snuff it in to get its odour". – *op. cit.*, p. 109.

[39] "Now they roam in the forest". – *op. cit.*, p. 108.

[40] "One says 'that there he charms. What about me?'" – *op. cit.*, p. 109.

[41] Fortune's account of Dobu provides such an excellent illustration of this point that it will be quoted at length. When he tried to find out if what the Dobuans said about the yams was a metaphoric expression or a statement of "literal" fact, this is what he found:

Another aspect of the general structure of plausibility is illustrated by this example. Physiognomic mobility as well as locomotion of yams are taken for granted by Dobuans. But, as facts in the everyday experience on Dobu, they rest on different kinds of evidence. Whereas the Dobuans *know* that yams roam about, they *experience* the changing expressions of yams. Generally speaking, the plausibility of facts that are part of socially derived knowledge may be more easily shaken than of facts based on "direct" experience. It was seen that on Dobu the overall plausibility of yams as persons was maintained. Under conditions that were described in general terms before, however, the plausibility of facts which require special explanation is more likely to give way.

Other things being equal, the ego thus perceives that some of the bodies to which the sense "living body" was originally transfered do not move about. Trees, for example, are seen to change expression. They change color; their branches and leaves move and rustle in the wind; they rot away. But they cannot be seen to leave their place, while many other bodies which were animated by the "universal projection" lie down and rise, walk, jump and run. The ability to move from one place to another is associated with the changing perspectives in which the environment appears to the ego. It is a constitutive element of ego's awareness of his body. Subjectively perceived mobility of bodies in the phenomenal field of the ego thus adds, for these bodies, specific and concrete support to the elementary sense-transfer. Conversely, if that quality is absent, the plausibility of the elemen-

"'Kinosi said in the garden yams are persons. How is this?' 'Yams are persons,' said Alo – 'what else? Like women, they give birth to children, among them my mother, as she gave birth to me and as my daughter will bear children, and then my grand-children, when I am dead – such is also the way of yams.' 'But,' I said, 'how is it yams are persons? Do persons stay still always?' Alo had his counter-statement. 'At night they come forth from the earth and roam about. For this reason, if we approach a garden at night we tread very quietly. Just as we startle a man with an abrupt shout – or with a dead snake concealed behind our back – he starts very quietly at night. We do not dig the harvest when the sun is low in the morning (the usual time for garden work). We wait till the sun has mounted. Then we know they are back. If we dig in the early morning how should we find yams? Nothing would be there. We do not dig early. It is *bomana* (our sacred prohibition) of the garden.' This statement proved to be no spontaneous argument, but a direct statement of traditional belief. I enquired if the vine and the root tubers walked about at nights entire. My enquiry was cast in all seriousness and received with all seriousness. 'No! The vines remain. You may see them steadfast any night in the garden. The tubers alone emerge from the ground and walk the bush tracks in the night.' ... After I had arrived at this stage, I once said, in the hope that provocation might eludicate matters further, that one man (whom I did not name) had told me that yams were not persons. This statement was strictly untrue. My two informants both assumed the extremely disgusted expression which means emphatic negation, and Alo said curtly and forcibly: 'Yams are persons, with ears. If we charm they hear.' Next day he showed me the ears, organs of hearing, the several

tary transfer of sense may be weakened. More precisely, if the absence of that quality is noted and if it is not neutralized by an internalized cultural system of classification and explanation, the plausibility of that sense-transfer *is* weakened.

In defining an ideal-typical world view that is based on a restriction of the "universal projection" both by physiognomic mobility and locomotion, we must remember that neither the former nor the latter need be identically perceived in different cultures. Seeing a body change expression or move about depends, of course, on elementary perceptual processes that are independent of historical cultures. But it depends, at the same time, on the interpretational context of perception. In other words, it is codetermined by the internalized system of classification that originates in the concrete relevance structures shared in a historical society. And, *a fortiori,* if it is a matter of believing that something moves about, when there is no direct perceptual evidence for it, institutionally stabilized stocks of knowledge play a decisive role. Although the boundaries of social reality in world views of the third type correspond approximately to the division between plants and animals, the inclusion or exclusion of a given species in the social world is determined by differing "perceptions" of what is locomotion. World views of this type thus show considerable variation in detail.

This type of world view is approximated by many cultures which were traditionally classified as totemistic. Interesting examples are provided by the hunting societies of Siberia. These societies differ from one another in social organization and culture. They exist in different climates; there are significant differences in the ecology of their habitat; they are of different ethnic and linguistic stock; they have been exposed to varied cultural influences. And yet the world views of these societies have a common denominator. They rest on relevance systems that are determined by dependence on a limited number of animal species with severely restricted populations. Characteristically, no fundamental difference between man and animal is perceived.[42] Similarities are found in all important points of comparison, although it should be noted that here, too, some similarities are perceived "directly" while others are merely known to be facts.[43]

tendril buds about the growing point of the vine. The growing point buds are no more ears than an ear of corn is an organ of hearing. In Dobu the ears of the vine are most literally organs of hearing, however." *op. cit.* London 1963 (1932[1]), pp. 107–109.

[42] "D'espèce humaine à espèce animale, il ne saurait être question de supériorité: il n'y a pas de différence d'essence." – Eveline Lot-Falck, *Les Rites de chasse chez les peuples sibériens,* Paris, 1953, p. 19.

[43] "Il (le chasseur) le *voit* chasser, comme lui, pour se nourrir, lui *suppose* une vie semblable à la sienne, une organisation sociale du même modèle." (italics mine). *ibid.,* p. 19.

The plausibility structure of world views that approximate the type just described, too, is heterogeneous. The weakest element in this plausibility structure consists in the fact that normal and reciprocal communication is possible with some bodies to which the sense "living body" was originally transferred, whereas it fails with others. The potential threat to the plausibility of the world view is typically neutralized by specific explanations. A different but equivalent language is ascribed to plants[44] and animals.[45] But only some experts, after appropriate rituals, are initiated into the secret.[46] The internal consistency of world views on this level of restriction of the "universal projection" is thus reestablished – but at a price. Social relations with animals are transposed to a realm different from everyday life.

Comparison of fellow-men with animals reveals a potentially relevant difference. Under the general conditions for the breakdown of plausibility structures, this difference may become a criterion for separating the social from the non-social. If this happens, a decisive step in the de-socialization of the universe is taken.[47] On this level of restriction additional and highly specific criteria may combine with language, or even partially supersede language, in defining the boundary of morally relevant social relations. This boundary, it should be noted, does not separate "man" from "animal". It includes in the social world the speakers of *the* language, i.e., fellow-tribesmen, and perhaps certain animals with whom *ritual* communication can be established, while all others remain outside.

Examples of this type of world view are tribes in which the term that refers to the tribe is coextensive with the concept of "man". One also remembers the distinction between Greek and barbarian; in this connection one may recall that some Slavic languages refer to the Germans as "mutes". None of these examples approximates the ideal-typical construction very closely, but in all of them we find vestiges of an attitude which forms the psychological sub-stratum of that construction. We may assume that in all societies which approximated this type – and which were not totally isolated – the reciprocal translatability of languages was discovered sooner or later. This must have served as the basis for less particularistic conceptions of

---

[44] Thus, for example, yams are known to talk on Dobu. Cf. Fortune, *op. cit.*, p. 107.

[45] Cf., for example, Lot-Falck, *op. cit.*, p. 19.

[46] Cf., for example, Mircea Eliade, "Les Rêves chez les chamans", in: Roger Caillois and G. E. von Grunenbaum, *Le Rêve et les sociétés humaines*, Paris 1967, p. 319.

[47] A further restriction of the "universal projection" could only lead to the reification of the entire world, if one may choose this phrase to describe a pathological state that is usually called autism. Cf. Margaret S. Mahler, Manuel Furer and Calvin F. Settlage, "Severe Emotional Disturbances in Childhood: Psychosis", in: Silvano Arieti, ed., *American Handbook of Psychiatry*, I, New York 1959, pp. 816–839, esp. p. 824 f.

man that emerged in classical civilizations. The conception with which we are most familiar is of course one whose tradition links our own view of the world with the universalistic humanism of the Renaissance and, by way of Rome, with Greek philosophy. And yet partial, rather complicated regressions are not uncommon. One may forget the treatment meted out, not long ago, by representatives of an advanced civilization to the unfortunate Tasmanians. But latter-day reappearances of a similar attitude, adorned with pseudo-scientific and religious frills, can hardly be ignored by an observer of the contemporary scene, from South Africa to our own country.

It must be stressed again that the levels of restriction of the "universal projection", from physiognomic mobility over locomotion to reciprocal communication, represent ideal-typical constructions. Historical world views that approximate a given ideal type are not the "evolutionary" result of a transformation of a historical world view that approximates the "preceding" type. But a less stringent and rather obvious historical relation is indeed implied. World views which are based on the unrestricted "universal projection" have "phylogenetic" as well as logical priority. World views in which the social world is coextensive with human affairs are always transformations of world views in which the "universal projection" is less restricted.

Another general observation should be added. Once a given level of restriction of the "universal projection" is objectivated in a world view, the objects in the life-world that are no longer part of everyday social reality need not become part of a merely physical universe. Under certain conditions the sense "living body", acquired by these objects in consequence of the elementary transfer of sense, is modified rather than canceled. These objects may be henceforth experienced as incarnations of *extra-ordinary* powers, as representations in the everyday world of a transcendent realm.[48] There is a close connection between the de-socialization of the world and the articulation of a religious symbolic universe. The de-socialization of parts of the life-world may be paralleled, however, by de-animation. The historical uniqueness of such a development – predicated on such complex causes that it still represents a major challenge to the history of ideas, historical sociology and the sociology of knowledge – hardly needs to be stressed. The result, however, is with us: a mechanistic conception of the universe in which the "universal projection" is invalidated.

A final remark should be added on the relation of plausibility structures to changes in the world view and to shifts of the boundaries of the social

[48] For an interesting discussion of the socialization of the non-human universe cf. G. van der Leeuw, *Religion in Essence and Manifestation,* London 1938 (in German, Tübingen 1933).

world. World views in which the "universal projection" either remains un-restricted or is not narrowly restricted are prevalent in societies which – although differing in many details – share a considerable number of traits. They have a simple technology and are therefore profoundly shaped by, and directly dependent on, their natural habitat; their social structure con-sists essentially of interlocking primary groups that are circumscribed by kinship relations; the patterns of relevance are relatively homogeneous; the systems of classification are unitary while, at the same time, configurations of "theoretical knowledge" are hardly developed. Socialization processes lead to a high degree of congruence between the socially objectivated con-ception of the world and subjective reality. In other words, the plausibility of the institutionally stabilized world view is pervasive as well as compelling, and traditions change imperceptibly. Increasingly narrower restrictions of the "universal projection", however, characterize world views that are typi-cally associated with societies of greater cultural and structural complexity and correspondingly faster rates of change. Knowledge tends to be special-ized and the world view is distributed in society in different "versions". The subjective plausibility of various interpretational schemes, bodies of "theo-retical knowledge" maintained by experts, and even of the "official" version of world view, tends to be less pervasively reinforced and less compellingly enforced by social institutions. Other things being equal, potential restric-tions of the "universal projection" that may arise in immediate, pragmati-cally determined contexts of subjective experience are less likely to be auto-matically neutralized by the "official" world view and are more likely to initiate processes that lead to a modification of the prevalent boundaries of the social world.

V. HUMAN SOCIAL STRUCTURE AND BOUNDARIES OF THE SOCIAL WORLD

The relation of the boundaries of the social world to the social structure was discussed in its chief aspect in the preceding section. Although the boundaries of the social world take their common origin in an elementary activity of human consciousness, they vary greatly in historical world views. This variation is indirectly connected with divergent social structures. The boundaries of the social world are the axis of an encompassing system of classification which is concordant with the established patterns of relevance. The degree to which the "universal projection" is restricted is thus dependent on the patterns of relevance that prevail in historical societies – patterns that are bound by the specific requirements of (human) social structure.

There is another aspect of this relationship that stands in need of elucidation. A social world that is identical with human intersubjectivity does
not belong to the elementary structures of the life-world. But only in a life-
world in which the social and the human coincide, are the social world
and the social structure conspicuously homologous. In other historical life-
worlds, the everyday patterns, at least, of social interaction would seem to
be incongruent with the prevalent conception of the social universe. It is
not unreasonable to ask, therefore, whether the individual who, according
to the precepts of his world view, is linked to animals, or plants, or all
nature, perceives such kinship to be peculiarly limited in comparison to the
bonds that unite him with his fellow-men.

One must remember that an individual who has internalized a world view
in which sociality is not limited to human beings, finds support for it not
only in many external traits of the personal beings in the life world but
also in their behavior. Whereas personal beings are comparable in that they
sleep, eat, run, fight, mate, growl, scream, dance, die, they are different in
that they are male or female, young or old, big or small, friendly or hostile,
dangerous or innocuous, edible or interdicted. Of the innumerable perceptible differences some are selected as relevant categories of discrimination
and incorporated in an obligatory scheme of classification. Some may become pivots of the scheme, others may constitute subsidiary categories, yet
others may serve to typify the life-world in ways that are neither habitual
nor obligatory. But no universal principle decides which will become which.
To be sure, all world views differentiate degrees or kinds of sociality. But
the difference between human beings and animals may be subordinated to
cardinal distinctions of another kind. Differences in the relations between
human and non-human personal beings may be therefore experienced as
less important than other differences in the relations between personal beings
– as, for example, those of age, sex and clan membership. What to us appear
to be obvious limitations in the relationship between human beings and
animals, need not, to others, undermine the plausibility of a scheme of classification in which animals are personal beings. In the absence of an abstract
conception of humanity, relations with members of a hostile tribe, or, for
that matter, mothers-in-law, may appear equally limited.

A universally relevant distinction arises elsewhere. Before a child inter-
nalizes the world view of the society into which it was born, before it acquires
a classification system that provides support for the subjective working of
the "universal projection" (while, at the same time, setting limits to it), it
enters the socialization process in a human social structure. In other words,
before the range of social relations is defined for the child by a historical

world view, it begins to participate in social processes in which the partners are human beings. A child's early years consist of almost continuous and highly regular face-to-face encounters with a numerically restricted group of persons. The relationships in which these persons are partners include frequent bodily contacts, are charged with a wide range of emotions and satisfy concurrently all the needs of the infant. The empirical dependence of human children on what is, in effect, a minimal human social structure has, of course, the greatest general significance. Its special importance in the present context is obvious. Although the apperceptive transfer of the sense "living body" is not, at this stage of the socialization process, limited to the persons who play a significant role in it, the fact that these persons are human provides the fullest, the most reliable and the most plausible confirmation for the earliest operations of the "universal projection".

The conduct of human partners in the earliest social relations reflects, more or less consistently, the child's conduct. Different actions meet with different responses. Mother, father or other significant individuals in the socialization process reward and punish the child, feed it, coddle it, play with it, talk to it approvingly and reprove it on occasion. By virtue of differentiated actions they shape and stabilize the infant's pliable and diffuse awareness of the world and of itself. The child begins to look at its own conduct from the "outside". In ongoing reciprocal relations with human partners the child acquires control over its instinctually rather indeterminate behavior. The child finds itself reflected in human partners as in mirrors; they present from different perspectives and in many facets one Self.[49] The cognitive and emotional richness and the full reciprocity, over a significant stretch of biography, or social relations with human partners constitute the empirical basis for the stabilization of experience in the life-world and, concurrently, for the crystallization of personal identity. The minimal *human* social structure in which socialization takes place leaves a lasting imprint on the effective orientation of the individual in everyday life, whether the objective and "official" system of classification that is internalized in the process of socialization recognizes the special "human" features of the early social relationships or not. The child may learn that its ancestor was a bear, but the fact will not escape its notice that its "real", everyday father – although classified as a member of the bear clan – acts in ways that "real", everyday bears do not.

The complement to the genetic priority of human social structure is its pragmatic precedence in the everyday life of the adult. Without regard to

[49] This account summarizes and combines some well-known theories of George H. Mead and Charles H. Cooley.

what world view was internalized and irrespectively of where the boundaries of the social world are drawn "officially," the adult's life involves certain social relations, with human partners, that have an eminent pragmatic significance. These relations, too, consist of regularly recurring face-to-face encounters some of which are associated with intimate bodily contacts. They are predictable in great detail, a fact that permits collaboration on vital tasks that cannot be performed individually. The full reciprocity of such relationships, ranging from sexual intercourse to hunting campaigns is not only essential for survival but also provides continuous support for the objective reality of the world of everyday life and for the maintenance of personal identity. Such reciprocity is not constitutive of relations with other persons in the life-world – whether these are animal or, in fact, human (as, for example, members of another tribe).

The genetic priority and pragmatic precedence of social relations with human partners bestow on the latter a privileged position among the personal beings in the life-world. The position is privileged in relation to individual biographies. It need not find an objective expression in the classificatory schemes of the world view. The incongruence between the boundaries of the social world and the patterns of orientation in ordinary social relations may be neutralized, provided that the incomplete reciprocity of relations with personal beings other than the partners in everyday life is plausibly explained. As indicated earlier, this is usually accomplished by a transposition of such beings to a symbolic domain and by ritualization of relations with them. Awareness of the incongruence between the human social structure and the "official" boundaries of the social world is suppressed by splitting the social universe. On the other hand, such incongruence can become a motive for increasing restrictions of the "universal projection". Under conditions that guarantee the maintenance of the plausibility structure which supports the world view, the motive remains latent. If, however, the plausibility structure is weakened, the "universal projection" is restricted until the "official" boundaries of the social world reflect more closely the social structure of everyday life.

As soon as the boundaries of the social world converge with the human social structure, a different kind of incongruence arises. The working of the elementary sense transfer is habitually confined to that part of the life-world which is enclosed by the "official" boundaries of the social universe. But the "universal projection" is not extinguished. Where the world view is not yet fully internalized, as in children, or where the plausibility structure that supports the world view is weakened for one reason or another, as among socially rather isolated persons, the lonely and the elderly, the elementary sense transfer may be rekindled. Would anyone but an adherent of the most trivial conception of normalcy stand aghast when a person swears at a stone against which he stubbed his toe, snigger when a lonely individual forms what appears to be a satisfying social relationship with a pet, and feel superior to a child that weeps for the injustice of a Christian heaven without animals?

ALFRED SCHUTZ ON SOCIAL REALITY
AND SOCIAL SCIENCE

by

MAURICE NATANSON

> Familiar things happen, and mankind does not
> bother about them. It requires a very unusual mind
> to undertake the analysis of the obvious.
>
> Alfred North Whitehead

It has taken American philosophers and social scientists thirty-five years to catch up with the early work of Alfred Schutz. His *Der sinnhafte Aufbau der sozialen Welt: eine Einleitung in die verstehende Soziologie* was first published in 1932. An English version has recently appeared under the title, *The Phenomenology of the Social World.*[1] It is clear that the German edition was closely studied by some of the ablest minds of the thirties and forties who were concerned with problems of the philosophy and methodology of the social sciences. References to Schutz's book appear in the writings of such thinkers as José Ortega y Gasset, Ludwig von Mises, Raymond Aron, and Felix Kaufmann. Although it is not unlikely that the English edition will be studied with equal care by American scholars, the fundamental assumptions of the European reader about the relevance of philosophy for social science have heretofore been rather different from those of his counterpart in the United States. Thus, for example, Ludwig von Mises, unlike most American economists, begins his treatise on economics, *Human Action,* with a substantial section on "The Epistemological Problem of a General Theory of Human Action." The fundamental assumption is that to be concerned with man in the social world is necessarily to explore the reality which underlies and characterizes "Man," the "Social," and "World." Philosophy is inescapable for the social scientist who seeks clarity and rigor in his work, who takes the term "discipline" seriously. Nor is it solely a question of interest in the logic of scientific inquiry, a matter of paying attention to the status of propositions, models, and laws. Philosophy is rather concerned with the *phenomena* of the social world: men acting in the context of an intersubjective reality, shared and sustained by temporal beings aware of themselves no less than of each other. Oddly enough, today's reader of *The Phenomenology of the Social World* may be closer to his European

---

[1] Translated by George Walsh and Frederick Lehnert with an Introduction by George Walsh (Evanston, Illinois: Northwestern University Press, 1967).

counterpart than would have been the case even fifteen years ago, for the recent interest in phenomenology ,existentialism, and existential psychology and psychiatry has brought many individuals to the realization that the very language of social science bears the philosophical inflections inherent in its presuppositions, presuppositions which cannot be examined within a methodological orientation without danger of entering a circle vicious not only for its logical distress but also for its conceptual insularity. A good measure of responsibility for creating the audience for his book belongs to Schutz himself. Through his teaching in the United States and the publication of the three volumes of his *Collected Papers,* phenomenology has found its way into social science. If we have had to wait thirty-five years for *The Phenomenology of the Social World,* it should be remembered that during those years a new philosophical force has risen to shape significantly the audience appropriate to the book, a force which owes much of its quality and momentum to the career of Alfred Schutz.

I

In its historical focus, *The Phenomenology of the Social World* is an attempt to vindicate and deepen Max Weber's theory of social action by providing for it a philosophical grounding which derives from some of the central ideas of Edmund Husserl and Henri Bergson. In its systematic aspect, the *Phenomenology* is an effort to establish the outlines of a conception of meaning whose constitutive character is grounded in the reality of inner-time consciousness. In its programmatic dimension, the *Phenomenology* is an adumbration of a philosophy of social reality, not simply a methodology but an anatomy of man's existence with his fellow-men in the midst of everyday life, within what Husserl called the "natural attitude." The axis on which this triple-fold movement turns is phenomenology itself, taken both as a method and as a mode of philosophical comprehension. The best way to approach Schutz's phenomenology is to see it at work in his characterization of the social world.

The social world is primarily the world of everyday life as lived and appreciated and interpreted by common-sense men carrying on the cognitive and emotive traffic of daily life. "Common-sense men" includes all of us insofar as we act in the world rather than observe it formally as disinterested scientists. Thus, although philosophers and sociologists are also common-sense men, philosophy and sociology are not part of the fabric of daily life. Philosophy is, in fact, a reversal of the underlying attitude of common-sense life, a primordial glance at what the mundane eye has simply accepted without even the intimation of serious question. Within the "natural attitude" of daily life, epistemology and metaphysics have no status, their fundamental problems are unadmitted because they are unrecognized, and their implications for a philosophy of human existence are simply and ingenuously excluded. To begin with, then, man in the natural attitude takes for granted his being in a world, his *having* a world, the existence of Others like himself, the on-going reality of communicating with those fellow-men, and, just as important, the assumption that everything just said holds equally well from the standpoint of the "other guy," the alter ego. Daily life – mundane reality – is "ours" from the outset, i.e., all elements of the world of everyday existence are taken as "real" for you as well as for me and for anyone who enters the human scene. The "taking as real" which is involved here is not a matter of inference or formal predication but an initial seeing and grasping, a perceptual seizing of the object or event *as real* and *as real for all of us*. Later we will turn to the phenomenological grounding for the "taken-as-real," but for the moment it is the naive, the "prepredicative" grasp of the experienced world as "ours" which needs consideration.

To say that the world is experienced as "ours" from the outset is to hold that my fellow-man is initially recognized as a "someone" (not a "something") and, further, a "someone like me."[2] In my face-to-face encounter with the Other, it is he as *person* who is grasped rather than a creature with the anatomical features which permit the human observer to classify him as a member of the same genus. It is in what Schutz terms the "Thou-orientation" that the Other is experienced as a person: "I am already Thou-oriented from the moment that I recognize an entity which I directly experience as a fellow-man (as a Thou), attributing life and consciousness to him. However, we must be quite clear that we are *not* here dealing with a conscious *judgment*. This is a prepredicative experience in which I become aware of a fellow human being *as a person*."[3] The social world is an inter-subjective one in several senses: first, it is the locus of my encounter with the "Thou"; second, it is the scene of my own action which is directed toward my fellow-men. My action reveals the world as "ours" no less than does my encounter with you as my "Thou." And of course, the social world does not spring magically into being with my birth or yours; it is historically grounded and bears the marks and signs of the activity of *our* ancestors,

---

[2] A few cautions are necessary: "from the outset" and "initially" are not to be taken as chronological terms, referring to events in the early lives of individuals. It is the phenomenological genesis and not the causal origin of experience which is at issue here.

[3] *The Phenomenology of the Social World*, pp. 163–164 (hereafter referred to only by page number).

most remarkable of all the typifying medium of language. Finally, the intersubjective world has an open horizon; it is in movement toward a future which is partly "ours" and in large part "theirs," the possession of future generations. In sum, the intersubjective world is the epistemic context for human action, the significative horizon in terms of which individuals, events, and even things are understood. It is now possible to turn to the phenomenological grounding for some of these claims.

The intersubjective world of daily life, our social world, is the domain of action, and the analysis of action is a central theme of Schutz's *Phenomenology*. In many ways, the problem of social action traverses and connects all of his work. In the *Phenomenology,* the starting point is Weber's conception of action. Although Schutz accepts and follows Weber's postulate of the subjective interpretation of meaning (the meaning which the actor bestows on his own act and for which he is responsible as distinguished from the interpretation which the observer makes), he presents some salient qualifications. First, and most generally, Weber explored the philosophical foundations of his theories only as deeply as the demands of his empirical research and the application of related theoretical investigation required; the vast insight and power of his methodology were not accompanied by equivalent philosophical analysis. Second, and more specifically, his conception of social action took for granted the very problem of intersubjectivity which lies at the basis of all theory of action. Concretely, the charges are that Weber does not recognize the complex time-structure of action, failing to distinguish between on-going action and the completed act; that his analysis of motivation is faulty because he does not allow for the difference between motivation whose explanatory principle lies in the past and that which demands the consideration of the future; that the entire status of *meaning* in social action has not been fully clarified because the structure of intention has been left philosophically unexamined. Schutz's position is perfectly clear at this point: convinced of the fundamental correctness (let alone greatness) of Weber's entire approach to the phenomena of the social world, he conceives his task to be that of a digger of foundations, to provide a philosophical underpinning for the sociology of *Verstehen* by clarifying its phenomenological presuppositions. It is in this perspective that Schutz's own formulation of the nature of action is to be understood.

There is a serious ambiguity in the term "action," for it can refer to the on-going course of an action's development or to the completed, finished product. Moreover, action may be presented to the ego in one of three temporal dimensions: "My *action as it takes place* presents itself to me as a series of *existing* and *present* experiences, experiences that are coming to be and passing away. My *intended . . . action* presents itself to me as a series of *future* experiences. My *terminated, completed act* (which is my expired action) presents itself to me as a series of *terminated* experiences which I contemplate in memory." [4] The meaning of an action is bound up with these temporal distinctions; further refinement is necessary. Schutz distinguished between action and act. The on-going constitution is termed "action"; the completed unit is the "act." Action is subject-bound, it builds up in a temporal development, and its full significance is always on the far side of the actor's intention. The act is a unitary phenomenon which is object-oriented and whose meaning is graspable. Since "meaning" is introduced here in a particular way, it is necessary to include some explanation of the phenomenological position in which it is embedded. Action (including act) and meaning are integral in their epistemic function. Meaning is not "added" or "attached" to action by way of some sort of predication or interpretive addendum. Instead, meaning is bound to the very conception of action and must be understood as vital to its formation. Meaning and action are both grounded in temporality: ". . . *meaning is a certain way of directing one's gaze at an item of one's own experience.* This item is thus 'selected out' and rendered discrete by a reflexive Act. Meaning indicates, therefore, a peculiar attitude on the part of the Ego toward the flow of its own duration." [5] These distinctions make it possible to see the dialectical relationship between "action" and "act."

In the process of its formation, social action is oriented toward certain goals; it is project-directed, we might say. The way in which a goal is entertained by the ego involves the following procedure: the individual projects his desired goal as having already been fulfilled and fancies it as completed, as though it now were, in Schutz's formulation, in the future perfect tense. The goal thus imagined is the projected act; it is the meaning of the corresponding action meant to realize it. The projecting, of course, takes place in a present. The goal projected is time-transcendent, for unlike the action within which its formation occurs, the *meaning* of the goal, the projected act, is merely intended by the consciousness of the imagining ego and not an actual part of his stream of awareness. In phenomenological terms, the intentional unity *meant* (the projected act, in this instance) is independent of the intending on the part of the ego. A mathematical proposition is true or false independent of the fervency with which the student asserts its truth or falsity and regardless of the idiosyncratic techniques he may use in fig-

[4] P. 39.
[5] P. 42. Note the distinction between "act" (*Handlung*) and "Act" (*Akt*), the latter referring to the spontaneous rather than the passive aspect of the ego's experience.

uring. What is *meant,* then, in social action is meaningful in the present to the extent (and for Schutz only to the extent) that a fancying or phantasying consciousness projects a corresponding act. Thus, "the meaning of any action is its corresponding projected act." [6] Apart from such projection, however, action, strictly speaking, has no meaning. [7] We have been discussing action in the present. Clearly, past action is taken up anew in the present and considered in its completed character as act. Instead of fancying an event as already having taken place, we have the event as actually having taken place. In an irreal or in a real way, the future is essential to the comprehension of action in the present, and within the present the history of acts is relived. One is tempted to speak with Augustine of a present of action present (the projected act), a present of acts past (the act remembered), and a present of action future (the anticipated act). [8] The structural grounding of the distinction between action and act in temporal considerations has decisive importance for the theory of meaning that emerges. Not only the ongoing action but the entire range of awareness requires a reflexive moment in consciousness, a looking-upon, if there is to be meaningful experience. That reflexiveness is made possible by inner time or durée which generates and sustains the multivalent order of human reality. It is precisely here that Husserl's and Bergson's analyses of human temporality provide Schutz with the foundation for a phenomenological account of the constitution of meaning.

The projected act, it has been suggested, requires a phantasying ego who imagines an event planned for the future as already having taken place. Phantasying is a complex activity in which the imagined objects are granted a peculiar ontological status: they are taken as "irreal" or fictive beings. Husserl speaks of them as "neutral" (as distinguished from "positional") projections. What is thus phantasied is "real" in the mode of being entertained by consciousness but not real in the sense of being taken as actually existent or having in fact transpired as a mundane event. The activity of phantasying is similar to Husserl's notion of a "neutrality modification" through which the aesthetic object emerges as "real" in the experience of the art work. [9] Phantasying, then, means presenting to oneself a possible

---

[6] P. 61.

[7] Though it may still be considered as part of "behavior" in the generic sense of that term.

[8] Perhaps the temptation ought to be avoided, for it is not altogether clear on this account what the relationship is between the futurity of the projected act and that of the anticipated act.

[9] ". . . let us suppose that we are observing Dürer's engraving, 'The Knight, Death, and the Devil.' We distinguish here in the first place the normal perception of which the correlate is the *'engraved print'* as a *thing,* this print in the portfolio. We distinguish

state of affairs and taking that state of affairs as consequent. One phantasies what his alter ego will do in response to a possible course of action whose projected act is now envisaged as finished and done with. If that course of action is indeed followed and the projected act becomes a reality, if what was phantasied does in actuality take place, then the mode of attention given to the act by the ego in reflective attitude changes into the "positional" attitude of consciousness. It is essential to consciousness that phantasying have the crucial reflective moment in its procedure for the experience in question to be meaningful. Reflection marks the difference between life and thought.[10] Phantasying, it must be added, covers a variegated range of attention, going from rich and dramatic envisagement to highly abstract and unlikely possibilities and resultants. The question of which possibilities are selected or chosen in the phantasying of projected acts leads to what Schutz calls the problem of "relevance," a topic I will turn to later. It is important at this point to recognize that the theory of phantasying has serious implications for social action at all levels of human experience because the projection of acts underlies the meaningful structure of the social world from the domain of face-to-face experience of the Thou to typifications of quite remote and distant fellow-men and their cultural realities.

Social action takes place in a context; it is situationally limited and defined. Even the fictive aspects of phantasying are qualified and restricted by the context within which the act is projected. What is deemed to be "likely," "possible," or "out of the question" depends, in part, on the situation at hand and the actor's assessment of it. To understand action, then, it is necessary to turn to what motivates the actor in a situation. One of Schutz's criticisms of Weber, it may be recalled, concerned his account of motivation. What Schutz objects to in Weber's treatment is that both the actor's subjective feeling about the context of meaning which is the ground

in the second place the perceptive consciousness within which in the black lines of the picture there appear to us the small colourless figures, 'knight on horseback,' 'death,' and 'devil.' In aesthetic observation we do not consider these as the objects (*Objekten*); we have our attention fixed on what is portrayed *'in the picture,'* more precisely, on the *'depicted'* realities, the knight of flesh and blood, and so forth. That which makes the depicting possible and mediates it, namely, the consciousness of the 'picture' (of the small grey figurettes in which through the derived noeses something other, through similarity, 'presents itself as depisted), is now an example for the neutrality-modification of the perception. This *depicting picture-object* stands before us *neither as being nor as non-being,* nor in any *other positional modality;* or rather, we are aware of it as having its being, though only a quasi-being, in the neutrality-modification of Being." (Edmund Husserl, *Ideas: General Introduction to Pure Phenomenology,* translated by W. R. Boyce Gibson (London and New York: George Allen and Unwin Ltd. and The Macmillan Co., 1931), p. 311).

[10] See p. 70.

of his behavior and what the observer supposes that ground to be are indiscriminately put together in the concept of motive.[11] Since it was Weber who introduced the postulate of the subjective interpretation of meaning, which insists on attention being paid to the meaning an act has for the actor who performs that act, it is curious that he failed to keep separate the subjective and objective aspects when discussing motivation. The reason for the confusion is the failure to explore the temporal foundation of action. Thus, " 'behavior' or 'action' is for Weber a discrete datum with which one can operate immediately, without further inquiry as to the principle of its unity." [12] A consequence of ignoring the temporal grounding of motivation is that the orientation of action toward a future event or its reference to a past experience cannot be distinguished. The difference, however, is a profound one, for the logic of future-directed action is qualitatively different from that of its past-related corollary. Schutz marks the difference by naming the former the "in-order-to" motive of action and the latter the "because" motive. The *Phenomenology* includes a detailed discussion of the meaning of these terms.

The central insight of the subjective interpretation of meaning hinges on the question of how we are to understand the motive of the actor. In response to the question, "Why are you doing X?" two answers are both common and appropriate: "I am doing X in order to accomplish Y" or "I am doing X because of Y." In many cases it is possible to translate one form into the other: "I am entering the diplomatic corps in order to serve my country" translates into "I am entering the diplomatic corps because I want to serve my country" (and vice versa). When translation of this sort is possible, we are dealing with what Schutz calls a "pseudo-because statement." In the case of a "genuine because statement" translation is impossible: "I left the diplomatic corps because I was fired" cannot be translated into an "in-order-to" equivalent. The motive of the genuine because statement lies in a completed experience in the past. Access to it temporally must be by way of the pluperfect tense. The in-order-to motive is not only directed toward the future but presupposes the project which characterizes the course of action phantasied by the ego. In the in-order-to relation, the project does the motivating; in the genuine because relation, the project itself is motivated.[13] The larger consideration involved here is that social action is initially defined by the project, not the causal antecedents of the project. This in turn means that social action is fundamentally motivated by in-order-to rela-

---

[11] See p. 86.
[12] P. 87.
[13] See p. 92.

tions which are, as they develop in the actuality of life, basically taken for granted by the actor. It is precisely here that we locate the root of Schutz's entire theory of "the world as taken for granted." The situation within which the projection of action by way of in-order-to motives takes place presupposes the past acts of the ego and the history of his antecedent projections. The practical efficacy of past performances in a variety of situations assures a base from which each new present projecting is oriented. Pragmatic justification of that base in turn renders new projects of action typically assured. In the moment of reflection the ego looks back on its fund of knowledge gained from past acts and makes the assumption that what has typically worked reasonably well in the past will also work equivalently well in the future. Of course, there is nothing automatic about the decision as to whether what was appropriate in the past is appropriate for the future because the "Here" and "Now" status of the individual is never quite the same as his earlier placement in life. Within the span of the project of the in-order-to relation, the problematic aspect of experience is placed in abeyance. Thus, the taken-for-granted "is always that particular level of experience which presents itself as not in need of further analysis. Whether a level of experience is thus taken for granted depends on the pragmatic interest of the reflective which is directed upon it and thereby upon the particular Here and Now from which that glance is operating." [14]

If action is always situated, it is a world of fellow-men which guarantees the sociality of man's existence. The human situation is essentially intersubjective. At the same time, the range of the intersubjective world is far larger than is ordinarily recognized, for in addition to my contemporaries (and the narrower but overwhelmingly important class of those contemporaries with whom I share a face-to-face relationship – Schutz calls them "consociates") there are my predecessors, those who lived before I was born, and my successors, those who will be born after I die. It is a mistake to limit the analysis of social action to the sphere of contemporaries, though it is indeed true that what I know of my predecessors and successors is dependent on the model of my experience of contemporaries. The beginning point for an analysis of the intersubjective world is the We-relationship I share with those fellow-men with whom I participate in direct spatial-temporal encounter – my consociates. The experience of the We is primordial. It is gained by the presence of men in the world, not by induction or a theoretical proof. We come here to an experiential bedrock of the social: the We of direct, shared, face-to-face encounter is, from the standpoint of the ego's *participation* in the social world, an experience *sui generis*. The prob-

[14] P. 74.

lem of intersubjectivity *is* a problem because of the fact of the We-relationship. In this sense, the We is experientially prior to the philosophical problem it generates for those who seek to understand how a social world is possible. Nor is the We-relationship to be explained on the basis of a logical construction of the social made by the ego. Rather, "the world of the We is not private to either of us, but is our world, the one common intersubjective world which is right there in front of us. It is only from the face-to-face relationship, from the common lived experience of the world in the We, that the intersubjective world can be constituted. This alone is the point from which it can be deduced." [15] Within the social world thus understood, however, there still remains the question of *how* knowledge of Others is possible. At one level this is a distinctively philosophical problem; at another level, it is a systematic issue for the methodology of the social sciences.

Even in the face-to-face relationship with a fellow-man, the individual knows only an aspect of the Other. Although the Thou is given as a person, the mode of givenness is essentially adumbrated. Some aspects of the Other are manifest, others are presented in shadowy form or are completely opaque. To say that I have knowledge of the Other is then to say that I know him directly in very limited measure but indirectly in vast degree, through typified constructs which I form of him and of human behavior generally. Of course, the paradigm Thou in the relationship of love or friendship presents himself vividly and thoroughly, and in all face-to-face encounters the reality of the Other is more or less vibrantly presented. But when we move from consociates to contemporaries, a radical change is introduced: the ego knows his contemporary by way of typifications and constructions, models of how "someone" traditionally behaves or is expected to behave in certain situations. In short, the ego knows his contemporaries chiefly through a complex, concatenated system of ideal types. Schutz distinguishes between two meanings of the concept of ideal type of human behavior: "It can mean first of all the ideal type of another person who is expressing himself or has expressed himself in a certain way. Or it may mean, second, the ideal type of the expressive process itself, or even of the outward results which we interpret as the signs of the expressive process. Let us call the first the 'personal ideal type' and the second the 'material' or 'course-of-action *type*.'" [16] What happens then to the theory of the subjective interpretation of meaning is that the social world is constituted, in large measure, by personal ideal types and by course-of-action types, varying

[15] P. 171.
[16] P. 187.

from more or less specific acquaintance with a fellow-man to almost complete anonymity in relationships. The means by which such types are constituted involves the postulation of a person and the attribution to him of those typical attitudes, motives, interests, skills, and techniques which would be sufficient to account for the kind of act in question we seek to understand. The analysis may begin either with the person and end with the act or start with the act and from its typical structure work back to the construction of the kind of person capable of behaving in that way. What decides the perspective from which the construction will be made is the interpreter's point of view. The personal ideal type *"is a function of the very question it seeks to answer."* [17] Finally, the personal ideal type is intimately related to the course-of-action type and indeed must utilize its model if it wishes to create its own. By means of both forms of ideal types, the ego is able to advance from the experience of the Thou in the We-relationship to the increasing stages of anonymization which mark its genesis and destiny as a contemporary with other contemporaries, as a successor to predecessors, and as a predecessor to successors.

II

"Whoever . . . wishes to analyze the basic concepts of the social sciences," Schutz writes, "must be willing to embark on a laborious philosophical journey, for the meaning-structure of the social world can only be deduced from the most primitive and general characteristics of consciousness." [18] This turn to the "subjective" must be understood in phenomenological terms; otherwise we are in danger of repeating what is by now the classical error of interpreting "consciousness" in individual, "interiorized" terms. It is not private contents of an introspective awareness but the structure of intentionality which is meant in the phenomenological conception of consciousness. The perceptual model, then, is not that of a container with an "inside" and an "outside," hooked up by wires to receive messages from the "real" world, nor is it the consequence of a separation between mind and body, a case still pending before the philosophic domestic relations court. Rather, for phenomenology consciousness is conceived of as a unity in which the "subjective" is already in direct connection with the objects of its intentional concern because those "objects" are parts of the unified structure of the streams of consciousness – not "things" but meant correlates of the acts which intend them. To turn to consciousness, then, is to locate the essential features of

[17] P. 190.
[18] P. 12.

meaning-structures whose universality is guaranteed, in part, by the fact that no predication of existence, ontological status, or psychological specificity is either being made or is at issue in the phenomenological attitude. Schutz's analysis of the time-structure of social action is concerned with what is necessarily presupposed for *any* ego which phantasies a projected act, not with the concrete, historical individual and his particular and special characteristics. It is irrelevant to the analysis to suggest, then, that the capacity to phantasy varies from individual to individual. It is because we can understand phantasying as such that it is possible to speak here of individual differences. Certainly, there are considerable and important variances in individual psychological capacities and operations, but they are measures of the ways in which the essential response is made. There are more or less gifted phantasiers but not more or less gifted phantasying.

Subjectivity, for the phenomenologist, is then to be understood as a domain which is readily accessible to the inspection of any investigator who cares to make the effort, provided that he equip himself properly. More important than special knowledge of methodological techniques is the broad recognition that consciousness is not an idiosyncratic spring to be tapped by a haphazard or esoteric method of intuition but intentionality itself, that which by its very nature is as "public" and as "intersubjective" as its intimates, mathematics and language. Nor is subjectivity to be approached through more sophisticated theories of personal intuition and empathy. Schutz explicitly repudiates the translation of *verstehende Soziologie* into either an irrationalism which tries to seize the vital aspect of life in some non-reductive way or a hermeneutics of fellow-feeling which tries to enter directly into the actuality of the Other's lived experience:

All true sciences demand the maximum of clarity and distinctness for all their propositions. There is no such thing as an irrational science. We must never cease reiterating that the method of Weber's sociology is a rational one and that the position of interpretive sociology should in no way be confused with that of Dilthey, who opposes to rational science another, so-called "interpretive" science based on metaphysical presuppositions and incorrigible "intuition."

It is true that the postulate of such an interpretive science arose historically from the necessity of breaking through the barriers that were erected between the rational special sciences and the understanding of living human experience. But it was forgotten by those proposing this new approach that life and thought are two different things and that science remains a matter of thought even when its subject matter is life. It cannot, therefore, base itself on some vague and confused empathy or on value presuppositions or on descriptions lacking in intellectual rigor.[19]

[19] P. 240.

There are a variety of reasons why the ego cannot seize the living actuality of the Other's experience: his Here and Now is unique, his stock of knowledge is built up and utilized from his perspective and by his choice, and he alone knows when his project begins and ends. As fellow-man, however, I can share a great deal with the Other: I *can* gain direct access to him as a Thou in the We-relationship and I *can* share a certain dimension of time through the fact that my alter ego and I grow older together. But even in these immediacies, I do not "become" the Other nor do I enter mysteriously into his lived experience. Sharing is not invading. The matter does not end there, of course, because my knowledge of the Other in its greatest complexity comes with the typifications and ideal types which form the matrix of social life. The description, analysis, and clarification of that matrix is nothing less than the subject matter of a phenomenology of the social sciences.

The distinction between life and thought which Schutz insists on demands a rigorous science of the subjective. It is not possible, in principle, for the scientist to enter directly into the life he observes and to build his science from the materials of direct encounter. At best these are points of departure for what may later develop into scientific work. Without doubt, the sociologist or anthropologist may live with his "subjects," share their daily lives, enter sympathetically and genuinely into their concerns and activities. It is from the standpoint of an observer, however, that the scientific reports of such participation are made and are methodologically warranted. The experience of the subject as a Thou in a We-relationship genuinely established by the scientist either remains part of daily life or is made an explicit object of reflective analysis. If it remains within life, it is no more a part of science than the corresponding experience of the subject. If it is examined and reflected upon, the experience is taken in its typified form and interpreted by means of constructions and ideal types. For Schutz, adequate scientific analysis must begin with the formation of objective types based on the knowledge gained of individuals through personal ideal types. The sociologic ascent, then, is from lived experience to typifications of mundane life to personal ideal types which account for individuals in action to objective ideal types which replace all prior constructs. With the final stage, the social scientist reaches his goal of establishing *"objective meaning-contexts of subjective meaning-contexts."* [20] And therewith he achieves the formalization and anonymization which rigorous science requires. In one sense, the scientist ultimately finds in the social world he describes the models he has placed there. Concrete human beings have been replaced by artificial crea-

[20] P. 241.

tures designed by the methodologist. Yet it is extremely important to remember that the genesis of construct and type-building goes back in naive form to the natural attitude within which men in daily life interact with one another. To paraphrase Kronecker's aphorism, we might say that the natural attitude gives us the primary constructs, the rest is the work of the social scientist. In a strange and tortuous way, it is through thought that life is able to return to its source.

The odyssey of Schutz's *Phenomenology* from the alone ego to the achievement of science is not without its internal discomforts and challenges. From within the orientation and outline of his work, there are three large issues which invite critical discussion: phenomenological method, the nature of intersubjectivity, and the problem of relevance.

1. Phenomenological Method: In an Appended Note to the first chapter of the *Phenomenology,* Schutz makes a systematic statement of the status of his investigation as phenomenological work. The analysis of inner time-consciousness is done within the phenomenological reduction. The rest of his book, however, is a phenomenology of the natural attitude which does not, for the most part, enter into the procedures or problems of transcendental phenomenology. It is the phenomena within the natural attitude which correspond to the correlative constituting phenomena of the phenomenologically reduced sphere that are considered the proper object of inquiry. The analysis of time is said to hold for mundane problems: ". . . since all analyses carried out within the phenomenological reduction hold true essentially also in psychological introspection, and thus within the sphere of the natural attitude, we shall have to make no revisions whatsoever in our conclusions concerning the internal time-consciousness when we come to apply them to the realm of ordinary social life." [21] Phenomenological method, of course, is not a special instrument which the phenomenologist uses as a jeweler his loupe. Use is bound at one end to a philosophy of perceptual experience and at the other to pragmatic considerations of what is being sought, what a

---

[21] P. 44. Compare the following formulations: ". . . a true *psychology of intentionality* is, according to Husserl's words, nothing other than a *constitutive phenomenology of the natural attitude.* In this eidetic mundane science (thus in the psychological apperception of the natural attitude), which stands at the beginning of all methodological and theoretical scientific problems of all the cultural and social sciences, all analyses carried through in phenomenological reduction essentially retain their validation. It is precisely here that the tremendous significance of the results achieved by Husserl for all the cultural sciences lies." (Alfred Schutz, *Collected Papers,* Vol. I: *The Problem of Social Reality,* edited and introduced by Maurice Natanson with a preface by H. L. van Breda (The Hague: Martinus Nijhoff, 1962), p. 132) and: ". . . Husserl himself has established once and for all the principle that analyses made in the reduced sphere are valid also for the realm of the natural attitude." (*Ibid.,* p. 149.)

problem calls for, and what level of clarification is appropriate to the goals of the inquiry. Understood in this way, the procedures of transcendental phenomenology may be unnecessary for the illumination of certain aspects of mundane existence. However, the various strata of phenomenological investigation mirror each other, are, in structural implication, isomorphic with each other. It follows that descriptive work done at one level has its direct implications and analogues for other levels. It is not altogether clear why Schutz restricts his transcendental glance to inner-time consciousness. Granted that time is the cardinal theme underlying social action, as it is of all social structure, it is still the case that the social itself, the current of mundanity, is not only equally deserving of transcendental investigation but in need of such inquiry if a variety of questions related to social action are to be analyzed out to their roots. The We-relationship, for example, is in many respects a primordial given for Schutz, i.e., his starting point in accounting for its form and function is its indubitable and immediate presentation. From the standpoint of the transcendental attitude, it is necessary to ask, How is it possible that there is such a structure? Within the natural attitude, the We-relationship is a fact of life, but in the phenomenological attitude it is deeply problematic. It is difficult to see how the question of the very possibility of the We-relationship can be given its full weight within the restrictions Schutz imposes. Obviously, it is the author's right to circumscribe the province of his investigation. What is at issue here is something else: how the analogue of the transcendental problem of sociality itself can be encountered within the limits of a phenomenology of the natural attitude. Perhaps an even deeper methodological difficulty appears when we seek to put into practice the Husserlian postulate of the correspondence of levels of phenomenological inquiry. Schutz accepts it as absolute that the correspondence holds. But that insight can be gained only from the vantage point of transcendental reduction. It would have been of enormous help to have had an account of what I have termed the isomorphism of levels instead of its being taken for granted as a principle of phenomenology. Such an account might show that the unity of phenomenological conception and practice permits the phenomenologist to limit himself to the mundane only by paying the price of excluding some of the constitutive questions ultimately necessary to the full illumination of the natural attitude.

2. *The Nature of Intersubjectivity:* Setting aside transcendental questions and method also has serious implications for Schutz's conception of intersubjectivity and his approach to an account of the ego's knowledge of his fellow-man. The acceptance of the We-relationship means that the epistemological issue of intersubjectivity is, in certain respects, set outside the

province of a phenomenology of the natural attitude. There is a sense of
alternation of emphasis in the account of these matters in the *Phenomenology,* for though we are clearly told that within the common-sense world
of daily life, intersubjectivity is a primordial fact of that life and so itself
taken for granted by common-sense men, still the problematic status of intersubjectivity and its prime importance as a philosophical theme for social
science intrudes obliquely into the discussion, a recognized, honored, but
still unadmitted guest.[22] Once again, it is not simply a matter of circum-
scribing the limits of the investigation. Inevitably in philosophical analysis
of social reality, there is a kind of circularity which has nothing to do with
deduction or the logic of inquiry but is instead a seemingly inescapable
correlation: the reality to be interpreted is already understood in a naive
or hidden way. Intersubjectivity, then, is not only a fact of life, it is imma-
nently comprehended as a fundamental accomplishment of the enterprise
of social existence. When the social scientist turns to the intersubjective
world and begins his description of it, the data he locates are already marked
and charged with intersubjective intent. When the philosopher turns to intersubjectivity as an epistemological problem, he is taking an odd stance with
respect to a familiar phenomenon, familiar in the sense of immanent pre-
acquaintanceship. *Not* to presuppose intersubjectivity in philosophical inquiry is hardly to erase it or make believe it never was; rather, it is to turn
to the conditions which account for the structure itself as a possible feature
of human reality. The circle is comprised of a "pre-existent" relationship of
man and fellow-man being interrogated by a philosopher who is already in
relationship with his fellow-men at the moment he asks how that relationship
is possible. Distinguishing between the logical and the chronological beginning of inquiry helps to show that the results of analysis are not vitiated by the
circle but does not alter the double pull of the questioner toward what he
knows on the one hand and toward a root unfamiliarity on the other. It is
in this way that a play develops in the *Phenomenology* between mundanity
as typically known and available to common-sense men and the structure
of mundanity as phenomenologically viewed by the philosopher-social scientist. The uneasiness I sense here may have something to do with Schutz's
position on Husserl's approach to the problem of intersubjectivity in *Formal
and Transcendental Logic* and the *Cartesian Meditations.* Like Husserl himself, Schutz was not completely satisfied with the attempt to account for
intersubjectivity in terms of the doctrine of the transcendental ego. It may
of course be the hindsight provided by his essay of 1957 on "The Problem
of Transcendental Intersubjectivity in Husserl" which leads me to offer this

[22] Cf. pp. 33 and 98.

suggestion, but I think that on the basis of the *Phenomenology* alone it would be possible to say that part of the reason for Schutz's curtailment of his use of transcendental phenomenology was the increasing realization that it could not provide a solution (apart from the clarification of the constitutive process) to the philosophical problem of intersubjectivity and that, in principle, intersubjectivity is an irreducible given within which and over against which philosophy struggles.[23]

3. *The Problem of Relevance:* Both social action by men in daily life and the observation and analysis of that action by social scientists presuppose a fundamental *interest* in goals taken to be desirable or necessary for carrying out the affairs of life and the work of science. Projects of action situated in complex systems of preferences and needs reflect the basic energy of man as a choice-making creature. The entire discussion of motivation, because and in-order-to statements, phantasying, and the construction of types turns on a concept of vast proportions which Schutz terms the general problem of relevance. It does not feature as a chapter or section of the *Phenomenology,* yet there is hardly a page of the book which does not imply or refer to aspects of the problem. It is only in the Conclusion that a direct statement of the nature of relevance occurs, and then it is only indicated in fleeting form as a subject which requires future development. Most simply, the problem of relevance is posed by "... the question of why these facts and precisely these are selected by thought from the totality of lived experience and regarded as relevant."[24] The question strikes all levels of man's involvement in the social world as well as his involvement in science, art, and religion because it points to the source of his *agency* in life, the vital principle underlying what I would call the motility of consciousness. Since the problem of relevance requires "an over-all phenomenological analysis,"[25] it is hardly surprising that Schutz was unable to include a treatment of it in the *Phenomenology.* A separate treatise would have been necessary. Nevertheless, we do have hints in later publications (brought together in his *Collected Papers*) of how he proposed to approach the problem. I am not interested here in summarizing or outlining the details of his views on relevance; rather, I am concerned with displaying the taproot of the problem.

[23] For the Intersubjectivity essay see Schutz's *Collected Papers,* Vol. III: *Studies in Phenomenological Philosophy,* edited by I. Schutz with an introduction by Aron Gurwitsch (The Hague: Martinus Nijhoff, 1966). Elsewhere Schutz writes: "... we may say that the empirical social sciences will find their true foundation not in transcendental phenomenology, but in the constitutive phenomenology of the natural attitude." (*Collected Papers,* Vol. I, p. 149.)

[24] P. 250.

[25] P. 249.

What is profoundly presupposed in and necessary to the argument of the *Phenomenology* is an account of the motile impulse of subjectivity, the valence of action. In all motivation, choice, projection, phantasying, and decision there is the force which drives the action and expresses the vitality of the actor. I suggest that the identification and comprehension of that nisus of consciousness would be the solution to the source of relevance. The *Phenomenology* gives us some reason to think that relevance is grounded in the phenomenology of inner-time consciousness, and a remarkable passage in a later essay "On Multiple Realities" may lend support to that claim:

> ... the whole system of relevances which governs us within the natural attitude is founded upon the basic experience of each of us: I know that I shall die and I fear to die. This basic experience we suggest calling the *fundamental anxiety*. It is the primordial anticipation from which all the others originate. From the fundamental anxiety spring the many interrelated systems of hopes and fears, of wants and satisfactions, of chances and risks which incite man within the natural attitude to attempt the mastery of the world, to overcome obstacles, to draft projects, and to realize them.[26]

The fundamental anxiety is necessarily bound to the meaning of inner-time consciousness not only because death is the negation of temporality but because intentionality is sustained and expressed in the temporality which the fear of death menaces. What strikes me as certain in this very hypothetical tracing of the source of relevance is that however earnestly and persuasively the analysis of the problem is carried out within the natural attitude, it is only through transcendental phenomenology that its foundation can be exposed and reconstructed. Perhaps paradoxically, it is through the horizon of relevance that the critical issues of transcendental phenomenology make their appearance in a phenomenology of the natural attitude.

Turning from the *Phenomenology* to the more than twenty-five years of work which followed, one is struck by the consistency of Schutz's thought as well as the richness and clarity of the initial statement of his position in 1932. It is not only the cardinal vision of a philosophical reconstruction of the essential structure of the taken for granted world of daily life which is sustained and amplified in his *Collected Papers,* but the detailed analyses of fundamental features of social reality which are deepened and extended in being applied to a variety of problems which were foreseen in the *Phenomenology* but left for future treatment. Although its author was in his early thirties when the *Phenomenology* was published, it is evident that this was the work of a mature philosophical mind, that the contents could easily

---

[26] *Collected Papers,* Vol. I, p. 228. Cf. Aron Gurwitsch, *The Field of Consciousness* (Pittsburgh: Duquesne University Press, 1964), pp. 342–343 and 394 ff.

have been expanded into a volume twice the size but for the fact that the author chose to wait for the time when the most rigorous and meticulous statement of his findings could be presented on themes he was still in the process of examining. The early work is an accurate prediction of what was to follow, despite the fact that the *Collected Papers* contain essays on many new topics and ideas not included in the *Phenomenology*. And in addition to the freshness of essays like "On Multiple Realities," Schutz enlarged his sociologic and philosophic horizon by studying the works of such thinkers on the American scene as George H. Mead, W. I. Thomas, and Charles H. Cooley, as well as Santayana, Whitehead, and Dewey. Although there are repetitions in the formulation of certain notions in the *Collected Papers,* there is no sense of conceptual redundancy. The career of Schutz was a unity devoted to an exploration of the true philosophical grounds of social reality in the intentional structure of human consciousness. Within that career, the *Phenomenology* marks a major event in the history of the philosophy and methodology of the social sciences. To be sure, it is perfectly reasonable to take the book as a sympathetic corrective for certain philosophical inadequacies in Weber's sociology; it is equally permissible to classify the work as an application of Husserl's ideas to the field of the social sciences. Yet such accounts would miss the nerve of what is truly original in Schutz's effort to come to terms with a philosophy of man in the natural attitude. The root originality is the illumination of mundanity as typified by the intentional structure of inner-time consciousness. Everything comes back to that – action, projection, phantasying (and ultimately even relevance, in my opinion) are all the materials of a typifying consciousness for which temporality is the secret of the social world. The choice of a phenomenological approach to such problems is hardly casual, for the very concept of the natural attitude demands a wrenching transformation of that very attitude, a reflexive procedure which Husserl calls "reduction" and which itself can be understood only in phenomenological terms. In phenomenology, then, Schutz found the meaning of temporality, and with that the clue to social reality.[27]

The *Phenomenology* is remarkable, though, for its sociological insight no less than for its philosophical brilliance. It is, in fact, the union of philosophy and social science in Schutz's thought which accounts for its power

[27] Interestingly enough, it was the problem of temporality which presented the philosophical meeting place between Husserl and Schutz. The first work he read by Husserl was the *Logical Investigations,* which at the time he found impressive and important but, he once told me, "not really for him." Later he turned to the *Lectures on the Phenomenology of Inner-Time Consciousness* and was catapulted into phenomenology.

and establishes its importance for present-day social science. There are, of course, many ways in which an alliance between philosophy and social science can take place. Looking at the matter from the standpoint of sociology, one might say that for the sociologist philosophy may offer a general perspective in terms of which certain methodological problems and theoretical questions can be approached. But there is also a deeper dimension of the relationship, one in which the sociologist absorbs the full weight of a philosophic position and sees basic aspects of his sociologic problems through the conceptual eyes of that position. A sociologist who is a convinced Deweyan, for example, may find that the very syntax of his thought and expression is molded or fundamentally affected by naturalistic categories and concepts. Schutz's indebtedness to Husserl was profound but it was not of the sort that I have just mentioned. To understand Schutz's sociology it is imperative to realize that he was not influenced by philosophy; he was a philosopher! He was not influenced by phenomenology; he was a phenomenologist! Before asking the question, Was he then also a sociologist? it is necessary to look more carefully into the claim that he was a philosopher and a phenomenologist. The matter of training is not at issue here. There are other scholars who, like Schutz, were thoroughly trained in both philosophy and social science but for whom the proper characterization would be, "He's a sociologist who knows a great deal about philosophy." Schutz was neither a philosopher who knew a great deal about sociology nor a sociologist intimately acquainted with philosophy. Still less was he an historian of ideas. As philosopher and phenomenologist, Schutz took as the content and focus of his work precisely that field of action whose sociologic status is defined by the system of constructs endemic to the natural attitude and the ideal types of the social scientist as well as that ground of intentional consciousness the investigation of which is the privileged responsibility of the phenomenologist. In this focus it is impossible to effect a division of labor and say that the sociologist concerns himself with ideal types whereas the philosopher takes up intentionality. It should be clear by now that in Schutz's sociology, taking up ideal types is exploring the intentionality constitutive of all typification. Conversely, in Schutz's phenomenology, turning to the nature of inner-time consciousness is investigating the exemplifications of intentional life in the natural attitude. At their theoretical fundament, sociology and philosophy are one.

I suggested at the outset that today's reader of the *Phenomenology* has a different relationship to the book than would have been the case some years ago. It is interesting to speculate on the career of the book had its English version appeared twenty-five years ago. Whether or not the time was right in America for the reception of such a volume is debatable, but it is certain at this time that the publication of the *Phenomenology* comes at last at a point in the development of philosophy and social science when it is necessary to make new demands on the book's audience. The period when phenomenology was considered a Germanic mystery is over. Accordingly, it is time for both philosophers and social scientists to declare a moratorium on, if not a final halt to, the pseudo-questions and academic clichés which have clung about the corpus of phenomenology, not as gadflies but as fruit flies, buzzing and pestering without knowledge or purpose. The time has come to leave behind such by now weary queries as "How does one phenomenologist check up on the report of another?" "What if phenomenologists disagree?" and "How can private intuition ever be expected to yield intersubjectively verifiable results?" or, "What does phenomenology look like in practice, when it's *done*?" With the publication of Schutz's book, phenomenology has finally come of age in America. And with that coming of age arise serious and inescapable pedagogic questions for a new generation of philosophers and social scientists: What kind of training is appropriate for work in the philosophy and methodology of the social sciences? Are graduate faculties equipped to guide students in the exploration of phenomenological research? How are students whose philosophical orientation in the social sciences is genuinely indebted to phenomenology to be encouraged to pursue their work? Squabbles about labels and slogans have no place in this discussion; what matters is the reality denoted. There, in the systematic endeavor of scholars and aspiring scholars is to be found the urgency of our questions. Toward the resolution of those questions, the *Phenomenology of the Social World* offers both a promise and a warning. Phenomenology is a way into the common source which unites philosophy and social science; its fulfillment would mean the illumination of life by thought. The refusal of philosophy, however, will fault the ultimate effort of social science to understand man as a mundane being, for "when common-sense assumptions are uncritically admitted into the apparatus of a science, they have a way of taking their revenge."[28]

[28] P. 9.

HOMO OECONOMICUS AND HIS CLASS MATES

by

FRITZ MACHLUP

PREFATORY NOTE

A French rendition of this essay, under the title "L'Homo oeconomicus et ses collègues," was included in *Les Fondements philosophiques des systèmes economiques,* a volume published in 1967 in honor of Jacques Rueff, member of the Académie Française. Since the ideas presented in my essay have been significantly influenced by the work of Alfred Schutz, since my intellectual debt to him is gratefully acknowledged in text and footnotes, and since my strong emphasis on some Schutzian theses can be regarded as homage and obeisance to my old friend and mentor, the inclusion of the English version of my essay in this volume in memory of Alfred Schutz is entirely appropriate. At the editor's suggestion, a section on Schutz's disquisitions on the "ideal type," which I had originally published in a German article, was inserted.

I have been working on a short biography of *homo oeconomicus* and have found it fascinating. The history of this idea is largely a history of misunderstandings and misinterpretations reflecting the course of the debate of the methodology of the social sciences. Reserving most of this ideological history for a longer publication, I propose to offer here my observations on some of the controversial issues involved.

Two problems should be clarified right at the outset: One is the question of the legitimacy and expediency of selecting specific traits or objectives of men through the mental construction of an abstract, partial man (*homo partialis*), in the face of the strong opposition of many writers who reject such a willful dissection of whole man (*homo totus*). The other problem relates to the difference, too often overlooked, between the construction of personal types for the understanding of particular men – historical personages, men in the news, acquaintances, friends – and the construction of personal types designed to aid in the analysis of things, events, and observed changes which are interpreted as the results of actions or reactions by persons who may be unknown and unidentified.

THE DISSECTION OF HOMO TOTUS

Writers without analytic tastes or talents have strongly protested against breaking up "whole man" into ideal types each endowed with only one quality (or a small selection of qualities) or exhibiting the pursuit of only one motive or objective. This anti-analytic position, the resistance to the analytical dissection of *homo totus* into many separate constructs isolating particular human traits or functions, is difficult to understand, let alone defend. After all, no real man could possibly have all the qualities or pursue all the objectives singled out in separate conceptual constructions needed for the understanding of human action. For example, *homo cholericus* and *homo phlegmaticus* are mutually exclusive types, who could not *both* be "embodied" in one real person. To be sure, we may need dozens of ideal types to interpret the conduct of any one person of our acquaintance or to understand different aspects of his behavior in particular situations; but never can *all* possible types become relevant in connection with any real man.

Analysis of human action with the aid of constructs isolating, idealizing, and exaggerating some human trait or function is needed both for historical and for theoretical investigation. That is to say, the "breaking up" of "whole man" is needed for understanding the actions of *historical* persons, known to us either personally or indirectly through reports, as well as for explaining and predicting the probable consequences of actions of *anonymous* persons known to us merely in their general roles in society. Such social roles may be those of consumers, producers, buyers, sellers, employers, workers, lenders, borrowers, landlords, tenants, bankers, depositors, and so forth, all social roles involved in generalizations in economics; or of voters, candidates, rioters, soldiers, officers, worshippers, priests, judges, thieves, actors, spectators, and in hundreds of other roles involved in generalizations in political science and sociology.

THIS ONE VERSUS ANY ONE

Having mentioned a variety of social roles, I should make it clear that every real person acts at various times in many different roles and that the interpretation of his actions presupposes the availability, in the minds of the interpreters, of a large collection of ideal types. Thus, our friend, Mr. *This*

One, may be a consumer, buyer, seller, worker, borrower, tennant, deposi-
tor, voter, worshipper, spectator (to choose from our list) and also a husband, father, trade unionist, tax payer, glee-club member, bowler, poker
player (to mention a few additional roles he plays in society). To understand Mr. *This One's* movements, gestures, and words, interpreters need to
be familiar with at least as many ideal types of behavior as there are roles
in which he acts, and probably many more since in each of these roles there
are several possible ways of acting.

The simultaneous or consecutive use of many separate ideal types is
usually required in inquiries about *particular* persons, acting alone or in
groups. In inquiries about events explainable as consequences of actions of
anonymous persons, the interpreters can often do with a very small set of
ideal types. For example, for the explanation of a rise in the price of a
commodity in a competitive market it will, as a rule, be quite irrelevant that
the buyers are also voters, husbands, poker players, and what not, and
whether they are choleric or phlegmatic, selfish or altruistic, pious or irre-
ligious. In such inquiries the bloodless type of a Mr. *Any One*, representing
a mere buying robot equipped with a stipulated "behavior equation" or
"objective function," will be the most serviceable analytic instrument.

FOUR CONTROVERSIAL ISSUES

Homo oeconomicus should be understood as an anonymous type, constructed for the interpretation of effects of human action. Economists, but
also sociologists, philosophers, historians, and other writers, have debated
a large variety of issues concerning the nature and the standing of *homo
oeconomicus.* Among other things, they have argued whether Economic
Man could serve as a realistic description of human decision-making or
only as a heuristic fiction; whether the authors who had used Economic
Man in their theoretical inquiries had actually believed him to be realistic
or only fictitious; whether Economic Man was employed in explanations of
decisions of businessmen only or also of consumers; and whether Economic
Man should or should not be regarded as an ideal type (in Max Weber's
sense). These four controversial questions, particularly the fourth one, will
be selected for discussion in the present essay.

The points of view about the "realism" of Economic Man range from
assertions of reasonable *lifelikeness* to characterizations as pure and useless
fiction. No writer, to my knowledge, has ever claimed that all men were
always actuated by egoistic motives or by a desire to maximize money
gains. All that supporters of Economic Man as a "realistic type" of man

engaged in economic activities claimed was that enough people often enough followed the lure of pecuniary advantage to make the outcome of market activities roughly correspond to the conclusions deduced from the assumption of profit-maximizing behavior.[1] Others claimed much less; and a few asserted that it would make no difference if the hypothesis of maximizing behavior were entirely unrealistic, provided only that the use of this theoretical postulate led us to deductions useful in predicting correctly the consequences of changes in observable data.

On the other hand, those who repudiated *homo oeconomicus* as a useful aid in economic theory denied not only the realism of the assumption of "maximizing behavior" but also its methodological standing as a heuristic fiction. They contended that abstraction from the large bulk of reality, and isolation of a small fragment of it, was an arbitrary and illegitimate procedure and they rejected the methodological tenet that unrealistic, fictitious constructions could be of any use in the explanation of real phenomena.

This controversy, as an issue in methodology, cannot be settled either by empirical tests or by formal logical demonstration. The second controversy, however, as a question about the history of economic thought, is easy to decide. One merely has to take the trouble to reread what the authors who befriended *homo oeconomicus* actually wrote about him.

The critics of "classical" economists derided them for their alleged failure to recognize that *homo oeconomicus* was a fiction (or caricature) and for their alleged naiveté in mistaking him for a true picture of reality. This charge was repeated over and over in the writings of the historical schools. But these critics had evidently neglected to check the sources, or they would have found very clear statements of the real position of the theorists whom they attacked. John Stuart Mill, for example, said most explicitly that "Political Economy presupposes an arbitrary definition of man, as a being who invariably does that by which he may obtain the greatest amount of necessaries, conveniences and luxuries, with the smallest quantity of labour and physical self-denial . . ." He stressed that "Political Economy . . . reasons from *assumed* premises – from premises which might be totally without foundation in fact, and which are not pretended to be universally in accordance with it . . ." And, in justifying the isolation of economic motives, he

---

[1] "The propositions of the theory of variations do not involve the assumption that men are actuated *only* by considerations of money gains and losses. They involve only the assumption that money plays *some* part in the valuation of the given alternatives." Lionel Robbins. *An Essay on the Nature and Significance of Economic Science* (London: Macmillan, 2nd ed. 1935), p. 98.

exclaimed: "Not that any political economist was ever so absurd as to suppose mankind are really thus constituted . . ." [2]

It is almost comical how the anti-theorists reveled in delight when, having demonstrated the fictional and fictitious nature of Economic Man, they believed they had refuted the classical school and demolished economic theory. One especially quixotic knight errant must have been terribly pleased with himself when he characterized "pure theory" as a big "circus of commodities with value-and-price acrobats on the mathematical trapeze and the *homo oeconomicus* as clown." [3] Evidently he did not realize that his supposedly devastating analogy would be quite acceptable to many a theorist. Not a circus but a puppet stage was the simile used for pure economic theory by Alfred Schutz, one of the most profound writers on the methodology of the social sciences. [4] Max Weber, likewise, fully accepted the critics' contention that the "rational constructions" of "pure economics" were "pure fictions." [5]

Sombart summarized the argument nicely when he spoke of "the legendary *homo oeconomicus*, the spook and bogie against whom generations of economists of the historical schools have waged their embittered windmill

---

[2] The last sentence is part of Mill's statement on the method of political economy as the science concerning itself only with "such of the phenomena of the social state as take place in consequence of the pursuit of wealth. It makes entire abstraction of every other human passion or motive; except those which may be regarded as perpetually antagonizing principles to the desire of wealth, namely, aversion to labour and desire of the present enjoyment of costly indulgences . . . The science then proceeds to investigate the laws which govern these several operations, under the supposition that man is a being who is determined . . . to prefer a greater portion of wealth to a smaller, in all cases, without any other exception than that constituted by the two counter-motives already specified. Not that any political economist was ever so absurd as to suppose that mankind are really thus constituted, but because this is the mode in which science must necessarily proceed. . . . In order to judge how he [man in society] will act under the variety of desires and aversions which are concurrently operating upon him, we must know how he would act under the exclusive influence of each one in particular . . ." John Stuart Mill, *A System of Logic*, Vol. II (London: Parker, 1843), pp. 570–572; "On the Definition of Political Economy; and on the Method of Investigation Proper to It," *Essays on Some Unsettled Questions of Political Economy* (London: Parker, 1844), pp. 137–139, and 144.

[3] Friedrich von Gottl-Ottlilienfeld, *Wirtschaft als Leben*, (Jena: Gustav Fischer, 1925).

[4] ". . . the [social] scientist replaces the human beings he observes as actors on the social stage by puppets created by himself and manipulated by himself." Alfred Schutz, "The Problem of Rationality in the Social World," *Economica*, New Series, Vol. X (May 1943), reprinted in *Collected Papers*, Vol. II (The Hague: Martinus Nijhoff, 1964), p. 81.

[5] *Max Weber on the Methodology of the Social Sciences* ed. Shils and Finch (Glencoe, Ill.: Free Press, 1949), p. 44. Translated from *Gesammelte Aufsätze zur Wissenschaftslehre* (Tübingen: J. C. B. Mohr, 2nd ed., 1951), pp. 190 ff.

battles, but who in the bright light of reason turns out to be a very harmless creature, namely, the fictitious subject deciding on the fictitious actions in our explanatory rational models [*Schemata*]." [6]

The third controversial issue is on the question whether *homo oeconomicus* is a businessman or a consumer or both. It is true that the writers of the classical school were more concerned with production, costs, and profits than with consumption and utility. But it is probably a misunderstanding to hold that "the classical scheme is not at all applicable to consumption or the consumer." [7] The hypothesis of utility maximization in the theory of the household is methodologically on a par with the hypothesis of profit maximization in the theory of the firm. Most expositors of economic theory have therefore decided to treat all "maximizing behavior" as the fundamental assumption implied in the "economic principle."

The fourth issue – whether *homo oeconomicus* is or is not an ideal type in the sense of Max Weber – has led to an extensive literary feud, especially among German writers (for whom methodological problems, however subtle, often assume an importance beyond the comprehension of the more pragmatic Anglo-Saxon economists). The literature on this subject, though impressive, is almost unknown outside the circle of Max Weber-exegetes. I think a taste of this debate on the "ideal type" will be worthwhile.

Merely in order to document the differences of opinion on this point, we may cite a recent history of theory in which Economic Man is, without the shadow of a doubt, treated as an ideal type, [8] and an epistemological discourse in which this characterization is emphatically rejected. [9] In general,

[6] Werner Sombart, *Die drei Nationalökonomien* (München und Leipzig: Duncker & Humblot, 1929), p. 259. The English translation is mine.

[7] Ludwig von Mises, *Epistemological Problems of Economics* (Princeton, N.J.: Van Nostrand, 1960), p. 179.

[8] "In spite of many disagreements, Menger, Jevons, and Walras claimed that only the economic man evaluates goods and services according to marginal utility. This fictitious man, an heritage of early classicism, had no clear-cut profile. As an ideal type he was sometimes identified as a materialist utilitarian, and then again as a bookkeeper who balances thoroughly cost and utility." Emil Kauder, *A History of Marginal Utility Theory* (Princeton, N.J.: Princeton University Press, 1965), p. 116. Still more recent is the brief assertion that " 'Economic man' is an 'ideal type.' " Jerome Rothenberg, "Values and Value Theory in Economics," in Sherman Roy Krupp, ed., *The Structure of Economic Science* (Englewood Cliffs, N.J.: Prentice-Hall, 1966), p. 228.

[9] "Yet neither is the *homo oeconomicus* an ideal type in Max Weber's sense." Ludwig von Mises, *op. cit.,* p. 180. "It was a fundamental mistake of the Historical School ... and of Institutionalism ... to interpret economics as the characterization of the behavior of an ideal type, the *homo oeconomicus*. According to this doctrine traditional or orthodox economics does not deal with the behavior of man as he really is and acts, but with a fictitious or hypothetical image ... Such a being does not have and never did have a counterpart in reality, it is a phantom of a spurious armchair philosophy ...

the contradiction could be due to disagreements on the meaning of "Economic Man" or on the meaning of "ideal type". Both these disagreements exist, but it is chiefly the second that explains why writers either affirm or deny that *homo oeconomicus* is an ideal type.[10]

THE IDEAL TYPE OF THE "IDEAL TYPE"

While it was obvious to all that any concept classified as "ideal type" was a mental tool, helpful in thinking and talking about certain phenomena, writers have differed on whose tool it was and for what purposes. Some claimed it as an exclusive property of historians for use in their interpretations of individual historical personalities, actions, events, institutions, and ideas. Others claimed the ideal type for exclusive use in sociology, others again for use in both history and sociology. Several writers assigned it to all social sciences, but solely for purposes of reasoning and generalizing, that is, for general theory, not for historical description. Others, however, regarded the ideal type as the appropriate concept for both historical and theoretical investigations of any phenomena, processes, personalities, and artifacts of the cultural world, hence for the social sciences, history, and the humanities. Finally, there were some who included the theoretical natural sciences among the users of ideal types.

Even if this really were the meaning of classical economics, the homo oeconomicus would certainly not be an ideal type. The ideal type is not an embodiment of one side or aspect of man's various aims and desires. It is always the representation of complex phenomena of reality; either of men, of institutions, or of ideologies." Ludwig von Mises, *Human Action: A Treatise on Economics* (New Haven: Yale University Press, 1949), p. 62.

[10] A survey of some of the literature on Max Weber's "ideal type" yields a conspicuous division on this question. Among those who affirm that Economic Man is an ideal type are Schelting, Spranger, Eucken, Spiethoff, and Schutz; among those who deny it are Hans Oppenheimer, Mises, Sombart, and Weippert. See Alexander von Schelting, *Max Webers Wissenschaftslehre* (Tübingen: J. C. B. Mohr, 1934); Eduard Spranger, *Der gegenwärtige Stand der Geisteswissenschaften und die Schule* (Leipzig-Berlin: B. G. Teubner, 1925); Walter Eucken, *Grundlagen der Nationalökonomie* (Berlin-Göttingen-Heidelberg: Springer-Verlag, 1st ed. 1939, 6th ed. 1950); Arthur Spiethoff, "Anschauliche und reine volkswirtschaftliche Theorie und ihr Verhältnis Zueinander," *Synopsis: Festgabe für Alfred Weber*, ed. Edgar Salin (Heidelberg: Verl. Schneider, 1948); Alfred Schutz, *Der sinnhafte Aufbau der sozialen Welt* (Wien: Springer, 1932); idem, *Collected Papers* (The Hague: Nijhoff, Vol. I, 1963, Vol. II, 1964); Hans Oppenheimer, *Die Logik der soziologischen Begriffsbildung, mit besonderer Berücksichtigung von Max Weber* (Tübingen: J. C. B. Mohr, 1925); Ludwig von Mises, *Grundprobleme der Nationalökonomie* (Jena: Fischer, 1933); Werner Sombart, *Die drei Nationalökonomien* (München und Leipzig: Duncker & Humblot, 1929); Georg Weippert, "Die idealtypische Sinn- und Wesenserfassung und die Denkgebilde der formalen Theorie," *Zeitschrift für die gesamte Staatswissenschaft*, Vol. 100 (1940).

But this is not all. Some wanted to reserve the designation "ideal type" for class concepts – though it would probably be a null class if one were to look for empirical counterparts of "ideal" types designed for theoretical investigations – whereas others extended the designation to refer to the mental image of any particular person or individual member of a class. (Thus, not only the class "economist" but also "Jacques Rueff" would be an ideal type; not only "city" but also "Paris"; not only "battle" but also the "Battle of the Marne"; not only "depression" but also the "Great Depression".)

Most of those engaged in the debate on the ideal type attempted to restrict the use of this appellation in one way or another. Since they pretended to interpret what Max Weber "really meant" (or "ought to have meant") it is noteworthy that Weber himself wanted none of the restrictions proposed by his interpreters, with one exception: he did consider the ideal type as a concept particularly appropriate for human action and effects of human action. (This is because the ideal types involve "meant meanings" attributed to the actors in question, which is not relevant for concepts pertaining to things in inanimate nature.) The other restrictions, however, were not intended by Weber, and he said so without reserve.

How was it then possible for the Weber interpreters to arrive at so many divergent interpretations of his ideas about the ideal type? There are probably several explanations, apart from the infelicitous choice of words – of whose most common meanings the reader has to be disabused before he can begin to grasp what Weber meant. (Only after the normative connotation of "ideal" and the empiric-taxonomic connotation of "type" have been exorcized can the intended meanings of "mental construction" emerge.) Foremost among the possible explanations are, it seems to me, Weber's writing style and people's reading habits. Weber developed his concepts only slowly and therefore could not at the outset present a comprehensive exposition showing their full scope. Thus he would at one place discuss the ideal type employed in historical research, at another place the ideal type in sociological theory, elsewhere again the ideal type in pure economics. Most readers approach a work with rather firm preconceptions and, though ready to accept gladly what fits in with their own position, are not receptive to ideas drastically deviating from their own; they either fail to notice them or they consciously reject them.[11]

[11] Perhaps there is no excuse for the denial that Economic Man is an ideal type in Max Weber's sense, since Weber himself had affirmed it explicitly. For example: "Economic theory is an axiomatic discipline . . . Pure economic theory . . . utilizes ideal-type concepts exclusively. Economic theory makes certain assumptions which scarcely ever correspond completely with reality but which approximate it in various degrees and

Thus, if a reader approaches Weber's writings convinced that the concepts of history must be differently constituted from the concepts of theory, he may accept a newly proposed phrase for one notion but not for another He may have been so impressed with the undeniable differences in concept formation in different areas of discourse, that he is willing to embrace a new designation for one kind of concept, in order to contrast it with others, but quite unprepared to adopt new language that brackets ideas which he is anxious to keep apart. Thus Weber was singularly unsuccessful in persuading his readers of the basic similarities in the formation of concepts in the domain of human action. These similarities were of great importance to Weber. He failed to get the common characteristics of these concepts across, largely because he violated the expository rule that one should not be silent about differences when one wishes to stress similarities, or about similarities when one wishes to stress differences.

If "Protestantism" is an ideal type, how could I agree that my "Aunt Molly" is also an ideal type? If "slavery" is an ideal type, how can I understand that "architecture" is also one? If "socialism" is an ideal type, how come that "Saint Augustine," "Egyptian hieroglyphs," "Spanish literature," "Robinson Crusoe," "Napoleon Bonaparte," "constitutional monarchy," "oligopoly," "witch hunting," "Arthur Miller," "tragedy," "International Monetary Fund," "deposit banking," and *homo oeconomicus*" are all ideal types too? The point is that *all* these persons, activities, institutions, constellations, artifacts, ideas, etc., can be understood only in terms of "meant meanings" by (particular or anonymous) actors of whom we have formed some mental image, however unrealistic or selective.

The differences among these ideal types are, of course, important too. But only later, Alfred Schutz provided us with a more discriminating terminology. Thus, for example, he pointed out the differences between various kinds of "personal ideal types," not only according to their place in time but also according to their place in our thought systems (e.g., "characterological ideal types" and "functional ideal types"). And, most significantly, he taught us that the ideal type is not only the fundamental concept of the social scientist and the historian but also, or even primarily, the basic concept of the ordinary man thinking about his everyday experiences with and relations to his partners and contemporaries. "The construction of the

---

asks: how would men act under these assumed conditions if their actions were entirely rational? It assumes the dominance of pure economic interests and precludes the operation of political or other non-economic considerations." Max Weber, *On Methodology of the Social Sciences,* pp. 43–44.

categories and models of the social sciences is founded on the pre-scientific common-sense experience of social reality." [12]

THE IDEAL TYPE ACCORDING TO ALFRED SCHUTZ

I regard the work of Alfred Schtuz as one of the most original, significant, and illuminating contributions to the methodology of the social sciences. Schutz expounded the functions of ideal-typical interpretation in his first book, *Der sinnhafte Aufbau der sozialen Welt* [The meaning-structure of the social world], published in Vienna in 1932. An English translation was published in 1967, nine years after his death, under the title *The Phenomenology of the Social World*.[13] No one who thinks or speaks about ideal types can afford to miss reading this work. But since the English version has only so recently become available, a few paragraphs quoting and paraphrasing some of Schutz's statements may be helpful here.[14]

A fundamental point is that "the ideal types vary and shift in accordance with the observer's point of view, the questions he is asking, and the total complex of his experience" (p. 192). This sounds ridiculously simple and trite but must be brought out because the learned professors keep arguing about the logical nature of the ideal type and whether it must be constructed this way or in some other way – questions which can be answered only with reference to the particular problems that concern us at the particular moment.

Schutz distinguishes between personal ideal types and material or course-of-action types, but he recognizes an "inner relation" between the two (p. 187). The personal ideal type is constructed as "one who acts in such and such a way and has such and such experiences" (p. 190). It is the type to which one can attribute a given ideal-typical course of action; that is to say, in order to understand a particular course of action we construct a

---

[12] Alfred Schutz, *Collected Papers*, Vol. II (The Hague: Martinus Nijhoff, 1964), p. 21.

[13] Translated by George Walsh and Frederick Lehnert (Evanston: Northwestern University Press, 1967). A part of Schutz's book, Section IV, had been translated by Thomas Luckmann and published, under the title "The Dimensions of the Social World" in Alfred Schutz, *Collected Papers*, Vol. II (The Hague: Nijhoff, 1964), pp. 20–63. Luckmann's translation is more faithful to the original and therefore more difficult to comprehend on first reading. The reader might benefit by studying first the Walsh-Lehnert rendition and then going to the more advanced Luckmann version. The German original is the most difficult.

[14] I have used the same samples of Schutz's presentation in my essay "Idealtypus, Wirklichkeit und Konstruktion," *Ordo,* Vol. 12 (Düsseldorf and München: Helmut Küpper, 1960–1961), pp. 40–42.

model of a conscious mind for whom this type of acting is motivationally meaningful. Hence, ". . . it is so constructed that it must subjectively attach to its acts precisely the meaning that the interpreter is looking for" (p. 190).

The private world of the man in the street, who thinks about the actions of the persons around him and who acts in anticipation of their reactions, is "constituted" of the ideal types he has constructed on the basis of his experiences. Any scientific analysis of the "social world" has to begin, therefore, with the problems of the acting individual, but must soon proceed to ideal-typical concepts of reduced concreteness, of lesser specific content; it requires ideal types of greater "anonymity," because "the concreteness of the ideal type is inversely proportional to the level of generality of the past experiences out of which it is constructed" (p. 195).

Personal ideal types may be "characterological," "habitual" or of "greater degrees of anonymity," down to the "absolutely anonymous" ones needed when the focus is on tools and utensils. (There, "from the means-end relation in terms of which the tool is understood, one can deduce the ideal type of user or producer without thinking of them as real individual people.") The class of "social collectives," such as state, economy, nation, working class, and the class of tools and artifacts "illustrate the progressive anonymization and corresponding loss of concreteness" of the ideal types constructed for the interpretation of the social world (p. 201). Schutz shows that "the concepts of social action and social relationship undergo many modifications, depending on whether the object of the Other-orientation is an alter ego of directly experienced social reality, the world of mere contemporaries, the world of predecessors, or the world of successors" (p. 219). What is "thematically pregiven to . . . every . . . social science is the social reality which is indirectly experienced (never immediate social reality)"; it follows that, "even when social science is dealing with the action of a single individual, it must do so in terms of types" (p. 227).

Schutz makes an "important distinction between the construction of the ideal type and the application of this type as an interpretive scheme to real concrete actions" (p. 228). He also distinguishes between "direct social observation" and "indirect social observation". In the latter, "there is no difference between the meaning-context of the observer and that of the actor." For, "if there is a real person corresponding to the observer's postulated ideal type, then he will by definition intend what the observer has in mind. However – and this is the basic postulate of social science – the motives ascribed to the ideal type must be both causally adequate and adequate on the level of meaning" (p. 229).[15] The double requirement that the

---

[15] I am quoting these phrases although I fear that many readers may fail to recognize

constructed types must be acceptable as efficient causes of the effects that are to be explained and, at the same time, plausible in the sense of reflecting the meant meanings in the minds of acting individuals implies that each of the ideal types "must be formulated as a *pure* construct without any admixture of type-transcending behavior" and that it "must be compatible with our experience of the world in general, and therefore with our experience of other people in general," and, in addition, "that the construct be based only on repeatable behavior" (p. 236).

With regard to the application of "ready-made ideal types" to concrete courses of action and processes, the requirement of "adequacy" implies that the attribution of a concrete course of action to a particular ideal type should serve as a sufficient explanation of these actions, fully consistent with previous experience. There must, therefore, be a definite "objective change" (probability) that the assumed ideal-typical motives were in fact present and effective. But there is no limitation whatsoever regarding the ways of constructing ideal types or regarding the techniques or principles of their formation. What a type posits as "invariant" may have been obtained by processes of generalization, abstraction, formalization, idealization, or imagination; what matters is only that the type is understandable and acceptable as corresponding to possibly intended meanings of acting individuals.

In Schutz's view, "pure economics is a perfect example of an objective meaning-complex about subjective meaning-complexes, in other words, of an objective meaning-configuration stipulating the typical and invariant subjective experiences of anyone who acts" as an economic man (p. 245).

In the German literature on "types" much is made of a distinction between "ideal" and "real" types. It should be noted that neither Weber nor Schutz has ever mentioned "real types". The man-in-the-street in his everyday relations with his fellow-men and contemporaries, the historian in his interpretation of the records of the past, and the theorist in his formulation of general laws of the social world, none of them has anything to do with real types so-called; but they all make constant use of ideal types and cannot help doing so since there is no other way of making decisions, of explaining past events, or of developing general theories of the social world.

Whether by providing these samples from Schutz's works (in translations and paraphrases that cannot do justice to the original) I have done a service or a disservice to the reader and to the general understanding of Schutz's methodological contribution, I do not know. Perhaps I have frightened him

them as the English equivalents of Max Weber's terms, *Kausaladäquanz* and *Sinnadäquanz*.

off rather than encouraged him to make a heavier investment in Schutz-
ianism. In any case, I shall return to my attempt at popularization by
presenting the main propositions on ideal-typical thinking in the simplest
possible ways.

The key to the understanding of the ideal type is the realization that not
only scholars – historians, economists, social theorists – think about their
subjects with the aid of ideal types, but that *everybody does so in his everyday life*.

Even the small child has probably formed his ideal type of his mother,
whom he expects to comfort him with her gentle voice, stroking hands, and
warm breasts. The schoolboy has formed ideal types of his teacher, his
classmates, the doctor, the minister, and his favorite television personalities.
The adult has formed ideal types of many people whom he meets repeatedly
face-to-face as well as of others whom he does not know personally but
with whose reactions he reckons in several connections. For example, he
may expect a policeman to blow a whistle and give him a summons if he
fails to stop his car at a red traffic light, or a postman to collect a letter
which he deposits in a mailbox. The ideal type I have formed of my wife
has something to do with my punctuality in coming home for supper, for it
includes her getting worried if I am late.

There is no essential difference in the construction of ideal types as com-
monsense concepts of ordinary people and as scientific concepts of the
historian or social scientist, except of course that the concepts designed for
scholarly investigation have to satisfy certain requirements of consistency
and relevance, requirements which are usually not checked by the ordinary
man in everyday life. Perhaps, though, a middle category should be distinguished between that of the ordinary man in his own social relations and
the scholarly observer engaged in serious professional investigations, namely, the category of the non-scholarly observer of the social scene. The by-
stander, onlooker, spectator, the listener and viewer of broadcasts, the
audience in theaters and cinemas, the reader of books, stories and news –
all these can understand what they see, hear, or read only to the extent that
they have formed the ideal types relevant to the scenes observed or described.

The lines separating acting man, lay observer, and scientific observer
look rather definite. *Acting man* is engaged in practical activities and relies
on his collection of ideal types in the interpretation of the actions, and in

predicting the reactions, of his "partners". The *lay observer* is an outsider, merely a curious audience, relying on his collection of ideal types in the interpretation of the actions of the people observed or described. The *scientific observer* is also an observer, making use of ideal types and models in his collection, but his interest in the matter investigated stems from his desire to add to the body of scientific knowledge. Upon closer inspection, however, the lines of separation among the three kinds of interpreters of the social stage become less definite. The lay observer, for example, may identify himself so intensively with one or more of the actors observed that his involvement in the scene may be such that he thinks and feels as if he were himself participating in a real-life situation affecting his own welfare. A man acting in his personal affairs may have scientific training enabling him to apply the techniques of his science, say, economics or psychology, to advantage in interpreting and predicting the actions and reactions of his "partners". By and large, however, we may take the distinctions to be valid and significant.

SELECTING THE RELEVANT TYPE

We spoke of the collection of ideal types at the disposal of actors and observers for use in their interpretations, but we have not indicated how they select the type relevant in the specific situation. Ordinarily, the necessary skill is acquired by experience. Know-how cannot easily be taught in any other way; and with regard to some ideal types, a stock of "inner experience" is necessary for a full understanding of the movements, gestures, or words of other people. Explicit directions or rules would more often mislead than help.

Assume, for example, that some primitive soul, having been exposed to a disquisition to the effect that the *homo oeconomicus* has to do primarily with money matters, propounded the rule that all situations involving money and its expenditure or nonexpenditure are most appropriately interpreted with the aid of the ideal type of Economic Man. Anyone who followed this rule would be sadly frustrated in his attempts to understand what goes on. Any number of situations involving money require a variety of characters – logical, psychological, and functional types – for their interpretation and could never be elucidated by the application of the ideal type of the *homo oeconomicus*, no matter whether he be regarded as a profit maximizer or a maximizer of utility.

To illustrate the principle that the money theme is not decisive in the selection of the appropriate ideal type, I shall present a sequence of vignettes, each in form of a scene with two persons on the stage, which can be understood only with the aid of special personal ideal types. After each "scene" I shall designate the ideal type in evidence.

Scene 1

"How dare you," Robert shouted in a husky voice, staring at the ten-dollar bill which George had put on the table before him. His face was flushed with anger, his eyes protruding, the veins at his temples formed thick blue cables. He took the bill, tore it into small pieces and threw them into George's face.
[The relevant ideal type is *homo cholericus*.]

Scene 2

"Boss, we've got to close down the mill at Hungerville. Our new plant in the city can easily take care of all our orders at a cost 36 per cent below that of the Hungerville mill."

"How many people would lose their jobs at Hungerville?"

"Six hundred and fifty, boss."

"I cannot do it. Most of these people have been with us for years. Who will take care of them if we don't?"

"They can go on relief. Every week that we keep the mill open means a net loss of 50,000 dollars. Are you running a business or a charity?"

"Call it what you will, the mill stays open as long as I have the money, or as long as I can borrow or steal it. I am not going to lay off any of my workers."
[The relevant type is *homo caritativus*.]

Scene 3

"Another shot of gin," he ordered in a bellowing voice.

Jim, the saloon keeper, reached for the bottle and said casually: "It's all right with me, Dick, but your wife won't like it if you spend half your week's pay on getting drunk again."

"This'll be the last one," promised Dick.

"The last till the next," teased Jim.

"What business is it of yours? I can do what I please with my own money." He emptied his glass in one gulp. "Okay, give me another. No one's going to tell me what I can't do."

"Dick, I'm glad to sell you all you can pay for. Here's your drink. But you told me you wanted the kids to get enough to eat. And your wife said you promised to reform and bring the money home for the rent and the grocery bill."

"The hell with her, and the hell with the kids. Give me another shot. I need my gin and, by gosh, I'm going to have it."

[The relevant ideal type is *homo alcoholicus*.]

Scene 4

John looked at her, took her hands, and then spoke in a low voice. "Listen, darling, I'm letting you have the money. But you should know: This money would not only have paid the note that falls due tomorrow but also for the half-interest I hoped to buy in the firm. Without this money I'll lose my option to become a partner and, what's more, by not paying the note I'll lose my honest name. But I don't care what happens. There's only one thing I care for: you. I love you. I adore you."

He tooks her into his arms and pressed her against his body. He drew her face toward his and let his lips touch hers.

[The relevant ideal type is *homo amorosus*.]

Scene 5

"This machine will pay for itself within eight months; it's the best investment you've ever made, Mr. Halo."

"You're absolutely right, Mr. Newtime," the industrialist replied solemnly, "but as long as I can't pay for it in ready cash on delivery, Halo and Son is not going to order the machine."

"But, Mr. Halo, we'll be delighted to take your note payable in six months, or, indeed, to let you have it on open terms of credit."

"Sir, Halo and Son, will not borrow. The First National has been trying to talk us into taking a million-dollar loan at 3½ per cent. No, we shall remain true to the traditions of our firm as they have been observed by my father, my grandfather, and my great-grandfather, Mr. Polonius Halo. We are neither borrowers nor lenders, and this, sir, is final."

[The relevant ideal type is *homo traditionalis*.]

Scene 6

"That's bunk!" He puffed several times on his cigar, dropping some of its overload of ashes on his bulging vest. "That's sheer bunk! You don't win an election with good intentions and such stuff. I've been running this machine for twenty-six years and I know it must be greased. After all, we nominated you not just because you're a reputable businessman, but a successful one with all the dough it takes to grease the party machine."

"Sorry, much as I want to win the election, and much as I recognize your experience as party boss, I don't want to buy votes."

"Well, well, we can put it differently. You're not buying votes, you're selling yourself. As a businessman, you know that you can't sell anything without paying for advertising. Political patronage is fine, it costs you nothing and gets you support. But it ain't enough. We need money. And one more thing: you'll have to create a few jobs in your business for some trusted party workers."

"What'll my stockholders say to that?"

"Nothing if they don't know it. Moreover, they'll like it fine having a state senator managing their investments. This will be businesslike government and statesmanlike business."

[The relevant ideal type is *homo politicus*.]

Scene 7

"We've just learnt, J.C., that the Chicago order went to Gregg's. Those blasted chiselers must have made all sorts of concessions. I'd been promised the order and was sure we had it."

"Damn it, that order would have been just right for our Wisconsin mill. What are our chances on the big Cleveland deal?"

"You never know, J.C. The Gregg people are after it, too, and they tell me Cone Brothers are at least 2 points below our price. If we don't want to lose this order, we'll have to come down too."

"Nothin' doing. If we shade our price, the whole industry will be demoralized. Gregg's, Cone's, Gannef's and all the rest will just fall all over themselves and no one will know what the right price really is."

"Are we going to sit back, J.C., and watch one dirty chiseler after another steal the nicest orders from us?"

"No use getting mad. You have to let them get away with it once in a while, as long as they keep their senses most of the time. If we start cutting prices, the bottom drops out of the market, and we'll have to fight over every single order, even the smallest. Let's stick to our list prices and avoid chaos."

[The relevant ideal type is *homo oligopolisticus*.]

THE ROLE OF HOMO OECONOMICUS

I could easily have produced a scene depicting *homo oeconomicus* at work. I refrained from doing so, because it might have confused the reader about the proper role of this ideal type, a role quite different from that of those exhibited in the vignettes presented.

The point is that the personal types relevant in the seven scenes were suitable for interpreting observations of men's actions, whereas the ideal type of *homo oeconomicus* is designed for interpreting observed *consequences* of men's actions. The difference is significant. In the scenes presented we listened to what some people said and we watched their movements and gestures. (Only in Scene 1 was the "watching" important; in the other scenes we chiefly "listened" to the dialogue.) The purpose of the *homo oeconomicus* is not to help us understand observations of people – that is, we neither watch anyone's movements and gestures nor listen to their conversations – but rather to understand observations of records, such as reports on prices, outputs, employment, and profits, which are evidently *results* of people's actions. Almost never can we observe the actions themselves. (Exceptions are our self-observations – introspection – as we change our minds concerning things to buy, assets to hold, etc.).

We observe, for example, price data and attribute changes in some prices to changes in certain cost items or to changes in tariffs, excise taxes, or total incomes; or we attribute changes in price indices to changes in interest rates or the quantity of money. But these causal attributions presuppose our assuming the intervention of people making decisions in reaction to changes in their opportunities to buy, sell, work, hire, lend, borrow, produce, etc. The "scenes" of people making these decisions are not observed but only imagined. The ideal type relevant for these imagined scenes is *homo oeconomicus*.

TOWARD A SCIENCE OF POLITICAL ECONOMICS[1]

by

ADOLPH LOWE

I. THE CRITICAL VIEWPOINT OF A POLITICAL ECONOMICS

1. Political versus Traditional Economics

The dividing line between Traditional Economics – by which I refer not only to classical and neo-classical but also to the positive parts of Keynesian theory – and Political Economics, as I denote my own reformulation of economic theory, can best be approached if we begin from two premises that both procedures share.

The first of these is an emphasis on *"theory"* rather than taxonomic or historical description as the essential core of the discipline. Both Traditional Economics and Political Economics, in other words, proceed from a small number of explanatory principles to a large number of propositions about the facts of economic life. Second, both approaches share a common concern with *prediction.* I wish to stress this point from the outset, because the reservations as to the predictive powers of Traditional Economics which I expressed in my book *On Economic Knowledge* have occasionally been misinterpreted as a denial on my part of the possibility – or even the legitimacy – of economic prediction generally. Nothing could be further from my intention. Indeed the major incentive in my search for an alternative to traditional reasoning has been the wish to invest economic theory with the power of prediction that I believe it now lacks.

From this it does not follow that the ability to predict should be regarded as the decisive criterion for scientific Economics. As the examples of Geology or Crystallography show, this is not even true of the physical sciences, and much less so in the social sciences in which historical explanation and structural analysis play such a large role. If nevertheless the ability to pre-

---

[1] Occasional reference will be made to my book *On Economic Knowledge,* New York and Evanston, 1965, abridged as OEK.

Author's Note: I wish to thank Prentice-Hall, Inc., publishers of *Economic Means and Social Ends,* edited by Robert L. Heilbroner, 1969, which contains the original version of this paper, for permission to reprint it here in a slightly abridged form.

dict today serves more and more as the touchstone of economic science, the reason is *pragmatic*. By this I mean more than the obvious fact that the application of economic knowledge is conditional on our capacity to foresee the effect of economic actions. What matters is the growing realization that the adequate functioning of our kind of economic system requires public action informed of its consequences. In other words, whether Economics is, or is not, capable of prediction is no longer merely a methodological concern but a question of cardinal importance for the organization of economic life.

Thus in the search for explanatory principles from which deductions can be made, and in the common focus on prediction as the pragmatic aim of the analytical procedure, Traditional and Political Economics agree. The roads part when we ask: how can we obtain knowledge of the explanatory principles – be they laws or stochastic regularities – from which predictive statements can be derived?

In accordance with the procedure prevailing in the "hard" sciences, Traditional Economics tries to derive laws and stochastic regularities from the observation of *actual* economic processes and of the *actual* behavior of the elementary units of the economy – buyers and sellers, consumers and investors, etc. Political Economics does not reject this procedure on principle. On the contrary, it recognizes a limited period of Western economic history – the period of "classical" capitalism in the decades following the Industrial Revolution – for which the traditional procedure is well adapted. But it finds the predictive usefulness of the so-called "positive" method on the wane during the later industrial development, to the point where under contemporary conditions the failures seem far to outweigh the successes. Considering the recent progress in econometric techniques this trend toward decreasing reliability in prediction can hardly be blamed on a lack of refinement of prevailing research methods. Rather it looks as if something had happened to the underlying research object itself, which is making it progressively more refractory to conventional methods of investigation. The nature of this historical change has been described in OEK as an ever widening spectrum of behavioral and motivational patterns, with the consequence of increasing "disorder" in the autonomous processes of modern markets.

If this is true, we are confronted with a grave dilemma. In the interest of the proper functioning of the modern market this tendency toward disorder needs to be counteracted by appropriate measures of public policy. But in order to devise suitable policies we require a theory capable of predicting the effect of particular measures. However, it seems impossible to construct such a theory if the observable phenomena from which the explanatory principles are to be abstracted, lack that minimum of orderliness which is the prerequisite of any scientific generalization.

It is from the horns of this dilemma that Political Economics tries to lift economic analysis. But before showing how this can be done we should first examine more closely the two presuppositions on which our formulation of the problem rests. One refers to the "minimum degree of orderliness" on the presence of which both the practical functioning of an industrial market and the theoretical explanation and prediction of its movements are said to depend. The other concerns the empirical question of whether the actual movements of contemporary markets do indeed fall short of that "minimum", and what may be the reasons for such a "deformation" of mature capitalism.

2. The Role of "Order" in Economic Theory and Practice

There is probably agreement that in no field of inquiry can scientific generalizations be derived from the observation of truly "erratic" phenomena. This does not imply that a continuum of observations, which leads from "perfect" order – meaning invariability of structure and motion – to perfect "disorder" – namely, full randomization of events – is also a continuum of decreasing scientific tractability. Rather the scientifically inexpedient range lies around the middle of the spectrum, since both extremes and their neighboring regions are open to deductive or stochastic generalizations.

Now frequently as the extreme of randomization seems to occur in the realm of natural phenomena, in the social world it materializes only in exceptional cases when no interrelations exist among the members of a group, as e.g. in a crowd milling around idly. Nor can we, in view of the spontaneity of the units of social groups, expect the other extreme, invariability of behavior, to be the rule over any length of time. For all practical purposes the relevant region for social occurrences lies somewhere between the extreme of perfect order and the middle range of erratic behavior, a region in which orderly and disorderly tendencies combine in varying proportions. The critical question for the predictability of autonomous economic phenomena is, then, whether, in a given case, the prevailing degree of orderliness approximates the state of perfect order sufficiently closely to permit the application of a deductive procedure, taking into account certain disturbance variables, the estimate displaying a small standard error or, what amounts to the same, a small prediction interval.

There can be legitimate disagreement as to the size of the prediction interval which, in a given case, is still practically useful and thus compatible with orderly structure and notion. Take the problem of a "reference cycle" for industrial fluctuations. It is one thing to predict – even with a considerable prediction interval – the rates of change of output during an upswing or downswing. It is quite another, however, to predict whether a given economic movement will continue or will turn in a contrary direction to that in which it is headed at the moment of making the prediction. In the first case there is no doubt about the direction of the movement; the strategic variables at least have the proper arithmetic sign. In the latter case it is the sign itself and thus the direction that is in doubt. So, too, in micro-economics, when we predict the effect of a rise in prices on, say, supply. If the situation is orderly enough, we can at least assert that a price rise will bring some increase in supply. But the prediction interval may rise to the point where we may be unable to assert even that much, namely if price rises induce a speculative contraction in offerings. Therefore to give some precision to the notion of "disorder" I shall henceforth define it as any situation in which we cannot unambiguously predict the *direction* of economic change.

In contrast with much modern theorizing, I feel bound to emphasize the singular importance of such "order" and "disorder" also in micro-economic relations. With Professor Machlup I cannot regard any explanation of macro-processes as complete or any prediction of their future course as safe, unless the particular micro-processes can be demonstrated from the integration of which the macro-phenomena result.[2]

There the problem of order arises on two levels. First, for the observer of macro-processes to draw unambiguous predictive inferences it is necessary that the *behavior patterns* of the buyers and sellers of commodities and productive services form an unbroken chain of productive and distributive activities. But to do so – and there we reach the second level – the *motivational patterns* underlying the behavior of individual marketers must themselves be mutually compatible. These motivational patterns in turn fall into two groups. One represents the purposive strand of incentives or *action directives*, such as pecuniary maximization and minimization, maintenance of asset values ("homeostasis" in Professor Boulding's terminology), protection of market positions, etc. The other is the cognitive strand of a marketer's *expectations* as to future market conditions, and especially as to the price, supply and demand responses on the part of his fellow marketers to the price and quantity stimuli emitted by himself.

[2] See Fritz Machlup, *Der Wettstreit zwischen Mikro- und Makro-Theorien in der Nationaloekonomie*, Tuebingen, 1960.

These expectations of the actors are of the greatest importance for the construction of a scientific Economics because they themselves represent predictions, though formed on a common-sense basis from fragmentary experience and information. Only if the state of the market shows a degree of order in the sense defined above will the economic actors be able to form correct expectations with a high degree of subjective certainty. And only then will their overt behavior show patterns capable of sustaining the prevailing order and thus of enabling the scientific observer to predict within practically useful limits. It is this common-sense interpretation of the ultimate "facts" – buyers' and sellers' behavior – by the actors themselves, that so greatly encumbers the work of the economist, a difficulty which the student of molecules and planets, of cells and organisms, is spared.[3]

However, there is still another complication in the scientific treatment of social processes, which must be recognized if the relevance of "order" for economic theorizing is to be fully grasped. I spoke above several times of the "proper functioning" or the "efficient performance" of the market as a task to be achieved by orderly macro-motions and interlocking behavioral and motivational patterns, possibly supported by measures of public policy. This implies that orderly macro- and micro-motion and thus predictability, though necessary conditions for constructing an economic theory, are by themselves not sufficient ones. Assume a perfectly periodic business cycle in which the same amplitudes and duration of phases repeat in unbroken sequence, but in which the stagnation phase each time approaches the level of zero output and employment. Though such a process would be fully predictable, it would be rejected as incompatible with another kind of "order". This second type of order refers to those macro-states that will accomplish a certain "purpose" or "goal" – in the case above the steady employment of the average member of the economic society in question and his steady provision with goods and services.

There is no logical argument by which we could refute a radical Positivism interested only in the explanation and prediction of market movements "wherever they might lead." But it should be remembered that at least on the micro-level even the most radical positivist ascribes a definite "purpose" to economic action, conventionally defined as "a relationship between ends and scarce means," and thus imposes definite restrictions on behavioral motion. Moreover, it can hardly be doubted that some notion of the level of *aggregate* provision which is to arise from the interplay of

---

[3] For an extensive treatment of this problem, see Alfred Schutz, "Common-Sense and Scientific Interpretation of Human Action," in *Collected Papers,* Vol. I (The Hague, 1962), pp. 3–47.

such "purposefully ordered" micro-motions underlies the entire history of economic doctrines, even if it has been conceptualized only recently in the theorems of Welfare Economics. To put it differently, macro-economic states and processes have always been interpreted as something more than mere chance aggregations of events. They have been treated as phenomena of "organization" – whether autonomous organizations like the self-regulating market or contrived organizations held together through planned controls.

Therefore, the orderliness of a particular economic event does not consist solely in its regularity and consequent predictability; at the very least the event must also be compatible with the prime purpose of every economic organization: macro-provision through an appropriate use of available resources. Intentionally I do not speak of "optimum" provision or of the "efficient" use of resources. Over and above a socially accepted minimum of subsistence, in principle, any level of output produced by a technically suitable segment of the available resources and distributed in socially approved shares may satisfy the goals of a particular economic system.

At the same time, once this is admitted, there is no denying that the ongoing "revolution of expectations" in mature as well as in developing countries progressively reduces the acceptable range of provision and employment levels. This development is of great importance for the relationship of regularity of motion and predictability to goal-adequacy. At first sight these seem to be quite separate aspects of an inclusive definition of economic "order". As our earlier example has shown, we can have perfect regularity of motion combined with extreme goal-inadequacy. Conversely, so long as low levels of output and employment are accepted as macrogoals, we can conceive of highly irregular and thus unpredictable motions as compatible with goal-adequate states and processes. But since irregular motions are bound to impair allocative as well as productive efficiency, orderliness of motion turns into a prerequisite of goal-adequacy, once the socially tolerable provision and employment levels rise above a certain threshold. There is little doubt that, in the mature economies of the West, this threshold has reached the point where a degree of motional disorder, which in the nineteenth century would have been accepted with animistic fatalism, is no longer compatible with prevailing welfare aspirations. Or to put it differently: under contemporary conditions irregular and thus unpredictable economic processes are bound to lead to socially intolerable results.

3. How to Test Economic Predictions

It is the contention of Classical and Neo-Classical Economics that, disregarding minor reservations, the decentralized decisions of the marketers, when free of political and contractual constraints, are certain to accomplish macro-states and macro-processes that exhibit "order" in this inclusive sense. All movements are supposed to pursue a fully predictable, self-correcting and self-limiting course, tending toward the establishment of a network of balances conceptualized as "macro-equilibrium", a state which represents the production-consumption optimum attainable with the given resources under the prevailing order of income distribution. We shall presently examine the implicit sociological and technological assumptions on which this optimistic verdict rests. At this point, however, we are interested in appraising the classical and neo-classical models as a paradigm for predicting the course of contemporary industrial market processes.

Nothing is simpler than to compile a long list of failures in prediction if the above-stated criterion: accurate forecasting of the *direction* of macro- or micro-movements, is e.g., applied to the cyclical changes in the United States over the last two decades. I have dealt with this issue extensively in OEK (pp. 52–56, 60–61), pointing out there that even the show piece of recent predictive efforts – the Kennedy tax revision – proves inconclusive, since the upturn in investment preceded the actual tax reduction by a year. And a tug of war about the imminence of inflation or deflation, which rages while this is written in December, 1966, does not inspire any more confidence in our ability to predict.[4]

In this connection preliminary results obtained from a forecasting model, which post-dates the publication of OEK, teach an even more impressive lesson. I refer to the Quarterly Econometric Model for the United States, developed from Professor Klein's original model by the Office of Business Economics in the Department of Commerce.[5] The model, dealing with the period from 1953 to 1965, has managed to circumvent some of the basic obstacles which usually hamper economic forecasting. It is actually concerned with "postdiction" because a system of simultaneous equations incorporating what are regarded as the strategic cause-effect relationships is tested *ex post* on statistical material available from observations of the past.

---

[4] For many more examples and also for the variety of predictive techniques employed, see Sidney Schoeffler, *The Failures of Economics,* Cambridge, 1955, Chapters 5 and 6.

[5] See *Survey of Current Business,* United States Department of Commerce, Vol. 46, No. 5, May, 1966, pp. 13–29.

This procedure has made it possible to assign to the exogenous variables their actual values. Moreover, the results concern the very period to the data of which the equations of the model were originally fitted. In spite of these peculiarities, both of which carry a highly favorable bias, the predictions of cyclical turning points have consistently proved wrong when made for more than two quarters ahead.

Still, in trying to account for these failures, the champions of modern predictive techniques offer some weighty counterarguments. Do we not meet with similar difficulties, they ask, in Meteorology, difficulties which the workers in that field are confident to overcome with the improvement of their research tools? Should we not therefore check our impatience in an enterprise like Econometrics which is only two or three decades old? Moreover, is it not true that the observations on which the traditional hypotheses are to be tested, reflect an empirical state of affairs in which growing imperfections of competition have removed a prime condition of the traditional model: unconstrained freedom of decision-making on the part of the micro-units?

In deference to such apologies I have fallen back in OEK on some general methodological considerations which offer certain criteria for the predictability of economic events independent of the usefulness of any particular technique. These considerations center in the fact that economic systems are "open" systems in a very special sense.

As conventionally understood,[6] an open system is a configuration in which the interplay of the intra-systemic forces – the core process – cannot be insulated from the impact of extra-systemic or environmental factors. Under this aspect the comparison of Economics with Meteorology seems pertinent, since in both cases the nature of the research object makes it impossible to subject the intra-systemic variables to artificial isolation in the laboratory. And yet, this analogy begs a fundamental question. If what we observe are always the results of the "impure" experiments which nature and history perform for us – experiments in which intra – and extra-systemic variables are inseparably joined – how can we know that there is any independent core process on which a theory can be built?

As a matter of fact, a satisfactory answer to this question can be given so far as Meteorology is concerned. There all the forces, however complex their interplay may be, obey the laws of Physics and Chemistry, laws which

[6] See Schoeffler, loc. cit., Chapters 4 and 8. Also, Emile Grunberg, "The Meaning of Scope and External Boundaries of Economics," in The Structure of Economic Science: Essays on Methodology, Englewood Cliffs, N.J., 1966, pp. 148–165.
[7] See Grunberg, loc. cit., p. 151.

themselves have been tested outside the context in which the meteriologist uses them. In other words, the behavior of the elementary variables is not in doubt, and the true problem of the researcher consists in making the set of such variables inclusive enough to cover all essential influences. This is not an easy task, but a technical rather than a theoretical one, the solution of which modern computers greatly facilitate.

Alas, the economist has no such means of testing the elementary laws of motion outside of the economic circuit. And even if he had, he would only run up against another difficulty which his fellow workers in the physical sciences are apparently spared. A simple example will illustrate the salient point. To predict the actual movements of a projectile the physicist must "add" to the impact of the intra-systemic forces acting on a body falling freely in a vacuum the retarding effect of the atmosphere, the deflection due to movements of the air, and the measurable influence of any other relevant extra-systemic factor. Can we, in analogy with this procedure, predict the effect of a tax reduction on aggregate demand by adding to the current flow of spending a flow equal to the size of the tax relief of business and public, minus an estimated amount of this increment withheld from circulation, plus or minus any monetary flow which other extra-systemic forces may set in motion or shut off?

Suppose that all these latter influences can be strictly calculated, we shall still arrive at a confirmable prediction only if, in analogy with the situation in Mechanics, the tax reduction and the changes in other extra-systemic factors will not in turn affect the behavioral forces which govern the current flow of spending. But is it permissible to transfer the postulate of "non-interaction" between intra- and extra-systemic forces from Physics to Economics? Can we, in other words, predict the effect of a tax cut with the same precision with which we can predict the effect which the introduction of a new stream of water has on the total flow in a hydraulic system?

Let us suppose that in 1963 investors and consumers had interpreted the proposed tax cut as a public confession of grave trouble ahead – a response which was in fact feared by some highly experienced governmental experts. The total flow of spending might then have dropped well below the level prevailing before the tax cut. This is, of course, precisely the manner in which private investment reacted to increased public spending during the New Deal. All this only restates for a specific case what was pointed out in general terms earlier when market expectations were defined as common-sense predictions on the part of the economic actors. Here all methodological analogies between Physics and Economics break down. They overlook "the difference between insensitive particles responding blindly though lawfully to blind stimuli, and purposeful actors who 'move' only after they have interpreted their field of action in terms of their goals and their common-sense knowledge" (OEK, p. 61). And in these interpretations the impact of the environmental factors plays a strategic role.

As a matter of fact, the interdependence between the forces of the core process and those emanating from the environment is still closer. Not only are all significant *changes* of the extra-systemic variables bound to affect the intra-systemic ones, but even in a *changeless* environment behavior and motivations acquire their strength and direction from the continuous impact which natural, social, and technical factors exert on what for purely didactic purposes has been set apart as "economic" phenomena. For this reason economic systems are "open" in a more fundamental sense than is true of any physical system including Meteorology. Not even ideally can the autonomous economic core processes be treated as closed, and the validity of "mental experiments" based on the "ceteris paribus" condition cannot be taken for granted beyond the particular set of variables from which they are derived. Rather theoretical generalizations and, especially, predictions are contingent on what, from case to case, the environmental factors do to the core factors of behavior and motivations. If their impact creates and maintains "order" in the inclusive sense defined above theory and predictability are assured. However, whenever the uncontrolled impact of the environment tends to create "disorderly" micro-behavior, the viability of the industrial market as well as its theoretical comprehensibility depends on our ability to devise controls that, in fact and not only by methodological fiction, "close" the system against disruptive forces.

4. Disorder in Mature Industrialism

This now leads to the crucial issue. For it is my contention that orderly motion of the *intra*-systematic variables – behavior and motivations – although characteristic of the early phase of industrial capitalism, no longer prevails in the key sectors of contemporary markets. This is equivalent to asserting that the behavioral and motivational premises on which all classical and neo-classical theorizing rests, are progressively losing realistic significance.

The premises in question are, at the behavioral level, appropriate negative freeback responses to any change in the prevailing market balances, responses that hold all economic motions to an equilibrating course. This behavior pattern has been formalized in the so-called Law of Supply and Demand, and itself is supposed to arise as the joint effect of two motivational sub-patterns: first, the action directive of maximizing pecuniary receipts and of minimizing pecuniary expenditures – what in OEK has been defined as the "extremum principle" – and second, what is described there as "stabilizing expectations," namely price expectations with zero or at least less than unit elasticity and quantity expectations with positive elasticity. To be specific, given the extremum principle as action directive and stabilizing expectations, a present rise in price will induce buyers, in the interest of minimizing expenditures, to shift purchases from the present to the future, that is, to reduce demand. Sellers on their part will be induced, in the interest of maximizing receipts, to shift sales from the future to the present, that is, to increase supply.[8]

There is no doubt that these premises underlie all traditional economic analyses including the main body of the Keynesian system, not to mention the bulk of econometric models employed for prediction. What is more difficult to demonstrate, and has for this reason been the target of a good deal of criticism, is my contention that, on the one hand, these premises did depict the actual state of affairs in early capitalism and, on the other hand, do so no more today.

To the extent to which the "facts of life" are to give support to these assertions it is easier to prove the latter thesis, if only because we know so much more about contemporary behavior and motivations of marketers. OEK (pages 46–49) enumerates in some detail the many incentives which today contend with the single-valued extremum principle. As the reader can convince himself, this was not meant to deny that a subjective desire to maximize pecuniary receipts is still the dominant action directive of business. My essential point was and is that such maximization has itself lost its classical determinacy, because the time span over which profits are to be maximized can no longer be defined once and for all. In the modern technical and organizational environment, indivisibility of resources, periods of investment and production, the size of financial commitments, etc., vary from branch to branch, possibly from firm to firm and even in one and the same firm from occasion to occasion. Consequently, opposite actions such as an increase or decrease of output, raising or lowering of prices can each be justified as the most promising step for profit maximization.

The same indeterminacy of the economic time horizon has undermined the stability of expectations, inducing divergent actions even under the rule of the same action directive whenever the evaluation of future market conditions changes. There is, in addition, a disturbing feedback effect from uncertain expectations to action directives, because a lower level of profits

[8] For details see OEK, Chapter 2, section 2.

which is expected with greater certainty may well become preferable to a higher but less certain one.

Altogether I feel on rather safe ground in speaking of a wide spectrum of action directives and expectations as prevailing in the modern scene in stark contrast with the simplistic assumptions of Traditional Economics. If this is granted, it may appear a question of minor importance whether in an earlier stage of industrial capitalism actual behavior and motivations conformed more closely to the premises of Classical and Neo-Classical Economics. This would indeed be so were it not that the thesis offers important clues to the fundamental causes of present "disorder" in market behavior and the resulting impasse in traditional theory.

Briefly stated, the thesis of a more orderly motion of the processes of early capitalism is derived from the recognition of certain social and technical determinants of marketers' motivations, determinants which tended to bring the latter in conformity with the theoretical postulates of the extremum principle and of stabilizing expectations. Among these determinants were, first, the *automatic pressure* which mass poverty, unbridled competition and an intellectual and moral climate favoring the accumulation of wealth, exerted on the action directives of the several social strata, making the maximization of receipts and minimization of expenditures a condition of economic if not physical survival. A second determinant was the then prevailing *mobility of resources*, due to smallness and non-specificity of capital equipment and the newly won "free circulation of labor from one employment to another" (A. Smith). This mobility kept the time horizon for adjustment to changes in demand and technology to the short run – a prime condition for stabilizing expectations in a laissez-faire market. A third and supplementary determinant took the form of what in OEK is defined as *automatic escapements*, in particular the rising rate of growth through rapid population increase, a steady stream of innovations, and the opening of new markets. Through constant stimulation of aggregate demand these escapements compensated for temporary dislocations and strengthened the stability of expectations by limiting the amplitude and duration of cyclical downswings.

It must be admitted that the empirical data referring to the actual incentives and expectations of that period are much too scanty to serve as a reliable test for the above hypothesis, but they certainly do not contradict it. Moreover, the traditional formulation of the Law of Supply and Demand, in which the classical premises about economic motivations are embodied, dominated the folklore of that age and even today expresses the "conventional wisdom" with which the average business man tries to interpret his experience.

That these attempts are not too successful, because rising prices are nowadays accompanied often enough by rising demand and falling supply is not surprising in the light of what was said above about the growing indeterminacy of profit maximization, and about the prevailing uncertainty of expectations. What is important is the fact that such divergences of economic motion from the model of Classical and Neo-Classical Economics can be easily understood once we take note of the striking historical changes in the original determinants of action directives and expectations. Practically all the social forces which once combined to exert pressure toward extremum motivation have greatly weakened. The consummation of the Industrial Revolution and the democratization of the Western social systems have liberated the masses from the bondage of extreme scarcity; self-organization of producers, and interventions of governmental policy culminating in the public controls of the welfare state have mitigated the fierceness of competition; and the earlier system of cultural values extolling acquisitiveness is giving way to what by the criterion of the classical laws of the market must be judged as capricious behavior. At the same time large-scale technology and the long-term financial commitments it demands, coupled with the spread of monopoly in the markets of goods and productive services, are progressively immobilizing the flow of resources, thus extending the time span over which dispositions must be made, and reducing the subjective certainty and objective accuracy of business expectations. On the other hand, persistent international tensions and political unrest in many underdeveloped regions, coupled with growing resistance to foreign capital imports in mature economies, preclude the exploitation of vast potential investment opportunities, thus blocking one of the most effective escapement mechanisms of an earlier era.

Most of these changes can be taken as symptoms of an affluent society, and as such the inherent "disorder" of modern industrial markets represents a significant victory of Western man over his environment and a breakthrough into a new realm of freedom. However, we have received ample warning that we must not blindly surrender to this liberation of the behavioral forces. If anything, the Great Depression taught us a lesson about what is likely to happen to an industrial market society which is no longer disciplined by the automatic constraints of the past and, at the same time, lacks an arsenal of compensatory contrived controls. The shock of this experience marks the turning point toward Political Economics as here understood, both as a new theoretical frame of reference and a new practice of public policy.

II. THE CONSTRUCTIVE FUNCTION OF POLITICAL ECONOMICS

1. The Instrumental-Deductive Method

From the outset it was emphasized that Political Economics, like Traditional Economics, is a theoretical science. As such it tries to derive a past state of the system (explanation) or a future state (prediction) from the knowledge of a given state (initial conditions) and from some "law of motion". The difference between the two approaches lies in the manner in which the law of motion and its more remote determinants are established. In Traditional Economics they either result from a process of induction – that is, from the generalization of observations concerning, say, actual behavioral and motivational patterns – or they are postulated as heuristic principles independent of any observation, as e.g., the extremum principle is treated in "Positive" Economics. Still, whatever their origin, these generalizations or postulates serve as fundamental assumptions or highest-level hypotheses, and as such belong among the knowns of economic reasoning from which the unknown states of the system can be deduced.

As our critical comments have shown, Political Economics denies that, under the conditions of contemporary capitalism, either observation of actual phenomena or heuristic postulation can establish highest-level hypotheses functioning as once and for all valid premises from which confirmable predictions can de derived. Rather, it insists that the actual forces which rule economic movements and, in particular, bring about a change in their direction, cannot be known a priori but themselves fall in the category of unknowns. Therefore, a major task of Political Economics consists in devising an analytical technique through which these unknowns can be determined.

In order to understand the precise role of this technique – henceforth defined as instrumental analysis – we should compare it with the part played by induction in the traditional procedure of the so-called hypothetico-deductive method. In the practical employment of this method emphasis rests on deduction, that is, on the "progressive" inferences which can be drawn from the premises – the alleged laws of economic behavior and motivations – to conclusions concerning past or future states of the system. In other words, once these premises have been established, they are taken for granted; their validity is not checked each time anew when a concrete explanation or prediction is to be undertaken. But this concentration on deduction when it comes to the *application* of a theory must not blind us to the fact that in the original act of theory *formation* the premises of the deductive syllogism are themselves unknowns to be determined by a "re-gressive" procedure from known observations.

In the reasoning of Political Economics instrumental analysis is the equivalent to this original act of induction in the conventional method. It too searches for explanatory hypotheses which subsequently can serve as premises in a deductive syllogism. And it too applies a regressive procedure, arguing backward from a given phenomenon to its determinants. We shall presently see that such terms as "given phenomenon" or "determinant" take on a new meaning in instrumental analysis and that, substantively, we move there in quite another dimension of experience. But awareness of the formal similarity between the hypothetico-deductive method and what is called here instrumental-deductive method may facilitate the understanding of the latter.

Perhaps the easiest access to the core of instrumental analysis is through the inclusive concept of *order* we established earlier. We combined there the "positive" notion of order of state and motion with the "normative" notion of the satisfactory functioning of the economy as a "system" – satis-factory, that is, when judged by criteria such as a stipulated state of re-source utilization, of aggregate output, of income distribution, etc. Now it is a main characteristic of all traditional reasoning before Keynes that it concentrated on the positive study of micro- and macro-motions and the manner in which individual motions integrate themselves into aggregate states and processes, treating these states and processes as the more or less inexorable result of unalterable behavioral forces. This did not exclude the *ex post* evaluation of this result under the normative aspect referred to, nor did it rule out attempts to bring the outcome of the autonomous operation of the market in line with accepted welfare goals through measures of public control. But the idea that such goals might serve as *ex ante yard-sticks* for the conscious *shaping* of the macro-states and processes would have been regarded as a collectivist anomaly and as such incompatible with the nature of decentralized decision-making.

It is perhaps the most radical of Keynes' many innovations that he broke with this tradition. The following quote taken from OEK (Page 218) ex-presses what seems to me his decisive turn in the direction of instrumental analysis:

Though (Keynes') immediate problem is the disequilibria and pseudo-equilibria engendered by lapses of the market from the state of full employment, he does not confine himself to merely explaining and predicting these events which have no place in the orthodox model. By demonstrating that equilibrium and equilibration in the traditional sense are the exceptions rather than the rule in the real world, he has restored awareness of the normative character of these notions. And the entire analytical effort reveals itself as ultimately devoted to the task of determining the requirements for the attainment of a macro-goal – full employment – which is postulated independently of actual experience. Moreover, when the major condition for such attainment turns out to be the substitution, in the sphere of investment, of a novel behavioral force for the traditional decision-making of the micro-units, the realm of instrumental analysis has been entered.

Instrumental analysis is, then, a generalization of Keynes' concern with the requirements for the attainment of full employment; it extends the range of macro-goals, for which the requirements are to be determined, to any conceivable state or process stipulated as desirable. And it systematically analyzes these requirements – or as we shall henceforth call them: *conditions suitable for goal attainment* – into their macro- and micro-components. In doing so, instrumental analysis "inverts" the theoretical problem by treating some of the knowns of traditional analysis as unknown and, conversely, by treating the major unknowns of traditional analysis: the terminal states and processes, as known. Or to state the same idea in a different form, the traditional procedure of deriving the effect of given causes is transposed into a procedure by which suitable means are derived from given ends. Under this aspect instrumental analysis can be called the logic of economic goal-seeking.[9]

In explicating this logical structure we begin with the *unknowns*. They are enumerated here in the sequence in which instrumental analysis tries to determine them, each subsequent step depending on the successful accomplishment of the prior one: (1) the *path* or the succession of macro-states of the system suitable to transform a given initial state into a stipulated terminal state; (2) *patterns of micro-behavior* appropriate to keeping the system to the suitable path; (3) *micro-motivations* capable of generating suitable behavior; and (4) *a state of the environment* including, possibly though

---

[9] I refrain from calling instrumental analysis a "teleological" method of inquiry because this label is too often used to indicate that a given procedure is incompatible with causal analysis. That the instrumental approach is fully compatible with cause-effect relations follows from the subsequent application of its results to deductive inferences in which the originally unknown "means" appear, after their instrumental determination, as known "causes" of effects to be explained or predicted. At the same time it is true that the suitability of a "cause" as a "means" for bringing about a stipulated goal cannot be judged without knowledge of the goal itself. In this sense a "telos" enters the search procedure by which the suitable means-causes are to be discovered.

not necessarily, political controls designed to stimulate suitable motivations.[10]

These unknowns are to be determined with the help of the following *knowns*: (1) the *initial state* of the system under investigation; (2) a *macro-goal* specified as a terminal state, either by stipulating the "numerical values of the target variables" (Tinbergen), or by stipulating the qualitative interrelations among the target variables in terms of, say, a Pareto optimum, full resource utilization, a steady rate of growth, etc.; and (3) certain *laws, rules, and empirical generalizations* with the help of which the suitability of means for the attainment of ends can be established.

The specific procedure by which the unknowns can be derived from the knowns will be illustrated below in an elementary example. But before doing so a brief comment is due on the role that is assigned here to the macro-goals.

2. The Terminal State as Datum

The "inversion" of the analytical procedure referred to above finds one expression in the change of role of the terminal state from the major unknown into a datum. This change is less striking if we compare instrumental analysis, as we should, with its methodological simile: induction, rather than with deductive inference. Still, there remains an important difference between these two regressive procedures. It concerns the nature of the "facts" from which they take their bearings. In the case of induction these facts are *observed* terminal states, namely the realized effects of causes to be discovered. In sharp contrast, instrumental analysis starts out from a *stipulated* terminal state which, except in the marginal case when preservation of the initial state is stipulated as macro-goal, is beyond present observation and which, whenever Political Economics fails to solve its problem, may not even become observable in the future.

This is not to imply that the choice of an economic macro-goal is an arbitrary act. In the concluding section of this paper a few words will be said about this problem. But it is intuitively obvious that such a discussion will carry us beyond the realm of facts and factual relations into the region of value judgments – a region in which discursive thinking and thus scientific inquiry as the modern mind understands it, cannot by itself offer final

---

[10] In order to establish full generality for this logic of goal-seeking, we must speak of "suitability," "appropriateness," etc., rather than of "requirements," because there are, as a rule, alternative paths, behavior patterns, motivations and states of the environment all of which can serve as means to the stipulated end. Thus we deal on this level with sufficient rather than with necessary conditions.

answers. At any rate the processes by which goals are chosen are not the subject of *economic* studies, and in the latter the macro-goals of instrumental analysis would have to play the role of data, even if Reason or Revelation – Philosophy or Theology – were able to present us with "intersubjectively demonstrable" criteria.[11]

However, there is another issue connected with the choice of macrogoals, which poses a genuine scientific problem. It is mentioned in OEK (page 263) as an afterthought, but deserves stronger emphasis as a preparatory stage of instrumental analysis proper. It refers to the implicit assumption that all the different aspirations of a goal-setter are mutually compatible and can be translated into a consistent and realizable set of targets.

For a certain type of goals, namely those which are concerned with a rearrangement of employed or latent resources, these prerequisites are in the nature of the case always fulfilled. This is not so, however, if for example a certain level of output or a certain rate of growth is stipulated, especially if the terminal state is further qualified by optimization criteria, such as the maintenance of a minimum level of consumption or of a stable price level. In all such cases the search for the suitable means must be preceded by a study of the compatibility of the several goals with one another and with the stock of available resources. Fortunately the various

---

[11] In this context I have sometimes been asked why I had to coin the term "instrumental" analysis instead of simply speaking of "normative" analysis in line with the recent practice of distinguishing between "descriptive" or "positive" and "prescriptive" or "normative" Economics. In this dichotomy traditional theory is assigned to the first category, whereas, e.g., Welfare Economics is placed in the second. My answer is that I try to avoid a confusion which seems to be inherent in the current terminology.

There is little danger of misunderstanding so far as the first category is concerned. But when we classify Welfare Economics simply as a normative procedure, we fail to take into account that it is concerned with two quite different problems the solution of which requires quite different procedures. One refers to the choice of the most desirable objectives or, in another formulation, to the decision as to whether one collection of goods is greater in terms of welfare than some other collection. Such choices and decisions and the establishment of the guiding criteria indeed fall in the normative realm. This is by no means so with the other problem of selecting the means for achieving these objectives or the methods of producing the chosen collection. These are issues which are open to discursive reasoning and thus proper subjects of scientific analysis. This remains even true if the quest is for "optimum" methods of goal attainment. In that case the discovery of the criteria for optimization is again a normative problem. But the subsequent application of such criteria to the selection of means is a purely analytical task.

What instrumental analysis tries to achieve parallels the analytical part of Welfare Economics – determining the means suitable for the attainment of given goals. And though drawing for one of its *data* on the results of normative judgment it derives its own propositions by "positive" reasoning.

techniques of Mathematical Programming are providing us with a growing arsenal of tools with the help of which the "feasibility" of a "program" can be established, taking into consideration all encountered aud stipulated constraints.

In passing, it should be noted that such complementarity between instrumental analysis and Mathematical Programming is by no means accidental. Both procedures are goal-oriented, even if the analytical interest of Mathematical Programming, as that of Welfare Economics, is more limited. This interest is confined to the technical arrangements through which a stipulated bill of goods materializes or some objective function can be maximized or minimized, while it disregards the behavioral and motivational forces at work. Under this aspect the complementarity of the two procedures is mutual: Mathematical Programming provides the ground from which instrumental analysis takes its bearing, and the latter transforms the technocratic insights of the former into genuine socio-economic knowledge.

3. What Laws and Rules Link Ends and Means?

No other proposition relating to Instrumental Analysis has aroused as critical a response as did the alleged contradiction in my asserting, on the one hand, that there are today no reliable laws of economic behavior on which predictions can be based, and on the other hand that it is possible to derive, from the knowledge of an initial and a stipulated terminal state, paths and forces suitable to transform the former into the latter. What else is it but a prediction, the critics ask, if a particular behavior pattern is selected as suitable to set the system on a path that will lead to a stipulated goal? Or, more concretely, how does one know that, e.g., a rise in the rate of investment is a suitable means for promoting employment, or that the incentive of receipt maximization coupled with positive elasticities of price and quantity expectations is suitable to stimulate investment decisions? To make such statements need one not appeal to laws and rules which relate specific means to specific ends, and derive the latter as effects from the former as causes?

Far from denying any of these propositions I am in full agreement on this point with my critics. At the same time I must insist that the laws and rules which permit us to predict what means are suitable for the attainment of a given end are of a nature quite different from what passes in Traditional Economics as laws of economic behavior, such as the Law of Supply and Demand. At this point let me briefly indicate the nature of these differences, and subsequently discuss the details at greater length.

(1) The relationship between ends and means is a problem of Technology

in the broadest sense. Applied to the realm of Economics, in which the relation of matter as a means to human ends plays a strategic role, the problem is one of material technology. Therefore, to the extent to which the ends including their hierarchial order are stipulated, the suitability of means is determined, first of all, by the currently known Rules of Engineering.

(2) Knowledge of such engineering rules, and of certain mathematical theorems which permit the determination of suitable quantitative relations, is all that is required to establish goal-adequate paths and, within a given socio-psychological environment, also goal-adequate behavior. Since the question whether the goal-adequate path and behavior actually materialize is not posed at this stage, there is no need for any "laws of behavior" in the sense of: if event A occurs then behavior B will follow. Rather the "law" implied in these engineering rules states: if behavior B occurs the state C will follow.

(3) For the determination of goal-adequate motivations it is necessary to take into account, in addition to the knowledge of goal-adequate behavior, a psychological hypothesis which relates specific motivations to specific behavior. But if accepted at all this hypothesis is of such generality that its validity extends far beyond the economic realm.

(4) Only when instrumental analysis regresses to the point where economic motivations are to be related to environmental factors – a step which is necessary if the deductive part of Political Economics is to be assured – does a causal problem arise which is formally comparable with, but substantively quite different from, the cause-effect relations formulated in the laws of Traditional Economics.

ad (1) The Role of Technology

In placing the technological aspect of Economics in the center of instrumental analysis I do not wish to intimate that Economics is nothing but Technology, or that the investigation of Man-Matter relations is its only concern. Outside the methodological fiction of a Crusoe economy all real economic processes are the combined result of technological and sociological forces so that the Man-Matter relationships always operate through the prevailing Man-Man relationships. But this does not alter the fact, once a definite state of provision with goods and services, that is, a feasible program of production and (or) distribution has been stipulated, the search for the suitable means is first of all a study of the suitable materials, devices and processes – in a word, a technological problem. From this it follows that the socio-psychological forces which must be called upon for the realization of the stipulated program are themselves suitable only to the extent to which they are compatible with, and promoters of, the technological prerequisites.[12]

ad (2) Engineering Rules as Instrumental Criteria for Path and Behavior

Technological relations, such as those that determine the suitability of specific materials, devices and processes for the realization of a feasible program of production and distribution, are governed by Rules of Engineering, understood in the comprehensive sense of physical, chemical, and biological manipulations. These rules themselves are derived from the apposite Laws of Nature, which thus reveal themselves as the ultimate determinants of the instrumental relationships. To these determinants the rules governing socio-economic relations – behavioral and motivational patterns – will have to adapt themselves if the stipulated goals are to be attained.

In Chapter XI of OEK I have demonstrated this proposition on three test cases – maintenance of a stationary process; stabilization of a market economy in the sense of raising it from a level of underutilization to that of full utilization of resources; balancing a system undergoing growth by assuring continuous absorption of resource increments and of increases in productivity. In particular, it could be shown that application of the pertinent engineering rules to the creation of characteristic equalities and inequalities among the components of the system is all that is required for the determination of the *Path*, that is, a sequence of states of the aggregate suitable to transform the initial into the terminal configuration. I cannot repeat this demonstration within the limits of this paper. All I can do here is briefly to illustrate it with reference to the simplest – but for that reason least realistic – example: stationary equilibrium. For a discussion which goes beyond an elementary exercise the reader must consult the original text.

For our purposes stationary equilibrium must be understood, not as a methodological device, but as the structural model of an economic macro-goal. What is singular in this model is the fact that the initial state is struc-

---

[12] This is not the place to reopen the dispute between the "materialist" and the "praxiological" conception of economic theory. In OEK, Chapter I, section 2, and Chapter VIII, sections 3–5, I have restated the well-known reasons why the extension of economic theory into a "generalized theory of choice" is bound to deprive it of any substantive content, but reduces its propositions to mere tautologies. Professor Boulding's recent inclusion of painters among economic men because, just as the consumer may have to sacrifice "a little ham for a little more eggs in a breakfast," the painter "sacrifices ... a little red for a little more green" (*Scientific American*, May 1965, p. 139), has only strengthened my conviction. Or are we to assume that "optimum painting" amounts to maximization of colors per square inch of the canvas? Poor Rembrandt!

turally identical with the terminal state or, speaking in terms of a process, that the path of the system presents itself as a steady sequence of identical states.

Since by assumption we deal with an industrial system in which all productive processes are supposed to require the employment of real capital as an input, the stationary structure of production can be conceived as a three-sectoral model. Disregarding the input of natural resources we can say that in each sector certain quantities of labor and fixed capital or equipment goods combine to produce specific outputs, the sum of all sector inputs exhausting the available supply of resources so that full utilization is continually maintained. We also disregard the "vertical" order of stages in which, in each sector, natural resources are gradually transformed into finished goods. The outputs are then all of them finished goods and consist of three physical types: primary equipment goods issuing in sector I capable of producing equipment goods; secondary equipment goods issuing in sector II capable of producing consumer goods; finally consumer goods issuing in sector III. For simplicity's sake it is assumed that the specificity of the three types of output is absolute.

At first sight one might suspect that all that can be said about the path suitable for maintaining such a stationary process refers only to the continuity of the processes of production in the three sectors. Such continuity – the maintenance of well-circumscribed engineering processes – is certainly a necessary condition, but it is by no means sufficient. Continuity of outputs presupposes continuity of inputs. As far as labor input is concerned, we may conceive of it as a meta-economic issue, treating the steady "replacement" of "worn-out" labor as a datum. We certainly cannot do so with regard to equipment. Rather the assumed three-partite structure of production is a consequence of the technological fact that the provision of equipment is an intra-economic problem, equipment being not only an input but also an output. In other words, continuous output of consumer goods in sector III is conditional on the steady replacement of worn out secondary equipment through the steady output of such equipment in sector II. In turn, such output of secondary equipment depends on the condition that the primary equipment, which produces secondary equipment in sector II, is steadily replaced from the output in sector I. But sector I can provide such replacement only if its own equipment stock is steadily maintained. This amounts to the further condition that the aggregate output in sector I must be large enough steadily to replace the worn-out equipment in both sectors I and II.

From these elementary observations it follows that, to maintain steady production in the system, not only must each sector produce its respective output, but parts of this output must be "moved" by other engineering processes from the producing into some "utilizing" sector. The same is obviously true of the output of consumer goods, the aggregate of which needs to be distributed among the workers of all three sectors. Were we to adopt the classical position which, in some fashion, interprets the output of consumer goods as the "fuel" that rekindles the working energy of labor, the conception of the path as an engineering process would be further strengthened.

In these physical processes in which inputs are transformed and outputs are shifted, definite quantitative relations must be maintained between inputs and outputs within each sector, between the outputs of the three sectors, and between that part of each sector's output which is applied "at home" and that part which is "exported" to other sectors. We can indeed conceive of the stationary path in analogy with a system of triangular trade relations for which zero surplus balances are stipulated. Just as the determination of the size and proportions of the exchanges which there bring about such zero balances is independent of any prior knowledge of the "forces" – centralized or decentralized decision-making and the respective behavior patterns – through which such balances are established and maintained, the course of the *suitable* stationary path can be derived without any knowledge of the *actual* behavior of the productive agents, on which of course the realization of such a path depends. Rather the instrumental dependence is reversed: not until we know the technologically determined structure of the path are we able to "select" the behavioral patterns that are suitable to keep the system to that path.[13]

Thus the suitable behavior of human agents, whether these be productive factors offering their services, managers combining these services according to productive requirements, distributive agents moving the outputs toward their final destination as objects of consumption or replacement, etc., is nothing but a mode of application of the pertinent engineering rules. It throws some light on the merely "subsidiary" role which these human actions play that there is, at least in principle, an alternative means of realizing the engineering requirements: Automation. I am using the term here in the general sense of all mechanical, thermal, chemical manipulations which at earlier levels of technological developments were performed by

[13] For details see OEK, Chapter XI, sections 3–5. For a more extensive treatment including the quantitative determination of sector ratios and inter-sectoral equilibrium conditions, see my paper on "Structural Analysis of Real Capital Formation," in *Capital Formation and Economic Growth,* Princeton, 1955, esp. pp. 591–7.

human actors. For our present purposes it is convenient to imagine complete automation of all processes of production and distribution up to the point where human decision-making is limited to goal-setting – that is, to decisions which concern the content of the output menu, the specific techniques to be applied, and to the acts of programming the computers. Whatever probability we may want to assign to the eventual advent of such a regime, there are neither logical nor empirical inconsistencies in this image. It offers an intuitive confirmation of the fundamental thesis that, once the goal is set, the structure of the path and the operation of the active "forces" suitable for goal attainment – human or subhuman – can be derived from the knowledge of engineering rules alone.

This is not to say that, so long as human decisions participate in the application of these rules, we can disregard the social setting in which economic processes occur when we try to establish path-adequate behavior patterns. To take the two extremes of economic organization: monolithic collectivism and a laissez-faire market, it is evident that the behavior patterns appropriate to centralized command and subordinate execution differ drastically from the anonymous price-quantity manipulations through which the market operates. This remains true even if we interpret the respective behavioral patterns as elements of a vast information system – apparently the basis for another analogy with the cybernetics of a fully automated economy. But this must not blind us to the fact that, at least in the present state of our knowledge, the "sensorium" through which human agents communicate, the manner in which their "responses" are elicited, and the secondary responses ("sanctions") which the primary responses draw, seem radically different from the mechanical or electronic stimulus-response relations in an automated system.

So in order to translate the input-output configurations which represent the path, into a suitable chain of coordinated actions we must know the nature of the prevailing signal system and the social rules according to which information is communicated and thus specific action can be solicited. But it must be realized that the meaning of the signals through which information is conveyed is by no means fixed in a law-like manner. In principle, a market is operable just as well under the rule that rising prices indicate excess supply, as under the conventional rule according to which they indicate excess demand. All that is necessary to insure interlocking of behavior is consistency in the use of the informative symbols.

At the same time it cannot be stated often enough that even such consistency in interpretation can only tell us what action *if taken* will agree with the pre-established path, but cannot assure us that these actions *will be taken in fact.* It is true that even in a fully automated system, goal realiza-tion is threatened by mechanical or electronical failures. But the possibility of goal-*in*adequate responses is inherent in a system that must rely for its driving force on spontaneous human behavior.

Ad (3) The Nexus between Behavior and Motivations

This indeterminacy at the level of behavior responses is the reason why instrumental analysis cannot stop short at the study of Behavior, but must pursue its regressive course to the level of Motivations. In other words, we must inquire what motivations are suitable to induce goal-adequate be-havior. Naturally, this step leads beyond the territory where engineering rules dominate, into the realm of functional or dynamic Psychology. This is not the place to embark upon a systematic discussion of the relationship between behavior and motivations, and I certainly lack professional com-petence for such a task. Fortunately, all we need for our purposes is the acceptance of the hypothesis that, in the absence of external constraints, overt economic behavior can be predicted if the underlying action directive and expectations are known. This then makes it possible regressively to infer from a known behavior one or more motivational compounds that are suitable to induce that behavior.

To illustrate this proposition by our previous example, we start out from a behavioral rule formulated in accord with what was said above. Once the stationary path has been established (its establishment is a dynamic process with its own rules), suitable behavior to maintain it consists in routinized repetition of the actions which achieve the physical transformations and shifts prescribed by the pertinent engineering rules. Now we ask: what com-pounds of motivations are suitable for the establishment of such behavioral routine? Focussing on a market system, we come up with alternative answers: either the extremum incentive as action directive coupled with zero elasticity of price and quantity expectations, or homeostatic action directives coupled with the same type of expectations.

For a proof we assume – along the lines of modern stability analysis of which our discussion is an amplification – that, accidentally, managers in the consumer goods sector raise their demand for secondary equipment beyond their current replacement needs and, possibly, even offer higher unit prices. If the price and quantity expectations of the producers of secon-dary equipment are positive, the extremum incentive will induce them to expand output. Contrariwise, while striving for maintenance of asset values – a homeostatic incentive – the same expectations will induce them to contact output. Either response, instead of eliminating the accidental distortion, tends to perpetuate it. Only zero elasticity of expectations, namely disregard of present changes in demand and price, will in either case maintain the stationary relations among the sectoral outputs, and thus assure the stability of the system.

In studying growth processes I have come up against a number of quite varied motivational compounds as suitability conditions for behavior in successive stages leading to Balanced Growth. But once the behavior patterns themselves have been regressively derived from the engineering rules governing the path, it is, in principle, always possible to infer suitable motivational substructures.

Ad. (4) The Link Between Motivation and Control

Before carrying our regressive procedure to completion, we had better review what instrumental analysis has proved capable of achieving up to this point. It is meant to serve as an alternative to the traditional procedure by which the intra-systemic forces assuring orderly and thus predictable processes are either derived by induction or are postulated as heuristic principles. Instead, instrumental analysis claims to derive these patterns by regressively relating a stipulated terminal state to an observable initial state. And it claims to do so without recourse to any "laws of economic behavior," but by invoking pertinent "laws of inanimate nature" and engineering rules derived from them.

These claims appear as fully vindicated. Once we know the pertinent engineering rules and the social organization which sustains the economic process under examination (the latter datum included in the knowledge of the initial state), and once we accept the hypothesis that specific behavior can be derived from specific motivational compounds, we indeed arrive at a precise definition of the path and, especially, of the behavioral and motivational patterns which connect initial and terminal states.

But now suppose that we were to employ the patterns thus derived as highest-level hypotheses in a deductive model, could we expect the conclusion to yield confirmable predictions about the terminal state toward which the system in question will actually tend? The answer is obviously in the negative, since all we can assert with confidence is that the instrumentally valid intra-systemic forces will lead to the stipulated end, *provided that these forces are actually set in motion*. If, however, the forces at work at the time of observation differ from the goal-adequate ones, not only instrumental analysis but any theoretical procedure imaginable is by itself powerless to set "capricious reality" right. Only *practical acts* of altering the autonomous course of the real economic processes by changing the underlying motivational and behavioral patterns can make reality converge toward a state of goal-adequacy.

Even if this statement were to imply no more than that instrumental knowledge is a useful guide for the framing of economic policy, the analytical technique described would be vindicated. But much more is at stake. *Prior reorganization of economic reality* in line with the instrumental findings *is now a precondition for establishing a viable economic theory.* To be specific, once measures of economic policy – or, as we shall call them: of instrumentally guided public control – have succeeded in adjusting the actual behavioral and motivational patterns to the goal-adequate ones, we can indeed apply our instrumental findings in the deductive part of Political Economics. Thus *analysis and political practice appear as inseparately connected steps in the acquisition of economic knowledge* – the rationale for the use of the term Political Economics. And the instrumental-deductive method of Political Economics reveals itself as a *three-stage procedure*: "resolutive" discovery of what is goal-adequate, "compositive" prediction of what will happen once goal-adequate forces are active; these two theoretical stages linked together by an intermediate practical stage in which political control makes the actual forces coincide with the goal-adequate ones.

With these comments we have implicitly answered another question: to wit, how to test the theorems resulting from the instrumental-deductive procedure. Since these theorems are empirically true – and not merely logically consistent – only to the extent to which control succeeds in transforming real into goal-adequate states, testing can only be "indirect" through confrontation of the theorems of Political Economics with manipulated experience. But now the objects of experience are no longer "passively observed" as is the case in the traditional procedure. The theorems to be tested prove true to the extent to which political action succeeds in *making* them true.

If anything, it is this linkage of theoretical analysis and political practice which sets Political Economics apart not only from Traditional Economics, but from all conventional theory formation. It introduces an engineering element into the procedure by which knowledge is generated. The methodological implications for other fields of the social and perhaps even of some of the natural sciences are obvious, but cannot be explored here.

In the foregoing remarks we have linked actualization of goal-adequate motivations to public control. But in doing so we have skipped a problem without answer to which this link cannot be forged. What are the specific measures of public control which, in a given situation, are capable of transforming actual into suitable action directives and expectations?

Though the application of such measures is a political task, the discovery of what measures are suitable for the purpose is certainly a scientific one. And we realize that the work of instrumental analysis is not completed before we have succeeded in regressing from goal-adequate motivations to suitable measures of control.

To tackle this problem we must first place it in a wider context. When criticizing the procedure of Traditional Economics I advanced the hypothesis that its predictive success during the classical period of capitalism was due to a combination of exceptional environmental circumstances – automatic pressures, resource mobility, escapements – which influenced economic motivations in the direction of extremum incentives and stabilizing expectations. Such a hypothesis implies that it is, in principle, possible to trace a causal nexus from specific environmental conditions to specific economic motivations. Thus the search for an instrumental link between "contrived pressures" of public control on the one hand and goal-adequate action directives and expectations on the other hand reveals itself as a special case of the wider problem of "social causation," namely of the manner in which behavior and motivations generally can be related to the "forces" of the environment, and also of the strength of this relationship.

Here we are referred to another field of Psychology, unfortunately to one in which little progress has been made since J. S. Mill pondered the prospects of an "Ethology or Science of Character". There are at least three limitations to the efficacy of external influences on economic motivations. One is the multiplicity of such influences of which even a highly intervention-minded public authority can subject only a limited number to conscious control. Another are the "internal influences" arising from the psychosomatic structure of the individuals concerned, which may successfully compete with the pressures from without. Third, and most important, there is the ineradicable spontaneity of human decision-making which renders compliance with the prescripts of control conditional on affirmation on the part of the controlled. Such affirmation in turn presupposes that the intentions of the controllers are rightly understood and, if so, that both the ends and the measures taken are approved of.

In the circumstances, it is not surprising that Psychology has not yet presented us with any "laws of social causation" on which instrumental analysis could build. But this does not exclude a few empirical generalizations or rules of thumb which permit us to form an estimate of the probable effect of certain types of control on economic motivations. To state the conclusion bluntly, it seems safe to presume that the effect of control will be determinate and predictible whenever (1) the macro-goal at which control aims and the specific measures it takes coincide with the "freely chosen" micro-goals of the controlled; and (or) when (2) the sanctions imposed for non-compliance are severe and inescapable.

We shall presently see that these rules impose some limits on the choice of macro-goals. At this point it is worth noting that the impact which controls are likely to have on expectations is more easy to predict than the impact on action directives.

In a regime guided by Political Economics, *control of expectations* has a twofold function. First, it is to spread information about the future course of economic processes among the marketers, thereby rectifying their own independent guesses and reducing uncertainty of expectations below the critical threshold. Second, the content of such public information, that is, the course of events predicted by the public authority, must coincide with the goal-adequate path if the new expectations are themselves to be goal-adequate.

Judged by rule (1) above, there is every likelihood that such control through information will be highly effective. To quote from OEK (pages (155-6): ". . . every marketer is interested in improving his common-sense knowledge about his present and future field of action. Therefore . . . he can be supposed to accept gladly any public information capable of correcting the content of his expectations and reducing the uncertainty of their coming true." Nor is there any doubt that the public information thus broadcast can be made to conform to the practical requirements. "Once it has established the macro-goal and the optimization criteria, the controlling authority can acquire by a process of instrumental inference precise knowledge of the adjustment processes through which the system is to move toward the postulated terminal state . . . Thus the successive market constellations – the future field of action of the marketers – are known at the moment when the decision about the goal is taken, and can be communicated to the prospective actors as the body of facts on which correct expectations can be built."

No such prestabilized harmony exists for the *control of action directives*. In the short run, the controllers will have to accept the prevailing incentives as data, trying to neutralize any digression from goal-adequacy by compensatory public action. This presupposes a public sector so organized that it can expand at short notice whenever the private sector fails to respond in accord with goal requirements. Over the long run, the transformation of economic incentives is a problem of "education". In this respect the anonymous pressures of the past – poverty and unbridled competition – were probably more effective than the "humanized" sanctions of public control ever will be. The former were truly inescapable, whereas the latter can, in principle, be resisted by countervailing political power.

However, we should not underestimate the potentialities of social learning, which have been so impressively demonstrated by the change in attitude toward fiscal controls on the part of the U.S. business community, an educational advance achieved within one generation. This example highlights the significance of an enlightened public opinion. By spreading insight into the economic advantages which suitable micro-responses confer on the marketers themselves, the ground is prepared for a more cooperative reaction to public controls on the part of all economic strata. This is not least due to the more enlightened instruction which the present generation of economic leaders has received during their college days.

4. The Probabilistic Nature of Political Economics

Though they do not display the mechanical rigidity of engineering rules or the strict nexus which ties specific motivations to specific behavior patterns, there are ascertainable links which relate particular action directives and expectations to particular environmental forces, especially to public control. These links are likely to grow stronger as public understanding of what is required for goal achievement widens and deepens. And predictions about the efficacy of public controls will then prove confirmable in proportion to the strength of those links. But this does not alter the fact that so long as we deal with humans rather than with robots, "social" causation will be weaker than "natural" causation. Therefore, even if engineering rules and the behavior-motivation nexus make the instrumental analysis of path, behavior, and motivations fully determinate, the last link in the regressive chain – suitable controls – can be established at best with a high degree of probability.

This reservation hardly touches the instrumental part of Political Economics, the earlier steps of which are unaffected by the uncertainties which surround the last step. But it has an important bearing on the deductive part where the instrumental findings are applied as highest-level hypotheses. It is true that these hypotheses now have an empirical basis which the heuristic principles of Traditional Economics lack. Once the intermediate stage of the political-economic procedure, – activation of controls – has successfully been completed, a new reality confronts us which is "ready made" for confirmable predictions. Still, the probability limitations which attach to the effect of controls on economic motivations, are necessarily transferred to the highest-level hypotheses and thus to the predictive conclusions derived from them. Therefore, the explanations and predictions offered by Political Economics are essentially probabilistic.

From this one might draw the conclusion that Political Economics has little predictive superiority over Traditional Economics, since both are limited to stochastic propositions. Such a conclusion would miss the essential point made earlier, namely that it is precisely the *degree* of indeterminacy, as measured by the error term or the prediction interval, that matters for the practicability of an economic theory. Under the conditions of mature capitalism, the odds are all in favor of the instrumental-deductive approach. By setting contrived limitations to the "aberrations" of motivational and thus behavioral patterns Political Economics can insure that "there is one and only one 'mode' around which the observations . . . are grouped in such a way that the mean-square deviation is relatively small." [14]

These considerations make us aware of the important auxiliary role which the probabilistic techniques of modern Econometrics play in the context of Political Economics. As we now see, the doubts expressed earlier about the usefulness of these techniques in the framework of uncontrolled or haphazardly controlled market processes refer really to the *data* to which dynamic Econometrics is currently applied rather than to the method itself. "Even a market in good working order is likely to exhibit a considerable range of tolerance for minor deviations from the rules which adequate patterning must obey. Determining the actual range of such deviations and predicting the most probable course of the macro-process within this tolerable range will then be a legitimate task of statistical techniques" (OEK, page 117). What was said in a different context about Mathematical Programming can now be claimed for Econometrics: far from running counter to the procedure of Political Economics, both approaches are indispensable in making the instrumental-deductive method an effective tool for economic practice.

At long last we are in a position precisely to define the logical relationship between Political and Traditional Economics. Traditional Economics is confined to the analysis of that special instance in which the automatic forces of the environment keep the "aberrations" of the motivational and behavioral patterns within the "tolerable" range, tolerable both for the system's steady provision and for the predictability of its movements. We saw, however, that the empirical validity of the ensuing theorems is at best limited to a passing phase in capitalist evolution. Contrariwise, Political Economics, by substituting contrived for automatic controls, establishes an analytical frame of reference which, *mutatis mutandis*, proves valid as an

[14] See Hans Neisser, *On the Sociology of Knowledge*, New York, 1965, p. 90.

interpretation of all historical forms of economic organization. And thus one can assert that, logically, Traditional Economics is really contained in Political Economics as that marginal case in which the state of the environment makes it possible to keep controls near the zero level.

III. THE ECONOMIC POLICY OF POLITICAL ECONOMICS

1. Some Open Issues

". . . [E]ven if most of the building blocks are available, the systematic construction of a Political Economics is a major task, and one that far transcends the scope of this study . . . Once more it must be emphasized that our purpose is didactic, and that no more is intended than a demonstration of some principles of economic reasoning within a highly simplified frame of reference" (OEK, pages 250, 264-5). In a word, my book and also this essay move on a level of abstraction far removed from the field of economic-political action where the ideas discussed here are put to the real test.

Thus important work remains to be done at the level of applied theory before Political Economics can serve as a reliable tool for the framing of policy. Among the issues requiring further study I mention, e.g., the proper balance between what in OEK (pages 148-50) was labeled as "manipulative" and "command" controls respectively, a distinction related to, though not identical with, that between indirect and direct controls; the differential measures suitable for eliciting adequate response from different socio-economic strata; administrative techniques concerning the timing and sizing of intervention; and last but not least, the political problems that public control of the economic process raises in democratic societies. It is needless to add that the answers to these questions are bound to vary with the level of economic development and political maturity.

2. The Choice of Goals

I should like to conclude this essay with another word about the focal point of Political Economics: the choice of macro-goals. Earlier it was stressed that Political Economics qua Economics must accept the stipulated goal or sets of compatible goals as data. This would be no different if, as economists, we were not wedded to "scientific value relativism," but would be prepared to commit ourselves to a definite hierarchy of goals with the apex of a *summum bonum*, as offered by rivalling theologies and philosophies. Even then our problem would be the suitability of the means rather than the validation of the ends.

So the problem presents itself as long as we are engaged in the preliminary work of instrumental analyses. But in order to advance to the level of predictive theory, we must first pass through the practical stage in which the holders of political authority are to modify the original institutional environment in accord with their instrumental findings. This original environment, conceptualized as the structure of the initial state, revealed itself as a logical constraint in the analysis of the goal-adequate path. It is, however, no less a practical constraint when the instrumental findings are to be applied. To give an example, it is a feasible task for analysis to establish the path, the behavioral and motivational conditions and even the controls suitable to transform a primitive subsistence economy into a mature industrial system. But when we ponder the practical application of the controls thus designed, we may come to the conclusion that the institutional transformation required would have to be purchased at the price of a social revolution which, rather than setting the primitive society on the road to development, might well throw it back to a still lower level.

What we encounter here is a conflict between a particular macro-goal and the socio-economic environment from which the path toward the goal is to start. Stated in general terms, all macro-goals are not intrinsically compatible with any prevailing order of social relations. Whenever a conflict arises, we are compelled to choose between abandoning the goal or the existing order, the latter at the peril of applying means which may defeat the end.

Value absolutists may brush aside such pragmatic considerations, but I must admit that they govern my own thinking as expressed in the concluding chapter of OEK. Though I leave no doubt that the instrumental method is applicable to the elaboration of the means suitable to the attainment of *any* macro-goal, be it the size and composition of aggregate output, the level of resource utilization, the rate of growth, or the order of distribution of income and wealth, I have confined the practical test cases selected for detailed investigation to two: full utilization of resources and balanced growth. It is true, these particular goals pose a number of problems of great analytical interest. But my choice was ultimately determined by political considerations. These are the only macro-goals aiming at which is fully compatible with the institutional environment of mature capitalism.

The reasons for this belief are easy to state. Decentralized decision-making based in private ownership of the means of production being the core of capitalist organization, instrumental controls will be effective within this framework only if the aim for which they are applied meets with the *consensus* of the large majority of micro-units. Such consensus can indeed be anticipated for the two goals selected, since extending the opportunity for the utilization of present resources (stabilization) and assuring the absorption of newly accruing ones at a rising rate of productivity (balanced growth) seem to offer benefits to all.

I am aware that even in the pursuit of these goals, certain conflicts of interest may arise between particular sectors and social strata of the economy. But the ensuing objections to public interference with the *functional* performance of the economy are certainly minor compared with the likely breakdown of consensus in the face of *structural* transformations such as the central planning of investment and output would require, not to speak of a fundamental redistribution of income and wealth. Fortunately, the politically feasible goals – stabilization and balanced growth – seem to satisfy the basic requirements for restoring to the market of mature capitalism that minimum of "order" in the inclusive sense defined above, on which the preservation of the fabric of Western society may well depend.

But it should be stressed once more that "prudence" in the choice of macro-goals does not limit the universal validity of the scientific procedure of Political Economics, nor can such prudence itself be vindicated on scientific grounds. It expresses a value judgment emulating peaceful evolution even at the expense of uncompromising justice. If this reveals a conservative undercurrent in my thinking, as some critics have insinuated, I must bow to this as to the opposite charge that my advocacy of political control of industrial capitalism "gives aid and comfort to men who are neither wise nor gentle." Since the political economist contrives his research object as much as he observes it, he too is exposed to the risks of decision-making.

SOME NOTES ON REALITY-ORIENTATION IN CONTEMPORARY SOCIETIES

by

ARVID BRODERSEN

Alfred Schutz was not a political scientist in the conventional sense of the term, nor a political writer, stating his positions to the varying policy problems of his time. Yet his general social theory and philosophy, a body of thought on which he was working with persevering consistency throughout his entire scholarly life, contains at its core conceptions and categories that are eminently applicable to an analysis of the human polity, and which he himself on several occasions in fact applied to such an analysis.[1]

For this purpose he took as his point of reference the general proposition that every human society carries within it an *interpretation of itself,* an ensemble of notions, ideas, images and observations which as a whole inform the meaning-structure of the particular society in question. For illustration, Schutz on occasion quotes a passage from Eric Voegelin, with whom he shared much of his thinking during a life-long friendship.

Human society is not merely a fact, or an event, in the external world to be studied by an observer like a natural phenomenon. Though it has externality as one of its important components, it is as a whole a little world, a cosmion, illuminated with meaning from within by the human beings who continuously create and bear it as the mode and condition of their self-realization. It is illuminated through an elaborate symbolism, in various degrees of compactness and differentiation – from rite, through myth, to theory – and this symbolism illuminates it with meaning in so far as the symbols make the internal structure of such a cosmion, the relations between its members and groups of members, as well as its existence as a whole, transparent for the mystery of human existence.[2]

Within this general proposition Schutz makes two distinctions which to him are all-important to the sociological analysis. First, what we have in sum-

[1] Cf. for example the essays, "The Homecomer" (1944), "The Well-Informed Citizen" (1946), "Equality and the Meaning Structure of the Social World" (1955), "Some Equivocations of the Notions of Responsibility" (1957) – all reproduced in *Collected Papers*, Vol. II, The Hague 1964.
[2] *The New Science of Politics*, Chicago 1952, p. 27.

mary fashion called the "ensemble of notions, ideas, etc." includes a great variety of symbols, some denoting pure fantasies, some religious, cultural or political myths, while some refer to noetic data, and these again of varying degrees of closeness to factual reality. Voegelin hints at this when he refers to the sequence "from rite, through myth, to theory." A full catalogue of any particular symbol system, especially in the case of complex societies, would contain a staggering variety of constructs, and would (if it were worked out in detail) indeed portray the basic outline of the particular society and culture under investigation. However, the concern of Schutz was essentially a different one. Primarily interested in a general social theory, he focussed his attention on the distinction between two fundamental types of symbol-formation: the non- or prenoetic common-sense self-interpretation of a society, present in the minds of workaday people; and on the other hand, the noetic theory and knowledge about society pursued by the social scientist through the critical and systematic exercise of his discipline. Schutz referred to this feature of his thought as a theory of "the social distribution of knowledge." There are, according to this, highly significant relationships between the two universes of knowledge, the common-sense interpretation of reality, "taken for granted" by the general population, and the scientific interpretation achieved by observers professionally committed to critical procedures. The social scientists will use the "knowledge" of the general population *as their data* for three different operations: the first aiming at deriving tools and concepts for their own, objective type of interpretation by refining such popular notions as are found usable for this purpose (the "Aristotelian method"); the second aiming at a description and understanding of society as it exists and is represented in its particular universe of self-interpretation; and the third aiming at a critical assessment of the latter (or significant components of this) with regard to (a) its factual accuracy where this is verifiable by the standards of objective knowledge; and (b) its functionality or dysfunctionality as measured by the basic value-system of the society (ethical norms, political ideals, etc.).

In the present paper we shall be concerned with the third problem area. By breaking it down into two "subareas", as indicated above, we are serving mainly a purpose of logical exposition; in actual fact, i.e., in the context of our culture, there is an intimate connection, indeed a near-identity, between the two by virtue of our placing a highly positive value on objective truth as such and on a secure reality-orientation as a fundamental posture of members of our society. We consider the "well-informed citizen" indispensable to the soundness of the sociopolitical order to which we are committed.

There is an abundance of literature on this subject. Indeed, Western social scientists as well as countless private and governmental agencies constantly take upon themselves the responsibility of informing the public on all kinds of matters, economic, political, cultural, etc., of concern to the citizen in his own daily life and for his intelligent participation in the political process. Less ample is the literature dealing with the epistemological problems of such information policies, especially the resistance entrained in people's minds against correcting erroneous or distorted views. A recent study of this particular problem, Alfred Sauvy's book, *Mythologie de notre temps* (Paris 1965), examines a series of "myths" and misinterpretations current mainly in France, but in some cases existing in other western societies as well. There is, for instance, the notion that "the war will be short", firmly believed by most Frenchmen before both World Wars, and contributing to the psychological climate which, to some extent, facilitated the outbreak of hostilities. (A similar misconception was recently noted in regard to the American public's – and even some government officials' – views on the Vietnam war, in its earlier stages.)

Then there is the more specifically French *idée fixe*, that "Germany is going to pay" (l'Allemagne paiera). Behind this there lurks, as Sauvy demonstrates, another myth: that of "money." The fact of the matter is that payments of this magnitude (in the hundreds of billions) cannot be made entirely in money, but largely *in natura,* by huge deliveries of goods and services, and the reparations, in any case, will play havoc with the economy of the receiving country itself. A few clearsighted men saw this coming, but "they were smothered by the myth".

A particularly fertile field of myth-making to which Sauvy devotes much attention, is that of the economy in general. People's conceptions of prices and of price trends frequently contradict the facts. A popular myth says "prices never go down", which only means that up-trends are noted, down-trends not, although historically the severe deflation of the Thirties occurred in the life-time of a large part of the population.

Sauvy deals with many other economic myths, such as that of "the good old days", the notion that people lived better in former times; the belief somewhat inconsistent with this, that people today work less than formerly, whereas in fact the number of real working hours or years per one thousand inhabitants is higher than in the old pre-industrial age; the notion, fondly held by the French, that "France is a garden", meaning: the country is economically self-sufficient and not really dependent on trade with the rest of the world – a myth which he disposes of in short order.

Sauvy's examples (he also cites a series from demography) all have in common that they are falsifiable by supplying expert opinion. They may be hard to root out, having been reinforced by long habit, but should yield to persistent efforts of public information. Consequently, the course recommended by Sauvy, in the classical spirit of Enlightenment, is an "ideotherapy" to be administered by concerted actions of specialists in various fields and by agencies modeled on such precedents as the Economic Information Unit created by the British government in the early post-war period.

However, there are other types of myths which, being rooted in deeper psychological strata, generally do not respond to simple, rational cures like the ones Sauvy has in mind. Many of them are of a *political* nature, and their impact on society is often far stronger and far more critical than that of the demonstrable misconceptions in a field such as economics. They require a more searching – and more interesting – type of analysis, probing into the psychodynamics of political and politically potent ideas and into the relations between people inside a given society as well as between people of different societies. On the following pages we propose to offer, not a fullscale analysis of this kind, but a few preliminary notes on some problems connected with it, and, in one or two cases, some partial answers. The example to be principally considered is the case of Nazi (and to some extent post-Nazi) Germany. More by way of introduction we shall refer to certain other contemporary Western societies.

A single fact-of-life and of everyday experience which perhaps more than any other is active in shaping the political self-interpretation of a historically (i.e., nationally) mature population is the latter's numerical size and, as a concomitant of this, its power as a nation, both in itself and among other nations of the world. The age of imperialism before the two great wars and that of neoimperialism as well as neointernationalism after the second, combined with the vastly increased impact of global mass communication, have inevitably brought home to people everywhere, and particularly in Europe, in America (North and South), and in the sphere of Soviet dominance, the stark fact of the difference between big-power and small-power nations. This has long since been thoroughly assimilated by the consciousness of some nations, more recently by that of others. A recent case is that of the United States whose ascendancy to great (indeed super-) power status has been accompanied by a still growing public awareness of the fact, finding expression in everyday phrases, such as "we are the greatest power in the world", "we are the richest nation", etc. Another recent case is that of the United Kingdom, where the loss of a once great empire has forced the public mind to entertain a painful reshaping of the nation's self-image as a political and economic power. Cases of historically long-established self-interpretations of this kind are found, for instance, among the numerically small nations of Europe, such as Switzerland and the Scandinavian countries. (Belgium and the Netherlands are cases apart, having been, until recently, colonial nations.)

How do societies, in their conscious or subconscious public mind, deal with these acknowledged facts-of-life? Does power in itself, great or small, rising or diminishing, affect their self-estimation? A broad first answer is suggested by W. G. Sumner's theory – or rather, discovery – of ethnocentrism and the ingroup-outgroup pattern. According to this a social body will typically tend to attach a positive evaluation to itself, and to view other bodies (outgroups) with feelings of estrangement, if not hostility. This is particularly true of the smaller or primary groups, but recent empirical research, conducted under UNESCO auspices, has proven it to hold also in the case of entire nations, regardless of their size.[3] From this it would appear that a strongly positive evaluation of a nation other than one's own represents an exception from the normal posture. This is especially the case where a national outgroup is held in higher esteem than the ingroup, the case of what might be called "ethno-excentricism". Nevertheless, such "exceptions" do occur, and in some instances with interesting consequences. A Swiss historian, Karl Schmid, has recently published a book on this problem with regard to his own country, *Unbehagen im Kleinstaat* (The Small Nation and its Discontents), Zurich 1963. Referring to a series of Swiss writers – C. F. Meyer, H. F. Amiel, Jakob Schaffner, Max Frisch, and Jacob Burckhardt, he demonstrates how the fact that Switzerland shares its main languages, German and French, and much of its culture with large and powerful neighboring states, has caused some of its intellectual leaders to look upon the latter rather than their own nation as their reference groups, to which they aspire to belong. In the case of Schaffner, this discontent with his small home country led to outright ideological treason; he chose to turn Nazi during the war. The much earlier case of C. F. Meyer is that of a writer who sublimated his longing for "historical greatness" and for identification with the "power and glory" of the Second Reich in artful historical novels and poetry. Both are clearly exceptional cases in a nation whose ingroup image generally is unusually self-centered despite the diversity of its composition, and despite its location in the gravitational fields of

---

[3] Cf. W. Buchanan and H. Cantril, *How Nations See Each Other,* Urbana 1953. Jean Piaget, in a related study, found the bias toward the positive identification with the national ingroup to be typically formed during a relatively early phase of the child's personality development. Cf. J. Piaget, "The Development in Children of the Idea of the Homeland and of Relations with Other Countries," *International Social Science Bulletin* (Unesco, Paris), Fall, 1951, Vol. III, No. 2.

large kindred populations. The case of Jacob Burckhardt is a school book example of this general Swiss attitude. He lived and worked all his life in his native city, Basle, turning down the most flattering calls to highly prestigeful chairs at German universities. He consciously cultivated his Swiss "provincialism", and eloquently described its superiority, in cultural as well as political terms, over the contemporary national life of Germany, which for all its bigness and power was marred by raw commercialism, militarism, and lack of individual freedom as well as of good taste. In his books and letters Burckhardt never tires of praising the virtues of the small nations, as for instance in this passage from his famous *Reflections on World History*:

The small state exists in order that there be a spot in the world, where the largest possible portion of the subjects will be citizens in the full meaning of the term . . . The small state possesses nothing at all, except the real actual freedom, whereby it ideally altogether compensates for the enormous advantages of the big state, even the latter's power.

Here and in numerous other passages Burckhardt describes the ideal-type self-interpretation of the small European democracies in general, except for the fact that these have in the course of their more recent sociopolitical development come to place a heavier emphasis than the 19th century Swiss patrician on such values as social justice and egalitarian distribution of income. The public attitude predominant in these nations by consequence of such self-imagery, and, at least in part, its successful realization, is a certain civic and national pride sometimes bordering on smugness toward the outside world, and often taking on the color of provincial coziness and self-sufficiency. With this goes, as Harry Eckstein has shown in a recent study of politics in Norway,[4] a high degree of political cohesiveness and continuity, despite the existing cleavages of parties and interest groups in the society. The very smallness and resulting intimacy (primary-group or "family" character) of the latter seems to contribute to this relatively wholesome state of affairs. It probably also was one of the main reasons why the population stood the test of the Nazi efforts at breaking up its sociopolitical structure during the occupation in 1940–1945. It is of interest to note that the tiny minority which fell for the Hitlerite temptations was led by men who already for a long time had been harboring illusions of national power and grandeur quite out of line with the reality-oriented self-image of the population as a whole. Harking back to ancient history, they wanted to revive the Viking spirit of conquest, and recalling the loss of the old Norse colonies, such as Iceland and Greenland, to

[4] Harry Eckstein, *Cohesion and Division in a Democracy*, Princeton 1965.

Denmark, they were dreaming of a new North Sea Empire of their own making.

Among the several factors which immunized the general population against the "Nordic" mythology of the Nazis was the striking impression, in the popular mind, of the contrast in style of the power-images projected by the two rivalling nations, Nazi Germany and Great Britain. The small Northern peoples were traditionally very familiar with the British style; they, and particularly the Norwegians, were (and still are) confirmed Anglophiles. Among the characteristics that impressed them (as well as many other nations around the world) were the reserved, quiet self-assurance, the "silence" of British power, the unobtrusiveness of its language, the clear separation of the ingroup sphere and the rest of the world ("foreigners"), often giving the impression of indifference, if not arrogance, but leaving the others to themselves (no probing curiosity!), and intent on the rules of fair play. By contrast, the Nazi style by its stridency and agressivity evoked the suspicions of an underlying desperate insecurity – in psychological terms the very opposite of real power. And, paradoxically, the very fact that the Nazis, in line with an older and worthier German tradition, took a positive interest in the Northern peoples, studied their cultural heritage, and passionately wanted to identify themselves with these, caused the latter to reject them all the more vehemently. Nor was it lost on these "most-favored" nations, that the Nazis at the same time were taking a quite different line, one of murderous hostility, against some other peoples, large and small, over whom they held sway.

This brings us finally to the problem of Nazi Germany itself, and especially to that of the reception of the Nazi mythology as a part of the nation's self-interpretation during the Hitler regime. In the public vocabulary of the current postwar period in Germany few phrases recur with more frequency and regularity than *die Bewältigung der Vergangenheit* ("getting finished with the Hitlerite past"). The political and psychological pressure to achieve this, by way of rational, intellectual explanation of what really happened, and why; by way of emotional catharsis, of honestly facing up to guilt as well as seeking, wherever justifiable, exculpation in the eyes of the world and the nation's own conscience – the pressure to achieve this is enormous. So is the national effort, if measured merely by the number of words devoted to it. But the task is far from finished yet, and there are strong counterpressures to hold it back. Nor is the quality of the work done of a particularly high order, apart from a few exceptions.

The mental blockage constraining the public conscience from facing up to the full reality of the past constitutes a special problem by itself in

Germany today. Clear-eyed observers are inevitably aware of it, yet so far little serious study has been devoted to it. All the more significant is therefore the appearance and the resounding public success of a recent book in which two leading psychoanalysts and social scientists are coming to grips with the problem: Alexander and Margarete Mitscherlich, *Die Unfähigkeit zu trauern* (The Incapacity for Mourning) Munich 1967. The title sums up the authors' main thesis: the public conscience, stunned into apathy, is incapable of mourning, that is: of caring and being emotionally concerned with the past, and instead is turning mindlessly to the business at hand – hard work, money making, and the sensual pleasures of an affluent society. (Here, perhaps, lie the deepest psychological roots of the "German economic miracle" of the postwar period.) The book merits a detailed examination which the present context unfortunately does not permit.[5] Suffice it to say that the very existence of such a study, and of the intelligent concern from which it springs, may be taken as a sign of an awakening readiness among present-day Germans to face the realities of their past, and to regain the "capacity for mourning".

However, not this, but rather the matter of Nazi Germany as such, is our subject here. And it is fitting to ask: what do we really know about German society during that period? To be sure, the political and historical data are on record in massive detail. There is an ample literature on the Nazi period in a long series of aspects: on the police apparatus; on the armed forces; on the economy; on the propaganda machine; on what happened to the schools, the universities, the churches; the labor unions and other organizations; the professions; and so forth. Also, the various aspects of Nazi terrorism and repression: the persecution and the systematic extermination of Jewish people; the so-called "euthanasia" program, destroying thousands of crippled and mentally ill people; the horrors of the concentration camps, of the mass deportations, of the slave labor system, and so on – all of this has been described in countless studies and memoirs. Further, the cases of resistance against the regime by individuals and by groups, climaxed in several attempts on Hitler's life, have been treated in numerous publications. There is, however, one subject which so far has been almost entirely neglected if not forgotten, namely the matter of the vast masses of the population who were neither among the special victims of the regime, nor heroes opposing it, but who actively supported it or passively obeyed its commands. In other words, about the inside story of the

---

[5] Kurt R. Eissler, the American psychoanalyst, paid tribute to the work of the Mitscherlichs in the essay "Zur Notlage unserer Zeit" in *Psyche,* Vol. XXII, No. 9–11, pp. 641–657.

"ordinary" German people in general we know relatively far less than about most other aspects of the Hitler period. Yet this is for a true understanding of the nation's political and social behavior and of its psychological attitudes at the time the most important of all problems, especially with regard to the burning issue of the postwar years: the people's effort of "getting finished with its past". The ignorance in this vital respect is certainly not accidental, nor is it exclusively due to the nation's inability or unwillingness to recall painful realities. The task of a penetrating analysis depends in this instance on a series of conditions which were singularly hard of fulfillment during the circumstances: it would have to be conducted *during the course of the period in question*, a current, contemporary study of the social scene in Germany from the rise of the regime all the way to its end; it would require a keen and detached mind, a capacity for objective observation, and for systematic intellectual penetration. Very few individuals possess the skills and training of this kind even under normal circumstances, still less under those of a terroristic regime and a total war. A good many people must have kept diaries during the Hitler years, and these may be of some interest as source material, but by and large they would be purely personal, dealing with events in the private lives of the writers. Very few have been published. Studies of a more general nature are infrequent, and usually inadequate, as they rely on retrospective and hence selective reconstruction from memory or from secondary sources.

All the more to be welcomed is the extremely rare case of a writer and a book which fulfill all the requisite conditions in this forbidding field of research, and thereby contribute genuine insights and solid knowledge about the subject. Such a case is Wanda von Baeyer-Katte, *Das Zerstörende in der Politik* (The Destructive in Politics), Heidelberg 1958, a landmark in the literature on Nazi Germany. The fact that it has so far failed to gain anything like the public attention it deserves is due in part to its intellectual quality – it is a subtle, tightly reasoned, and compact book – and in part, one suspects, to the utter frankness with which it treats sensitive subject matter. The author, a trained, practising psychologist, already in 1931, when the Nazis first entered the political scene in force,[6] started making systematic observations, mostly among middle class people in a large Bavarian city. She continued her research during the entire Nazi period and well into the postwar years, when she attended the Nuremberg War Crimes Trials as an observer and reporter. Her book presents the essence of her findings, based on a vast amount of primary material, collected and interpreted over a span of twenty-seven years.

[6] Having won more than a hundred seats in a Reichstag election.

What the author is concerned with is neither indictment nor exculpation of her countrymen, but in her own words, "a conceptual clarification and 'demythification' (*Entmythifizierung*) of mental processes under political opinion pressure". This approach makes the book an exceptionally rich source for the type of analysis we are after in the present context. Within the space available here we must, however, limit ourselves to one or two examples for illustration.

One of her main theses, to which she devotes the long opening chapters, concerns the conjunction of two major figures in German society: the non- or apolitical man, and the "cultural pessimist" (Kulturpessimist). Middle class people were, in their masses, predominantly apolitical, disinterested in public affairs, confused and repelled by the complexities and controversies of the political scene, particularly during the last, stormy period of the Weimar Republic. Turning away, they were everything but "well-informed citizens". When Hitler arrived on the scene they were forced to take a stand, and many of them, before they knew it, joined "the movement" as activists or as fellow-travellers. A wave of political enthusiasm swept the formerly apathetic masses. Why? The psychology of this mass behavior is complex, and our author goes into it in depth in chapters on the Nazi family, on the impact of Hitler as a speaker, and so on. Elsewhere in the book, Dr. v. Baeyer-Katte has contributed an important new insight regarding the *role of the "cultural pessimist"* in this process of politization.

The *Kulturpessimist* is, or was, a familiar figure on the German intellectual scene. His ancestry goes back to such eminent thinkers as Nietzsche and more recently to Oswald Spengler, the prophet of decline and fall of Western civilization. On lower levels the tradition was continued by large numbers of contemporary intellectuals and quasi-intellectuals. And the philosophy was now directly applied to the interpretation of the present age and its crisis. It was an eschatological philosophy, or rather, mythology, announcing the end of Western culture and its values, the hopelessness of its causes and the withering of its power of survival. According to the author's diagnosis, the *Kulturpessimist* acted in the German situation of the Thirties as a most dangerous virus carrier, spreading the contagion of this mythology among the masses of apolitical citizens, in turn frightened and elated, with the effect that many of them, seeing no future for the old order of their world, embraced Nazism, which to their blinded eyes appeared at least to offer something "new", something "strong". The author describes a series of individual cases where this happened.

It was a deadly disease, and all the more so, because it spurred utterly destructive and self-destructive forces in the mental makeup of the nation.

The material ruins which later were to cover large parts of Europe, the millions of murdered, dead and wounded people, were all anticipated in this deformation of the German mind itself. The psychological processes which led to this are analyzed by our author in exemplary fashion. It is a story of a political myth conquering a nation in crisis, with what appalling consequences we know only too well.

In sum, the examples here cited from recent literature present various approaches of inquiry into the self-interpretation of societies with regard to its structure and contents, as well as functionality or dysfunctionality, as measured by the consequent patterns of political behavior.

THE ECLIPSE OF REALITY

by

ERIC VOEGELIN

By an act of imagination man can shrink himself to a self that is "condemned to be free". To this shrunken or contracted self, as we call it, God is dead, the past is dead, the present is the flight from the self's non-essential facticity toward being what it is not, the future is the field of possibles among which the self must choose its project of being beyond mere facticity, and freedom is the necessity of making a choice that will determine the self's own being. The freedom of the contracted self is the self's damnation not to be able not to be free.

The contraction of his humanity to a self imprisoned in its selfhood is the characteristic of so-called modern man. It becomes recognizable as a personal and social process in the eighteenth century, when man begins to refer to himself, not as Man, but as a Self, an Ego, an I, an Individual, a Subject, a Transcendental Subject, a Transcendental Consciousness, and so forth; and it reaches an intense clarity of its own structure in the twentieth century, when a Jean-Paul Sartre, whose formulae I have used in describing the contracted self, submits this type of deficient existence to the analysis of his *L'être et le néant*.

As neither the man who engages in deforming himself to a self ceases to be a man; nor the surrounding reality of God and man, world and society does change its structure; nor the relations between man and his surrounding reality can be abolished; frictions between the shrunken self and reality are bound to develop. The man who suffers from the disease of contraction, however, is not inclined to leave the prison of his selfhood, in order to remove the frictions. He rather will put his imagination to further work and surround the imaginary self with an imaginary reality apt to confirm the self in its pretense of reality; he will create a Second Reality, as the phenomenon is called, in order to screen the First Reality of common experience from his view. The frictions consequently, far from being removed, will grow into a general conflict between the world of his imagination and the real world.

This conflict can be traced from the discrepancy of contents between realities imagined and experienced, through the act of projecting an imaginary reality, to the man who indulges in the act. First, on the level of contents, a reality projected by imagination may deform or omit certain areas of reality experienced; reality projected, we may say, obscures or eclipses First Reality. Ascending from contents to the act, then, one can discern a man's intention to eclipse reality. This intention can become manifest in a large variety of forms, ranging from the straight lie concerning a fact to the subtler lie of arranging a context in such a manner that the omission of the fact will not be noticed; or from the construction of a system that, by its form, suggests its partial view as the whole of reality to its author's refusal to discuss the premises of the system in terms of reality experienced. Beyond the act, finally, we reach the actor, that is the man who has committed the act of deforming his humanity to a self and now lets the shrunken self eclipse his own full reality. He will deny his humanity and insist he is nothing but his shrunken self; he will deny ever having experienced the reality of common experience; he will deny that anybody could have a fuller perception of reality than he allows his self; in brief, he will set the contracted self as a model for himself as well as for everybody else. Moreover, his insistence on conformity will be aggressive – and in this aggressiveness there betrays itself the anxiety and alienation of the man who has lost contact with reality.

But what is Reality? Moving with conventional language, we had to use the term in more than one sense, and the several meanings seem to be at cross-purposes: A reality projected by imagination, it is true, is not the reality of common experience. Nevertheless, a man's act of deforming himself is as real as the man who commits it, and his act of projecting a Second Reality is as real as the First Reality it intends to hide from view. The imaginator, his act of imagination, and the effects the act has on himself as well as on other people, thus, can claim to be real. Some imaginative constructions of history, designed to shield the contracted self, as for instance those of Comte, or Hegel, or Marx, even have grown into social forces of such strength that their conflicts with reality form a substantial part of global politics in our time. The man with a contracted self is as much of a power in society and history as an ordinary man, and sometimes a stronger one. The conflict *with* reality turns out to be a disturbance *within* reality.

The multiple meanings of reality are not caused by loose usage of the term, but reflect the structure of reality itself. To be conscious of something is an experiential process polarized by the cognitive tension between the knower and the known. The several meanings of reality can be made intelligible by going through the successive acts of reflection on the process of consciousness: If, in a first act of reflection on the process, we turn toward the pole of the known, the object of cognition will be the something we acknowledge as real. If, in a second act, we turn toward the pole of the knower, the human carrier of cognition as well as his images and language symbols referring to the known, will move into the position of the something to be acknowledged as real. And if, in a third act, we turn toward the experiential process and the cognitive tension as a whole, the process will become the something we acknowledge as real. Following the acts of reflection, the meaning of reality moves from the known to the knower and ultimately to the process that is structured by the participation of, and by the cognitive tension between the knower and the known in the experience. The consciousness of reality becomes a process within reality.

Only on the level of reflection established by the third act there will come into view the problem of disturbances in the process. In the common sense attitude of everyday life, we take the experiential process as undisturbed for granted: The knower refers to the known through the images and language symbols engendered by the event or process that we call experience, and living in this attitude we assume the experiences will be reliable and the symbols engendered will truly refer to the known. Nor will the philosopher surrender common sense when he engages in reflective thought, but will assume reality to be knowable in truth – even to the limit of knowing in truth that some things are unknowable. In Hellenic philosophy, where the problem becomes thematic for the first time, the term *aletheia* is burdened, therefore, with the double meaning of Truth and Reality; and even a speculation that deviates in its course as widely from common sense as Hegel's does, starts from a reality known by sense perception with truth and certainty. This common-sense assumption concerning the truth of images, on which the main line of philosophy is based, will have to be qualified, however, when we encounter persons who produce imagery at variance with the images supposed to be true. Imagination, it appears, can cut loose from reality and produce the sets of images that we call Second Reality because they pretend to refer to reality though in fact they do not; and, setting aside the phenomena of error or of imperfectly articulated experience, imagination will cut loose in this manner, when the imagining man has developed centers of resistance to participating in reality, including his own, so that his imagery will no longer be true but

express reality in terms of his resistance to it. We are faced with the phenomenon of a cognitive tension of consciousness that will retain its form
of referring to reality, even when in substance the contact with reality has
been lost for one reason or another. Moreover, since imagination can eclipse
but not abolish reality, not only the form of consciousness will be retained,
but the whole reality of common experience that apparently has been lost
will remain present to consciousness, though its presence will now be
marked by various indices of non-reality according to the character and
degree of the disturbance. For reality eclipsed but not abolished will exert
a pressure to emerge into consciousness, and thereby to achieve full status
of reality, that must be countered by acts of suppression – a reality to be
eclipsed can be relegated to the limbo of oblivion that we call the unconscious; or it can remain semi-conscious as a disturbing background to
reality imagined; or it can be consciously denied the status of reality, as in
the dogma of no-God; or it can induce a state of revolt, because it cannot
be denied but is sensed to be hostile, as in certain Gnostic speculations. A
man deformed, thus, can well be conscious of his deformation, and indeed
may experience his existence as a hell in which he is condemned to act as if
he had the freedom of a man undeformed.

The major thinkers who suffer from the compulsion to deform their
humanity to a self are never quite unaware of what they are doing. From the
eighteenth to the twentieth century, the stream of Second Realities is paralleled, therefore, by a stream of self-analysis. There are the surprisingly
frank confessions of the intellectual tricks employed in accomplishing the
imaginative feat of the moment; there are the conscientious explanations
why the present Second Reality had to be produced in opposition to those
already encumbering the public scene; and there are the shrewd inquiries
into the author's self that compels him to do what, at the same time, he
senses to be a misdeed. Self-analysis is so much the accompaniment of
imaginative projections that the age of Second Realities has become the
great age of Psychology. A peculiar compound of insight and intellectual
dishonesty has developed; and this honest dishonesty has become an enduring twilight mode of existence, replacing the clear existential rhythms
of degenerative fall and regenerative repentance. A character of compulsive
action against better knowledge, very marked for instance in Marx and
Nietzsche, pervades the process of deformation and must be considered in
part responsible for certain oddities of its historical contour – such as the
tiresome elaboration of problems into irrelevant detail, the resumption of
problems exploded long ago, epigonal revivals of positions one would have
thought abandoned for good, in brief: a compulsive repetitiveness that defies

all rational predictions of an end when the problems are exhausted. When, for instance, an imaginative outburst of such grandeur as the Hegelian attempt at salvation through conceptual speculation (*Begriffsspekulation*) had run its course; when it, furthermore, had been followed by Max Stirner's exposure of the contracted self in its naked misery as the motivating core of all current philosophies of history, projective psychologies, and new humanisms; when, thus, the Second Realities protecting the self had been torn to shreds, and nothing was left to be done but to abandon the contracted self and stop the deformation of humanity; one might have expected *Der Einzige und sein Eigentum* (1844) to have a sobering effect on the intellectuals engaged in the game of deformation. But nothing of the sort happened. On the contrary, at the time when Stirner wrote and published *Der Einzige,* the young Marx prepared a new philosophy of history, improved on Feuerbach's projective psychology, developed one more humanism, and imagined a revolution that would metamorphose man into a Superman and thus redeem man, society, and history from the evil of alienation. That is not to say that we cannot discern an advance of insight through the cycles and epicycles of the process; today we certainly know more about its problems than the thinkers of the eighteenth century possibly could know. Nevertheless, neither the recognition of advancing insight, nor the increased sophistication of analysis or the aesthetic satisfactions it grants, must blind us to the fact that Sartre's *moi* of 1943 is still lost in the same dead-end as Stirner's *Ich* of 1844. The process has run itself to death, both metaphorically and literally, and yet it does not stop. Modern man has become a bore.

I have stressed the compulsive repetitiveness of the process, the atmosphere of slaves treading the mill without hope of escape. Perhaps I have stressed it too strongly. Existence in the twilight zone of projective imagination and self-analytical insight, it is true, pertinaciously preserves its structure during its long course from the middle of the eighteenth century to the present. Nevertheless, the manifestations of the constant mode of existence are more than individuals of a species, and their sequence in time is more than a series of interchangeable events. For deformed existence has its dynamics; and the dynamics intrudes a distinct pattern into the course. Let us list the rules of the dynamics:

(1) When imaginators of Second Realities proceed to act on their imaginative assumptions and try to make the world of common experience conform to their respective dreams, the areas of friction with reality will rapidly increase in number and size.

(2) As the world of common experience can be eclipsed but not abolished, it

will resist its deformation and, in its turn, force the imaginators to revise their Second Realities. Imaginative projecting will not be given up as senseless, but specific projects will be changed in detail or replaced by new ones. During the period under discussion, revisionism is a common phenomenon, caused by the refusal to dissolve the contracted self and to stop projecting.

(3) When conflicts with reality compel revisions with some frequency over a period, the activity of projecting can pass from a phase of comparatively naïve indulgence to one of a more critical occupation with the standards of projects. For a Second Reality must, on the one hand, satisfy the requirements of the contracted self and, on the other hand, contain enough uneclipsed reality not to be ignored as a crackpot scheme by the contemporaries. There is a remarkable advance from the comparatively loose anthropologies and philosophies of history of the eighteenth century to the tight interlocking of Hegel's *Phaenomenologie, Logik, Philosophie des Rechts,* and *Philosophie der Geschichte.*

(4) When a more or less stable balance between the contracted self and satisfactory Second Realities has been achieved – as it has by the work of Comte, Hegel, and Marx – the interest can shift from the construction of further Second Realities to the problems of deformation. The twilight mode of existence can become an independent field of study.

Under pressure from the dynamics just adumbrated, the process of deformation has developed a recognizable and intelligible pattern in history: There are to be noted two periods, of about equal length, marked by the shift of accent from the projection of new Second Realities to the inquiry into the type of existence that engages in their projection. In the century from Turgot, Kant, and Condorcet to Hegel, Comte, and Marx, the weight lies on the construction of philosophies of history, of the great designs that will justify the deformation of humanity as the meaning and end of history, and assure the contracted self of its righteousness when it imposes itself on society and the world at large. In the century from Kierkegaard and Stirner, through Nietzsche and Freud, to Heidegger and Sartre, the weight shifts toward the inquiry concerning deformed existence. The early philosophers of history and the late existentialist thinkers, thus, are more intimately related than the surface differences of their fields of interest would suggest. For the shift of weight means that the early constructs, purposely designed to eclipse historical reality, have performed their task so well that, to the late-comers in the movement of deformation, history is, if not altogether, at least sufficiently dead not to disturb by memories of a fuller humanity the concern with the contracted self.

To the texture of man's existence in general belong the moods. We must advert to the issue of the moods, because the age of the contracted self has engendered a whole sheaf of neologisms which express fluctuations of mood, such as *optimism, pessimism, egotism, altruism, egomania, monoma-*

nia, and *nihilism* – a fact which suggests that existence compulsively deformed has a mood peculiarly its own. Moreover, the dynamics of deformed existence has caused an historical polarization of the fluctuations similar to the shift of accent from the projection of Second Realities to self-analysis. For the shift of accents is accompanied by a change of mood from eighteenth century exhilaration by the projects of building a new world, and confidence of being equal to the task, to twentieth century disorientation, frustration, despair, and sense of damnation in face of the accumulated results of projecting.

We can approach the question of the peculiar mood through Hegel's recall, in his *Philosophy of History* (593), of the general excitement aroused by the events of the French Revolution:

As long as the sun stands in heaven and the planets revolve around it, has it not happened that man stood on his head, that is on his thought, and built reality in conformity to it. Anaxagoras had been the first to say that Nous governs the world; but only now has man gained the insight that thought should govern spiritual reality. This was a splendid sunrise; all thinking beings shared in celebrating the epoch. The age was ruled by a sublime emotion, the world trembled as the enthusiasm of the spirit *(Geist)* pervaded it, as if only now the divine had been truly reconciled to the world.

The text is of particular value to our purpose because it is couched in one of the several languages of deformation. The question of the new languages will be treated in a later context; let it suffice for the present that coining a new language, either by giving new meanings to familiar terms or by inventing new technical terms, is one of the most effective devices for eclipsing reality. That Hegel's recall is written in one of these newspeaks makes for certain difficulties of understanding, but it also makes us more sharply aware of the unity of texture, of the style that characterizes deformed existence from the compulsive deformation of humanity, through the deformation of language and the projection of Second Realities, to the odd moods that accompany the operation.

At first reading, the text seems to be a piece of nonsense because the sentences will apparently not render a coherent immanent meaning. If we assume both Thought and Spirit to be translations of the Greek Nous, and therefore to be used as synonyms, how can Thought have come to govern the Spiritual World? If we try again and assume Thought and Spirit not to be synonyms, but only Thought to translate Nous, what is meant by the Spirit it has come to govern? But when we read on and learn that the world has been pervaded by the enthusiasm of the Spirit, now that Thought has come to govern the world, it sounds as if Thought and Spirit were the same after all. Well, there are no answers to such questions arising from close reading; the text will remain unintelligible as long as we expect it to be consistent by common-sense logic. The difficulties will dissolve, however, and the text render its meaning, if we accept Hegel's dialectical logic, that is his project of a Second Reality. If we read the passage in the light of Hegelian dialectics of history, the Nous of Anaxagoras and Aristotle will be the divine Spirit that governs a world removed from divinity; Thought will be the name of the divine Spirit when, in the dialectical course of history, it has gained the "objective form" of human thinking which enables it "to reach effectively into external reality" because now it is immanent to the world in which it operates; and the Spiritual World will be the world of man, society, and history in which the divine Spirit, having gained the objective form of human thought, operates effectively. If in this manner we provide a dictionary for translating the language of dialectics into the language of common sense, the text will become intelligible: Hegel, it turns out, is a metastatic thinker who believes that man can transform the world, which exists in tension toward God, into the very Realm of God itself. Ordinary man, of course, cannot accomplish this extraordinary feat – first the divine Spirit must have become incarnate in the Thought of man, and that it has done in the events of the French Revolution. History has found a new epoch, for the divine, which had been only imperfectly reconciled to the world when God became man in Christ, has come to be truly reconciled to the world now that the Thought of man has provided the divine Spirit with its objective form. Hegel conceives history as moving from the Nous that governs the world, to the God who becomes man, and finally to the man who becomes God. To Hegel, God is dead because man-god at last has come to life and will create a new realm in his image. To sum it up: The Hegelian man-god has eclipsed the reality of God and history and thereby gained both the freedom and authority to project Second Realities and impose them on the world. Shorn of the paraphernalia of dialectics, Hegel's Thought is a contracted self that closely resembles Sartre's *moi*.

The mood of deformed existence is subject to remarkable fluctuations. Hegel recalls it as a state of elation – but he has to recall it. The elation of the years in which he worked toward the great outburst of his *Phaenomenologie* of 1807 is no longer quite the mood of the time when he wrote the recall, more than twenty years later – even though in his later years he had not at all abandoned his views of reconciliation or of salvation through projecting a speculative system. The milder fluctuations, it is true, can be explained by the disenchantment following the realization that an imaginative project does indeed not effectively transform reality. But how do we account for the great historical oscillations between the extremes of exuberant confidence and black despair?

The spiritual disease which causes such extremely disparate symptoms was diagnosed by a healthier mind than Hegel's, by Jean Paul, in his *Vorschule der Aesthetik* of 1804. At the time when Hegel was elated Jean Paul wrote:

When God sets – like the sun sets – on an age, then soon the world will be in darkness: the scorner of the All *(des All)* respects nothing but his own self, and in the ensuing night he is afraid of nothing but his own creatures.

As if he had Hegel's text lying before him and were devising the most suitable counterformula to the recall, Jean Paul describes the sunrise of Thought as the sunset of God. When the contracted self rises, the reality of God will be eclipsed; and since God can be eclipsed but not abolished, the mood of elation cannot be sustained; the presence of God makes itself felt in the fluctuation of the mood from the earlier confidence of self-assertation to the later anxiety and despair.

Moreover, when the phase of despair has been reached in the process, the man who experiences it must express it by means of the very symbols used by Jean Paul in his diagnosis. For Jean Paul's symbols of Night and Nothing reappear, when Nietzsche describes the mood of the men who murdered God, in *Froehliche Wissenschaft (Aphorism 125)*:

What did we do when we cut the earth loose from the sun? Whither is it moving now? Whither are we moving? Away from all suns? Are we not falling all the time? Backward, sideward, forward, in all directions? Is there still an above and below? Are we not groping as through an infinite nothing? . . . Is there not night falling and evermore night?

Hegel was elated because God at least was dead and the man-god had convincingly revealed himself in the events of the French Revolution; Nietzsche knew despair because by his time insight into the problems of deformation had advanced far enough to make him aware that God certainly had been murdered but that the man-god, the Superman, had yet to appear.

But let us return once more to Jean Paul; for not only had he diagnosed the darkness underneath Hegel's elation, eighty years before it was experienced and expressed by Nietzsche, he also knew why the Superman, in whom Nietzsche still placed his hope, would never appear and make an end to the falling and groping in the infinite Nothing. In the *Vorschule* he speaks of the spirit of the age (*Zeitgeist*), its "lawless arbitrariness" and its "egomania", and then continues:

It (the *Zeitgeist*) would egomaniacly annihilate the world *(Welt)* and the All *(All)*, in order to empty the field and to gain free play for itself in the Nothing.

The empty field of Nothing results from the eclipse of reality; Jean Paul has recognized its imaginary character. No projection of a man-god can overcome the Nothing, for the Nothing has been projected, by the man who deforms himself, for the very purpose of indulging in the projection of the man-god. Man can eclipse the reality of God by imagining a Nothing, but he cannot overcome the imagined Nothing by filling it with imagined somethings.

To recognize the empty field of the Nothing as resulting from an act of imagination, however, is not to to say that there is not a real problem of nothingness; on the contrary, man can project the imaginary field of the Nothing only when he has really fallen into nothingness by contracting his humanity to a self. Thus, on the level of the mood, with regard to Nothing and Anxiety, we encounter a compound of reality and imagination, corresponding to the compound of insight and intellectual dishonesty which characterizes deformed existence. Or inversely, the deformation of existence affects the whole of its texture down to the mood that moves in the amplitude of elation and despair.

ALIENATION IN MARX'S
POLITICAL ECONOMY AND PHILOSOPHY
by

PHILIP MERLAN

It is generally agreed that the concept of alienation as used by Marx [1] originated in German idealism. In this context, "German idealism" is mostly equated with Hegel's philosophy. This, however, is somewhat one-sided and prevents us from seeing the concept, and the problem behind it, in full perspective. It seems advantageous to start not with Hegel, but rather with Kant.

I. According to Kant, contrary to what is the case, consciousness (and many a philosopher) ascribes certain "qualities" to its objects. But actually these "qualities" are qualities of the consciousness itself. Space, time, quantity, quality, relation, modality are aspects (forms) of consciousness. However, it took Kant to discover this. Instead of realizing that what, in our perceptions and thoughts, presents itself as belonging to the realm of the objects, actually belongs to consciousness, uninstructed consciousness misunderstands itself: it does not recognize itself in all the aforementioned aspects of its objects.

---

[1] By "alienation" I am rendering Marx's *Entfremdung* rather than his *Entäusserung*. But to the extent that *sich entäussern* implies an abandoning of ... or a turning over to ... something which was mine, the act of *sich entäussern* may and often does result in *Entfremdung* – the object of *Entäusserung* has become alien to me = no longer mine. In the section of the *Phenomenology* (on enlightenment) the word *Entfremdung* is introduced as a technical term (*Der sich entfremdete Geist, die Bildung*). But the process resulting in *Entfremdung* is called by Hegel *Entäusserung* (and *Entwesung*) (pp. 316, 319f.). The same is true of the concluding paragraphs (pp. 518, 520). But if somebody insists that *Entäusserung* is a neutral term and designates simply the production of goods (e.g., G. Stiehler, *Die Dialektik in Hegel's "Phänomenologie des Geistes,"* Berlin: Akademie-Verlag, 1964, p. 280 note), there is nothing wrong with this. Stiehler's book is very important for the problem at hand; see especially its concluding chapter (pp. 241–306) on *Entfremdung*. Specifically, for the problem of translating *Entfremdung* and *Entäusserung* see the introductory note in Anonymous [Martin Milligan], *Karl Marx, Economic and Philosophic Manuscripts of 1884* (Moscow, 1961), pp. 11f. Cf. also note 8 below. Of prime importance on many aspects of the problem of alienation is D. Bell, "The 'Rediscovery' of Alienation," *The Journal of Philosophy* 56 (1959), pp. 933–952.

In taking space, time, etc., for "attributes" of objects, consciousness, as we would say, has alienated itself from itself.[2]

Now, as is well known, the very foundations of Kant's "limited" idealism ("limited" means: *only* the *forms* of the world of objects are the contribution consciousness makes to the world as sensed and perceived) have been shaken by two men (though neither of them can claim prime philosophic rank).

The first is Jacobi.[3] Kant's "limited" idealism presupposes that in part consciousness is determined by objects external to it. In Kant's language: the matter = content of experience is something given to consciousness. However, "to be determined" or "to be given" is only a somewhat non-committal expression for "to be caused by". But according to Kant, causality is one of the forms of consciousness which consciousness contributes to the edifice of the world of experiences. No causal relation can therefore obtain *between* consciousness and objects external to it. Kant's "limited" idealism is, according to Jacobi, self-contradictory. Realism seems to be preferable to Kant's "limited" idealism. And, as we know, Jacobi's variety of realism is what could be called "fideistic" realism.[4]

Just the opposite point of view is represented by Maimon.[5] He denies the difference between form and matter (content) of consciousness and essentially asserts that *all* modifications of consciousness are self-modifications. But of this conciousness knows nothing. Especially as far as sensations are concerned consciousness implicity asserts that their objects are *given* to it. How-

---

[2] In this context I cannot discuss the various interpretations of the relation between things-in-themselves and phenomena, nor between the empirical consciousness and trans-empirical (unique) one. On these problems see H. Herring, *Das Problem der Affektion bei Kant* (Kantstudien, Erg. Heft 67), Köln, 1953, with whose defense of Kant from Jacobi (p. 14) I, however, disagree; P. Lachièze-Rey, *L'Idealisme Kantien* (Paris, 2nd ed., 1950), pp. 443–463.

[3] Of prime importance in this context is the appendix to his *David Hume über den Glauben* [1st ed. 1787] (F. H. Jacobi, *Werke,* Leipzig, 1815), pp. 289–323, with the famous sentence that one cannot enter Kant's system without assuming the existence of things-in-themselves, but with this assumption one cannot remain in it (p. 304). On Jacobi see, e.g., the articles by V. Verra in the *Encyclopedia filosofica,* with bibliography, and by S. Atlas in the *Encyclopedia of Philosophy* (with whose interpretation and evaluation of Jacobi's criticism I, however, disagree).

[4] For this fideistic realism Jacobi is obviously indebted to Hamann. A skillful exposition of it by a contemporary is [T. Wizenmann], *Die Resultate der Jacobischen und Mendelsohnischen Philosophie kritisch untersucht von einem Freiwilligen* (Leipzig, 1786). On the other hand it is not sufficiently stressed that the late Fichte in turn took over Jacobi's fideism. See, e.g., M. Wundt, *Fichte* (Stuttgart, 1927), pp. 271f.

[5] On him see M. Gueroult, *La Philosophie transcendentale de Salomon Maimon* (Paris, 1929), especially ch. II; and S. Atlas, *From Critical to Speculative Idealism* (The Hague, 1964), especially pp. 20–37.

ever, Maimon shares Jacobi's conviction that givenness presupposes a causal relation, whereas causal relations do not obtain between consciousness and anything external to it; also according to Maimon, consciousness is mistaken (just as, according to Kant, it is mistaken when it takes space, time, etc., for qualities of things external to it). And now Maimon asks the decisive question which Kant has never asked: how shall we explain this self-misunderstanding? Implicitly Maimon answers: consciousness posits *unconsciously* the elements of which it builds what appears to it as external things. The root of consciousness is its unconscious activity.[6] The term "unconscious" does not appear in Maimon; instead we find the term "incomplete (*unvollständig*) consciousness" and a reference to Leibniz' *petites perceptions* (as Windelband says, in the language of today they would be unconscious mental states).[7]

Thus, the task of philosophy is in this respect much more comprehensive than it would be according to Kant. Kant overcomes the alienation of consciousness by "uncovering" the true character of space, time, etc.; Maimon faces the neverending task to "uncover" the original activities of consciousness or the elements of all phenomenal reality. But what Kant and Maimon have in common is their attempt to overcome the alienation of consciousness and make it possible for it to say to what seems to be given to it – tat twam asi – I am the giver and the gift.

Maimon's thesis became fully developed in speculative idealism. In one of their aspects, the philosophies of Fichte and Hegel can be interpreted as attempts to repossess what consciousness lost by not recognizing itself in its objects.[8]

In this context, as we have noticed above, alienation means that the subject does not recognize his own work (or his own property). The reason why he does not recognize it is that the production (or original possession) took place behind the back of consciousness – whether it is the empirical or the trans-empirical consciousness. This fact can be expressed either with the

---

[6] A neat formula we also find in J. S. Beck, *Erläuternder Auszug aus den kritischen Schriften des Herrn Prof. Kant,* vol. III (1796), p. 130: *Vorstellung* must be preceded by *Vorstellen.*

[7] See, e.g., W. Windelband, *A History of Philosophy,* paperback repr., New York: Harper, 1958, pp. 424–578. Whatever the reason, of older interpreters of German philosophy Windelband is particularly sensitive to the problems of the unconscious (in an entirely pre- and non-Freudian manner). See P. Merlan, *Monopsychism, Mysticism, Metaconsciousness* (The Hague, 1963), pp. 126–130; cf. Lachièze-Rey, *op. cit.,* p. 447.

[8] The tat twam asi in Fichte's *Die Bestimmung des Menschen:* everything you perceive outside yourself is always you yourself (Phil. Bibl.), p. 64; ed. of 1800, pp. 135–137; of 1834–46, pp. 20–28.

help of a concept like "the unconscious" or like "forgetting". In either case alienation presupposes some kind of "knowledge" (unconscious knowledge, knowledge forgotten) of the type "this is mine" or even more radically, "this is I," now gone.

Of course, it is possible to extend the concept of alienation by saying that he who does not recognize what is his own, does not recognize himself and is in this sense of the word alienated from himself. But clearly this is a derivative sense of "alienation" – the original is the non-recognizing *of* something which is mine (or I) as mine (or I), in the sense of having produced it.

As far as Hegel is concerned, it is not necessary to think exclusively of just one section of the *Phenomenology of the Spirit* [9] as elaborating the idea of alienation (*Entfremdung, Entäusserung*). Rather, the whole work is the presentation of the Odyssey of the mind which must become its other in order to become its own. It is therefore not surprising that Marx in discussing the problem of alienation (see below) concentrates on the concluding paragraphs of the *Phenomenology* in which Hegel describes the overcoming of any alienation by the self-appropriation of the Spirit.

For the sake of completeness it should be added: the consciousness of which we have spoken is, or should be, interpreted as a unique, transpersonal, non-empirical consciousness – but it is in any case tacitly taken for granted that it exists only in and through the empirical human consciousness. The controversies regarding, e.g., the nature of Fichte's Ego (is it transcendent or empirical?) seem to be, in the present context at least, irrelevant. In other words, alienation is essential to consciousness, be it trans-empirical, be it empirical.

But why this alienation? Is it a *factum brutum* or can we explain its cause or its purpose?

As far as Kant is concerned, it seems fair to say that it is easier to explain the reason of the forms of intuition (*Anschauung*) than of those of thinking. Consciousness, as Kant sees it, must be modified by its objects (whether by things-in-themselves, or by phenomena, is controversial) to become consciousness of them. But the unity of consciousness, i.e., the fact that modification does not result in complete alteration and thus discontinuity, obviously demands a kind of pin-point-like existence of consciousness. This was very well brought out in the formula of St. Augustine, according to which instead of saying a past, present, future, we should speak of a *praesens de*

---

[9] Section VI, B (*Der sich entfremdete Geist*). In this section, *Entfremdung* and *Entäusserung* seem to be used interchangeably. The section VIII (*Das absolute Wissen*), to which Marx refers (see below) never uses *Entfremdung*, but only *Entäusserung*.

praeteritis, praesens de praesentibus, praesens de futuris. Clearly the soul (or as Kant would say, consciousness *of* time) must be timeless or it would be completely dispersed. Therefore all modifications must be simultaneous and coplesent; any kind of extension (interval) presupposes previous complete compression, without which there could not be anything like unity of consciousness. But if consciousness is to be (and in fact is) consciousness of an extended multiplicity, it must, if we may say so, stretch itself and by so doing stretch out its modifications, time and space being the fundamental forms of "asunder". Unfortunately, no *equally* good reasons can be found why it should be just the categories of quantity, quality, relation, and modality which consciousness imposes on its modifications.

Moreover, it is well known that, according to Kant, the necessity of perceiving objects in space and time holds only for human minds; he, in other words, is ready to allow the existence of some kind of consciousness which would "intuit" its objects in a completely different way (non-spatial, non-temporal). We are left with the impression that the forms of both our perception and of our thoughts are entirely contingent.

With both Fichte and Hegel the situation is completely changed. The alienation of consciousness is interpreted as necessity if consciousness is ever to become consciousness in the proper sense of the word, actual rather than potential; and this means self-consciousness. The world of objects which consciousness posits as different from itself serves as the other without the cognition of which no self-consciousness is feasible. The multiplicity of the consciousness' content is its own purposeful work. To become self-consciousness, consciousness must become consciousness of its non-self. Self-appropriation must be preceded by alienation.

So much on the concept of alienation in German idealism.

II. Of the many ways to express the relation of Marx to Hegel[10] perhaps no other is shorter and easier than the interpretation of just one brief passage of his *Nationalökonomie und Philosophie.*[11]

---

[10] For a review of claims and counterclaims concerning the dependence of Marx on Hegel, see especially J. Barion, *Hegel und die Marxistische Staatslehre* (Bonn, 1963), pp. 83–85 with notes. Cf. *ibid.,* pp. 100–102; also pp. 144–147. For a review of the relation of Marx to philosophy in general, see especially J. Habermas, "Zur philosophischen Diskussion um Marx und den Marxismus," *Philosophische Rundschau* 5 (1957), pp. 165–235.

[11] The German text to which I refer is that in S. Landshut (ed.), *Karl Marx, Die Frühschriften* (Stuttgart, 1953), p. 271, English translation: Anonymous [M. Milligan], *op. cit.,* p. 153; T. B. Bottomore (tr.), *Karl Marx, Early Writings* (London, 1963), p. 204 (also in E. Fromm, *Marx's Concept of Man* (New York, 1961, p. 179). French translation: E. Bottigelli, *Karl Marx, Manuscrits de 1844* (Paris, 1962), p. 134. This is the passage in which Marx refers to the concluding paragraphs of Hegel's *Phenomenology.*

Hegel, so Marx says, identifies man with his self-consciousness. Therefore, for Hegel, all alienation is alienation of self-consciousness.

What Marx meant is clear. In speaking of man, Hegel, according to him,
abstracts from all concrete human qualities (e.g., that he has a body, occupies a particular place in society, etc.). Therefore, for Hegel, alienated
man means man whose consciousness has become alienated from itself.

It is obvious what Marx is aiming at. As a realist he must reinterpret the
concept of alienation so that it no longer would indicate a process or event
strictly internal to consciousness.

Thus he continues his criticism of Hegel and says: Hegel does not see
that alienation as an intraconscious process or event is only the mirroring
of an actual (real, *wirklich*) alienation (*im Wissen und Denken sich ab-
spiegelnder Ausdruck der wirklichen Entfremdung*)[12] – i.e., as we must
complete Marx – Hegel does not realize, that the *real* alienation has taken
place between real objects and the concrete (whole) man's consciousness of
them, to be only *mirrored* as a relation within consciousness.

With the help of the most famous pages from *Das Kapital* we can immediately understand Marx. Things which man has produced as means of
satisfying his needs, under the capitalist system of production appear to him
as commodities, with a life of their own, so that he does not recognize them
for what they are. And it is obviously this real alienation which appears
(only *appears!*) or is mirrored as the self-alienation internal to consciousness (one is almost tempted to say: of "pure" consciousness), where it is
discovered by the philosopher.

Marx continues with his criticism. After having discovered the phenomenon of alienation (and misinterpreted it as intrinsic to consciousness) the
philosopher now proceeds to overcome the alienation (to replace it by
anagnorisis or repossession). But how can he do it? Strictly by a movement
within consciousness. In other words, the philosopher will explain that what
consciousness perceives as different from itself is only consciousness in a
mask, if we may say so. Not that the philosopher is ever able to remove the
mask; he only can prove to us that if we could do it, we who are behind it
would perceive ourselves. Indeed, Marx could have quoted the famous
couplet by Novalis, which sums up an important aspect of idealism: the
only one who succeeded in penetrating the veil of the statue of Sais (i.e., to
discover the nature of reality) saw behind it nothing but himself. But let it
be repeated: the claim of the philosopher is even more modest. After he
uncovered the fact of alienation he cannot actually change it; consciousness

---

[12] I think the French and English translations of *abspiegeln* by *réfléchir* and *reflect*
are too abstract.

continues to perceive all reality as different from itself, as something given rather than something posited.

Thus, an analysis of this single passage is sufficient to establish the unity of Marx's thought – regardless of terminology (such as presence or absence of the term "alienation") [13] and – for better or for worse – the quantity and quality of his debt to Hegel.

We can now fully understand Marx's famous dictum that philosophers have limited themselves to interpreting reality, whereas man's true task is to change it. The reality which Marx wants to change is the capitalist system, and it is only after the system has been changed, which means only after things created by man for the satisfaction of his wants and needs and therefore destined to be freely appropriated by him according to his wants and needs have lost their character as commodities, the actual alienation will have come to an end; and therefore consciousness will also overcome its alienation which was only a mirror image of the actual alienation.

Thus, Marx accepts Hegel's concept of alienation: man does not recognize his own products. But while, according to Hegel (and Maimon or Fichte), these products are products of consciousness, Marx thinks of them as products of labor which man's consciousness now encounters qua commodities, endowed with a "life" of their own. It is these commodities which create the experience of alienation misinterpreted as an event intrinsic to consciousness. The consequences of this difference between Hegel and Marx are obvious. Consciousness, as Hegel conceives of it, *lives* always on the level of alienation and no matter what the amount of enlightenment with which the philosopher can provide consciousness, consciousness will always continue living on this level. After we have finished reading the *Phenomenology of Spirit* and absorbed all of its content, we still perceive the objects of sensible reality as external to our consciousness. But if Marx is right, a radical change is possible (see below). If we abolish the socio-economic order created by (and in turn creating) the illusion of commodities as entities having an existence of their own, we by the same token will have changed the nature of consciousness.

This difference between the philosopher who only interprets and the revolutionary who changes the world is brought out very well in a passage of Fichte's:

---

[13] Cf. on this passage Barion, *op. cit.,* pp. 106–110, especially note 358; Landshut, *op. cit.,* pp. xxxl–xxxv; on the problem of the unity of Marx's thought see E. Fromm, *Marx's Concept of Man* (above, note 10), pp. 69–74, especially 70–74. To a certain extent, I disagree with the conclusions of Bell, *op. cit.*

A philosopher says only in his own name – everything which exists *for* the Ego is *by* the Ego. But this Ego has his own philosophy and says: as truly as I am and live, there exists something outside of myself which is not by me. . . . The former point of view is the speculative, the latter that of life . . .[14]

Thus, the difference between the idealistic and the realistic (Marxian) interpretation of the phenomenon of alienation is, be it repeated, great and obvious[15] – both as to the causes and the cure. The famous 11th of the theses on Feuerbach to which we referred above[16] concentrates on the problem of the cure; but it becomes fully intelligible only if we do not forget that idealism considers alienation a kind of congenital "disease", while realism sees it as a "disease" contracted from without. And therefore alienation for idealism is in some sense of the word, incurable – or rather, the diagnosis is the only cure, whereas for realism an appropriate change in the environment will result in the restoration of full health.

But some fundamental similarities remain.[17] First, as to the inevitability of alienation. In the case of the idealist, especially of the Fichtean or Hegelian variety, the alienation is the necessary roundabout way – the only way open to this spirit (consciousness, the Absolute, the non-empirical Ego) on which it can find itself and by so doing, fully concentrate itself. If we want to keep our imagery of alienation as a kind of disease, we would be entitled to speak of a *felix morbus*. For the realist of the Marxian type, especially one sufficiently convinced of the importance of historic development, alienation is as inevitable as capitalism. Who would not be familiar with the admiration of capitalism expressed by Marx and Engels in the *Manifesto*! It unfettered – and with what stunning results – the productive forces manacled by the feudal order; it transformed the globe and made it ripe for communism. Seen from the point of view of the future, it could again be called a *felix morbus*.[18]

And above all we must not forget: neither the idealistic nor the econom-ico-realistic interpreter considers alienation as a private, individual process over which the individual as such could have any control. To the extent that the content of the empirical consciousness is *in the last resort* determined by the trans-personal Ego (spirit, consciousness, etc.) empirical conscious-

---

[14] *Zweite Einleitung in die Wissenschaftslehre*, § 2, note.

[15] In this respect I fully agree with the Old Marxian, Stiehler, *op. cit.*, p. 297.

[16] *Die deutsche Ideologie. A. Thesen über Feuerbach*, § 11 (Landshut, *op. cit.*, p. 341).

[17] Thus, I would side rather with the interpretation asserting the essential unity of Marx's thought. On this see, e.g., E. Fromm, *op. cit.*, pp. 69–83, and especially pp. 70–74.

[18] Cf. E. Fromm, *Beyond the Chains of Illusion* (New York, 1962), p. 57.

ness is, and will remain, aware of a reality other-than-itself. To the extent that the content of the empirical consciousness is *in the last resort* determined by the socio-economic system in which man finds himself, he as a private individual has no control over his consciousness. He must remain alienated until the system changes.

The well known problem of how then ever a change of consciousness can precede (let alone cause) a change in the economic-political system need not be discussed here.

III. Now, as it is well known, the concept of alienation is in the center of interest of many neo-Marxists.[19] But they considerably change its meaning. Let us limit ourselves to one respresentative – Schaff.[20]

We repeat: according to Marx, there is only one root of alienation – capitalism. With the abolition of capitalism all alienation should disappear. But Schaff denies the correctness of this "prophecy" of Marx's; according to him, the reality of socialism clearly proves Marx incorrect. In socialist society there is also alienation, and there is every reason to assume that alienation will exist in communist society too. It is not necessary for us to review Schaff's theory extensively; we limit ourselves to some salient points.

First, Schaff reminds us that there are different types of alienation (his classic example would be the religious alienation in the sense in which Feuerbach described it: man does not recognize that God is only man's idea and therefore man does not recognize himself).[21] Second, according to Marx, alienation under capitalism means not only that man does not recognize his product, i.e., the result of production, and takes it to be a commodity, but also that he does not recognize the process of production for what it is (free activity) but mistakes it for labor *the wages* of which will enable him to live (see below). Therefore, labor is for him a dire necessity, instead of being a joyful and spontaneous exercise of his capacities. Hence, according to Marx, in communist society labor will completely change its character.

This idea of Marx Schaff considers a relic of Marx's utopianism. Even communist society will have to subordinate itself to the demands of an ever

[19] A characteristic sui generis proof is provided by N. Birnbaum, "Eastern Europe and the Death of God," *Commentary* 44 (1967), pp. 69–73, especially pp. 71 and 73 (a report on a meeting of sociologists in Prague in December, 1966).

[20] A. Schaff, *Marksizm a jednostka ludzka* (Warsaw, 1965).

[21] In this paper for external reasons I excluded any discussion of the Feuerbach-Marx relation. For a review of its different interpretations see J. Barion, *op. cit.*, pp. 88–98.

[22] Schaff, *ibid.*, pp. 260–266. Cf. *Deutsche Ideologie: Feuerbach* (Landshut, *op. cit.*, p. 361).

advancing technology and therefore the process of production will dominate man even in communist society. On rereading the famous passage in which Marx describes how, in communist society, everybody will work at his discretion in everchanging occupations,[22] Schaff simply reminds us of the slavery imposed on man by the necessity of working at the assembly line (though he does not use the word *slavery*). The working hours will, to be sure, be shortened and working conditions made as pleasant as possible; to assume that working itself will, in communist society, be a pleasure is to forget the demands of modern, industrial technology and to see the worker as a kind of artisan, happy in his work.[23]

I used the word "artisan" (not used by Schaff) on purpose. It is (or should be) well known that Marx's contemporary, Ruskin, bitterly complained (as did others) of the effects of division of labor. "Men have become divided, not labor" is his formula,[24] and the words could have been written by Marx. What such words could mean, however, is the division of man into the man whose work is stultifying drudgery (done only for the sake of making a living) void of pleasure and into the man, the pleasure seeker, whose pleasures lack any serious purpose and are therefore insipid. This division of man is, we could say, marked by the clock telling the end of the labor day. Now, the remedy suggested by Ruskin is to restore labor to the condition under which the worker would enjoy it – a condition which, according to Ruskin, existed in the Middle Ages, when, to use a brief formula, the artist and the artisan were one and the same person. Ruskin is obviously thinking of the artisan who not only executes but also designs (the ideal of Morris); and what he suggests is a return to manual labor (or near-manual labor) – under the conditions of medieval methods of production.

Now, it is obvious that to Marx the idea of overcoming the division of man by such a method must appear simply ridiculous. What he wants is to do away with the divided man under conditions of a highly mechanized, industrialized society. If this cannot be done, the dream of Marxism breaks down – or, if we so prefer, its utopian component stands revealed.[25]

---

[23] Schaff, *ibid.,* p. 190.

[24] *Stones of Venice,* vol. II, vi, par. 16. But in spite of his objections to dividing mankind into thinkers and workers, see *Fors Clavigera* (Letter 89), § 11 with its assertion that there are essential and eternal divisions of labor (twenty-one of them).

[25] The whole problem can best be seen if we remember that, according to Marx, alienation implies not only alienation from the *products* of man's activity, but also alienation from the *process* of production (cf. on this, e.g., Bell, "The Debate on Alienation," in L. Labedz (ed.), *Revisionism* [London, 1962], pp. 195–211). In what way can this latter aspect of alienation be overcome in a communist society, as long as the

But let us go back to Schaff. He is not surprised at all that even in social-ist society there are clear and distinct proofs of the continued existence of alienation. He points to the well-known phenomena of vandalism, hooli-ganism, drunkenness, animal-like satisfaction of instincts, etc. (I am not sure whether he would include the provos, the mods and rocks, the Halb-starken and the Gammler, the beatniks, and the hippies) – which for him are only the reverse of the existentialist's loneliness – and of the interest which the literature of loneliness finds also in socialist countries.

But Schaff remains a Marxist in that he never even considers the possi-bility of treating hooliganism and related phenomena as characteristics of the individual as such. Nobody, he says, knows how to handle alienation expressing itself in actions such as the aforementioned ones.[26] And he only urges all socialist societies to remain aware of the problem and to try to remedy the situation.

Remedy – how? A Marxist should say: obviously again some transforma-tion of society is necessary – some collective action corresponding to the fact that alienation, as a Marxist (or as an idealist) sees it, is not a private affair. To put it pointedly: Schaff does not suggest that the economico-social revolutionary (or reformer, or simply the communist planner) be replaced by the psychiatrist (or, for that matter, the social psychologist). Nor does he, of course, recommend the use of criminal law to reform or to rehabilitate the offender-by-alienation, though it is difficult to imagine that he could entirely eliminate this kind of remedy if asked point blank.

But all his Marxism notwithstanding: by deciding to classify phenomena peculiar only to small segments of society as cases of alienation, Schaff implicitly suggests treating them on a strictly individual basis, i.e., handling them not (or at least: not only) from the point of view of society but from the point of view of the individuum. It is the individuum which should be "cured", not society. The cure of alienation could therefore consist in re-integrating the individual with society *as it is* – at least temporarily. The revolutionary implications of the concept of alienation have disappeared. There is no longer alienation; rather, there are alienations – and even if they will all be eliminated in the long run in an ideal (communist) society, in the short run they are cases – and require to be treated as such. One more step – and Schaff's concept of alienations can be taken over by non-Marxists and by non-idealists alike.

IV. Nobody has a monopoly on words; nobody can be blamed for using

technique of work (e.g., working at an assembly line) will remain the same as it was in the capitalist one?

[26] Schaff, *ibid.*, p. 319.

the word "alienation" in a sense different from that used either by German idealists or by Marx (non-recognition of what I myself have produced as *my* product and therefore misunderstanding the nature of the process of production). After all, as the *OED* tells us, the word has been used in a pretty technical but different sense since the 14th century. But neither this fact nor the possible protest from an alienist to the effect that the word should be exclusively used to designate mental illness, need overly influence us.

Here are some characteristic examples of such "free" use of the term.

a. The word could be used to express the human condition caused by the fact that man possesses (or is possessed of) consciousness. For, as Sartre has shown, consciousness means that we never are what we know us to be, but merely act out some part. We cannot be grief – we can only be grieving, and that means we know we are grieving and therefore there is some sham in our grief. We never can be joy – we can only enjoy ourselves and in so doing we show ourselves to a real or imaginary audience. Conscience makes bona fides impossible and injects a note of sham into whatever we are, do, or feel. There is no such thing as absolute sincerity; there is no such thing as stripping oneself of every mask. Only a thing is "sincere" – it is simply what it is, because it does not know itself. The knowledge acquired by the eating of the forbidden fruit may symbolize the acquisition of consciousness – man's original "sin": the acquisition of mala fides. And perhaps this condition could be called a condition of man's alienation from himself. From now on, he is split into the man who knows himself and the man who is – and the two never coincide.[27]

b. And the word could also be used to express some particular human condition. An example is provided by Natanson, who sees the problem of alienation from the perspective of role taking.[28]

c. And the concept can be extended so as to designate the relation resulting in any avoidable discontent, rooted in a chronic condition of the society to which the alienated individual belongs.[29]

---

[27] Another theory making alienation a universal human category regardless of economic conditions: J. van der Meulen, *Hegel* . . . (Hamburg, 1958), pp. 306–317.

[28] M. Natanson, "Alienation and Social Role," *Social Research* 33 (1966), pp. 375–388.

[29] A. S. Kaufman, "On Alienation," *Inquiry* 8 (1965), pp. 141–165. Modified: *idem,* "Diesing and Piccone on Kaufman," *ibid.,* (1967), pp. 211–216 as reaction to the article by P. Diesing and P. Piccone. "Kaufman on Alienation," *Inquiry* 10 (1967), pp. 208–210, in which it is stressed that, according to Marx, alienation is an unavoidable evil.

d. Finally, one can refer to the mood underlying gnosticism as the mood of feeling an alien in the universe.[30]

V. But, granting all these possible uses of the term, let us return to the concept of alienation in the narrow sense as defined in the beginning of this paper (with, however, a change in perspective).

As used in German idealism, the concept differs from its use in Marx also in this respect: that no human misery (merely philosophic ignorance) is implied in its idealistic use, whereas, according to Marx, the capitalist system as it creates alienation, *pari passu* engenders misery. Correspondingly, the abolition of alienation caused by capitalism, *pari passu* engenders the abolition of misery. Of *all* human misery? It is here where the ways of Old Marxists and Neo-Marxists are most likely to part and, in fact, do part.

Let us consider the alternative answers to this question.

A Marxist has the choice: either to assume that alienation is ultimately the root of *all* human misery and thus by implication assert that doing away with alienation will indeed guarantee general happiness; or to assume that there are several such roots, essentially independent from each other, in which case there would be no such guarantee.

Let us discuss the first alternative. To subscribe to it, a Marxist must accept a peculiar anthropology. Man, according to this anthropology, is "good" and capable of happiness, and it is only society (which, before the advent of communism, has always been an "evil" society) which "spoils" man and deprives him of his share of happiness. He, then, would unhesitatingly use the word "alienation" to describe the only cause of all human misery and unhappiness, and expect the communist society to consist of happy individuals.

It is plain how naive (Rousseauian) or utopian such an expectation will sound to many. How could it be defended?

It is well known that Marx often describes the human condition under the capitalist system as that of private (particular) existence, opposing it to the condition of universality (man as *Gattungswesen* – translated sometimes as "generic being", sometimes as "species being").[31] The abolition

---

[30] See, e.g., H. Jonas, *Gnosis und spätantiker Geist I,* 2nd ed. (Göttingen, 1954), pp. 96f., 143–145; and, most recent, E. Voegelin, "Immortality," *The Harvard Theological Review* 60 (1967), pp. 235–279, especially pp. 267–271.

[31] Some interpreters assert that by designating man as a generic being, Marx means that only in society is man truly man (so, e.g., Landshut, *op. cit.,* p. xxxix). I think this is too narrow an interpretation. On this problem cf., e.g., G. Petrovic, "Alienation" in *The Encyclopedia of Philosophy* (1967); *idem*, "Marx's Theory of Alienation," *Philosophy and Phenomenological Research* 23 (1963), pp. 419–426. The key passage is the concluding sentence of *Zur Judenfrage* I: Man will truly be emancipated only when

of alienation will, according to Marx, reestablish man as universal (generic, specific) being. There will be no split between man's private and public life. It is well known how sharply Marx criticized the concept of human rights as established by the American and French revolutions – to him all these rights were only rights to be a private person.[32] What, then, is man as a generic being?

It seems fair to answer: it is the man who does not differentiate in any essential sense between his own interests and the interests of society – in the long run from the one all-comprehensive human society, or from society at large. Man is a *zôion politikon* with the understanding that the *polis* to which he belongs is that embracing the whole human race; in other words, man is *kosmopolitês*. Man is in his essence not a *zôion idion* – but all pre-communist society changed him step by step into being just this, this change culminating in capitalism.[33] And this means in particular that the locus of his happiness and misery was (or, was considered) predominantly his private life. Not exclusively (though this point is never sufficiently stressed in considerations as the ones we are engaged in); it is virtually impossible for a human being not to be affected by the happiness and misery of the society to which he belongs. But still the happiness and misery stemming from this source is, in capitalist society, distinctly subordinated to man's private happiness and misery, his own health and sickness, his own life or death, his own happy or unhappy love, marriage, and so on. Marxism, which promises to restore man's generic nature, by the same token promises to reverse the relation: though undoubtedly there will continue to be private happiness and misery in man's overall life account, they will count much less than the happiness and misery arising from his "political" life. To illustrate this by a simple example: the unhappiness caused by an earth quake in a city from which he is very remote will affect the new man, i.e., the generic man, more profoundly and significantly than the misery caused by some accident in his own family. Though even in a communist society man will still be a *zôion idion,* everything which affects him in this capacity will be much less important than that which affects him as a *zôion politi-kon.*[34]

---

he will transform himself from an individuum = egoist, bourgeois into a generic being = citoyen (Landshut, *op. cit.,* p. 199).

[32] *Zur Judenfrage* (Landshut, *op. cit.,* pp. 191–199).

[33] In this context, *polis* obviously does not mean "state," but rather "community" (*Gesellschaft*) or a similar term.

[34] The point that Marx intends to abolish the contradiction between the particular and the universal, the private and the public, is strongly stressed in K. Löwith, "Man's

This is the way in which a Marxist could defend the thesis that the abolition of private property of means of production and therefore of *all* alienation, will at the same time mean the transformation of the "egoistic man" into the "generic man", whose happiness – if not entirely identical with the happiness of the *polis*, will by and large coincide with it, so that his private misery will count for little. Indeed, to quote Marx, for such a man even death will be much less of a calamity than for an "egoist", because he will know that he dies only as a member of his genus and is, as we can add, in this sense of the word, expendable.[35] In other words, the Marxist will not have to assume the *total* replacement of the particular in man by the universal. It is enough if he assert that the former will be subordinated to the latter. We could also say: the question is: Where is the *center* of man's happiness located and where is its periphery, and how long is the radius which connects the two? And on the whole it seems that no matter how greatly Marx was concerned with human happiness, by and large he would hold that the happiness and the misery of man *qua zôion politikon* are much more important and significant than of him *qua zôion idion*.

And it seems that this is the true issue between an Old Marxist and a Neo-Marxist.

When Hamlet ponders over the problem of suicide, he concludes that it is only the fear of what may wait for him in after-life that keeps a man in his senses from committing it:

> For who would bear the whips and scorns of time,
> The oppressor's wrong, the proud man's contumely,
> The pangs of disprized love, the law's delay,
> The insolence of office, and the spurns
> That patient merit of the unworthy takes,
> When he himself might his quietus make
> With a bare bodkin?. . .

Now, as for all these reasons, sufficient, according to Hamlet, to justify one's suicide, so the Neo-Marxist will say – shall we assume that they are ultimately rooted in alienation, this alienation, in turn being caused in the

Self-Alienation in the Early Writings of Marx," *Social Research* 21 (1954), pp. 204–230, especially p. 230.

[35] This seems to be the sense of the sentence: death seems to be the harsh victory of the genus over the individual and their unity and to contradict [scil. the coincidence of genus and individuum]; but the concrete [*bestimmte*] individuum is mortal only qua concrete [*bestimmtes*] generic being (Landshut, p. 239). Ultimately, *being* generic and being *conscious* of being generic will coincide (identity of being and knowing through their difference).

ultimate resort by alienated labor – alienated from its own work and its own process? Will they therefore all – including the pangs of disprized love and all other reasons akin to this one – disappear in communist society? Or if they do not disappear, will they at least approach the vanishing point?

Implied in this question seems to be the Neo-Marxist's conviction that even in the "new", generic man, the center of happiness will remain in him qua retaining his quality of a *zôion idion* – or, at least, that in the overall balance of his life the misery of which he is capable and which is likely to be encountered by him – the pangs of disprized love and everything akin to it – will forever remain a major, perhaps even a decisive, factor.

Now, there is hardly any doubt possible: in every utopia there is a strong tendency to eliminate or at least to minimize the importance of private problems, to assure us that in the ideal society such problems will either disappear or be of little significance, etc. – and at the same time insist that man when completely transformed into a *zôion politikon* will simultaneously be happy, if the *polis* is. Few utopians have the courage of Plato, who, when faced with the problem of whether his guards will be happy, said: we are trying to create an ideal (just) and therefore happy *polis* – we are not trying to create happy members of the *polis*.[36] And other utopians will try to defend their ideal of "collective" rather than individual happiness by insisting that they do not try to subordinate (or sacrifice) the individual completely to the collective, but to integrate him with his collective, which, they assert, permits him really to become what he as an individual cannot become: truly himself. Utopians of different brands will insist that true integration is possible only in their kind of society, whereas other, seemingly similar, kinds of society actually sacrifice the individual. Of this and related discussions there seems to be no end in sight.

We shall see this even better if we descend from the heights of Hamlet to the flatland of moviedom. A famous Russian movie ends by showing Russian soldiers returning as victors, from World War II, to their home town. They are greeted by the whole population, happy over the victory and happy to have their husbands, sons, sweethearts returned to them. One girl does not share in the general happiness: she now definitely realizes that her own sweetheart must have been killed. An old man sees her crying. He

---

[36] *Rep.* IV 1, 420 B. It is true that even Plato leaves himself an escape clause. Perhaps, he says, guards whom we deprived of everything which commonly is considered as essential to happiness will still be the happiest ones.

It would be equally appropriate in this context to refer to Rousseau's concept of the general will. The true citizen, as Rousseau sees him, has made the general will his own will; he has transformed himself from a "natural" into a "social" being. Whether Marx would accept such an interpretation of Rousseau cannot be discussed here.

comforts her with the thought, whatever the words, that she should submerge her personal grief in the universal joy.

If we translate this advice into somewhat more general terms, we could say: find yourself by losing yourself in a collective.

But is this possible? Is it human?

Let us remind ourselves how profound a change Marx expects as the result of the abolition of alienation (or restoration of man's generic nature). Seeing, hearing, smelling, tasting, feeling, thinking, perceiving, sensing, willing, acting, loving – all these will, in communist society, be completely different from what they are at present. The abolition of private property (and therefore of alienation) means at the same time that now all these activities will no longer be activities of the "egoistic" man.[37] Has ever an idealist claimed anything even approaching the enormity of Marx's claim? And it would be interesting to know whether many Old Marxists would be prepared to support him.

But let us limit ourselves to the problem of what the transformation of man into a generic being will mean in terms of happiness and misery.

Now, if Marx expected such far reaching changes in man, it would not be surprising if his humanism, so strongly stressed by Neo-Marxists, would have in mind the generic homo rather than the private, individual homo.

"What happens to you as a generic being is more important than what happens to you as an 'egoist'." This sentence seems to indicate the line separating the Old Marxist from the Neo-Marxist. The Old Marxist is committed to the point of view that as soon as alienation will be abolished and therefore man restored to his generic nature, participation in the new *polis* will make him happy – even though *some* shades of his private misery may detract *some* from his happiness. The Neo-Marxist will insist on the opposite point of view: that private misery will be mitigated in communist society which has done away with one type of alienation, but by no means

---

[37] Landshut, *op. cit.*, pp. 240, 243.

[38] This paper had just been completed, when I came across: A. Schaff, "Alienation and Social Action," *Diogenes* 57 (1967), pp. 64–82. In many respects, it deals with the same problems as does his book, but sometimes in a different light. Highpoints in our context: "Not all social evil is ... alienation," with suicide caused by unhappy love quoted as an example (cf. our quotation from *Hamlet*). On the other hand: "Any alienation can be overcome ... if one knows what conditions it socially ..." (pp. 71, 78). Most startling is the fact that the paper concludes with pointing at the problem of the "new" man as fluctuating "between the Scylla of anarchic individualism and the Charybdis of the destruction of personal individuality ..." (p. 82); thus our conclusions are virtually identical, even as to wording. Only I cannot and don't want to share his expectation that the solution of this problem might be provided by – biochemistry.

abolished nor even essentially reduced in weight. The Old Marxist will suspect the Neo-Marxist of advocating the claims of an a-social individual. The Neo-Marxist will suspect the Old Marxist of advocating the claims of totalitarianism.

THE PROBLEM OF MULTIPLE REALITIES:
ALFRED SCHUTZ AND ROBERT MUSIL

by

PETER L. BERGER

Robert Musil's great novel, *The Man Without Qualities*, constitutes an entire world.[1] This world has a vast multiplicity of facets, enough to keep a couple of generations of *Germanisten* fully occupied, and certainly far too many to attempt even an overview here. There are facets of this world that clearly refer to the external, historical situation of the novel – Austria on the eve of World War I. But, from the beginning, there are dimensions of the novel's world that have nothing to do with this location in space and time. Indeed, as the novel develops, it is these dimensions that move into the foreground of attention and give the socio-historical events the quality of a largely ironic preamble. What Musil attempted in his gigantic work was nothing less than a solution of the problem of reality from the perspective of modern consciousness – a consciousness that, unlike most others who have talked about it, he not only posits but painstakingly describes. A central theme in this context is what Musil calls the "other condition" (*"der andere Zustand"*) – another reality that haunts the reality of everyday life and the quest of which becomes the principal concern of Ulrich's, the novel's main protagonist. It is this theme that will interest us here.

The centrality of the "other condition" to *The Man Without Qualities* has been remarked upon by several critics and has recently been the subject

---

[1] We have throughout used the edition of *Der Mann ohne Eigenschaften* by Adolf Frisé (Hamburg, Rowohlt, 1952). All subsequent numbers, unless otherwise stated, refer to the pagination of this edition, which includes not only the part of the novel published in the early 1930's, but a vast bulk of material from the *Nachlass*. The edition has been severely criticized for its handling of the *Nachlass,* but has become standard nonetheless. Most of this literary controversy, of course, is irrelevant to our present purpose. To date, only the part of the novel published during Musil's lifetime is available in English – *The Man Without Qualities* (New York, Coward-McCann, 1953). The English translators have been among Frisé's sharpest critics. Cf. Ernst Kaiser and Eithne Wilkins, *Robert Musil – Eine Einführung in das Werk* (Stuttgart, Kohlhammer, 1962).

of a careful monograph.[2] But it is not our aim here to engage in literary criticism. Rather, we want to show this central theme if Musil's novel can be illuminated with the aid of certain Schutzian categories and, conversely, how Alfred Schutz's analysis of the problem of multiple realities can be effectively illustrated by means of Musil's novel.[3] Such a confrontation between Schutz and Musil has intrinsic plausibility to anyone familiar with their respective works. To what extent this could also be ascribed to the fact that they were both contemporaries and compatriots may be left open. One may recall, if one wishes, the opinion of yet another important Austrian figure of this period, Karl Kraus, to the effect that Austria served as a dress rehearsal for the apocalypse – an opinion echoed by Musil when he writes, in a note for *The Man Without Qualities*, that Austria is a particularly clear case of the modern world.[4]

The Man Without Qualities contains a veritable labyrinth of plots and sub-plots, but its major events can be easily summarized. Ulrich, a moderately well-to-do and highly promising mathematician in his early thirties (*nel mezzo del camin . . .*) decides to take a year's "vacation from life", with the purpose of dealing with a vague but general malaise concerning his manner of living. The entire action of the novel falls within this year, between the summers of 1913 and 1914, mostly in Vienna. During this period Ulrich becomes involved in two public affairs. The one is a large-scale undertaking, sponsored by the government but centered in the *salon* of Diotima, wife of a high government official and an "influential lady of indescribable spiritual grace". The aim of this undertaking, begun in competition with a similar enterprise in Germany, is to celebrate the 70th anniversary of the coronation of the Emperor Francis-Joseph in 1918 by proclaiming the true meaning of the Austro-Hungarian monarchy. The other affair is the trial of Moosbrugger, the demented murderer of a prostitute, in whose fate Ulrich and some of his friends have a mysterious interest. Both these affairs move into the background in the later stages of the novel. The turning point in Ulrich's year comes with the death of his

---

[2] Ingrid Drevermann, "Wirklichkeit und Mystik", in Sibylle Bauer and Ingrid Drevermann, *Studien zu Robert Musil* (Cologne, Boehlau, 1966). Drevermann's monograph has been useful for the present paper, but our approach to the problem, of course, is from a very different vantage point.

[3] The problem, of course, is taken up in several places in Schutz's opus. We would especially refer to the following articles: – "On Multiple Realities", in *Collected Papers*, vol. I (The Hague, Nijhoff, 1962), p. 207 ff.; "Symbol, Reality and Society", in *ibid.*, p. 287 ff.; "The Stranger – An Essay in Social Psychology", in *Collected Papers*, vol. II (The Hague, Nijhoff, 1964), p. 91 ff.; "Don Quixote and the Problem of Reality", in *ibid.*, p. 135 ff.

[4] 1577.

father. Ulrich returns to the provincial city, where he grew up and at whose university his father had been a professor of law, for the funeral and the settlement of the estate. There he meets Agathe, his "forgotten sister", whom he has not seen since childhood. Ulrich and Agathe, who has decided to leave her husband, return to Vienna and set up a common household, with the express purpose of together discovering the "other condition" that has become Ulrich's passionate goal. What remains of the unfinished novel, including the fragmentary material from Musil's posthumous papers, deals with the unfolding relationship between Ulrich and Agathe.

Ulrich is a man standing in the very midst of everyday reality – young, successful, open to the world. It is this everyday reality that we encounter with full force in the early chapters of the novel, beginning with the first paragraph, which gives us the exact weather report for central Europe for a lovely day in August 1913. It is this reality that, throughout the novel, serves as the departure point as well as the foil for Ulrich's ventures into other regions of being – the "paramount reality", in Schutz's sense, in which "normal life" takes place and which persists in its massive facticity even after various breakdowns in the fabric of "normality".

This reality is presented by Musil in its overwhelming richness, in itself a vast assemblage of different social worlds. In a rapidly revolving kaleidoscope we meet such different milieux as that of the higher officialdom, the military, the polite intelligentsia, the international business world, as well as the dank, subterranean sphere in which Moosbrugger has his social habitat. Various figures representing these milieux are drawn by Musil with almost ethnographic exactitude – for example, Count Leinsdorf (the tolerant, rather tired dignitary who first thought up the great patriotic *Parallelaktion*, so called because of its competition with the German undertaking), General Stumm von Bordwehr (a figure drawn with loving care, who tries honestly and hard to grasp the vagaries of the civilian mind within the orderly categories of military logic), Diotima (who escapes from the pedantic bed of her husband into the intoxicating realm of ideas and of the "soul") or Arnheim (the Prussian business tycoon, who is at the same time a man of "soul" and intellect, and of whom Musil gives us a portrait composed with the precision of acute antipathy). It is safe to say, however, that Musil does not present us with this array of sociologically specific figures with the intention of giving us an overall picture of Austrian society at that time (in this respect, one might profitably contrast Musil with his younger compatriot novelist Heimito von Doderer). The rich reality of the sociological assembly remains a foil for what is to come, a means rather than an end. *The Man Without Qualities*, Musil notes himself, is not a "great Austrian novel", nor a "historical report", nor a "description of society".[5] Rather, this particualr society is presented to us with the intention of bringing out certain key features of *any* society, that is, with the intention of delineating the essential structure of everyday reality.

While everyday reality is experienced as a totality, it is within itself variegated and stratified. Thus, for instance, Diotima and her maid Rachel (the little Jewish girl from Galicia who passionately reveres the glittering people she feels privileged to serve) share the same everyday reality, even live in the same house, yet are separated by an enormous gulf in terms of their respective social worlds. Because of this differentiation within everyday reality, the transition from one of its sectors to another can be experienced as a shock. This is felt, for instance, by Ulrich as he arrives in the cold splendor of the *Hofburg* for an audience with a high imperial official, or by the good General Stumm in his mounting perplexity at the intellectual debates in Diotima's *salon*. These shock experiences foreshadow the shock that accompanies any transitions *beyond* the domain of everyday reality, but they are both quantitatively and qualitatively more moderate, for the simple reason that the transition they signal takes place between sectors of *the same* comprehensive reality of the social world, that is, still takes place within the same ontological coordinates.

The world of everyday reality presents itself as self-evident facticity. In order to live a "normal" life in society, it must be taken for granted as such. Only then can one travel through time as on "a train that rolls down its own rails ahead of itself", thus "move within firm walls and on a firm ground".[6] This feat, however, requires a specific suspension of doubt – to wit, the *"epoché* of the natural attitude". As Ulrich puts it to himself on the nocturnal walk during which he decides to devote himself fully to the investigation of the "other condition", being at home in the world of everyday reality presupposes a "perspectival abridgment" of consciousness.[7] Only then does that reality take on the appearance of an "orderly, smooth roundness", within which the life of the individual becomes plausible to himself as an orderly and seemingly necessary sequence of facts.[8] Most people are satisfied with this accomplishment, because it gives them the impression that their lives have a definite course, an impression that protects them against the terrors of chaos. A life thus lived is suffused with the warm feeling of being at home that a horse has in its stable.[9]

[5] 1600.
[6] 445.
[7] 648 ff.
[8] 650.
[9] 1239 – "Stallgefuehl".

This security in everyday reality, precisely because it rests on the continuous effort of the "*epoché* of the natural attitude", is inherently precarious. From within its own perspective, everyday reality assigns to other ontological possibilities the status of "utopias". Upon closer scrutiny, however, everyday reality loses its taken-for-granted character and itself takes on the appearance of a "utopia" – that is, as the enactment of a highly artificial drama, and a poorly composed one at that. History, expounds Ulrich in a conversation with his friends Walter and Clarisse (two musical spirits who detest what they take to be his cynicism), consists of the dull repetition of the limited number of roles provided for in this "world theater".[10] History is thus based on routine and triviality, and even most murders are only performed because certain roles call for killing. As soon as this viewpoint is taken, everyday reality becomes problematic *as a whole*, over and beyond any specific problems *within* it (such as the political problem of ordering its stratified sectors – which is why Ulrich is un-political). Now, everyday reality is revealed as a tenuous balancing act between a multiplicity of forces bent on destroying it, "a middle condition made up of all possible crimes",[11] a compromise in which all passions check each other and take on a comforting gray coloration.[12]

In terms of the historical situation of *The Man Without Qualities*, the world of its everyday reality moves towards dissolution. Musil's original plan had been to bring the novel to an end with the outbreak of the war. The year 1918, as the reader is ironically aware throughout the whole presentation of the *Parallelaktion*, will see not the definitive proclamation of the true meaning of the Austro-Hungarian monarchy but its cataclysmic destruction. Ulrich's central concern, however, is in another dimension. It is not with this or that problem within the reality of what he calls the "existing system", but with the questioning of the latter's very universe of discourse – or, as he puts it repeatedly, with the "abolition of reality". The utopian vision of the "other condition" lies on the other side of this abolished reality. It is glimpsed, as it were, through the openings of this reality's crumbling structures.

What are these openings? They are the points at which the "*epoché* of the natural attitude" breaks down. These points then become possible transfer stations to the "other condition", not yet identical with the latter, but potential occasions for its attainment. While differing greatly in their experiential content, all these transition points have in common a violent

[10] 364.
[11] 474 – "ein Mittelzustand aus allen uns möglichen Verbrechen".
[12] 573.

breakdown of the taken-for-granted routines of everyday life and, *ipso facto*, an intimation of novel and strange modes of being.

The first allusion to this in the present text of the novel is instructive.[13] Ulrich, on one of his frequent nocturnal walks through the city, is attacked by a gang of hoodlums and knocked unconscious. Upon returning to consciousness, still lying in the street, he finds himself being attended to by a solicitous lady and her coachman (the lady is the ineffably silly and slightly nymphomanic Bonadea, who subsequently becomes Ulrich's mistress for a time). When the lady commiserates with him over the brutality of his experience, he launches into a somewhat feverish discourse in which he defends such brutal, totally physical experiences as most valuable in disrupting the ordinary habits of everyday living. Ulrich's discourse, which startles poor Bonadea in its inappropriateness to the situation, ends by comparing sports with mysticism and love in its capacity to transport the individual into a "truly bottomless, suspended state", suggesting that before long a theology of sports will have to be developed.[14] While this incident is the first one in which the breach of everyday reality is alluded to within the course of the novel, it is not the first such experience in Ulrich's memory. A number of times he recalls an experience he had at the age of 20, as a young lieutenant in the army, when he fell violently in love with the wife of a major and was so terrified by his own turbulent emotions that he fled to a distant and solitary island.[15] It was during this "island experience", indeed, that he had his first intimation of a possible "other condition", a strange and infinitely comforting peace that followed the preceding violence. Both in Ulrich's biography and in the action of the novel, then, the possibility of the "other condition" is first encountered in a sudden interruption of everyday routine, that routine which had been "taken for granted until further notice".

At times such an interruption can occur in the midst of otherwise ordinary events, which, in a flash, are seen as absurd. This absurdity then undermines the taken-for-granted reality of everyday life as a whole. On one such occasion Ulrich, who, against his will, has been made secretary of the *Parallelaktion*, returns home and starts to work through a collection of memoranda sent to him by Count Leinsdorf. This includes such items as a declaration of the archdiocesan ordinariate against confessional mixing in a proposed foundation for orphans and a rejection by the ministry of education of an appropriation requested on behalf of the stenographers'

---

[13] 25 ff.
[14] 29.
[15] 124 ff.

association. Ulrich reacts to all this by "pushing back the package of real world" and going out for a walk, which ends in a visit to Walter and Clarisse, during which Ulrich expounds the afore-mentioned thesis of history as a very dull and very repetitious *theatrum mundi*.[16] On another occasion Ulrich is interrogated in a police station in the wake of a street incident in which he has been unwittingly implicated. As customary in such situations, Ulrich is asked his name, age, occupation and domicile, and in a not too friendly fashion, since the street incident, created by a drunken and aggressively class-conscious worker, entailed the offence of *lèse-majesté*. All at once, Ulrich has the impression of being caught up in a machine that is grinding his customary identity to pieces, dissolving such seemingly durable elements of that identity as his scientific reputation or the sensitive complexity of his emotional life. He experiences a "statistical disenchantment" of his person and is more shaken by this than by the immediate inconvenience of his collision with the forces of law and order. It is still under the impact of this experience, weakened in the robustness of his accustomed way of life, that he accepts Count Leinsdorf's invitation to become secretary of the *Parallelaktion* on the following day.[17]

An important place is given in the novel to sexuality and sexual experiences, in terms of their efficacy in creating breaches in the structures of everyday reality. This, indeed, is a theme that runs through much of Musil's work outside *The Man Without Qualities*, with sexuality frequently appearing as a Dionysian, chaotic and ominous force.[18] Sexuality violently interrupts the ordinary routines of life, tearing the masks of their social roles from the faces of men and women in its grip and revealing a howling animality beneath the civilized decorum. As Ulrich observes after one of his wild bouts with Bonadea, it suddenly transforms individuals into "raving madmen", and it is in this capacity that sexual experience is "inserted" into everyday reality as an "island of a second condition of consciousness".[19] Interestingly enough, in the same passage, Ulrich compares sexuality with other interruptions of everyday reality, specifically the theater, music and religion. The violent eruption of sexual frenzy into everyday life marks a threshold of a disparate sphere of reality, a "finite province of meaning" existing as an enclave within the "paramount reality" of everyday life, as does the raising of the curtain on the theatrical stage, the raised baton of the conductor at the opening of a concert and the introit of the

---

[16] 363 ff.
[17] 159 ff.
[18] Cf., for example, Musil's first novel, *Die Verwirrungen des Zöglings Törless* (Hamburg, Rowohlt, 1959).
[19] 115.

liturgy. It is not surprising, then, that Ulrich is not so much sad as contemplative *post coitum*. It is after the afore-mentioned sexual bout with Bonadea, while the latter interminably prolongs the process of getting dressed and getting out, that Ulrich has a vision of Moosbrugger.[20] And it is after Bonadea has finally made her departure that Ulrich, walking through the streets, engages in a long meditation on the fictitiousness and arbitrariness of ordinary social life.[21]

Violent aesthetic experience is another mode of interruption. Musil was particularly fascinated by music in these terms. In the novel it is especially represented by Walter and Clarisse, Ulrich's friends, who exist in the midst of violent emotional upheavals, mainly directed against each other, to the accompaniment of an ongoing musical turbulence. The piano in their apartment is always open, ready to start the tumult all over again, reminding Ulrich of the bared teeth of an all-devouring idol.[22] Clarisse moves ever more deeply into this "spirit of music" as the novel develops. It is in this spirit that she becomes fascinated with Moosbrugger (a murderer, she exclaims at one point, who is musical and must therefore be helped) and the possibility of liberating him from prison, that she is drawn irresistibly to the company of madmen, until she finally succumbs to madness herself. One should not lightly surrender to the dark power of music, Musil suggests – nor to that of mathematics. The quality of mathematics as an interruption of everyday reality is not developed in detail in *The Man Without Qualities* (despite the fact that Ulrich, like Musil himself, was trained as a mathematician), but the idea is already fully expressed in Musil's first novel, *Die Verwirrungen des Zöglings Törless*. The world of mathematics, like that of sexual and aesthetic experience, establishes a separate universe of discourse existing within everyday reality as an alien intrusion, superficially contained, made into an "island", by the habits of social routine, but always threatening to break out of this containment and to shatter the fabric of taken-for-granted "normality".

Everyday reality contains alien enclaves and, to protect its own integrity and the peace of mind of its inhabitants, it must control these enclaves. It is this necessity of control that is illustrated most sharply in the figure of Moosbrugger, who represents the criminal possibility found in every society and *ipso facto* threatens the "middle condition" that is social reality. To be sure, Moosbrugger, who goes about "senselessly" murdering people, poses a problem of social control in the trivial criminological sense. Much more

---

[20] 117 ff.
[21] 128 ff.
[22] 48.

fundamentally, however, he poses a problem of reality control. For the most dangerous thing about Moosbrugger is not that he murders people, but that he has no socially understandable motives for doing so and, worse still, actually feels innocent of any crime. He inhabits that "second home-land, in which everything one does is done innocently".[23] The law, there-fore, is not just an instrument to control and punish Moosbrugger's criminal acts. More importantly, the law is the agency of society that solemnly negates Moosbrugger's *criminal reality* – a reality that, unless negated, threatens the suspension of doubt on which all social order rests. This negation is undertaken by means of the juridically precise assignment of culpability, that is, by *translating* Moosbrugger's acts from his reality to that of society. It is just this that is done by the judges in Ulrich's vision. The counter-image to the judges, society's most impressive definers of reality, is the "dancing Moosbrugger", a mythological figure of threatening chaos.[24] Yet, ironically, Moosbrugger foreshadows the interruption of every-day reality by the collective crime of the coming war, which, in its own way, also posits another "condition".[25] Crime and war, then, replicate on the level of public life the reality-shattering effect of sexual and aesthetic experience in the life of individuals.

The first part of *The Man Without Qualities* ends with Ulrich's decision to take up seriously the guest of the "other condition", in two chapters entitled "The Way Home" and "Turning Point".[26] The background of the decision lies in the breach experiences just discussed, in the fully reflected-upon relativization of everyday reality brought on by these experiences, as well as in the instinctive rejection by Ulrich of inferior approximations of the "other condition" (notably, those represented by Clarisse and Moos-brugger). Ulrich is walking in the direction of his home. It is a beautiful but dark night, the streets are empty, there is a feeling of impending events as in a theater. Ulrich is walking along the Ringstrasse, the broad circular bou-levard that encloses the inner city of Vienna. Instead of crossing it, which would take him towards his house by the most direct route, he goes off on a tangent, following a stretch of sky visible above the trees of the boule-vard. He feels a sense of great peace, but immediately reflects that this very peace, this sensation of at-home-ness, is only the result of that "perspec-tival abridgment" that makes "normal" life possible – a feat that he can no longer accomplish satisfactorily. He recalls the "island experience" of his

[23] 119 – "eine zweite Heimat, in der alles, was man tut, unschuldig ist".
[24] 393 ff.
[25] 1496.
[26] "Heimweg", 647 ff., and "Umkehrung", 654 ff.

early youth, its feeling of liberating simplicity, and recognizes that his life
will never again follow a straight line, but must henceforth move on an
infinitely expanding plane. It is in the midst of these reflections that he is
accosted by a streetwalker. For a moment he is tempted to accept her
invitation for a few moments of uncomplicated pleasure, but then he recalls
that it was under just such circumstances that Moosbrugger must have met
his victim. He gives the customary fee to the girl, says a friendly word to
her, and walks on. It is in this instant that he understands Moosbrugger's
meaning for him – "an escaped parable of order" – and a parable to be
rejected for ever.[27] And, an instant later, he says to himself: – "All this will
have to be decided!" He understands that he must choose, decisively,
whether to live like other men for attainable goals or to take seriously the
"impossibilities" haunting him.

Ulrich hurries towards his house now, strongly sensing that an important
event is about to take place. Upon coming home, he sees that the lights are
on. His first thought is that a burglar has entered the house (the German
word *Einbrecher* indicates the, let us say, ontological association intended
by Musil), but upon entering he finds that the "burglar" was Clarisse (who,
in one of her increasingly frequent frenzies, has decided to seduce Ulrich).
The real nature of the "forceful entry" (*Einbruch*), however, is revealed a
moment later, when Clarisse hands him a telegram announcing the death
of his father. It is this death that inaugurates the decisive rupture in Ulrich's
year of "vacation". It is an intriguing question whether Musil here intends
an allusion to the "death of the father" in Nietzsche's sense – the "un-
intended solomnity" of Ulrich's announcement to Clarisse, "my father has
died", and Clarisse's previously expressed interest in Nietzsche give a certain plausibility to the thought.[28] In any case, the news of his father's death
leads to Ulrich's fateful journey to the provincial city of his childhood,
where his father is to be buried, and to the encounter with his sister Agathe.
And that encounter, indeed, takes place under the shadow of this death, in
a "house of grief".[29] It is thus in the presence of the ultimate "interruption"
of everyday reality that Ulrich's deliberate quest for the "other condition"
begins in earnest. On the night of his decision Ulrich gets rid of the in-
opportune Clarisse, almost absent-mindedly, and prepares himself to meet
"this business" with the same mixture of irrational peace and observant
rationality that he had felt earlier on his walk home.

The presupposition of the "other condition", at least in Ulrich's case, is

[27] 653 – "ein entsprungenes Gleichnis der Ordnung".
[28] 655 – "mit einiger unwillkürlicher Feierlichkeit".
[29] 686.

the relativization of everyday reality. The theoretical content of this relativization is nicely summed up in what could be called Ulrich's negative credo, a set of propositions propounded in answer to a question by Agathe as to what he believes in.[30] It opens, systematically enough, with the statement that all existing morality is a concession to a society of savages, that none of it is correct, and that behind it glimmers "another meaning", which has the potentiality of consuming fire. The "other condition", however, is not experiencing the world. As such, it is located "tangentially" with reference attainable by means of theoretical propositions. It is a different mode of to the reality of everyday life, which it "touches" at unexpected places. It can only be entered from the domain of everyday reality by going off at a "tangent", as Ulrich did in his nocturnal walk home. Putting the same thing in Schutzian terms, the "other condition" constitutes a "finite province of meaning", disparate with reference to the common-sense reality of everyday life, and possessing a distinctive "cognitive style". What, then, is this cognitive structure?

An indication is already given in Ulrich's first recollection of his "island experience".[31] There is a dissolution of differentiations, particularly of the differentiation between subjective consciousness and the objective, external world. There is a feeling of oneness with the "heart of the world", of being carried by being as such, a cessation of movement, an overwhelming lucidity. Already here there is an explicit reference to mysticism, though Ulrich (or Musil) hesitates to fully identify his experience with that of the mystics. In Ulrich's first communication about this to Agathe there is added the element of isolation from other men, of alienation from the world and even one's own body, which, however, is not only not terrifying but acutely happy.[32] What the novel tells us about the character of the "other condition" is then developed mainly in the ongoing communication about it between Ulrich and Agathe, particularly in the so-called "holy conversations".[33] It is clear that it entails a different mode of experiencing not only the world but also the self and others. The world is seen as full of hitherto unsuspected interconnections. making up an all-embracing totality that is experienced in a state of profound calm.[34] There is a feeling that nothing more can happen – and yet that everything is happening. There is further a loss of self, a surrender to the stillness of being, an abandonment of all

---

[30] 769 ff.
[31] 125 f.
[32] 723 f.
[33] Beginning with 746 ff. and taken up *passim* through what remains of the text.
[34] 762 f.

desire, even the desire to ask questions.[35] Very importantly, the experience is one of intense love, for all others and for the whole world, which is now understood to be founded on love.[36] The experience also includes a different mode of time (or *durée*). One now no longer lives "for" things, but "in" them – that is, one no longer exists in projects into the future ("moving, striving, weaving, ploughing, sowing . . ."), but in the *hic et nunc* of an eternal present.[37]

Although the passages in which the "other condition" is described extend to impressive lengths, they are disappointing to a degree. Despite Ulrich's (or Musil's) valiant efforts to articulate what is, almost by definition, inarticulable, the reader fails to obtain a coherent idea of just what the nature of the experience is. This is hardly surprising. Language originates in and is primarily geared to the reality of everyday life. The attempt to use language to refer to experiences that are totally outside this reality is predestined to fail, almost *a priori*. It is made very clear that the "other condition" is, if not completely the same, yet closely analogous to the experience of mystical union – an experience that, whatever its ultimate ontological status, has proven to be intensely resistant to linguistic communication. Yet it is also made very clear that Ulrich's mysticism, if such it is to be called, is a mysticism "with all exactness" – that is, a mysticism that does not abandon itself to orgiastic ecstasies but always retains its linkage to rational lucidity.[38] It is also a mysticism without any theological presuppositions, indeed without any positive religious faith.[39]

The entrance into any reality alternative to that of everyday life requires a breach of the "*epoché* of the natural attitude" upon which the latter is founded. The new, alternative reality (that is, the reality of any "finite province of meaning"), however, requires *its own "epoché"* – once more, one can only exist within *this* reality by suspending doubts about *it*. Such a secondary "*epoché*", as we might call it, is part and parcel of the "cognitive style" of every "finite province of meaning". Without it, the new reality is threatened with the same kind of collapse that it originally "inflicted" upon the reality of everyday life. What is more, to the extent that the new reality is removed from the massive reality-confirmations of every-

---

[35] 1143 ff. This is the chapter entitled "Atemzüge eines Sommertags", possibly the last one written by Musil before his death and containing the most intense description of the experience.

[36] 1240 f., but also *passim* throughout the "holy conversations".

[37] 1331 f.

[38] 665 – "mit aller Exaktheit".

[39] 1604 – as Musil notes about the novel as a whole, "religiös" unter den Voraussetzungen der Ungläubigen".

ιay life, it is *more* susceptible to disintegration than the latter, therefore *more* in need of a determined suspension of doubt. And, indeed, we find that the "other condition" is a very fragile business. Every little interruption of the experience by the trivialities of ordinary life threatens to upset the precarious reality of the "other condition" – and then it is "as if a goddess were running after a bus".[40] As the attempt is made to retain the experience over a period of time, moments of apodictic certainty alternate with the suspicion of madness.[41] Ulrich and Agathe, in their "magic forest", experience something that they take to be eternal – and yet fear that it may dissolve into nothingness in the very next instant.[42] This contradiction increasingly preoccupies them.

The basic empirical problem of the "other condition" is succinctly stated by Ulrich himself when he says: "Faith must not be one hour old!"[43] But those who hold the faith are getting older every hour – older not in the timeless reality of the "other condition" but in the concrete "standard time" of that everyday reality in which, despite everything, they continue to live. Their problem is thus one of "synchronization". Put differently, they face the problem of legitimating the coexistence of the "other condition", in which time stands still, with the world of everyday reality, in which all things continue to move through time. In this, of course, they are not alone. To the extent that, at any rate, approximations to the "other condition" permeate everyday reality, the problem exists wherever everyday reality is "invaded" by other realities. From the perspective of *either* reality, the old *or* the new, there is the problem of "translating" the alternative reality into terms appropriate to the reality in which one has chosen to stand. This, as Schutz has shown, is a central problem of *Don Quixote* – the problem that Quixote himself tried to solve by his theory of the "enchanters", those powerful magicians who can change things back and forth between the two contending realities.[44]

Seen in the perspective of everyday reality, the problem is to explain and thus to neutralize the alien presence of the "other condition". There are a number of ways by which this can be accomplished. One common and theoretically unsophisticated way is to look upon the eruptions of "otherness" into everyday life as a stimulating interlude, from which one may then return, refreshed, to one's ordinary routines as one returns from a

---

[40] 1209.
[41] 1213.
[42] 1246.
[43] 755.
[44] Cf. *Collected Papers*, vol. II, p. 142 ff.

vacation.[45] The "other condition", or whatever approximations to it are experienced under such circumstances, is trivialized as sentimentality. Its reality is accepted, without undue disturbance, "for the duration of the vacation" (and, as Ulrich remarks, mysticism, by contrast, is the intention to go "on vacation" permanently). This way of coping with the "other condition" is even employed by businessmen, who, on vacation in the Alps, enter into a quasi-mystical contemplation of bucolic scenery.

On a more sophisticated and institutionalized level, organized religion has always coped with the "other condition" by encapsulating it in ecclesiastical routines of one kind or another.[46] Ulrich, who keeps on reading classical mystical texts during the whole period of the "holy conversations", hypothesizes that the "other condition" represents a human capacity *older* than the historical religions. These, in their ecclesiastical organizations, have always tried to keep the "other condition" under control. Their representatives have always viewed the "other condition" with the suspicion of bureaucrats in the face of private enterprise and have consistently (and, says Ulrich, with apparent justification) sought to replace it by a generally understandable morality. What Ulrich refers to here is, of course, the same phenomenon that Max Weber called the "routinization of charisma" – indeed, the parallel is striking. The Catholic procedure of containing mystical explosions within the "safe" institutional enclaves of monasticism may serve by way of illustration. But, as Ulrich quickly points out in the same discussion, secularization has not eliminated the problem. The alien intrusions still occur and, in the absence of the old ecclesiastical "therapies", new ways must be found to cope with this. One of these ways is provided by modern science, which can explain and thus legitimate the "other condition" in psychiatric categories.[47] Later in the novel, in connection with Clarisse's descent into madness, we encounter this function of psychiatry in the figure of Dr. Friedenthal, whose mental hospital serves as a bulwark in the defense of the "island of sanity" that is everyday reality.[48] The psychiatric "treatment" of reality-shattering experiences illustrates very clearly the double character of such defensive operations – the "other condition" is physically, institutionally contained and, simultaneously, theoretically liquidated. In a much more general way, there is the peculiarly European or western methodology of "treating" the "other condition" by regarding it, along with the emotional life as a whole, as a preamble or

---

[45] 767.
[46] 766.
[47] 767 f.
[48] 1391 ff. and 1517 ff.

accompaniment of purposeful activity in the empirical world.[49] This general orientation makes it possible to view the "inner world" of the mind as a beautiful and profound thing (that which Diotima and Arnheim call "the soul"), but nevertheless deal with all this beauty and profundity as mere appendages to the "real life" of activity in the world as socially defined. Thus the "vacation" status of all alien states of consciousness is guaranteed both practically and theoretically. By contrast, oriental cultures have much more readily made concessions to the "other condition" as an autonomous ontological state – with arresting effects on this-wordly activity. Again, the parallel with some of Weber's analyses (specifically, in his comparative sociology of religion) is striking here.

Seen in the perspective of the "other condition" itself, the problem of legitimation is, of course, the reverse – how to protect the fragile reality of the "other condition" from the massive threat of the surrounding reality of everyday life. This "maintenance" problem can be put in sociological terms by saying that the "other condition" requires a specific "plausibility structure" – that is, specific *social* relations that serve to confirm and sustain its reality.[50] This sociological principle (which can be elaborated theoretically not only in Schutzian terms but in terms derived from the social psychology of George Herbert Mead) is stated explicitly by Ulrich himself. Ideas require social resonance to attain and to retain their plausibility. A young man, says Ulrich at one point, sends out ideas in all directions – but only those that obtain a response from those around him come back to him and attain a certain "density".[51] Man is, above all, the talking animal – he even requires conversation in order to procreate.[52] It is in conversation with others that an ordered reality is built up and kept going. This social construction of reality extends to identity itself. Thus, among lovers, "one constructs the other, as a puppet with which one has already played in one's dreams".[53] And when Agathe asks Ulrich "but how am I really?" he can only laugh and point to this reciprocal construction – "I see you as I need you" – and no one can say what either of them is "ultimately".[54]

In the novel it is the relationship between Ulrich and Agathe, and *only*

---

[49] 1315 f.

[50] The term "plausibility structure", unlike the previous analytic concepts in quotation marks, is not directly Schutzian, though it can readily be integrated with Schutz's analysis of the problem of multiple realities. Cf. Peter Berger and Thomas Luckmann, *The Social Construction of Reality* (Garden City, N.Y., Doubleday, 1966), especially, p. 144 ff.

[51] 116.

[52] 1130.

[53] 1131.

[54] 1177.

this relationship, which serves as the "plausibility structure" of the "other condition". Seen sociologically, this alone will predict the extreme fragility of the latter. As Georg Simmel has shown, the "dyad" is the most tenuous of social relationships – consequently, the reality constructed and maintained by a dyadic "plausibility structure" will be very tenuous. Yet the presence and response of the other, specifically one who is as much a "significant other" (to use Mead's term) as Agathe, bestows a reality-accent upon the "other condition" that it never had for Ulrich alone.[55] During the earlier "island experience" he could only give "density" to the experience by writing long letters to his "distant lover" – and, understandably, this effort failed very quickly. But now Agathe "is really here".[56] She listens, confirms and, above all, shares the experience. And precisely in moments of doubt about the whole thing, Ulrich can reassure himself by exclaiming "how beautiful is Agathe's voice!".[57]

The relationship of Ulrich and Agathe is entered with the explicit purpose of experiencing the "other condition" in common. It is in this sense that it is a "journey to the border of the possible" and a "marginal case".[58] It is in the "real presence" of each other's company that the "other condition" is to be experienced and articulated. The analogy with a religious community is thus perfectly logical. Indeed, there are sections in the "holy conversations" that have the quality of liturgical diaphony. The essential "maintenance" problem of Ulrich and Agathe is thus similar to that of any religious community whose members must continue to live "in the world" – but aggravated by the fact that their community, after all, has only two members.

When Ulrich and Agathe decide to live together in Vienna, after their father's funeral, they conceive of this as an "entrance into the millenium".[59] They will live, they say, like hermits – and already at this point Agathe is a little worried that such a millenial existence might be rather boring. Upon their return to Vienna they first plan to remodel Ulrich's house, but soon abandon this plan and decide to leave it as it is – after all, physical surroundings are irrelevant by definition to one living in the "other condition". It turns out that they do not quite live like hermits, partly because old friends and acquaintances (led by the indomitable General Stumm) manage

[55] In the sense of reality construction, Ulrich is truly "married" to Agathe – quite apart from the question of incest between them. *Cf.* Peter Berger and Hansfried Kellner, "Marriage and the Construction of Reality", *Diogenes,* Summer 1964.

[56] 892 – "Agathe ist wirklich da".

[57] 1209.

[58] 761.

[59] 801.

to penetrate their isolation, partly perhaps because of the very boredom that Agathe foresaw. But they look upon their "worldly" involvements as an "interlude".[60] Like the early Christians and sectarians everywhere, they live "in the world, but not of it" – or so they hope. They walk through the streets together, relishing the thought that they seem like ordinary people and that nobody can suspect their secret existence.[61] They are drawn to the world of ordinary people, yet shrink from it, because any real immersion in it threatens the precarious fabric of their "holy" life together.[62] They feel that they "ought to do something", but do not know what, and their life together is burdened by this absence of activity – that is, by the absence of the reality-giving force of *praxis*.[63] Because of this separation from *praxis* (which is the genetic matrix of language), their conversations ever again take on an accent of "irreality" to themselves. Thus the fence around the garden of their house both separates them from and binds them to the world of ordinary life – an ambiguous and disturbing boundary.[64]

What goes on behind this barrier can well be described as "total conversation". For Ulrich and Agathe not only converse about the "other condition", but literally about everything. In the course of this conversation they even re-define (or, if one wishes, re-construct) each other's respective pasts.[65] The relentless mutual openness and the loss of previously held identity that this entails frightens both of them. Both make some attempts to withdraw from this intensity, but the attempts are half-hearted and partial – they feel guilty about these withdrawals, which appear to them as betrayals, and return from them into the ongoing "totalization" (to use a term of Sartre's) of their privileged conversation. One may say that, *mutatis mutandis*, they experience what in Catholic monasticism has been called the sin of "particularity" – the withdrawal, sinful by definition, from the totalizing community. A lot of time is spent in reading, much of it of mystical texts. They do read books separately, but the "particularity" of this is neutralized by their subsequent joint discussion of these books. Ulrich, in a deliberate effort to control the power of "reciprocal suggestion" of his conservation with Agathe, starts keeping a diary, which contains highly rational and even skeptical psychological observations about what

[60] 936.
[61] 943.
[62] 1095 ff.
[63] Schutz, of course, emphasized the centrality of practical activity and projects in the constitution of everyday reality. This can, we think, be linked with the Marxian category of *praxis*.
[64] 1162 ff.
[65] 953 ff.

is going on between them.[66] His diary, though, perhaps by subconscious design, is left lying about in such a way that Agathe finds it. Only after they have included *it* in their endless conversation do they feel that "everything is in order again".[67] Agathe reacts to her discovery of the diary by taking revenge and cultivating a relationship from which Ulrich is excluded. This is with Lindner, a widowed pedagogue she meets on a walk in the woods during a fit of intense depression and who has the erotically tinged ambition to "educate" her. She does not openly tell Ulrich about her meetings with Lindner – but he knows about them, and she knows that he knows. In one way or another, then, the integrity of the separate reality of the "other condition" is maintained. At least in the material (most of it from Musil's posthumous papers) directly pertaining to the Viennese "hermitage" of Ulrich and Agathe, the attempt to maintain the "other condition" as a plausible reality is successful to a considerable degree.

Perhaps enough has been said to indicate that *The Man Without Qualities* contains perspectives of some interest for a phenomenology of the *Lebenswelt* and for the general problem of multiple realities. Musil's great novel, however, has a more timely significance. Ulrich, "the man without qualities", is deliberately presented by Musil as a prototype of modern man. As has been remarked upon by several critics, Ulrich is one of the most "faceless" characters in modern literature – and this in a novel that abounds in sharply profiled characters. This is not due to some artistic failure on the part of the author. Ulrich's "facelessness", his deprivation of "qualities", is deliberate and essential. The "man without qualities" is, at the same time, the "man of possibility".[68] He is marked by two distinctively modern traits – an openness to all possible modes of experience and interpretation – and a persistent, highly rational reflectiveness about the world and himself. Thus Musil, in his painstaking literary delineation of this, creates a paradigm of modernity that bears striking resemblance to a number of non-literary conceptualizations of modern man – such as David Riesman's conceptualization of the "other-directed character", Arnold Gehlen's of "subjectivization", and Helmut Schelsky's of "permanent reflectiveness" (*Dauerreflektion*). Only if this is seen can one grasp the true scope of what Musil attempted to do in his nearly life-long struggle with this book – and, one may say, with Ulrich.

Modern man, as the "man without qualities", is open to an indeterminate

---

[66] 1205 ff. The diary contains, among other things, a very interesting theory of the emotions, which, however, is not of direct interest to us here.

[67] 1322.

[68] 1579 – "Möglichkeitsmensch".

number of reality – and self-transformations. Put differently, modern man is prone to "alternation" between discrepant worlds of reality.[69] The reasons for this (which are far from mysterious, but empirically available to historical and sociological analysis) need not concern us here. But in this sense one can view the novel as a whole (not just Ulrich's "experiment" with the "other condition") as a vast treatise in "alternation". Thus most of the important characters in the novel serve as "embodiments" of alternate possibilities for Ulrich and/or Agathe. There is a whole "chorus" of characters representing the constant possibility of returning to ordinary life through an abandonment of both excessive openness and excessive reflectiveness. There is Arnheim, a sort of "master of realities", who appears *as if* he fully controlled his own life and any possible transformations in it, who manages to combine his commercial interests in Austrian oil wells with a magnificent sensitivity of the "soul", who, indeed, seems to combine in his person all the "qualities" that others have separately – and who, probably for this very reason, is detested by Musil.[70] There are several figures, notably Count Leinsdorf and General Stumm, who represent a conservative pessimism that sees in political order the only viable bulwark against reality-disintegrating chaos. Lindner, Agathe's semi-secret mentor, embodies the security of conventional morality and religion – a security to which, we are told, he fled in his early youth after a terrifying encounter with religious ecstasy.[71] Walter and Clarisse, and the poet Feuermaul who plays an important role in their lives, present Ulrich with the tempting possibility of Dionysian intoxication – at the end of which stands the sinister figure of Moosbrugger, the mad murderer. There are even fairly detailed representations of most timely political possibilities in the novel – a proto-Nazi romantic nationalism, represented (ironically) by the Jewish girl Gerda Fischel and her "Aryan" boyfriend Hans Sepp [72] – and revolutionary socalism, represented by Schmeisser, the son of the gardener of Ulrich's father.[73]

All these figures, along with Ulrich and Agathe, have one common problem that appears to be endemic to their historical situation – that of maintaining or establishing anew principles of order in the face of threatening chaos. This is also the essential problem of the *Parallelaktion*. As we know from the beginning, of course, the attempt to root order in the public reality

---

[69] Cf. Peter Berger, *The Precarious Vision* (Garden City, N.Y., Doubleday, 1961), p. 8 ff., and Berger and Luckmann, *op. cit.*, pp. 144 ff. and 155 ff.

[70] Cf. the poisonous portrayals of Arnheim on 26 ff., 47 ff. and 95 ff.

[71] 1299 ff.

[72] 307 ff. and later, *passim*.

[73] 1322 ff. and 1328 ff.

of the monarchy fails, and Musil makes it very clear that he has no great hopes for political projects for a "new order". But what about Ulrich's and Agathe's attempts at order-construction in their private reality?

It is on this issue that the literary controversy over the posthumous material for *The Man Without Qualities* is interesting for us. There are two principal positions on Musil's intentions with regard to the end of the unfinished novel. In terms of literary criticism, they hinge on the status of a passage in the posthumous material, entitled "The Journey into Paradise", that describes a journey by Ulrich and Agathe to Italy, where they commit incest and eventually become disillusioned with each other as well as with their "experiment".[74] Adolf Frisé, the editor of the standard edition of the novel, places the passage towards the end of the last part, *after* the "holy conversations". This editorial decision has important consequences in interpretation. The incestuous journey here represents the climax of the "experiment", the decisive attempt to attain the "other condition" through a violent break with "normality". The "experiment" fails, the "other condition" collapses, and Ulrich and Agathe return to the "utopia of the inductive attitude", a phrase of Musil's understood by Frisé as an acceptance of the primacy of ordinary, social life. Frisé's post-incestuous Ulrich even turns his attention to political matters, such as the coming role of China on the world scene.[75] Frisé's critical position, as well as the interpretation it entails, have been sharply attacked, particularly by the English translators of the novel.[76] The latter take the position that the disputed passage was a draft discarded by Musil long before his final years, that in his later plans for the novel there was to be no incest and no physical "journey into paradise", and therefore no collapse of the "experiment" in the wake of such a journey. According to this position, the final plan of the novel did not envisage any developments beyond the stage of the "holy conversations".

Obviously, no layman who has not delved into what must be the labyrinthine depths of Musil's posthumous papers can make a defensible judgment on the issue. Equally obviously, on such a judgment hinges the decision as to whether Musil finally intended Ulrich's attempt to "abolish" reality to succeed or fail. It is quite possible that Musil himself did not know until the end – and, indeed, that this may be at least one of the reasons why the novel remained unfinished at his death. In any case, as things are, Musil leaves us with an unanswered question. But to bring home

---

[74] 1407 ff.

[75] 1609.

[76] Cf. Kaiser and Wilkins, *op. cit.* Frisé has defended himself against this attack in several articles and in a postscript to the 5th printing of his edition, 1618 ff.

to ourselves the import of the question it may be useful to think once more of the analogous problem of Cervantes. Ulrich and Agathe are "Quixotic" figures in a very profound sense. It is not without interest to recall here that, at their very first meeting in the novel, they appear dressed in "Pierrot costumes".[77] There is a "ludic", a "clownish" dimension to their entire "experiment". The two putative outcomes of the latter can be readily put in "Quixotic" terms. If the one outcome is posited, Ulrich's final fate is essentially the same as that of Cervantes' tragi-comic hero – in Schutz's words, "a homecomer to a world to which he does not belong, enclosed in everyday reality as in a prison, and tortured by the most cruel jailer: the common-sense reason which is conscious of its own limits".[78] The other outcome implies a different conclusion. It has been put eloquently by Enid Welsford in the last paragraph of her great history of the clown as a social and literary figure: "To those who do not repudiate the religious insight of the race, the human spirit is uneasy in this world because it is at home elsewhere, and escape from the prison house is possible not only in fancy but in fact. The theist believes in possible beatitude, because he disbelieves in the dignified isolation of humanity. To him, therefore, romantic comedy is serious literature because it is a foretaste of the truth: the Fool is wiser than the Humanist; and clownage is less frivolous than the deification of humanity".[79] In that case, *The Man Without Qualities* would not be a replication of Quixote's tragedy, but a vindication of his comic triumph.

---

[77] 675.
[78] Schutz, *op. cit.,* p. 157.
[79] Enid Welsford, *The Fool* (Garden City, N.Y., Doubleday-Anchor, 1961), p. 326 f.

PHENOMENOLOGY, HISTORY, MYTH

by

FRED KERSTEN

At the end of his *Formale und transzendentale Logik,* Edmund Husserl delineated the boundaries of what he called the "Logos of the aesthetic world" (the passive synthesis of the unity of nature). He then went on to say that founded on that "world" is a multi-leveled structure which eventually acquires the form of "exact natural science (Galilean physics), a science aware of a new style, a non-'descriptive' science, i.e., not a science which typifies and apprehends in concepts 'aesthetic' formations, givenness in pure intuition, but instead an idealizing and logicizing science. As is known, its first historical form and, later on, its guide, was Platonic geometry which did not speak of right-angles, circles, etc. in the 'aesthetic' sense, nor of their apriori which appears in actual and possible *appearance*; it spoke instead of the (*regulative*) *idea* of such a space of appearance, the 'ideal space' with 'ideal right-angles', etc. All of 'exact' physics dealt with such 'idealities'; thus underlying actually experienced nature, the nature of actual living, was a nature as idea, as a regulative ideal norm, as its Logos in the highest sense."[1] In the *Krisis der europäischen Wissenschaften,* Husserl examines in detail that first historical form of science, enlarging his philosophical method to uncover the constitutive sense of nature investigated by modern science.[2] Indeed, not only Husserl's own discussion, but also discussion and development of his work has chiefly centered on its relevance for modern science, thus having the unfortunate effect of confining the results of Husserl's insights to a certain period in history.

However, were one to take Husserl seriously as regards the context of his analysis of science in the "higher sense", then the "Logos of the aesthetic world" cannot be neglected as that methodological confinement would sug-

---

[1] Edmund Husserl, *Formale und transzendentale Logik* (Halle, 1929), p. 257. The translation is mine.

[2] Edmund Husserl, *Die Krisis der europäischen Wissenschaften und die transzendentale Phänomenologie,* ed. Walter Biemel (Haag, 1954). Cited hereafter as *Krisis.*

gest. The principal purpose of this essay is to overcome that neglect by extending Husserl's method in its historical range to other and, in a sense, more remote areas of Western thinking upon which "Platonic geometry", as an idealizing and logicizing science, has been built. Accordingly, our inquiry, which will see the "Logos of the aesthetic world" as a determinative moment in the first historical form of modern science, is an inquiry into origins in a two-fold sense. In the first place, it is an inquiry into the actual giving of a certain concatenated set of affairs as "they themselves". In the second place, it is an inquiry into the development of those affairs over a period of time. Both senses of "origin" are mutually inclusive. But the first sense is equivalent to the essence of phenomenological inquiry at large, while the second makes up a special area of endeavor: *the phenomenology of history*. The present essay falls within that special area, although we shall be more concerned to employ the phenomenology of history than to develop it as a theoretical body of doctrine.

To set the problems with which we shall have to concern ourselves, we shall begin by formally delineating the premises of phenomenological-historical inquiry; we shall then concretize those premises with an account of mythical thinking in general and of Homeric myth in particular as characteristic examples of empirical typification constituting the "Logos of the aesthetic world". An account of Plato's challenge of Homeric mythical thinking, out of which geometry is produced as an idealizing science, i.e., a science of ideal typification, and of the "fate" of that challenge in modern science, will bring us to the threshold of a discussion of the relation of "science aware of a new style" to the "Logos of the aesthetic world".

I. THE BASIC PREMISES OF PHENOMENOLOGICAL-HISTORICAL INQUIRY

The world we inhabit has been interpreted and reinterpreted by science understood in the broadest possible sense. Yet that interpretation and reinterpretation is hardly exhaustive of the world in its temporal meaning. In one way or another, science attempts to meet the demands of the actual historical situation, and to that extent science takes on the shape of history. And also to that extent no scientific claim, or alleged claim, to universality can be relieved of its bond to the present Now:

as regards the Now with the contents it presents, it figures as the *present* Now within a horizon of modified Nows, sc. of the present past which it retains in its depth and the present future into which it passes. The sense in which this passage takes place constitutes the living and therefore, plastic meaning of past and future. "The past" – so we hold with G. H. Mead – "refers to that conditioning phase of the present which enables us to determine conduct with reference to the future which is also arising in the present." Phenomenology of History will have its starting point in the analysis of the present and its inner historicity. It will extract sediments of the past which the present contains as its foundation. This understanding of the present will be, at the same time, a revision of the past and its ends – a critical and historical introspection, a revaluation of traditional motives and a clarification of the tasks – the common tasks – with which the present is charged.[3]

The present, living moment of our orientation to past and future is the starting point for an inquiry into the historical origin of the meaning of the world in respect of those "sedimentations" of the past contained by the present as its foundation. As we shall see, those sedimentations ultimately concern the constitutional sense of the "Logos of the aesthetic world". To elucidate that sense it will be necessary at the beginning to set aside all the valuational and existential meanings bestowed on the world in consequence of scientific interpretations and reinterpretations.

That is to say, beginning with our own living present we shall attempt to say something true of the constitutional sense of the world in which we live regardless of how it has been scientifically understood. By disregarding *en bloc* for the moment any understanding of the world provided by science, we can discover a "sub-scientific" dimension of mundane reality haloed by a unitary horizon of humanity, the "absolutely unconditional accessibility to everyone which belongs essentially to the constitutional sense of Nature".[4] This dimension of the world is a common-sense one taken for granted. In the words of Alfred Schutz: "To take the world for granted beyond question implies the deep-rooted assumption that until further notice the world will go on substantially in the same manner as it has so far; that what has proved to be valid up to now will continue to be so, and that anything we or others like us could successfully perform once can be done again in a like way and will bring about substantially like results."[5]

---

[3] Fritz Kaufmann, "Phenomenology of the Historical Present," *Proceedings of the 10th International Congress of Philosophy,* Amsterdam, August 11–18, 1948 (Amsterdam, 1949), pp. 967f.

[4] Edmund Husserl, *The Cartesian Meditations,* trans. Dorion Cairns (Hague, 1960), p. 132; cf. p. 133. For Husserl's concept of horizon, uncritically employed in the present study, see *ibid.,* §§ 19f., and Edmund Husserl, *Erfahrung und Urteil,* ed. L. Landgrebe (Hamburg, 1954), §§ 8, 10, 22f., 32ff. An important correction and critical evaluation of the concept can be found in Aron Gurwitsch, "Contribution to the Phenomenological Theory of Perception," *Studies in Phenomenology and Psychology* (Evanston, 1966), pp. 343ff.

[5] Alfred Schutz, "Equality and the Meaning Structure of the Social World," republished in Alfred Schutz, *Collected Papers,* ed. A. Brodersen (Hague, 1964), Vol. II, p. 231.

The taken-for-granted world presents itself as a non-scientifically categorialized and conceptualized world penetrated by intersubjective, socially derived and distributed meanings of many kinds conferred on it by members of the community living in that world [6] – the "necessary communalization" of one's life and the lives of others which fashions the same Nature in which we all live into a cultural world.[7] This sub-scientific dimension or world may also be said to be a cultural world with a unitary mental connotation which constitutes the tradition of our own historical age.[8] For the sake of precision, it is worth-while citing Husserl's review of the affairs here under discussion:

Each man understands first of all, in respect of a core and as having its unrevealed horizon, *his* concrete surrounding world or *his* culture; and he does so precisely as a man who belongs to the community fashioning it historically. A deeper understanding, one that opens up the horizon of the past (which is co-determinant for an understanding of the present itself), is essentially possible to all members of that community, with a certain originality possible to them alone and barred to anyone from another community who enters into relation with theirs. At first such an individual necessarily understands men of the alien world as generically men, and men of a "certain" cultural world. Starting from there, he must first produce for himself, step by step, the possibilities of further understanding. Starting from what is most generally understandable, he must first open up ways of access to a sympathetic understanding of broader and broader strata of the present and then of the historical past, which in turn helps him to gain broader access to the present.[9]

Accordingly we may say that the world in which we live and find ourselves regardless of what science may tell us about it, is through and through historical. As the passage from Husserl suggests, to be aware of a present cultural formation is to be aware of it not only as occurring "in" history, but also as essentially alive and significant in the present.[10] As formulated by Alfred Schutz, the past still forms part of our "stock of knowledge at hand", still figures into our lives as part of our "preacquaintedness" with the world.[11]

[6] See Husserl, *Cartesian Meditations,* §§ 56ff. For the concept of world employed here, see Aron Gurwitsch, *The Field of Consciousness* (Pittsburgh, 1964), pp. 410ff.

[7] Husserl, *Cartesian Meditations,* p. 133.

[8] See Edmund Husserl, "Ursprung der Geometrie," published as Appendix III in *Krisis* (pp. 378ff.).

[9] Husserl, *Cartesian Meditations,* p. 133. Cf. Alfred Schutz, "The Stranger: An Essay in Social Psychology," and "The Homecomer," both republished in *Collected Papers,* Vol. II, pp. 91–105, 106–119.

[10] See José Ortega y Gasset, "Die Krise der Vernunft," *Europäische Revue* (1942), XVIII, pp. 144ff.

[11] Alfred Schutz, "Tiresias, or Our Knowledge of Future Events," *Collected Papers,* Vol. II, pp. 283ff.; see also Alfred Schutz, *Der Sinnhafte Aufbau der sozialen Welt* (Vienna, 1960²), §§ 33ff.

Adhering to our example of "Platonic geometry", we may say that in any awareness of such a historical form we can always distinguish a co-awareness, often largely implicit, that such a formation is the result of human work or production. "Production" is taken here in a sufficiently broad sense to comprise constitution of categorial as well as practical meanings of the world and things in it. Owing to human constitutive activities a cultural formation possesses a sedimented structure having a tradition which can be reactivated and rendered explicit, performed once again in a like way with substantially like results.[12] Indeed, our entire cultural, living present implies a continuity of sedimented pasts, each in itself a past cultural present with its own present future into which it has passed. Not only is the whole continuity of pasts traditionalized, handed over to and into one another, and upon which the present stands, but the plastic, living present itself is also a continuous process of traditionalizing.[13] In one sense, at least, it follows that to make the origin of any present cultural formation evident is to disclose or re-perform in substantially like ways the production of sedimented meanings. For our purposes here it is sufficient to note in this connection that we hold with Husserl the view that in principle anything whatever presented through acts of consciousness possesses an inner structure of meaning which can be re-performed, reactivated and made a theme for inquiry.

But an inquiry into the origin of a cultural formation such as "Platonic geometry" is also an inquiry into the "first time" that a given structure was established and, correlatively, into the concatenated acts of consciousness through which that structure is most originally presented as "it itself". However, what does "first" signify here, and what is the concept expressed by the term? A preliminary answer can be given by sketching the basic features of any actual or possible historical living present – basic (or "eidetic") features which serve as the premises of phenomenological-historical inquiry.

With Husserl we shall call the historical living present, the unitary horizon of humanity, the "all-embracing community of actual and possible mutual understanding."[14] Mutual understanding is related to a common frame of reference, namely the one objective spatio-temporal world believed in as existing not only by me but by others as well. Others are experienced by me as experiencing this common spatio-temporal world in ways typically similar to those in which I experience it. Communicating with my fellow-men, we understand each other and apprehend each other as belonging to one and

---

[12] Husserl, *Krisis*, p. 379.

[13] *Ibid.*, p. 380. For a discussion of Husserl's use of the term "tradition", see below, pp. 256f. See also Kaufmann, *op. cit., loc. cit.*, pp. 967f.

[14] See above, p. 237.

the same world, as members of an open plurality of humans standing in mutual understanding.[15] Experience of the world is a communal affair, not private or just private. As communal, experience of the world is practical, religious, moral, aesthetic, political, scientific and so forth. Even though the awareness of this world-experience may not always be explicit, notwithstanding it shows itself in all our activities as the most general "premise", as the silently efficacious foundation and background of our activities. Most immediately this world for us all is confronted by me as having the sense, "'my' world", "'my' community", group or class of people standing in a relationship of mutual understanding. "'My' world" is the world for everyone, where "everyone" signifies "everyone of the corresponding cultural community, such as the European or perhaps, more narrowly, the French cultural community."[16] Founded on mutual understanding of "my" community is a We-relationship obtaining between myself and others, a commonality of the community, experience of the world in the first person plural.[17] Here, too, it is necessary to discriminate the stratified structure of bonds of personal associations (classes, groups, collectivities).[18] Through our gearing into a common external world not only is the reciprocity of social relationship constituted, but also the nature of our surrounding world as a communicative one, which is the basis, in turn, for still higher personal unities such as Church and State. The meaning which the world acquires in virtue of constitution of a group or collectivity of personal associations is the "cultural world" in the strict sense of the term.[19] At still higher levels of constitution, international associations and the like are to be mentioned. What is important to emphasize here is that the world is always presented as relative to a certain structure of the meaning of sociality at a certain time in history. The world must be regarded in this connection precisely and purely as experienced and conceived by the community whose world it is.

[15] See Husserl, *Cartesian Meditations*, p. 133; and Edmund Husserl, *Ideen zu einer reinen Phänomenologie und phänomenologischen Philosophie* (Halle, 1929), Vol. I, §§ 29, 59, 150ff. (Hereafter cited as *Ideen*, I).

[16] Husserl, *Cartesian Meditations*, p. 92.

[17] For the relevant constitution of the third person plural, see Jean-Paul Sartre, *Critique de la raison dialectique* (Paris, 1960), Vol. I, pp. 200ff., 320ff. The "seriality" of the third person plural is a founding stratum for constitution of the first person plural.

[18] Edmund Husserl, *Ideen zu einer reinen Phänomenologie und phänomenologischen Philosophie*, ed. Walter Biemel (Haag, 1954), Vol. II, § 51. (Hereafter cited as *Ideen*, II.) Cf. Alfred Schutz, "Husserl's Ideas, Volume II," *Philosophy and Phenomenological Research* (1953), XIII, pp. 394ff.

[19] See Alfred Schutz, "Common-Sense and Scientific Interpretation of Human Action," *Collected Papers*, ed. M. Natanson (Hague, 1962), Vol. I, p. 16; R. Toulemont, *L'Essence de la société selon Husserl* (Paris, 1964), Chapters III, V, IX.

On the ground of the world we confront each other as human beings, the world acquiring at the same time its meaning from our collective, communalizing consciousness, from our progressive and progressing, traditionalizing and totalizing acts of experiencing and conceiving it. The collective and communal achievements of these experiences and conceptions become part of the world which, in turn, is transformed by them, contributing to the continual growth of the world relative to a living community.

The structure just sketched in an abstract and formal way furnishes us with essential guidelines for a phenomenological-historical inquiry. It forms what may be called the basic "premise" of such an inquiry. To be sure, as yet no commitment has been made to a *theory* of history – for example, a theory which would hold that history is an indefinite process of objectification in which cultural systems are built up.[20] All that is being said so far is that if one is interested in the historical origin of a certain structure of meaning in our own living present, it is necessary to inquire into the materials inherent in it, "presupposed" by it in the cultural surrounding world. What is then historically first is our own living present: we already always "know" about our own present surrounding world and we also "know" that this historical present has *its* historical pasts which themselves arise out of one another in a continuity of pasts, each of which is presented as a past-present tradition. We "know" also that the on-going, living and concrete historical present belonging to our own surrounding world, with the weight of historical time implicit in it, is the historical time of a humanity univocally bound through generations, continuously cultivating in a community what has always already been cultivated.[21]

All of this indicates in a rough way an awareness, to be made explicit, of a universal horizon of "knowledge" into which an inquiry must go if it is to discover the inner structures of meaning in history. This "knowledge" is *non-scientific, non-philosophic* in nature; it is a thinking and experiencing always at the margin of, hence presupposed by, scientific and philosophic knowledge about the world, through which the world is given as existing in certain ways, as being of a certain kind, largely taken for granted.

To restate the matter in another way, were we to compare the stream of historical events with the stream of our own past experiences, we would find that they are alike in both being continuous and manifold, and that although the historical stream contains anonymous events, and although homogeneous events are repeated, those events can, nonetheless, be taken as the experiences of others – experiences which have occurred in the indivi-

---

[20] See Kaufmann, *op. cit., loc. cit.,* p. 967.
[21] Cf. Gurwitsch, *op. cit.,* pp. 384ff., 391f.

dual and communal lives of others living in a historical present of their own.[22] Indeed, they may be regarded as experiences having occurred in (past) first and third person plural so that we may speak of continuous experience from the beginning of mankind down to our own times. Precisely for this reason a phenomenology of history need not commit itself to a theory of history. "This view of history", Alfred Schutz has said, "while permitting of metaphysical interpretations, is not in itself metaphysical but, rather, the necessary condition for the unity not only of our experience of the world of predecessors but of social reality in general."[23] A basic implication of this view of history is that "belief in a historical law above history by which not only the past and the present can be explained but also the future predicted evidently has no foundation in the nature of human experience of social reality."[24]

II. THE NATURE OF HISTORICAL KNOWLEDGE

The term "ontological experience" will be employed to designate the non-scientific, non-philosophic knowledge at the root of our daily confrontation with historically conditioned social reality.[25] An idea basic to the present study is that the direction taken by philosophical and scientific thinking in the West is, as a rule, implicitly referrable to an experience of reality at large which is not itself necessarily philosophic or scientific in nature.[26] Without wishing to oversimplify too far the history of philosophy, it may be said that Hegel's philosophical system is the last great attempt to formulate the experience of reality on the part of "natural" or non-philosophic consciousness which has been dominant in Western tradition since its inception. In Hegel there is, perhaps for the last time, the attempt to clarify the ways in which we "know" what a thing is, what its properties are, what a universal is, what a particular is, what the one and many are, what essence, actuality and possibility are, etc. It is in these terms that we are still accustomed to think about and understand the world and on which, generally speaking,

---

[22] See Alfred Schutz, *Der Sinnhafte Aufbau der sozialen Welt*, p. 245. (An English adaptation is published in *Collected Papers*, Vol. II, by T. Luckmann, under the title of "Dimensions of the Social World," pp. 20–63. The quotations cited in the text are taken from this adaptation.)

[23] Schutz, p. 61.

[24] *Ibid.*, p. 62.

[25] See Eugen Fink, "Zum Problem der ontologischen Erfahrung," *Actas del Primer Congreso Nacional* (Buenos Aires, 1949), Vol. II, pp. 733ff.

[26] Cf. Alphonse de Waelhens, *La Philosophie et les expériences naturelles* (La Haye, 1961), pp. 11ff.

philosophic and scientific knowledge are based.[27] We already "know" what things, animals, people, truth, etc. *are*, we live within a horizon of categories of reality which have a sedimented but still living tradition. So far as our daily confrontation with reality is concerned, regardless of our vocations or avocations, these categories form our "stock of knowledge at hand", the categorialization and conceptualization of reality at large with which each of us is familiar and employs in his everyday praxis. Past, present and future lives in the world are continually interpreted in terms of the "preorganized stock of knowledge" which "we have at hand at any moment of our existence".[28] The stock of knowledge at hand, of which the ontological experience is a part, is directly tied up with the all-embracing community which we previously identified with the plastic meaning of past and future characterizing our understanding of the present.

Peculiar to a large part of the stock of knowledge is the fact that it is *socially derived:*

it consists, that is, of experience lived through directly and originarily by my fellowmen, who communicated them to me. Hence I assume – or better, I take it for granted in the practice of everyday life – that other people's knowledge at hand is to some extent congruent with mine, and that this *holds good not only in respect to knowledge of the world of nature, common to us all, but also in respect to knowledge of the social and cultural world I am living in.*[29]

It is at this level of mutual understanding that the sedimented meaning of the ontological experience and its continuous traditionalization must be considered. This is because, as Schutz points out, the stock of knowledge at hand is not homogeneous with regard to its traditionalized inner structure of meaning. It is, rather, surrounded by various "zones" of vagueness, obscurity, clarity, ambiguity.[30] There are three other features of the stock of knowledge which must be mentioned here. In the first place, there are segments of the stock of knowledge which are more distinct than others, some of which are problematic while others go largely unquestioned. In the second place, the stock of knowledge is not something fixed once and for all; instead it is in constant flux, enriched or impoverished as the case may be by supervening experiences. In the third place, "all forms of recognition and identification, even of real objects of the outer world, are based on a *generalized*

---

[27] For the notion of "natural consciousness" and the "history of its formation into science", see Hegel, *Phänomenologie des Geistes*, ed. J. Hoffmeister (Hamburg, 1952²), pp. 67ff.

[28] Schutz, "Tiresias, or Our Knowledge of Future Events," p. 281.

[29] *Ibid.*, p. 282. (The emphasis is mine.)

[30] In the discussion of Homer, below, pp. 248ff., two of these zones will be made thematic: the zone of ambiguity and the zone of neutrality.

knowledge of the *type* of these objects or of the *typical* style in which they manifest themselves."[31]

Although ontological experience shares all three of the features just mentioned, it is particularly in respect of the third feature that its significance can be seen. This is because the typical experiencing of realities and idealities as of kinds depends on a primordial confrontation with the real and the ideal. It is with respect to this confrontation that the stock of knowledge at hand subdivides itself into what is and what is not relevant, and so far as it is operative, of what is and what is not distinct. Ontological experience is, so to speak, the "measure" of the real and the ideal, the clear and the obscure, the relevant and the irrelevant, the distinct and the ambiguous, the principle of division of zones of knowledge. When applied to our own living present and its tradition, this signifies that reality at large is experienced with regard to "genera" and "species", with respect to the various ways in which the "whatnesses" of things are articulated.[32] "Genera" and "species" are spelled out in terms of categories; leaving aside the problem of how such categories emerge from non-philosophic and non-scientific confrontations with reality, once made explicit and clarified in philosophic and scientific thinking they become through their embodiments part of our tradition, forming sedimentations of both scientific and non-scientific thinking and experiencing.[33] In this connection, a basic feature of ontological experiencing to be singled out for consideration is its *projective* feature.

Briefly stated, ontological experience involves a pre-organized planning which governs our dealing with and gearing into the world of daily life; it is a pre-organized planning in somewhat the same sense that the painter's sketch governs the step-by-step actualization of the painting itself. Among other things this signifies that "according to my present knowledge the projected action, *at least as to its type,* would have been feasible, its means and ends, *at least as to their types,* would have been available if the action had occured in the past . . . It is not necessary that the 'same' projected action in its individual uniqueness, with its unique ends and unique means has to

[31] Schutz, "Tiresias, or Our Knowledge of Future Events," p. 284. For a concise summary of these and other aspects of the stock of knowledge at hand, see Aron Gurwitsch, "The Common-Sense World as Social Reality: A Discourse on Alfred Schutz," *Social Research* (1962), 29, pp. 50ff.

[32] Fink, *"Zum Problem der ontologischen Erfahrung," loc. cit.,* pp. 737ff. Needless to say, the concepts expressed by "genus" and "species" require clarification; see Husserl, *Ideen,* I, pp. 22ff.

[33] See Maurice Merleau-Ponty, *La Phénoménologie de la perception* (Paris, 1945), pp. 120ff. Merleau-Ponty's discussion of the experiments of Gelb and Goldstein in this connection illustrates well the non-philosophical basis for the categorialization and conceptualization of the confrontation with reality in daily life.

be pre-experienced and, therefore, known. If this were the case, nothing novel could ever be projected. But it is implied in the notion of such a project that the projected action, its end and its means, remain compatible and consistent with these typical elements of the situation which, according to our experience at hand at the time of projecting, have warranted so far the practicability, if not the success, of typically similar actions in the past." [34]

Stated in a different and more general way, the sedimented structures of meaning, cultural formations, are human productions, and in those productions man is not entirely free. In one sense, the project of those productions depends on the typification and categorialization governing their formation. In another sense, the project of those productions depends on their fittingness to reveal or make manifest the relevancies and significancies of the world in which they are inserted. For instance, a table is not merely a plank of wood standing on four legs, but the place of eating and drinking which, most originally, is a "cult, perhaps the most ancient one that exists:" [35]

In eating and drinking mythical man celebrated his incorporation into the earth, enjoying the gifts of soil and light in bread and wine . . . Eating and drinking represent their origin in a celebration, and celebrations suggest divine presence – not diversions peculiar to man at the margin of his relation with the world. Work and rest, . . . visible man and invisible gods, are all gathered around the table. The table is not a mere object of use, employed simply in accordance with its practical end, but it is also something before which men come together to experience the gathering of the world which draws them together . . . Human mutual understanding is not based on a mere finding of ourselves together, or in mutual fellow-feeling or in looking at one another. It originates in the function the world has of drawing us together. Things are simply the places of that function. [36]

The passages just cited express the primordial confrontation with the real and the ideal, the experience of the world as drawing us together on the basis of which mutual understanding arises, determining the nature of our world-projects. Those projects of ontological experience establish the basic ways in which the unquestioned yet always familiar stock of knowledge at hand refers us to what is real and ideal so far as it holds good regarding the spatio-temporal world common to everyone, the frame of reference of the all-embracing horizon of humanity, as well as to given social and cultural environment. The kind of inquiry to be developed in the present essay at-

[34] Fink, *op. cit., loc. cit.,* p. 739; Alfred Schutz, "Choosing Among Projects of Action," *Collected Papers,* Vol. I, p. 73.

[35] Eugen Fink, "El problema del modo del ser de la comunidad humana," *La Torre* (San Juan, 1956), 15–16, p. 515. (The translation is mine.)

[36] *Ibid.,* pp. 515f., 517. (The translations are mine.)

tempts to reactivate as to their types the sedimented ontological experiences on which mutual understanding depends for its efficacy in terms of world-projects. A case in point, as we shall see, is the first historical form of a science built up on the "Logos of the aesthetic world". To analyze that form, we shall inquire into the kinds of original ontological experiences in which that form is constituted precisely and purely as such. By reconstituting those experiences it will be possible to rethink them again within the horizon of present historical actuality to which they belong as traditionalized sedimentations. In the preceding section we sketched the basic premise of our inquiry – the purely formal structure of the world regardless of how it may be interpreted or reinterpreted scientifically, especially as regards its function of drawing us together. In the present section, the nature of non-philosophic, non-scientific knowledge, also as to its structure, about the world has been sketched. The task which now confronts us is to make those correlative structures concrete and specific within the extended historical scope of analysis suggested by Husserl's investigations mentioned at the beginning of this essay. Accordingly, the next sections report, first, an analysis of an experience of reality not necessarily philosophic or scientific, and second, an analysis of the ways in which it determines a philosophic, scientific experience of reality.[37]

III. HOMERIC MYTH AND THE EPIC SIMILE

So far as the "Homeric world" is concerned, the specifically ontological form of the unitary horizon of humanity is expressed mythically, and the most direct way to approach it is through a brief characterization of myth as the stock of knowledge at hand for the Homeric Greeks. As the stock of knowledge fundamental to actual and possible mutual understanding, myth has a variety of functions, of which the following must be mentioned:[38]

In the first place, comprised of more or less coherent accounts of the deeds and lives of gods and certain mortals, myth provides a global account of the unitary horizon of humanity. Equivalently stated, myth expresses a totalizing attitude toward the universe at large; at the same time that myth speaks of the deeds of individuals, it also speaks of man at large, of divinity at large, etc. In the second place, myth is historically oriented in the sense that, on the one hand, it expresses a timelessness peculiar to deeds, events, actions at large true for all time – thus deeds, events, actions which can be

---

[37] See above, pp. 234f., 241f.
[38] For a concise summary of the functions of myth, see Paul Ricoeur, *Finitude et culpabilité* (Paris, 1960), Vol. II, pp. 153ff.

repeated over and over again, which can be "imitated".[39] On the other hand, mythical history is seen in the perspective of both beginning and end – though, to be sure, they need not be purely chronological.[40] A third function of myth is to articulate not only the harmonious, organized aspects of reality, the invariant patterns of deeds and events, but also to spell out those disharmonies protruding into human and divine affairs.[41] As a consequence, suffering and struggle, doom and guilt are among the chief themes of Homeric myth.[42] In the fourth place, myth is symbolic: a particular evil befalls a given person who also at the same time symbolizes the force of evil which befalls man at large. By virtue of rites, celebrations, magical signs, things of a sacred nature, myth can keep this symbolization alive, guarantee actual and possible mutual understanding by continuously manifesting the capacity of individuals to symbolize something higher and greater. The world so presents itself that everything occurring in it is symbolic of what happens at a higher plane of reality, and in this way draws men together into the cosmos at large. Finally, myth is "imitated" in epic poetry, which signifies that the higher order of reality is made up of invariant deeds, events and actions subject to continuous repetition dramatic and ritualistic in nature, hence which can be re-enacted, recited.

As a result, we may say that the mythical stock of knowledge at hand is largely of certain more or less unchanging and stable structures pertaining not only to the cultural world itself but also to the material world as the common frame of reference of mutual understanding. This latter reference, as we shall see, makes possible the epic simile, the ontological experience at the heart of the mythical stock of knowledge at hand. Because of the familiarity with those structures, the stock of knowledge at hand is not made up so much of *specific* and detailed information about things, deeds, events, as it is of *typical* ways of knowing about them in typical situations. In that sense, nothing which occurs is ever completely novel: in general contour at least it is automatically recognized as similar to what has happened before. Moreover, owing to typical and generalized patterns of believing and knowing, and the more or less invariant structure of reality presented through

---

[39] For the constitutive structure of the concept of imitation, see Husserl, *Cartesian Meditations,* § 27.

[40] The mythical history of the *Odyssey,* for instance, begins with the dual movement of Telemachus initiating the search for his father, and his father at the same time leaving the island of Calypso. This is in contrast to the purely chronological beginning which reaches back to the Trojan War. See Werner Jaeger, *Paideia: The Ideals of Greek Culture,* trans. G. Highet (New York, 1945), Vol. I, p. 30.

[41] Thus the councils of the gods at the beginning of the *Odyssey,* or Book XV of the *Iliad.*

[42] Cf. Ricoeur, *op. cit.,* pp. 154ff.

them, there are always "grounds" or "causes" for this or that deed or event. The "grounds" are largely taken for granted, and language, signs, behavior all point to the relative unchangingness of the structure of the world.

We may illustrate the functions of myth by confining ourselves to a single example, the *Odyssey* so far as it can be understood as narrating a contest between Odysseus and the disordering forces of society and nature. Indeed, the poem itself was recited in the context of contest by rhapsodes vying with each other to provide the greatest performance of the poem. In this sense, the poem, like the drama, is a form of contest, i.e., a ruling and ordering of the forces of violence and destruction, a continuous transformation of those forces into order. Containing those forces in the form of a re-enactable work of art allows the poet to mold order, ultimately to rescue society from evil – hence the great "educational" force of poetry.[43]

In what way, one may ask, was the poet fitted by the gods for this crucial rôle? At first sight the answer is paradoxical: *blindness*. Not only was Homer reputed to have been blind, but the two poets of importance mentioned in the *Odyssey* were blind: Demodokos and Tiresias. Here, of course, we are not interested so much in blindness in the literal sense as we are in its symbolic significance. Poets such as Demodokos and Tiresias have certain powers, namely the ability to recount the past and to foretell the future. To what, then, are they blind? They are blind to the present: what men have done is known, and what men should do and *will have done* is known. To the present alone the poet is blind. As Alfred Schutz has observed, Tiresias does not forecast what will happen, but what will have happened: "In a certain sense his forecasting would be a vaticination after the event (*vaticinium ex eventu*) for, although in reality the event is still in the future at the time of the vaticination, the seer anticipates it as if it were a past one."[44] Although he finds some truth in this view, Schutz considers it incongruent, indeed, ultimately unintelligible, with regard to the manner in which we anticipate the future. However, by regarding the epic simile as expressive of the ontological experience of the "Homeric world", hence by referring mythical thinking back to its foundations in the "Logos of the aesthetic world", I believe that it is possible to suggest an entirely different view of the Tiresian theory of knowledge which is in keeping with some of Schutz's own views as to how we anticipate the future.

Consider the example of Aigesthus mentioned at the beginning of the *Odyssey:* he knows the past and was forewarned of what will have happened

---

[43] See Jaeger, *op. cit.*, Chapter 3, especially pp. 39f. See also Hannah Arendt, *The Human Condition* (New York, 1959), §§ 42ff.

[44] Schutz, "Tiresias, or Our Knowledge of Future Events," p. 279.

were he to kill Agamemnon. In spite of the warning, Aigesthus proceeds to commit the crime. The present figures as a force in the action, disrupting, as it were, a "perfect" foretelling of the future. Action in the present contradicts everything Aigesthus knows about the past. The implication is that man is blind to what he is presently doing in the face of his knowledge of past and future.

Knowledge of the past and future allows for the assigning of responsibility for past and future deeds. But what about deeds in the present? The present is given *as ambiguous,* as a *zone of ambiguity,* thus subject to "irrationality" over which neither men nor gods have full control. It is a zone in the midst of reality where man can be overpowered and where, if he succeeds at all, it is purely by virtue of something utterly inexplicable, almost nameless: fate. Yet so far as knowledge of the past and the future is concerned, one cannot plead blindness. What happens does so by necessity, although it is never a firm necessity since there is a moment when neither gods nor men can be entirely responsible for what occurs. The zone of ambiguity, the present, is, accordingly, a sort of ballast of the project of action, a limitation to the freedom of the project.[45] As a consequence, overpowering evil can never be fully contained: the plasticity of meaning of the transition of the present Now into the present future, retaining the present past. Blindness to the present constitutes the essential *heterogeneity* of the Homeric stock of knowledge at hand, organized around a *problematic* segment of that stock of knowledge – problematic in virtue of that very heterogeneity and forecasting in the mode of what will have happened, of a generalized type of behavior in a typical style.[46]

There is a way out of the dilemma regarding the present, a way of overcoming the heterogeneous nature of the stock of knowledge at hand. Using myth, the poet can continuously hold up to man what has happened and what will have happened. Great "examples" can be presented for scrutiny as ideals, standards, in such a manner that this typified and generalized knowledge becomes a fusion of what has happened with what will happen.[47]

---

[45] See above, pp. 243f., and below, p. 252.

[46] See above, p. 242.

[47] In this connection, see Erich Auerbach, *Mimesis: The Representation of Reality in Western Literature* (New York, 1957), pp. 4f.: "And this procession of phenomena takes place in the foreground – that is, in a local and temporal present which is absolute. One might think that the many interpolations, the frequent moving back and forth, would create a sort of perspective in time and place; but the Homeric style never gives any such impression." Auerbach proceeds to show how Homer avoids perspective in the syntactical structure of the Recognition Scene in the *Odyssey.* Continuing, he says: "But any such subjectivistic-perspectivistic procedure, creating a foreground and background, *resulting in the present lying open to the depths of the past, is entirely foreign*

That is to say, the poet attempts to gloss over what is occurring *now* in such a manner that the plastic meaning of the present is compressed into the greatness of the past and a future sharply defined beforehand, i.e., a future on which is bestowed the contour of the past. The present is "de-thematized", deliberately overlooked. This compression or fusion of the past and future is the root of the *timelessness* of myth, and the poetic form employed to express it in Homer is the *tertium comparationis,* the epic simile. As we shall now see, the consequence of this fusion is the substitution of a *zone of neutrality* for the zone of ambiguity. A series of examples of the epic simile from the *Odyssey* will clarify what we have in mind here.

The first example is that of Penelope listening to the report of the beggar bringing the first news of Odysseus:

> Now all these lies he made appear so truthful
> she wept as she sat listening. The skin
> of her pale face grew moist the way pure snow
> softens and glistens on the mountains, thawed
> by Southwind after powdering from the West,
> and, as the snow melts, mountain streams run full:
> so her white cheeks were wetted by these tears
> shed for her lord – and he close by her side.[48]

Both snow and skin are alike in being white; water and tears flow, wind and mood change, and so forth: in short, Homer presents us with the comparison of different affairs with something "third" which they share. However, the comparison embraces the whole of Penelope's life; looking at the mountains, snow, streams, we see her becoming cold, rigid through the long years of Odysseus' absence. But we also see her whole being soften and brighten when the snows will melt, when mountain streams will run full in the Spring. The imagery of Homeric thinking produces the confrontation with the long, terrible winter in the mountains and the freshness of approaching Spring in such a manner that a dead process, Winter, gives life to a living process, Spring, in comparison with a woman's barrenness, frigidity,

to the Homeric style; the Homeric style knows only a foreground, only a uniformly illuminated, *uniformly objective present* ... and the story of the wound becomes an independent and exclusive present." (The emphasis is mine.) The zone of neutrality is precisely such a present, except that I would add that not only does it not lie open to the depths of the past, but it is also closed to the depths of the future.

[48] Homer, *The Odyssey,* trans. Robert Fitzgerald (New York, 1963), Book XIX, p. 360. For the selection and explication of examples I have drawn on Kurt Riezler's excellent study, "Homer's Contribution to the Meaning of Truth," *Philosophy and Phenomenological Research* (1943), III, pp. 326ff. However, I do not accept Riezler's conclusions, nor follow in every case his interpretation of the epic simile.

giving life to the fertility of womanhood. A mutual animation is at work between the living and the dead, between opposites: Penelope's tears animate the melting of the snow, itself inanimate. But the inanimate melting snow in turn animates the woman who comes to life again. As Riezler has observed, this double animation is the true function of the simile, and in this connection he refers to the continuation of the lines just cited:

> Imagine how his heart ached for his lady,
> his wife in tears; and yet he never blinked;
> his eyes might have been made of horn or iron
> for all that she could see. He had this trick –
> wept, if he willed to, inwardly.

Here, again, there is the contrast of hard and soft. The snow remains on the surface, but within it has melted, while in the previous lines cited it melts on the surface; here it has become hard on the surface, frozen, and soft, melted, within.

Of importance to us in this connection is the nature of the basis for the comparison such that mutual animation takes place. There is an apprehension of "qualities" which man and nature share – the something "third" in respect of which the comparison is made. Moreover, certain of these "qualities" can be mutually transferred from man to nature, from nature to man. Riezler notes that these "qualities" go nameless, and that it is the art of the poet to weave them together. But of what type must thinking be such that these "qualities" are presented in their most original manner as "they themselves"?

Certainly one essential constituent involved in this type of thinking is what Alfred Schutz has called an "equalization of traits relevant to the particular purpose at hand for the sake of which the type has been formed." "Typifying consists in passing by what makes the individual unique and irreplaceable" and considering certain "traits as equal . . . in all the objects falling under the same type," thus presupposing that things and events are already constituted as of kinds.[49] So far as Homeric thinking is concerned, the unique and irreplaceable occur in the present; past and future are typified to such a degree in the *vaticinium ex eventu* to such a degree that, as it were, there is no room for what is unique. Precisely the epic simile achieves the "equalization", hence the "overlooking" of essential differences among traits which contributes to making the stock of knowledge homogeneous. The kind of apprehension which produces the epic simile is, then, the foundation for the *vaticinium ex eventu* on which action is predicated and in the light

---

[49] Schutz, "Equality and the Meaning Structure of the Social World," p. 234.

of which action is judged. It must be noted here that "equalization" involves more than traits of things of the same order; it concerns as well different planes of reality such as the animate and the inanimate. As a consequence, the zone of neutrality is like a net or web (the simile) in which the most disparate elements of reality are caught and held in tension through a typification of reality such that past and future are made homogeneous, the ambiguous present thus being "overlooked". This is a case of ontological experience where, upon apprehension of those nameless, animating "qualities", the domains of relevance and irrelevance are distinguished, the boundaries of responsible human action are established. It is not difficult to anticipate the further *and philosophical* objectivation of this experience in, for instance, the *Parmenides* of Plato, which is concerned with the elucidation of the animating invariants, "qualities" or "ideas" in which opposites partake, the "something third" and One in accordance with which the world of human affairs is understood. The warrant for this anticipation will be treated in the next section in discussing Plato's challenge of Homeric typification. Before we can turn to that challenge, however, several other essential constituents of Homeric thinking must be made thematic as regards the simile.

The Homeric simile is not confined to the expression of similarities. Consider the description of the flight of Hermes:

> No words were lost on Hermes the Wayfinder,
> who bent to tie his beautiful sandals on,
> ambrosial, golden, that carry him over water
> or over endless land in a swish of the wind,
> and took the wand with which he charms asleep –
> or when he wills, awake – the eyes of men.
> So wand in hand he paced into the air,
> shot from Pieria down, down to sea level,
> and veered to skim the swell. A gull patrolling
> between the wave crests of the desolate sea
> will dip to catch a fish, and douse his wings;
> so higher above the whitecaps Hermes flew
> until the distant island lay ahead,
> then rising shoreward from the violet ocean
> he stepped up to the cave.[50]

Following the poet's eye we experience the breakdown of the simile since Hermes does not catch the fish; as it were, Homeric thinking transcends

[50] *Odyssey,* Book V, pp. 82f.

the comparison of similarities. What is seen with the imagery of the gull is the wistful and playful ease without effort – a characteristic of divine action. The flight of Hermes anticipates Odysseus' voyage over the sea: the next day Odysseus will build a raft which will break up in a storm. The gull catching fish stands in contrast to the helplessness of the raft (Riezler). On the one hand, by comparing Hermes to the gull there is a contrast between the ease of the gods and the clumsiness of man.

Our final example of the simile describes Odysseus' plans for revenge:

> His rage
> held hard in leash, submitted to his mind,
> while he himself rocked, rolling from side to side,
> as a cook turns a sausage, big with blood
> and fat, at a scorching blaze, without a pause,
> to broil it quick: so he rolled left and right
> casting about to see how he, alone,
> against the false outrageous crowd of suitors
> could press the fight.[51]

The roasting of the blood sausage unites in one image Odysseus turning over and over in bed with the ripening of his plan for revenge on the suitors, a plan to be considered with the maw of a hungry man. But here the comparison ends; the sausage is done and eaten, but Odysseus' plans remain incomplete. With all his turning nothing comes to a broil, the solution is not found, and Odysseus finally falls asleep without a plan.

In their proper contexts, shipwreck and the extreme risk involved in not having a plan, these two similes suggest that the making homogeneous of the stock of knowledge at hand is not complete, that the typification of the ways of knowing about deeds and events is always only more or less perfect, that the feasibility of projected action, as well as of means and ends, as to their types, is nonetheless uncertain even were they available in the past. Accordingly, the *vaticinium ex eventu* is never a perfect merging or fusion of what has happened with what will have happened. Were the typification and fusion perfect and complete, the *tertium comparationis* would always be of similarities. However, Homeric thinking discovers borderline cases where objectivation of what will have happened, hence of typification, remains unfulfilled, where "equalization" of traits cannot be fully achieved, where the zones of neutrality and of ambiguity intrude upon one another. "Irrationality" can never quite be eliminated; the present is still a ballast

---

[51] *Odyssey,* Book XX, p. 376.

of the project of action.[52] Roughly speaking, for Homeric mythical thinking the human condition consists in living between knowledge and blindness.

IV. THE FIRST HISTORICAL FORM OF EXACT NATURAL SCIENCE

Two final tasks remain in order to carry out the account of the historical "premise" of modern science. The first consists in stating the nature of the sedimentation of meaning disclosed by the reconstitution of Homeric thinking. The second consists in elucidating the significance of that reconstituted sedimentation of meaning, i.e., clarifying the way in which it figures as a "premise" or "presupposition" for the first historical form of modern science. The carrying out of both tasks will disclose the way in which the "Logos of the aesthetic world" is a determinative moment of the first historical form of modern science. The two tasks will be carried out by sketching the development of Homeric thinking in Plato and by comparing the results of that development with the development of thinking in the "Galilean style" studied by Husserl in the *Krisis der europäischen Wissenschaften*. In other words, we shall see how the ontological experience underlying Homeric thinking becomes tradition for the ontological experience at the heart of "Platonic geometry".

So far we have considered some of the principal features of the all-embracing community of mutual understanding in Homeric thinking by focusing mainly on the structure of the stock of knowledge at hand in the *vaticinium ex eventu*. A further study would have to be made to account for the stratified organization of objectivities of a higher order (laws, classes, etc.).[53] Among other things, that stock of knowledge at hand involves an existential confrontation with the world taken for granted in daily life. But that confrontation already involved typifyings and generalizings of deeds, events, actions of the sort formally conceptualized in the *vaticinium ex eventu*. This knowledge holds good not only with regard to the common frame of the spatio-temporal world and, through mutual animation, the social and cul-

---

[52] In passing it may be noted that already in Homer the present emerges as a problem not "resolved" until later Roman and Roman-Greek-Christian thought where the present becomes an attribute of God (the "nunc stans"), hence only derivatively a feature of the human condition. In that transformation the present loses its ambiguity and, in turn, past and future become the carriers of sin and salvation. This "temporal displacement" would require a separate study to reactivate and evaluate it. For the Greek experience of the present, see also Oskar Becker, "Mathematische Existenz: Untersuchungen zur Logik und Ontologie mathematischer Phänomene," *Jahrbuch für Philosophie und phänomenologische Forschung,* ed. E. Husserl (Halle, 1927), Vol. VIII, pp. 641ff.

[53] See Eric Voegelin, *The World of the Polis* (Baton Rouge, 1957), pp. 77ff.

tural world; it also guarantees and warrants mutual understanding as regards existential and valuational meanings (e.g., evil) in typified ways, thus making the flux of knowledge more homogeneous (the presumptive character of the present), achieving a more or less stable substitution of the zone of neutrality for the zone of ambiguity. In addition, that knowledge establishes the limits of relevance and significance – the epic simile being, accordingly, much more than simply a matter of "artistic economy".

All of this points to the fact that mythical thinking in the Homeric style is not autonomous. Equivalently stated, mythical thinking has certain "premises" in the world of daily life, "presupposes" a taken-for-granted world already typified and generalized (the "Logos of the aesthetic world"). Certain aspects of this "presupposition" must be made explicit to understand the traditionality of the meaning-structure constituted in Homeric thinking – aspects tacitly present in our analysis of Homeric thinking. The *vaticinium ex eventu* is founded on an experiencing of events, things, deeds, etc., as repeatable and re-enactable, and that signifies that they have already been constituted as of kinds, types, that individual traits have been "equalized" regarding certain goals and purposes. *This, in turn, is founded on an apperceptive confrontation with the world, and it is this "premise" of Homeric thinking which will now be made explicit to illustrate the dependence of Homeric thinking on the "Logos of the aesthetic world" (the "prepredicative" world).*[54]

In *Erfahrung und Urteil,* Husserl has shown that an essential feature of our daily encounter with the world, regardless of our vocations or avocations, is apperception.[55] We confront things and events as "preorganized" with the characteristics of typical familiarity and unfamiliarity. Even things and events met with for the first time are apperceived as of kinds, although the kinds themselves may be largely undetermined, presented as having inner and outer horizons of further determinableness. Accordingly, things and events are not presented simply as things and events in all their individual particularity, but as being of a particular type – as *an* external thing, *a* plant, *an* animal, etc. Equivalently stated, things and events are presented and appresented not only as to individual particularity, but also as to "genera" and

---

[54] In the following discussion, the whole problem of symbolism is set aside in favor of a more general account. However, what is said about the "prepredicative", appresensational basis of experience of typification would also serve for an account of the symbolic character of the Homeric experience of the world. In this connection, see Alfred Schutz, "Symbol, Reality and Society," *Collected Papers,* Vol. I, pp. 287ff.

[55] See especially *Erfahrung und Urteil,* §§ 15ff.; and the summary by Alfred Schutz, "Type and Eidos in Husserl's Late Philosophy," *Philosophy and Phenomenological Research* (1959), XX, pp. 147ff.

"species" – a horizon of structurization characteristic of consciousness of the world which can be made concrete in the further course of experiencing in accordance with typical perceptual or explicative styles.[56] In daily life, as a rule, these styles are habitual and conform to an empirical and presumptive certainty about the world – presumptive because it is a certainty good only until further notice.[57] The point is that things are apperceived as having further determinations both as to individual particularity *and as to types.* It is the latter which is important here since it provides a degree of typification allowing for repetition of like events and deeds under typically similar circumstances. And it is this structure of apperceptive presumptiveness which is the origin of the experience of the world as drawing us together.

In addition to acts characteristic of daily life for fulfilling undetermined yet familiar horizons in the on-going course of praxis, there are specific acts of consciousness which make kinds, types, thematic. The *vaticinium ex eventu* is one such act which, among other things, involves an "overlooking" and an "equalizing" of individual particularities in order to objectivate affairs appresented as of kinds exemplified by those traits.[58] In short, the *vaticinium ex eventu* is akin to what Husserl calls "ideation", a making thematic of kinds or types in their exemplifications based on apperceptive experiencing.[59] The epic simile represents a further step in *thematic explication* based on such objectivation. The kinds or types are already there beforehand, as it were, waiting to be "wakened" (Husserl) by apperceptive syntheses in ideation.[60] This also involves an extension of typicality as seen in the simile; it is an extension which "discloses itself merely in the fulfillments of the anticipations, and can be conceptualized by particular intentional acts in hindsight only" (Schutz). This is the basis for the project of action whose ends and means must remain "compatible and consistent with these typical elements of the situation which, according to our experience at hand at the time of projecting, have warranted so far the practicability, if not the success, of typically similar actions in the past." [61] The project is a form of conceptualization in hindsight, but in Homeric thinking of a specific kind: namely, one where what has happened and what *will have* hap-

[56] See above, pp. 243f.

[57] See above, p. 242; see also Husserl, *Cartesian Meditations*, § 28; José Ortega y Gasset, *Man and People,* trans. W. R. Trask (New York, 1957), pp. 95ff.

[58] One must carefully distinguish between those acts of consciousness in which something individual is presented as of a kind, and those acts in which kinds themselves are presented as exemplified by that individual. The *vaticinium ex eventu* is an act of the second kind.

[59] See Husserl, *Erfahrung und Urteil,* § 87.

[60] *Ibid.,* §§ 16ff.; *Cartesian Meditations,* §§ 38f.

[61] See above, pp. 243ff.

pened coincide. In this connection something of radical significance must be observed.

The *vaticinium ex eventu* is an act of ideation and thematization of what is already appresented as to kind, and as such it is largely restricted to what Husserl calls "empirical types". That is to say, whereas things, deeds, events, are apprehended *as of kinds* thematically, explicatively and relatingly, there is no explicit apprehension of the kinds or types themselves as exemplified by appresented individual particulars. The latter requires an entirely new kind of act. The epic simile is, to be sure, a further step in thematization since it forces the (at least implicit) distinction between non-essential and essential empirical types.[62] Hence it is highly selective; the mutual animation expressed in the simile is not just of anything by anything else at all, but of traits essential to, e.g., gods and men (Hermes and Odysseus), and this, as has been noted, establishes the relevance and significance of the stock of knowledge at hand. But in Homeric thinking there are no acts distinguished in which, for instance, "the typically generic itself" is constituted, "as whose 'representative' the individual object is apperceived, that is, as an *objectivity of this kind, of this type. . . .* The generality of the empirical presumptive type is merely one among them and a relatively low one; at the highest level are the pure or eidetic universals and, based on them, judgments which no longer originate in the thematization of the relations of the objectivities to their empirical types of familiarity . . ."[63]

As Husserl has shown with regard to the Galilean style of thinking in modern science,[64] unless such "premises" as appresentation of things as of kinds and the constitution of empirical types are kept in mind, one becomes captive of the structures of meanings produced. That is to say, at least part of the meaning of *tradition* is to regard the products of Homeric (or also Galilean) ideation as autonomous, with no "premises" outside themselves, thus obviating any inquiry into the origins of these products.[65] Indeed, this is precisely the form in which Plato encounters Homeric ideation as a sedimented meaning-structure of tradition. Moreover, Plato is the first to successfully challenge the traditionality of meanings produced in Homeric thinking and experiencing by inquiring into the apperceptive experience underlying Homeric ideation, i.e., into the way in which the "Logos of the aesthetic world" figures into Homeric thinking such as the *vaticinium ex*

[62] See Schutz, "Type and Eidos in Husserl's Late Philosophy," pp. 153f.

[63] *Ibid.*, p. 155.

[64] See above, pp. 234f.

[65] See Aron Gurwitsch, "Comments on Herbert Marcuse, 'On Science and Phenomenology,'" *Boston Studies in the Philosophy of Science* (New York, 1965), pp. 299f. (Hereafter cited as "Comments".)

eventu and the relatively low generality of the presumptive empirical types constituted. Although Plato carries out his inquiry with regard both to the content as well as to the style of Homeric ideation, it is his inquiry into the Homeric style of thinking which directly concerns us so far as we are interested in making thematic the Homeric tradition as a "presupposition" of the first historical form of modern science.

It is perhaps in the *Ion* that Socrates most graphically attacks the "premise" of the ontological experience of reality as repeatable, re-enactable, hence re-presentable.[66] But since Plato does not reject this experience as being illegitimate, but instead as requiring restatement and clarification, it is possible to set aside a discussion of the *Ion* in favor of a consideration of Book X of the *Republic*. That part of Book X of interest here begins with the words: "Could you tell me in general what imitation [*mimesis*] is? For neither do I myself quite apprehend what it would be at."[67] "Imitation" is the conceptual sense of the ontological experience of reality as repeatable, re-enactable, re-presentable *based upon empirical typification*. Socrates states that we should follow the standard procedure to find out what it is: "Shall we, then, start the inquiry at this point by our customary procedure? We are in the habit, I take it, of positing a single idea in the case of the various multiplicities to which we give the same name."[68] What is it that a multiplicity of things share such that they look like what they are and in virtue of which they are given the same name? In the ensuing discussion, two ways of speaking of things are distinguished. We may either speak of "this house", "this table", "this thing", in which case we speak of them only with regard to individual particularity. Or we may speak of this thing *as* a house, *as* a table, *as* a thing, in which case we speak of it with regard to its *eidos,* as exemplifying a kind or type. "Imitation", accordingly, is not just a re-presentation of anything at all, but of what already has a name, hence of what is already apprehended as to generic or specific kind. Plato takes a specific case out of daily life to illustrate this, namely the case of the craftsman who makes beds or tables (596 b). The craftsman fabricates a table out of wood, and to do so he must obviously know what a table looks like – a basic condition of repetition and re-presentation. The wood acquires a shape and contour, a purposefulness and meaning within a certain context (see above, pp. 244ff.) which appresent what a table shows itself as being such that we are drawn together around it. However, *what* the table is like

[66] Plato, *Ion,* 537ff.
[67] Plato, *The Republic,* 595c. The translation is by Paul Shorey, *The Collected Dialogues of Plato,* ed. E. Hamilton and H. Cairns (New York, 1961).
[68] *Republic,* 596a; cf. *Meno,* 74ff.

is not fabricated by the craftsman. Taking the fabrication of the table as a paradigm case of practical activity, practical activity at large may be said to be re-presentative and appresentative in the same way: as imitative, it always articulates what is not fabricated, namely what things are.

Plato advances the problem by taking an exceptional case of craftsmanship: the craftsman who can produce everything (596c). It is the extreme case of *empirical* "imitation" where things are produced appresenting, re-presenting, and re-enacting utensils, plants, animals, gods, deeds, etc. It can be conceived best "if you should choose to take a mirror and carry it about everywhere. You will speedily produce the sun and all the things in the sky, and speedily the earth and yourself and the other animals and implements and plants and all the objects of which we just now spoke" (596d-e). The example illustrates the basic sense of "imitation": presentation of what a thing is (e.g., plantness) in something else (a reflection in the mirror of *a* plant) – this, Plato asserts in effect, is the true nature of appresentation of things as of kinds. And just this sort of appresentation of something in one plane of reality (Ideas) in another plane (the spatio-temporal world) is involved in the epic simile with its expression of that nameless "something third".[69] However, what is reflected in the mirror (or in verbal expressions), what is repeated and re-enacted, only resembles what something really looks like, whereas the wooden table is confronted *as* a table. As Heidegger has observed, Plato accordingly distinguishes two distinct ways in which the *eidos* of something is appresented: 1) the way an *eidos* is appresented in something other than what something is – the reflection of the table in the mirror; and 2) the way something shows itself *as what it is* in wood (the table).[70] We need not rehearse further Plato's well-known discussion; what is of importance is the conclusion drawn from the distinction between the two ways of empirically appresenting things as of kinds in daily life.

Plato's inquiry into the appresentational "premise" of Homeric thinking allows of a three-fold distinction: 1) the *eidos* or type of something; 2) the something fabricated by a craftsman; and 3) a reflection, a painting or verbal description of something.[71] Correspondingly, there are three ways of apperceiving what something is: 1) direct apprehension of the *eidos* itself, the typically generic itself; 2) fabricating, or more broadly, using something which exemplifies what *a* given thing shows itself as being and which conse-

---

[69] This is the phenomenon at the core of symbolism; see Alfred Schutz, "Symbol, Reality, Society," pp. 331ff.

[70] Martin Heidegger, *Nietzsche* (Pfüllingen, 1961), Vol. I, pp. 207ff. See also Oskar Becker, "Platonische Idee und ontologische Differenz," reprinted in *Dasein und Dawesen* (Pfüllingen, 1963), pp. 157ff.

[71] See Heidegger, *Nietzsche*, pp. 213ff.

quently has a name; and 3) apperceiving the appearing of something in something else – the reflection, the painting of the verbal description. Once this distinction has been made, Plato proceeds to incorporate it into his *method* of ideation, just as the third kind of apperceiving in an extended form is incorporated into the method of the *vaticinium ex eventu* and the epic simile in Homeric ideation.

That is to say, by seeing the *difference* between the second and third ways of apperceiving, it is possible to apprehend, as different from both, the *eidos* or generic type itself. The comparison and difference in the epic simile leads to a grasping of affairs as to their kinds. But in the case of Plato the seeing of *appresentational* differences leads to a grasping of the *kinds themselves* exemplified by presented and appresented particulars. Platonic ideation, the foundation of "Platonic geometry" in the Renaissance, as a consequence, transcends empirical types. And it is in just this respect that we may say with Husserl that it does not "speak of right-angles, circles, etc. in the 'aesthetic' sense, nor of their apriori which appears in actual and possible *appearance*"; i.e., it does not speak of them as regards their presumptive empirical types. "Platonic geometry", instead, spoke of the generically typical itself, of ideal types. But this is only possible if, as in the case of Homeric ideation, the results of the method are taken for what is real: Platonic ideation becomes tradition, and, as a living tradition, a regulative norm. And like Homeric tradition, the Platonic tradition has its "premises" in the "prepredicative" presentational and appresentational experiencing of the real and the ideal, i.e., in the "Logos of the aesthetic world".

The effect of the Platonic inquiry into the "origin" of the Homeric tradition as an essential constituent of the present historical situation for Plato is to transform the stock of knowledge at hand with regard to the inner core of its ontological experience. Apprehension of the typically generic itself "demythologizes" the Homeric ontological experience by its transcendence of empirical types, thus attaining to the "Logos in the highest sense". That signifies, among other things, that the typically generic itself functions as an "ideal pole", a "limit-form" (or regulative norm) produced in ideation and which is approximated to a greater or lesser degree by actual and possible exemplifications of the types themselves.

It would be impossible here to develop the whole history of this "new" process of traditionalizing; to capture its significance we need only briefly dwell on one aspect of it which is handed over to that tradition of Euclidean or "Platonic geometry" which serves as the immediate "premise" of Galilean physics: the science aware of itself as of a new style.

Just as empirical typification of the "prepredicative" world, in and of itself, would never lead to the *vaticinium ex eventu* and from there to the epic simile, or to the apprehension of *eide* through comparisons and differences, so the more or less vague but typical confrontation of spatial forms would never produce Euclidean geometry. That geometry is produced by a process of ideation of the Platonic kind, in and through which ideal limit-forms are constituted – an ideation in which the typically generic itself is constituted *originaliter* as exemplified by particulars. Such figures can be produced with absolute exactness, unlike spatial shapes encountered in daily life whose precision depends not only on the purpose at hand but also on the relative perfection of the instruments of measurement. Geometrical limit-forms or ideal poles, the regulative norms, are grasped as more or less approximated by perceived and apperceived shapes, lines, angles, etc. As noted in the case of Homeric ideation, the stock of knowledge at hand bears a reference to the common spatio-temporal world serving as the basis for mutual understanding and communication. This reference is significantly changed in Platonic ideation, particularly as regards Euclidean geometry in its traditionality for thinking in the Galilean style. That is to say, instead of mutual animation of the organic and inorganic, of the animate and inanimate,

in physics of the Galilean style, all happenings and changes which concern the specific qualities are referred to spatio-temporal events in such a manner that all qualitative aspects of the world are conceived of as causally dependent upon spatio-temporal events . . . i.e., events completely describable in terms of spatiality and temporality and, hence, accessible to mathematization.[72]

In consequence thereof, the geometrical method provides a body of knowledge possessing universal validity. It is a case of Platonic ideation, "Platonic geometry", developed over centuries, as a consequence of which that method becomes a habitual technique in much the same way that Homeric thinking had become a habitual technique for rhapsodes such as Ion. And like Homeric thinking, "Platonic geometry" lost sight of its experiential "origin", the "Logos of the aesthetic world" and the tradition which it implies. Accordingly, "Platonic geometry" seems to rest on its own grounds.

Galilean science inherits geometry in its traditionalized form, and through abstraction and mathematization is developed and considered as autonomous. In elucidating the proper perspective in which to understand Husserl's analysis of the first historical form of modern science, hence of phenomenology of history as defined earlier in this essay, Aron Gurwitsch observes that

[72] Aron Gurwitsch, "Husserl's Last Work," *Studies in Phenomenology and Psychology*, p. 410.

it is the right of the positive scientist, the logician, mathematician, and physicist, to remain within this scientific tradition and to abstain from concerning himself with its origin and institution. It is the duty of the philosopher to raise precisely that question in order to clarify and account for the very sense of modern science.[73]

It has been our purpose to raise the question of "origin" of "Platonic geometry" by examining in some detail the nature of the reference borne by several cultural formations to the "Logos of the aesthetic world", the sub-scientific dimension of the world. More specifically, that reference has been considered in its traditionalizing character, in the first place, as regards the actual giving of empirical types at the heart of the stock of knowledge at hand around which the taken-for-granted world of daily life is fashioned. And in the second place, that reference has been considered with respect to the ontological experience at the basis of empirical typification historically developed through a series of objectivations. In turn, this is nothing but a clarification of our own living present extended into its roots, i.e., the extracting of "sediments of the past which the present contains as its foundation" (Kaufmann): the Homeric-Platonic-Galilean traditionalized and sedimented structure of our own living present.

V. CONCLUSION

In brief outline, we have attempted to carry out several steps of a phenomenological-historical clarification of a cultural formation in our own living present. We have done so by disregarding the autonomy which science bestows upon itself as a cultural formation – a formation, which, after all, is but one case of scientific interpretation of the world. Both the Homeric and Platonic-Galilean interpretations and objectivations bear within themselves the "premise", the silent ground, of the "Logos of the aesthetic world". This was seen in the discussion of the epic simile as well as in the elucidation of the grounds on which the Platonic-Galilean style of thinking challenges the Homeric, i.e., *apperceptual rather than ideational grounds*. It is precisely in this manner that the present essay attempts to overcome the seeming methodological confinement of Husserl's analyses to modern science. However, the development of those analyses here does no more than raise the question of "origin". It would be the task of a further study to consider the dynamic process of origination itself of that "origin". Such a study would exhibit all the particulars concerning the relation of "science aware of a new

---

[73] Gurwitsch, "Comments", p. 299.

style" to the "Logos of the aesthetic world".[74] Ultimately, this would involve revisions of the analyses of Husserl and Schutz on whose insights we have primarily relied in the present study. Leaving the nature of those revisions implicit, it is worth while, in concluding, to reconsider the phenomenological-historical analysis developed in the preceding pages in terms of a phenomenological inquiry into "origin" in the wider sense.[75] That is to say, it is necessary now to rethink the Homeric, Platonic and Galilean ontological experiences within the horizon of our present actuality to which they belong as traditionalized sedimentations.[76]

§ 1. The Nature of "Ad libitum" Consciousness in Homeric Ideation

Earlier we noted that in itself empirical comparison of perceived and apperceived particulars would never lead to the apprehension of empirical, let alone pure, types.[77] As we have seen in the *vaticinium ex eventu* and the epic simile, the apprehension of empirical types rests on the consciousness of a varying and variable series of presented and appresented particulars exemplifying presumptive empirical types in accordance with a prototypical or pre-organized project.[78] Such a prototypical project is the story of Aigesthus,[79] mentioned at the very beginning of the *Odyssey,* and which serves throughout as an action of return projected as to type;[80] it is a prototype of action which stands out as identical in contrast, hence with reference, to a series of variations, of transformations, modifications, which, presented together, display concrete similarities to the prototypical project.[81]

In this connection we noted that differences among the perceived and apperceived variant examples are "equalized" (under the pre-condition of "overlooking" the ambiguity of the present[82]), thus giving the *actuality of the past* a privileged position. Homeric, or presumptive typical ideation provides in this way sufficient typification to construct the repetition of like events and deeds under like circumstances; the empirical type stands out as that in respect of which the variations are all coincident. This, of course, does not signify that all possible variations are by any means developed in

---

[74] See above, pp. 235, 236ff., 253.
[75] See above, p. 235.
[76] See above, p. 245.
[77] See above, p. 260.
[78] See above, pp. 243f.
[79] See above, pp. 247f.
[80] See Schutz's statement cited above, pp. 243f.
[81] See Aron Gurwitsch, "Gelb-Goldstein's Concept of 'Concrete' and 'Categorial' Attitude and the Phenomenology of Ideation," *Studies in Phenomenology and Psychology,* pp. 370ff.
[82] See above, pp. 248f.

Homeric ideation. However, the fusion of what has happened and what will have happened not only produces the basis for ritual repetitiveness in Homeric myth, but also for the timelessness of myth, the unobjectivated awareness of an "and so on, at will" in the generation of variant examples out of the original prototypical project.[83] In other words, there is an *ad libitum* consciousness in Homeric ideation of an infinity of variations generated out of an *actual* example from the past. What will happen is linked irrevocably to what has happened; further and future examples can never appear other than in the mode of what will have happened.

More specifically with regard to empirical ideation, to speak of an infinity of possible variations signifies that it is not evident whether or not in the further course of *actual* experience the variations will be cancelled out as exemplifying an identical *eidos* (here, an empirical type).[84] Empirical ideation is always presumptive, good only until further notice.[85] A case in point is the episode in the *Odyssey* where Odysseus' plan for overthrowing the suitors remains incomplete; the simile involving the roasting sausage remains uncompleted, the projected action as to type remains unfulfilled, the requisite "equalization" of perceived and apperceived traits belonging to Odysseus and the hungry person cannot be fully achieved.[86] The presumptive character of the ideation is never transcended because the prototype (the result of the meeting of Aigesthus and Agamemnon) does not determine a necessary bond between the variations it generates.

This signifies that a presumptive *eidos,* standing out as "something third" and identical over against the multiplicity of variations is not only open in the sense that it can always undergo change and correction, or in the limiting case, cancellation – hence is dependent on the contingencies of actual experience;[87] it also signifies that the empirical type is open in the sense that no *a priori* limits for variation are ever or can be established: *any limits established are always found in hindsight only and hold good only until further notice,* which is the sense of the *vaticinium ex eventu.* As is clear from Plato's critique of the basic premises of Homeric ideation,[88] no foundation is provided for differentiating between essential and non-essential types, something testified to by the very namelessness of that "something third" with respect

---

[83] See above, pp. 246f., 249.
[84] Cf. Husserl, *Erfahrung und Urteil,* p. 410.
[85] See above, p. 236.
[86] See above, pp. 252f.
[87] It is precisely in neutralizing the present that the Tiresian theory of knowledge tries to free itself from such contingencies.
[88] See above, pp. 254, 256ff.

to which apperceived particulars are compared.[89] As we shall see, this is a consequence of making an actual case serve as the prototypical project in accord with and out of which variant examples are generated.

As a consequence, the *ad libitum* consciousness of an "and so on" continuation of variations from an initial project remains confined to a rather rigid present shaped on the unambiguous, unyielding irrevocableness of the past owing to the methodological blindness of the Homeric poet. Indeed, precisely the reification of the ambiguity and plasticity of the present is at stake in neutralizing the present since it is only in virtue of the ambiguity and plasticity of, for instance, the apperceptual field of particulars that "equalization" is possible in the first place.[90] Without ambiguity and plasticity, ultimately without the heterogeneous character of the stock of knowledge at hand,[91] perceived and apperceived affairs would be just that and nothing more – mere actualities exhibiting no reference to "something third", to empirical types which, in their identity stand out over against, yet in reference to, them. In this sense the *vaticinium ex eventu* is faulty, because Homeric ideation must at the same time both confine itself to a rigid past-present (the zone of neutrality) and still consider it as plastic enough to refer to another order or plane of reality, i.e., as appresentational. It must both look over and at the present. A chief merit of Plato's revision of Homeric ideation, leading him to the discovery of the typically generic itself, pure types, is restoration of the ambiguity and plasticity of the perceptual and apperceptual present, hence allowing for transposition of actualities into pure possibilities in consequence whereof the project need not be a past and only a past actuality.

§ 2. *Empirical and Pure Types in Platonic Ideation*

Even though Platonic ideation transcends empirical types in apprehending the typically generic, pure types, it nonetheless is also "imperfect"[92] as regards the *ad libitum* consciousness of an infinity of variations. To be sure, in the case of Platonic ideation *a priori* limits are apprehended, but still with

[89] Cf. Husserl, *Erfahrung und Urteil*, § 83, pp. 402f.; Schutz, "Type and Eidos in Husserl's Late Philosophy," pp. 153f.

[90] For example, "equalization" of such items as white, snow, skin, iron, horn etc., in the similes considered. It is interesting to note in this connection that pathological studies of brain-injured patients show that the ambiguity and plasticity of the perceptual field acquires a rigidity in consequence of which the patient is confined to the perceptual field and to the perceptual field alone. See Gurwitsch, *op. cit., loc. cit.*, pp. 379f.

[91] See above, pp. 242f.

[92] See Aron Gurwitsch, review of James Street Fulton, "The Cartesianism of Phenomenology," in *Philosophy and Phenomenological Research* (1940/41), 2, pp. 557f., for Husserl's sense of "imperfect" used here.

reference to an actual situation: namely, in the difference between actually emergent cases – e.g., the table and the reflection of the table in the mirror. These are cases which are not in themselves regarded as purely possible examples; apprehending the "mimetic" difference in no way divests them of their status of perceptual actuality, although it de-emphasizes it.[93] That is to say, the pure type does not stand out as identical throughout variation in contradistinction and with reference to given as well as more *possible* examples *ad infinitum*. Accordingly, the extension of the type includes real objects *rather than pure possibilities alone*. Neither the table nor its scia-graphic representation are transposed into the purely possible. For instance, it may be postulated that an *eidos* such as Geometrical Figure be bounded by a certain number of sides: three. To apprehend that *eidos* it is necessary that there be the appresentation of variant examples of the *eidos* in two different media – e.g., wood and the mirror (or a verbal expression, such as the definition of "triangle").[94] The apprehension of the *eidos* is not only referred to, *but confined to* actualities perceived and apperceived. What Plato considers are variant examples which, *in virtue of their difference,* make the *eidos* stand out *as actualized in both cases.*

As a result, a serious consequence of Platonic ideation is that it arbitrarily limits the very "specification" of the *eidos* (Husserl). In this case ideation is dependent on the "Logos of the aesthetic world" in the sense of being limited to the *a priori* "which appears in actual and possible appearances".[95]

§ 3. Difference and No Difference in Ideation

If we now contrast Platonic ideation as found in Plato with Platonic ideation as found in the Renaissance, in the first historical form of modern science, we can see that the arbitrary limitation of the "specification" of the pure type is transcended and that there is a more originary apprehension of the typically generic. "Platonic geometry" in the Galilean style of physics [96] has undergone a radical change in the nature of the *ad libitum* consciousness of an infinity of variations and, accordingly, in the way in which the "Logos of the aesthetic world" is related to the "Logos in a higher sense". For both Homeric and Platonic ideation, the actual status of the variant and varying examples was at stake; only in view, for instance, of the different status of presented and appresented particulars in perception was the *eidos* apprehended in and of itself as exemplified in those variants. This

93 See above, pp. 257f.
94 Cf. Plato, Seventh Letter, 342ff.
95 See above, p. 234.
96 See above, pp. 259f.

is true of "mimetic" ideation whether it is of the *tertium comparationis* or the Platonic dialectic. But the situation changes with the introduction of mathematization in the Galilean style.[97] This is a case where the difference in status of the variant examples *makes no difference*. Consider a case of "Platonic geometry" late in the modern period: the possible displacements of a three-dimensional space of constant curvature as treated in projective geometry. Here any example whatever will serve as prototype; "figures that belong to a given group constitute a unity, no matter whether and how they be representable in an intuitive way" (Felix Klein [98]). Here the apperceptive basis of Platonic ideation is transcendend because, in Plato, the basis for such ideation is precisely whether and how figures are intuitively representable so that their differences can be grasped. In Galilean ideation, instead, by the *ad libitum* modification of figures, passing from form to form owing to continuous modifications it is sufficient that in seeing the limits of one set of figures another set can be generated in ideational variation. And any example will do. More specifically stated, in the case of a three-dimensional space of constant curvature whose possible displacements depend upon six parameters, the motions of three-dimensional space are a sextuple infinity.[99] The study of the sextuple infinity of possible motions in this connection leads to a "group of transformations": "Given a multiplicity and a group of transformations referring to the former; the problem is to study the elements of the multiplicity with regard to those properties which are not affected by the transformations of the group" (Klein). In this connection, Ernst Cassirer makes the following observation: "Every system of geometry is characterized by its group: It deals only with such relations of space as remain unchanged through the transformations of its group." [100]

This example is important because, if generalized to all regions (Husserl) of being, it suggests the way in which "Platonic geometry" as a science aware of a new style apprehends *eide* exhibiting themselves in the very process of variation (the multiplicity and group of transformations). To be sure, it obviously would be impossible to survey all of the sextuple infinity of possible movements. But even though the process of ideation may be broken off after a certain number of steps, it could nonetheless be carried out *ad infinitum*. It is the awareness of an *eidos* whose extension is not exhausted by actual and possible variants; it is an *eidos* not confined to perceived and

---

[97] See above, p. 260.

[98] Cited by Ernst Cassirer, "The Concept of Group and the Theory of Perception," *Philosophy and Phenomenological Research* (1944), V, p. 2.

[99] Cassirer, pp. 2f.

[100] *Ibid.*, p. 3.

apperceived actualities. Indeed, if relations among pure types hold, for instance, even *a priori* for perceptual and apperceptual affairs, that is because actual occurrences can be considered now as *purely possible* (although not imaginary) varieties which happen to be actualized. In other words, for the generically typical to apply to what is actually given in perceptual experience, the real existent must be "divested" of its actuality, transformed into one pure possibility among others – though, as just suggested, this by no means entails *elimination* of actuality:

Plato's *Chorismos* is to be upheld, without, however, being interpreted in the sense of metaphysical realism. Eide do not present themselves in isolation from one another. Rather they appear in systematic orders and form *eidetic domains.* Such domains are exemplified by the system of colors, of musical notes, the number systems, any system of geometry, or any multiplicity in the mathematical sense. *Every eidetic domain must be considered as an autonomous order of existence.* In contradistinction to the above-discussed worlds of imagination, eidetic domains are essentially atemporal; they do not exhibit structures even of quasi-time. To account for their essential atemporality, we have to consider that, when throughout the process of free variation in imagination, we proceed from one variety to the next we are not contriving a coherent and continuous quasi-world. We are rather in search of an invariant which, because it is realized in every variety, is not one more variety among others. Free variation in imagination thus prepares the way for a real *Metabasis eis allo genos.*[101]

The pre-condition for achieving a genuine *Metabasis eis allo genos* is the transformation of actuality into pure possibility such that the occurrence of a possible example is unimportant and hence may accordingly be disregarded.[102] And it is the very ambiguity and plasticity of perceptual experience which allows for this divesting of the real of its character as actual (rather than neutralizing it, or remaining confined to it, or even eliminating it[103]), so that from variant to variant all the specifications of a given *eidos* emerge in the overlapping coincidence of the variations regarded as pure possibili-

[101] See Aron Gurwitsch, *The Field of Consciousness,* pp. 390f. Confinement to the actual in ideation prevents accounting for the atemporality of eidetic domains. Even the timelessness of myth is not atemporal; rather it is quasi-temporal; see note 40 above.

[102] See Gurwitsch, *The Field of Consciousness,* pp. 192ff., and 195: "The 'possibilities' and 'impossibilities' appearing in the course of the process of free variation are not of a subjective nature. They do not originate from limitations or other contingencies of human mental capacities, but rather refer to eidetic laws a priori grounded in the very natures of the contents concerned."

[103] The confusion of the transposition of actuality into pure possibility with the elimination of actuality is called by Cassirer, *op. cit., .. , loc. cit.,* p. 22, a "sensationistic deduction" in contrast to Kant's transcendental deduction; see also Ernst Cassirer, *Das Erkenntnisproblem in der Philosophie und Wissenschaften der neueren Zeit* (Berlin, 1922³), Vol. II, pp. 713ff.

ties. Only when this is the case are *a priori* limits established with necessity in the sense that they allow ascertainment of the essential possibilities (which may or may not be actualities), the essential impossibilities (which cannot be actualities), and the essential necessities (which must be actualities) in any possible realm of being whatever.[104]

§ 4. The Relation of the "Logos of the Aesthetic World" to the "Logos in a Higher Sense"

As a result of re-constituting the traditionalized sedimentations of the cultural formations of Homeric, Platonic and Galilean ideation, and of then redeveloping them as steps toward more original givenness of empirical and pure types, we may say 1) that regardless of how the world may be interpreted scientifically and philosophically, the "aesthetic world" has already undergone a vast and complex typification; 2) that the very pre-condition for non-scientific and non-philosophic typification is the appresentational plasticity and ambiguity of the perceptual present; 3) that to the extent that "equalization" of perceived and apperceived particulars is "imperfect", that non-scientific and non-philosophic ideation is confined to and dependent on the presumptive experience of actuality, i.e., that the transposition of actuality into pure possibility is limited, non-scientific and non-philosophic typification is arbitrary and unfulfilled; and 4) to that extent scientific and philosophic typification, hence categorialization, is also limited, itself dependent (as in the case of Plato) on actualization of types. Confinement and adherence to the actual allows for "overlooking" the plasticity and ambiguity of the present, hence yields the illusion of the autonomy of typification both as regards apprehension of the generically typical itself and as regards scientific and philosophic thinking understood in terms of cultural formations such as "Platonic Geometry". Only in virtue of a return to the full ambiguity of the perceptual-apperceptual present in all its plasticity, i.e., the full concreteness of the "Logos of the aesthetic world", is it possible to achieve a typification not arbitrarily restricted to the "Logos of the aesthetic world".

In this sense, preserving the full access to the sub-scientific dimension of the world is the pre-condition for scientific interpretation of the world.[105] Indeed, we may now say that all typification, empirical or pure, hence all categorialization and conceptualization, philosophic and scientific or not, bears a constitutive reference to the "Logos of the aesthetic world" which shapes, guides and warrants that typification, categorialization and concep-

---

[104] See Husserl, *Cartesian Meditations,* § 34, p. 106.
[105] See above, pp. 240f.

tualization (although, to be sure, it does not establish their validity). The very presumptiveness of the "aesthetic world" is the pre-condition for it not being merely an "aesthetic world", but the foundation for a "Logos in a higher sense". This dependency on the "Logos of the aesthetic world" allows for a "revaluation of traditional motives and a clarification of the tasks . . . with which the present is charged" (Kaufmann): In consequence of the transposition of actuality into pure possibility, all other domains of being refer to the "aesthetic world" – the sense of Nature to which everyone has unconditional accessibility.[106] Using traditional terms and adopting the formulations of Aron Gurwitsch, it follows that "*episteme* in the traditional sense also falls under the concept of *doxa*" or the "aesthetic world". Instead of being opposed to *doxa, episteme* is then the "*episteme* of the very *doxa, of all possible doxa,*"[107] hence of those projects of ontological experience which, in constituting the basic ways in which we confront the real and the ideal, serve as the principles of organization of the unquestioned yet always familiar stock of knowledge at hand pertaining to the common-sense, taken-for-granted world.[108]

[106] See above, p. 236.
[107] Gurwitsch, "Husserl's Last Work," *loc. cit.,* p. 447.
[108] See above, pp. 236, 243, 245.

THE ROLE OF MUSIC IN LEONARDO'S PARAGONE

by

EMANUEL WINTERNITZ

PREFATORY NOTE

Alfred Schutz was profoundly musical, and a study such as the present one on Leonardo's Paragone would, no doubt, have led to one of those long, nocturnal discussions which we used to have through forty years in Vienna and then in New York. We first met as students of law at the University of Vienna in 1918, but it was music which really brought us together. We ran into each other on the steps leading to the standing room section high up under the roof of the Vienna Opera House, both of us duly equipped with the score of the "Entführung aus dem Serail."

Schutz had a broad and intense knowledge of German and French literature, and he had his favorites among painters: he could become ecstatic before a Giovanni Bellini "Pietà" or Rembrandt's "Jewish Bride," but his beloved art was music. Even in his student days, his knowledge of the theory and history of music would have done honor to any musicologist. His interests and his tastes were catholic, and reached from Pachelbel and Heinrich Schütz to Alban Berg's "Wozzeck." He knew by heart J. S. Bach's Passions, most of his Cantatas and the Goldberg Variations; he was equally at home with Mozart's Masses and operas and the chamber music of Brahms. One of his special idols was Gluck; he knew every page of the standard treatises by Spitta, Schweizer, Chrysander, Jahn-Abert and Thayer. He played the piano with little technique, but the form and emotional content were magically conjured up by his enthusiasm. We played four-hand music throughout all the years of our friendship, and though we often squabbled over Brahm's triplets or Bruckner's hemioles, his shining face and radiant pleasure and our ensuing arguments belong to my dearest memories. We often discussed the experience provided by music, and analyzed the nature of flow, succession and time and their relation to Bergson's durée, and the musical structure as a model of the role and function of memory as creator of form and flux.

Alfred Schutz's concern with the phenomenon of music deeply influenced his philosophy. It will be a task for his philosopher friends to explore this connection and to continue his work.

INTRODUCTION

It is not generally known that Leonardo da Vinci was deeply engaged in Music, not only as an admired performer, improviser and teacher, but in many avenues of research such as acoustics, musical aesthetics and the invention of numerous ingenious musical instruments.[1] Some of his most interesting ideas about the nature of Music and her noble status as an art are included in his Paragone (comparison of the arts), a treatise animated by the visible intention to exalt the noblest of all arts, Painting, "the grandchild of Nature and relative of God." Yet for the reader between the lines it is a fascinating spectacle to see how Music, the inferior sister of Painting, and "ill of many defects," appears at closer study and at second thought to be an art equally as noble as Painting and a discipline in her own right, the "figuratione dell' invisible."

The Paragone, or Comparison of the Arts, is part of the Trattato della Pittura, a book arranged after Leonardo's death from his writings on the arts scattered throughout many of his manuscripts, including some now lost, by his pupil Francesco Melzi. Melzi's manuscript is now in the Vatican library, known as Codex Vaticanus (Urbinas) 1270. We can only guess why Leonardo did not himself arrange and edit these ideas in book form[2] – most probably he did not have the time. Often in his manuscripts, he reminds himself to write "a book" on this or another matter, but none of these have come to us.

The first printed editions of the Trattato appeared in 1651, in French as

---

[1] E. Winternitz, *Keyboards for Wind Instruments Invented by Leonardo da Vinci*, the Raccolta Vinciana, Fasc. XX, Milan, 1964; *Leonardo's Invention of the Viola Organista*, Raccolta Vinciana, Fasc. XX, Milan, 1964; *Melodic, Chordal and Other Drums Invented by Leonardo da Vinci*, Raccolta Vinciana, Fasc. XX, Milan, 1964; *Leonardo da Vinci*, in "Die Musik in Geschichte und Gegenwart," Vol. 13, Bärenreiter, Basel, London, New York, 1966; *Anatomy the Teacher – On the Impact of Leonardo's Anatomical Research on His Musical and Other Machines*, Proceedings of the American Philosophical Society, Vol. III, No. 4, Aug. 1967.

[2] The most recent accounts of the Trattato are: Anna Maria Brizio, *il Trattato della Pittura di Leonardo*, in Scritti di Storia dell'Arte in onore di Leonello Venturi, Rome 1956; A. Philip McMahon, *Treatise on Painting by Leonardo da Vinci*, Princeton University Press, 1956; Kate Trauman Steinitz, *Leonardo da Vinci's Trattato della Pittura, a bibliography*, Copenhagen, 1958; Carlo Pedretti, *Leonardo da Vinci, On Painting, A lost Book*, Berkeley 1964.

well as Italian. The Paragone forms the first chapter of the Trattato, and is comprised of 45 small sections, which we will call chapters, retaining the numbers given to them in the edition by Heinrich Ludwig.[3]

If we seek to clarify the role and rank assigned to Music by Leonardo, we find that the existing translations do not suffice, because the translators were not familiar enough with all the evidence of Leonardo's theoretical and practical concern with the art of Music; nor were they sufficiently acquainted with the structure of Music as an aesthetic phenomenon and with the musical thought and terminology of Leonardo's day. Thus, I had to make my own translations of the chapters, or parts thereof, relevant to Music.

Whenever my translation of certain passages did not seem to me to be the only possible one, or when no exact equivalent existed in English, I inserted an alternative and marked it by [   ].

TEXTS AND COMMENTS

Trattato 21:

CHE DIFFERENTIA È DALLA PITTURA ALLA POESIA

La pittura è una poesia muta, et la poesia è una pittura ciecha, e l'una e l'altra va imitando la natura, quanto è possibile alle loro potentie, e per l'una e per l'altra si pò dimostrare molti morali costumi, come fece Apelle con la sua calunnia. ma della pittura, perchè serue al' occhio, senso più nobile, che l'orecchio, obbietto della poesia, ne risulta una proportione armonicha, cioè, che si come di molte uarie uoci insieme aggionte ad un medesimo tempo, ne risulta una proportione armonicha, la quale contenta tanto il senso dello audito, che li auditori restano con stupente ammiratione, quasi semiuiui. ma molto più farà le proportionali bellezze d'un angelico uiso, posto in pittura, della quale proportionalità ne risulta un' armonico concento, il quale serue al' occhio in uno medesimo tempo, che si faccia dalla musica all' orecchio, e se tale armonia delle bellezze sarà mostrata allo amante di quella, da chi tale bellezze sono imitate, sanza dubbio esso resterà con istupenda ammiratione e gaudio incomparabile e superiore a tutti l'altri sensi. Ma della poesia, la qual s'abbia à stendere alla figuratione d'una perfetta bellezza con la figuratione particulare di ciaschuna parte,

---

[3] Heinrich Ludwig, *Leonardo da Vinci: Das Buch von der Malerei;* Vol. XV of the *Quellenschriften für Kunstgeschichte,* Vienna, 1882.

della quale si compone in pittura la predetta armonia, non ne risulta altra gratia, che si facessi à far sentire nella musicha ciaschuna uoce per se sola in uarj tempi, delle quali non si comporrebbe alcun concento, come se uolessimo mostrare un' uolto à parte à parte, sempre ricoprendo quelle, che prima si mostrano, delle quali dimostrationi l'obliuione non lascia comporre alcuna proportionalità d'armonia, perchè l'occhio non le abbraccia co' la sua uirtù uissiua a' un medesimo tempo. il simile accade nelle bellezze di qualonque cosa finta dal poeta, le quali, per essere le sue parti dette separatamente in separati tempi, la memoria nō ne riceue alcuna armonia.

WHAT THE DIFFERENCE IS BETWEEN PAINTING AND POETRY

Painting is mute Poetry, and Poetry is blind Painting, and both aim at imitating nature as closely as their power permits, and both lend themselves to the demonstration [interpretation] of divers morals and customs, as Apelles did with his "Calumny." But since Painting serves the eye – the noblest sense and nobler than the ear to which Poetry is addressed – there arises from it [from Painting] harmony of proportions, just as many different voices [tones of different pitch] joined together in the same instant [simultaneously] create a harmony of proportions which gives so much pleasure to the sense of hearing that the listeners remain struck with admiration as if half alive. But still much greater is the effect of the beautiful proportions of an angelic face represented in Painting, for from these proportions rises a harmonic concent [chord [4]] which hits the eye in one and the same instant just as it does with the ear in Music; and if such beautiful harmony be shown to the lover of her whose beauties are portrayed, he will no doubt remain struck by admiration and by a joy without comparison, superior to all the other senses. But if Poetry would attempt a representation of perfect beauty by representing separately all particular parts [features] that in Painting are joined together by the harmony described above, the same graceful impact would result as that which one would hear in music, if each tone were to be heard at separate times [in different instruments] without combining themselves into a concert [chord], or if [in Painting] a face would be shown bit by bit,

[4] The terms "chord" and, for that matter, "polyphony" were not yet idiomatic in the musical treatises of Leonardo's time, though polyphonic musical practice used chords increasingly. In fact, full triads had become fashionable about one generation before Leonardo.

always covering up the parts shown before, so that forgetfulness would prevent us from composing [building up] any harmony of proportions because the eye with its range of vision could not take them in all together in the same instant – the same happens with the beautiful features of any thing invented by the Poet because they are all disclosed separately at separate [successive] times [instants] so that memory does not receive from them any harmony.

Comments on Trattato 21:

The precedence of the eye over the ear – or rather, of sight over hearing – is mentioned throughout almost all chapters of the Paragone that deal with the comparison between Painting and Poetry. But as soon as Leonardo sets out to demonstrate this preeminence of the eye, he seems to fall immediately into contradictions, for the distinction of Painting is based on a fundamental feature of music – harmonious proportions; and Painting is accorded precedence over the arts of the ear because it shows harmony, just as does an art for the ear – music. Very clearly, Leonardo describes the phenomenon of the chord – the simultaneous occurrence of several tones – though the term "chord" is not yet in his vocabulary; he rather speaks of the *armonico concento* created simultaneously by proportions – evidently the proportions between tones of different pitch.[5]

While Music is a temporal art like Poetry, it has proportions, of which Poetry is deprived. And this is demonstrated by comparing a poem with a piece of music performed, not by all voices simultaneously, but one voice after another (in vari separati tempi), an absurd procedure that would prevent the formation of vertical harmony.

Memory[6] is briefly mentioned in the last sentence, but its basic function in the temporal arts of retaining the past sections of the work is not described. Otherwise, Leonardo would have been forced to acknowledge, besides pitch proportions of simultaneous musical tones, proportions between successive portions of works of music or poetry.

---

[5] Leonardo was, of course, well versed in the tradition of Pythagorean proportions, and entirely at home in the theory of harmony, especially the musical treatises of his friend, Franchino Gaffuri. He also was familiar with Leonbattista Alberti's theory of proportions in *De Re Aedificatoria,* completed 1452, published 1485. There, Alberti recommends borrowing the laws of visual shapes (*figure*) from the musicians since "the same numbers that please the ears also fill the eyes and the soul with pleasure."

[6] About Leonardo's notion of memory as victor over time, see the Epilogue.

Trattato 23:

DELLA DIFFERENTIA ET ANCHORA SIMILITUDINE, CHE HA LA PIT-
TURA CO' LA POESIA

La pittura ti rapresenta in un' subito la sua essentia nella uirtù uisiua
e per il proprio mezzo donde la impressiua riceue li obbietti naturali,
et anchora nel medesimo tempo, nel quale si compone l'armonicha
proportionalità delle parti, che compongono il tutto, che contenta il
senso; e la poesia rifferisce il medesimo, ma con mezzo meno degno
che l'occhio, il quale porta nella impressiua più confusamente e con
più tardità le figurationi delle cose nominate, che non fa l'occhio, uero
mezzo infra l'obbietto e la impressiua, il quale immediate conferisce
con somma verità le vere superfitie et figure di quel, che dinnanzi se
gli appresenta. delle quali ne nasce la proportionalità detta armonia,
che con dolce concento contenta il senso, non altrimente, che si fac-
ciano le proportionalità di diverse uoci al senso dello audito, il quale
anchora è men degno, che quello dell' occhio, perchè tanto, quanto
ne nasce, tanto ne more, et è si veloce nel morire, come nel nascere.
il che intervenire non pò nel senso del vedere, perche, se tu rappresen-
terai all' occhio una bellezza humana composta di proportionalità di
belle membra, esse bellezze non sono si mortali nè si presto si strug-
gono, come fa la musica, anzi, ha lunga permanentia e ti si lascia vedere
e considerare, e non rinasce, come fa la musica nel molto sonare, né
t'induce fastidio, anzi, t'innamora ed è causa, che tutti li sensi insieme
con l'occhio la uorrebbon possedere, e pare, che a garra uogliono
combatter con l'occhio. pare, che la bocca se la uorebbe per se in
corpo; l'orecchio piglia piacere d'udire le sue bellezze; il senso del
tatto la uorrebbe penetrare per tutti gli suoi meati; il naso anchora
vorebbe ricevere l'aria, ch'al continuo di lei spira . . . .

. . . un medesimo tempo, nel quale s'include la speculatione d'una
bellezza dipinta, non può dare una bellezza descritta, e fa peccato
contro natura quel, che si de'e mettere per l'occhio, a uolerlo mettere
per l'orecchio. lasciaui entrare l'uffitio della musica, e non ui mettere
la scientia della pittura, uera imitatrice delle naturali figure di tutte le
cose.

OF THE DIFFERENCE AND AGAIN THE SIMILARITY BETWEEN PAINT-
ING AND POETRY

Painting presents its content all at once to the sense of sight [and it does so] through the same means [organ] by which the perceptive sense receives natural objects, and it does so in [at, within] the same span of time, in which there are established the harmonic proportions of those parts which together make up the whole that pleases the sense; and Poetry presents the same thing, but through a means [organ] less noble than the eye, and brings to our perception with more confusion and more delay the shapes [forms, delineations] of the designated [verbalized] things [the things presented]. The eye [on the other hand], that true link between the object and the sense of perception, presents [supplies] directly and with greatest precision the actual surfaces and shapes of the things appearing before it. From these [surfaces and shapes] arise those proportions called harmony which in their sweet combination [unity, concord] please the sense, in the same manner in which the proportions of diverse voices please the sense of hearing which again [as I said before] is less noble than the eye, because there [in the sense of hearing] as soon as it is born, it dies, and dies as fast as it was born. This cannot happen with the sense of sight; for if you [as a painter] represent to the eye a human beauty [the beauty of the human body] composed by the proportions of its beautiful limbs, all this beauty is not as mortal and swiftly destructible as music; on the contrary, it [beauty] has permanence [long duration] and permits you to see and study it [at leisure]. It is not reborn [does not need to reappear, come back] like music is when played over and over again up to the point of boring [annoying] you; on the contrary, it enthralls you [makes you love it] and is the reason that all the senses, together with the eye, want to possess it, so that it seems as if they wanted to compete with the eye. [In fact] it seems as if the mouth wants to swallow it bodily, as if the ear took pleasure to hear about its attractions [the beauties of it], as if the sense of touch wanted to penetrate it through all its pores, and as if even the nose wanted to inhale the air exhaled continually by it [by beauty] . . . . The same instant within which the comprehension of something beautiful rendered in Painting is confined cannot offer [give] something beautiful rendered by [verbal] description, and he who wants to consign to the ear what belongs [must be consigned] to the eye, commits a sin against nature. Here, let Music with its specific function enter, and do not place here [into this role] the science of Painting, the true imitator of the natural shapes of all things . . . .

Comments on Trattato 23:

Though here only painting and poetry are compared, music comes into the argument. The argument focuses on the simultaneity of all elements of a painting ("in un subito," "nel medesimo tempo"). The main argument contrasts the eye, as the more noble instrument of perception, with the ear. The eye as the real ("vero") mediator between the world of objects and human receptivity presents shapes at once and simultaneously. Only in this way harmony based on proportions can materialize. The ear, or rather the sense of hearing upon which poetry depends, furnishes the shapes of things less clearly and with delays. "Delay" ("tardità") evidently means "not in medesimo tempo." "L'armonica proportionalità delle parti" is evidently synonymous with expressions used frequently later such as "proportionalità detta armonia." The discussion of this *armonia* gives occasion to throw a side glance upon music which, paradoxically enough, is considered to lack this harmony that is made possible only by a simultaneously composed object such as the limbs of a beautiful harmonious body and their proportions. Music suffers from the defect of repetitiousness or rather its need to be performed over and over again ("molto sonare"), which creates nausea, boredom ("fastidio") *. This implies, of course, another flaw of music, its main defect, namely, its quick passing or fading away; in Trattatos 29, 30 and 31b Leonardo again refers to this flaw.

After this brief side glance at music, Leonardo returns to poetry and painting, and arrives at a sharper formulation of their basic difference by introducing the concept of, as we would call it today, art in space versus art in time. In poetry, time separates one word from the next; oblivion interferes and prevents any harmony of proportions.

This is a rather naive and unfair criticism of poetry. Oblivion does not prevent the listener and even less the reader of Poetry from retaining past parts of the work of art; there is *memory,* for the function of which Leonardo finds beautiful formulations, for instance in C.A. 76a and C.A. 9a, and a poem can be envisaged in retrospect as a harmony of its successive parts. More important for our purpose, Leonardo himself seems, later in the Paragone, to suggest proportions between successive parts. But he does so only for Music, not for Poetry (see Trattato 30 and 32 and also perhaps 29). Here, however, Leonardo does not elaborate any further on successive parts and their proportions. Yet he makes an important statement that seems to take Music out of its position as sister of that other temporal

---

* Leonardo does not explain whether poetry is not affected by this same disadvantage.

art, poetry, and seems to suggest that if the flow in time prevents harmonious *proportionalità* in Poetry, this is not necessarily so in Music, if only Music is considered by its own rights and merits. Poetry, as we must read between the lines, cannot legitimately do for the ear what Painting can do for the eye, and he insists it is a sin against nature to blur this borderline. But where does this leave music? "Here let music with its specific function take its own place [assume its specific role] and do not confuse it with the science of painting, "that true imitator of true shapes of all things."

Two words deserve comment here: "l'uffitio della musica" and "imitatrice." The first emphasizes music's characteristic role and realm; it doesn't aim at imitation, but is *hors de concours,* in a class of its own and not inferior to either painting or poetry. This term of the argument anticipates the more explicit definition of music in Trattato 32 as *figuratione delle cose invisibili.* In his writings on anatomy, Leonardo gives a long and careful outline of a planned book on anatomy. Immediately after this outline, he says: "Then describe perspective through the office of the sight or the hearing. You should make mention of music and describe the other senses." (Fogli B 20 v.)

"Imitatrice" and "imitare" in general must not be understood as literal, or rather passive copying, but as the act of re-creation of shapes and figures; only this interpretation of the function of painting supports its claim to being the most noble and most scientific of the arts.

Trattato 27:

RISPOSTA DEL RE MATTIA AD UN POETA, CHE GAREGGIAUA CON UN PITTORE

> Non sai tu, che la nostra anima è composta d'armonia, et armonia non s'ingenera, se non in istanti, ne quali le proportionalità delli obieti si fan uedere, o' udire? Non uedi, che nella tua scientia non è proportionalità creata in istante, anzi, l'una parte nasce dall' altra successiuamente, e non nasce la succedente, se l'antecedente non more? Per questo giudico la tua inuentione esser assai inferiore à quella del pittore, solo perchè da quella non componesi proportionalità armonica. Essa non contenta la mente del' auditore, o' ueditore, come fa la proportionalità delle bellissime membra, componitrici delle diuine bellezze di questo uiso, che m'è dinanzi, le quali, in un medesimo tempo tutte insieme gionte, mi danno tanto piacere con la loro diuina proportione, che null' altra cosa giudico essere sopra la terra fatta dal homo, che dar la possa maggiore.

Con debita lamentatione si dole la pittura per esser lei scacciata del numero delle arti liberali, conciosiachè essa sia uera figliuola della natura et operata da più degno senso. Onde attorto, o scrittori, l'hauete lasciata fori del numero delle dett' arti liberali; conciosiachè questa, non ch'alle opere dit natura, ma ad infinite attende, che la natura mai le creò.

REPLY OF KING MATHIAS TO A POET WHO COMPETED WITH A PAINTER

Do you not know that our soul is composed [made up] of harmony, and that harmony is generated only in those instants in which the proportionality of things can be seen or heard? Do you not see that in your art [Poetry] proportionality is not created in an instant, but that on the contrary, one part is born from the other, succeeding it, and that this succeeding one is not born if the preceding one does not die? Therefore I regard your invention [art] much inferior to the painter's for the sole reason that in your art no harmonious proportionality is formed. Your invention [art] does not satisfy the mind of the listener or beholder like the proportionality of the beautiful parts that together form the divine beauties of this face here before me, which joined together in the same instant give me so much pleasure with their divine proportion, that I believe there is no man-made thing on earth that can give greater pleasure . . . . It is a justified lamentation if Painting complains of being expelled from the number of the Liberal Arts, [justified] because she [Painting] is a true daughter of nature and serves the noblest of all senses. Therefore, it was wrong, oh writers, to have left her out from the number of the mentioned Liberal Arts; because she devotes herself not only to the creations of nature, but to countless others that have never been created by nature.

Comments on Trattato 27:

Trattato 27, which introduces King Mathias Corvinus, does not contain a direct reference to music; still it is important in our context because of its reference *to armonia, proportionalità,* and *divina proportione* in relation to the minds of the listener and the onlooker. Harmony is denied to poetry, because in poetry one part is born from its predecessor "successively." Here, if a reference to music would have been made at all, it would have become clear that music knows at least one form of harmony, namely, harmony in simultaneity (nel medesimo momento) i.e., as a combination of tones of

different pitch into chords; and this alone would have established the superiority of music over poetry. As it is, this is suggested only later in Trattato 29. By the way, Leonardo does not recognize explicitly harmony or
proportionality between successive portions of a poem or any work of poetry
– for instance, the formal balance between the strophes or the lines of a
sonnet, though he seems to recognize this kind of proportionality in music
(see Trattato 29).

The last two phrases of Trattato 27 are of interest, because here Leonardo
proffers openly his complaint that painting is unjustly omitted from the ranks
of the liberal arts, which is especially unfair if one considers that painting
is not only dedicated to the works of nature, but can create infinite works
never created by nature.

Trattato 29:

COME LA MUSICA SI DE' CHIAMARE SORELLA ET MINORE DELLA
PITTURA

La Musica non è da essere chiamata altro, che sorella della pittura,
conciosiach' essa è subietto dell' audito, secondo senso al occhio, e
compone armonia con le congiontioni delle sue parti proportionali
operate nel medesimo tempo, costrette à nascere e morire in uno o
più tempi armonici, li quali tempi circondano la proportionalità de'
membri, di che tale armonia si compone non altrimenti, che si faccia
la linea circonferentiale le membra, di che si genera la bellezza umana.
ma la pittura eccelle e signoreggia la musica, perch' essa non more
imediate dopo la sua creatione, come fa la sventurata musica, anzi
resta in essere e ti si dimostra in vita quel, che in fatto è una sola
superfitie . . . .

HOW MUSIC SHOULD BE CALLED THE YOUNGER SISTER OF PAINTING

Music cannot be better defined than as the sister of Painting, for
she depends on hearing, a sense inferior to that of the eye, and establishes harmony by uniting her proportional parts [elements] that are
performed simultaneously [i.e., the voices or melodic strands that run
at the same time, that is, in juxtaposition within the polyphonic web],
elements that are destined [forced] to be born and to die in one or more
harmonic sections which confine [include] the proportionality of the
elements [members], a harmony composed [produced, established] the
same way as is that outline of the members [of the human body] which

creates human beauty. But Painting surpasses and outranks Music since it does not die instantly after its creation as happens to unfortunate Music; on the contrary, it stays on [remains in existence] and so shows itself to you as something alive while in fact it is confined to a surface . . .[7]

Comments on Trattato 29:

Trattato 29 begins with a meditation on music itself and is fraught with seeming contradictions. Clear is the statement that painting excels and lords over music because music dying immediately after birth lacks permanence. Leonardo has stressed this aspect before (Trattato 23). Yet music, in spite of its flow, is credited with harmony of proportions, which poses the question of whether Leonardo means proportions between successive portions of the work of music. It is here that the text seems obscure or at least inconsistent. For first harmony is described as a conjunction of proportionate parts performed simultaneously ("nel medesimo tempo"); but right afterwards the text introduces the plural: "in uno o più tempi armonici," and this seems ambiguous. It could mean that chords occur one after each other and that each is equipped with harmony in the sense defined. But it could also refer to successive portions of music and in favor of this interpretation is the formulation that the "Tempi armonici circondano la proportionalità de membri," which could be translated as instants in the flow that include between them sections of music proportionate to each other. If this interpretation is correct, then Leonardo, in a remarkably independent approach to the phenomenon of music, would have applied the concept of proportion to the relation between successive portions of music and thus established the notion of a quasi-spatial structure of portions balanced against each other.

There are two facts that would invite such an interpretation of Trattato 29: first, it falls in with Leonardo's definition of music as the *figuratione del invisible* (figuration evidently meaning shape or from – see Trattato 32); second, the text of Trattato 29 goes on to compare the proportional sections ("membri") of music with spatial portions or members that by their proportions produce the beauty of the human body. The limbs of the body could, of course, hardly be compared with musical chords, but only with sections of the musical flow.

It is thus the painter Leonardo who, starting from his most beloved art, painting, finds similarities with music, an approach basically different from

---

[7] The remainder of Trattato 29 is of no interest as for music.

that of the musical theories of his time. As far as I can see, no treatise on music of Leonardo's days developed this notion of musical form as a balance between the parts of a composition, although contemporary treatises abound, of course, with the notion of numerical ratios between tones of different pitch. Leonardo must have been familiar with this traditional element in musical theory, at least through the treatises of his friend, Gaffuri, the *maestro della capella del Duomo* during Leonardo's stay in Milan.

Trattato 30:

PARLA IL MUSICO COL PITTORE

Dice il musico, che la sua scientia è da essere equiparata a quella del pittore, perchè essa compone un corpo di molte membra, del quale lo speculatore contempla tutta la sua gratia in tanti tempi armonici, quanti sono li tempi, nelli quali essa nasce e muore, e con quelli tempi trastulla con gratia l'anima, che risiede nel corpo del suo contemplante. ma il pittore risponde e dice, che il corpo composto delle humane membra non da si se piacere a' tempi armonici, nelli quali essa bellezza abbia a variarsi, dando figuratione ad un altro, ne che in essi tempi abbia a nascere e morire, ma lo fa permanente per moltissimi anni, et è di tanta eccellentia, che la riserva in vita quella armonia delle proportionate membra, le quali natura con tutte sue forze conservare non potrebbe. quante pitture hanno conservato il simulacro d'una divina bellezza, ch'el tempo o' morte in breve ha distrutto il suo naturale esempio, et è restata più degna l'opera del pittore, che della natura sua maestra!

THE MUSICIAN SPEAKS WITH THE PAINTER

The Musician claims that his science is [of a rank] equal to that of the Painter because it [music] produces a body of many members whose whole beauty is contemplated by the listener [observer, contemplator] in as many sections of musical time [8] as are contained between birth and death [of these sections]; and it is these [successive] sections with which Music entertains the soul residing in the body of the contemplator.

But the Painter replies and says that the human body, composed of many members, does not give pleasure at [successive] time-sections

---

[8] Mistranslated with "rhythms" by J. P. Richter and Irma Richter, *Paragone*, London, 1949, p. 75.

in which beauty is transforming itself by giving shape (form) to something else, nor that it [beauty] needs, in these time-sections, to be born
and to die, but rather that he [the Painter] renders it [the body] permanent for very many years and the painting is of such excellence that
it keeps alive that harmony of well-proportioned members which nature
with all its force would not be able to preserve – how many Paintings
have preserved the image of divine beauty whose real model has soon
been destroyed by time or death, so that the Painter's work has survived
more nobly than that of nature, his mistress.

Comments on Trattato 30:

Trattato 30 actually does not expound any new arguments in favor of
the Musician, but repeats his claim that his science equals that of painting
because it operates by combining one "corpo" out of many members.
Whether these members are successive sections of the musical flow is not
entirely clear, but would seem to be suggested by the term "tanti-tempi
armonici" confronting the contemplation of the listener – if "speculatore"
could be at all translated by "listener."

When the Painter, however, tries to defend his claim of superiority, he
adds to his old arguments one new angle: he credits painting with the capacity
of "figurationi," implying that this capacity is lacking in music. We must
emphasize this here, because later in Trattato 32 that "figurationi" is regarded also as a characteristic of music, although, unlike the "figurationi"
used by painting, it is the figuration of the invisible.

The end of chapter 30, emphasizing the power of Painting to preserve
the image of a person beyond his death, echoes Ovid, *Metamorphoses,*
Book XV, with the famous lamentation of the aging Helen of Troy observing
in the mirror the wrinkles of her face and weeping about Time, the great
destroyer of things, and Leonardo's own paraphrase in Codice Atlantico
71 r.a.:

"O tempo, consumatore delle cose, e, o invidiosa antichità, tu distruggi
tutte le cose e consumi tutte le cose da duri denti della vecchiezza a poco
a poco con lenta morte!

Elena quando si specchiava, vedendo le vizze grinze del suo viso, fatte
per la vecchiezza, piagnie e pensa seco, perchè fu rapita due volte.

O tempo, consumatore delle cose, e o invidiosa antichità, per la quale
tutte le sono consumate."

O Time, thou that consumest all things! O envious age, thou destroyest
all things and devourest all things with the hard teeth of the years, little by

little, in slow death! Helen, when she looked in her mirror and saw the withered wrinkles which old age had made in her face, wept, and wondered to herself why ever she had twice been carried away.

O Time, thou that consument all things! O envious age, whereby all things are consumed."

Trattato 31:

IL PITTORE DÀ I GRADI DELLE COSE OPPOSTE ALL' OCCHIO, COME 'L MUSICO DÀ DELLE VOCI OPPOSTE ALL' ORECCHIO

Benchè le cose opposte all' occhio si tocchino l'un e l'altra di mano in mano, nondimeno farò la mia regola di XX. in. XX. braccia, come ha fatto el musico infra le voci, che benchè la sia unita et appiccha insieme, nondimeno a pochi gradi di voce in voce, domandando quella prima, seconda, terza, quarta e quinta, et così di grado in grado ha posto nomi alla varietà d'alzare et bassare la voce.

Se tu o musico dirai, che la pittura è meccanica per essere operata con l'esercitio delle mani, e la musica è operata con la bocca, ch'è organo humano, ma non pel conto del senso del gusto, come la mano senso del tatto. meno degne sono anchora le parolle ch'e' fatti; ma tu scrittore delle scientie, non copij tu con mano, scrivendo ciò, che sta nella mente, come fa il pittore? e se tu dicessi la musica essere composta di proporzione, o io con questa medesima seguito la pittura, come mi vedrai.

THE PAINTER USES DEGREES FOR THE OBJECTS APPEARING TO THE EYE, JUST AS THE MUSICIAN DOES FOR THE VOICES RECEIVED BY THE EAR

Although the objects confronting the eye touch one another, hand in hand [one behind the other], I will nevertheless base my rule on [distances of] XX to XX braccia, just as the Musician has done, dealing with [the intervals between] the tones [voices]: they are united and connected with each other, yet can be differentiated by a few degrees tone by tone, establishing a prime, second, third, fourth and fifth, so that names could be given by him to the varieties [of pitch] of the voice when it moves up or down.

If you, oh Musician, will say that Painting is mechanical because it is performed by using the hands, [you should consider that] music is performed with the mouth which is also a human organ though not [in this case] serving the sense of taste, just as the hands [of the Painter] do not serve the sense of touch – [and as for word-arts] words are even more inferior than actions [such as those just described] – and you, oh Writer on the sciences, doest thou not copy by hand, like the Painter, that which is in the mind? And if you say that Music is composed of proportion, then I have used the same [method] in Painting, as you will see.

Comments on Trattato 31:

Trattato 31 touches on another comparison between music and painting which is farfetched but reveals how anxious Leonardo is to do justice to music within the Paragone. He compares the objects as they confront the eye in a continuous receding row or chain (opposte all' occhio si tocchino l'un altra di mano in mano) with the gradation of tones, that is, with the musical tones that by their numerical ratios ("gradi di voce in voce") form a scale. The mathematical rationalization of pitch values of tones is, of course, old Pythagorean and Boethian tradition and was commonplace in Leonardo's time; it is this mathematical quality of music that gave it a place among the liberal arts, but to credit painting with a similar rational basis was a relatively novel idea. Leonardo's argument is expressly, though only in passing, stated in Trattato 31-b: "Since you accorded to music a place among the liberal arts, either place there painting also, or remove music from there."

It is, of course, the science of perspective which Leonardo has in mind when he speaks of "la mia regola di XX in XX Braccia" (receding of objects from the eye by a standard distance of 220 yards). It is easy to see how forced the whole comparison is – a much more substantial comparison between linear perspective and acoustical phenomena is found in Ms. L, 79 v. where Leonardo tries to find the ratios of fading sound, or more precisely, the proportions between the volume of sound and the distance between the ear and the source of sound; there he establishes a "regola" which in his own language could be termed a perspective of sound.

Trattato 31-a deals with the art of sculpture.

Trattato 31b:

>   Quella cosa è più degna, che satisfa a miglior senso. Adonque la pittura, satisfatrice al senso del vedere, è più nobile che la musica, che solo satisfa all' udito.
>   Quella cosa è più nobile, che ha più eternità. Adonque la musica,

che si va consumando mentre ch'ella nasce, è men degna che la pittura, che con uetri si fa eterna.

Quella cosa, che contiene in se più universalità e varietà di cose, quella fia detta di più eccellentia. adonque la pittura è da essere preposta a tutte le operationi, perchè è contenitrice di tutte le forme, che sono, e di quelle, che non sono in natura; è più da essere magnificata et esaltata, che la musica, che solo attende alla voce.

Con questa si fa i simulacri alli dij, dintorno a questa si fa il culto divino, il quale è ornato con la musica a questa seruente; con questa si dà copia alli amanti della causa de' loro amori, con questa si riserua le bellezze, le quali il tempo e la natura fa fugitive, con questa noi riserviamo le similitudini degli huomini famosi, e se tu dicessi la musica s'eterna con lo scriverla, el medesimo facciamo noi qui cō le lettere. Adonque, poi chè tu hai messo la musica infra le arti liberali, o tu vi metti questa, o tu ne levi quella, e se tu dicessi li huomini vidi la d'operano, e così è guasta la musica da chi non la sa.

That thing is more worthy which satisfies the higher sense. Thus, Painting, since it satisfies the sense of seeing, is more noble than Music, which only satisfies the ear.

That thing is more noble which has longer duration. Thus Music, which withers [fades] while it is born, is less worthy than Painting, which with the help of varnish renders itself eternal.

That thing which contains within itself the greatest universality and variety of objects may be called the most excellent. Thus Painting is to be preferred to all other activities, because it is concerned [occupies itself] with all the forms which do exist and also with those which do not exist in nature; it is to be more praised and exalted than Music which is only concerned with sound [voice].

With Painting one makes the images of gods, around which divine rites are held which Music helps to adorn; with the help of Painting, one gives lovers likenesses [portraits] of those who aroused their ardor; through Painting one preserves the beauty which time and nature cause to fade away; through Painting we preserve the likenesses of famous men, and if you should say that Music becomes eternal when it is written down, we are doing the same here with letters. Thus, since you have given a place to Music among the Liberal Arts, you must place Painting there too, or eject Music; and if you point at vile men who practice Painting, Music also can be spoiled by those who do not understand it.

Comments on Trattato 31b:

Trattato 31b, combining earlier and new arguments, expounds various reasons for the preeminence of painting over music: 1) Painting satisfies the highest sense, sight, music only the sense of hearing – but why sight should be more noble than hearing is not elaborated. 2) Painting is permanent, music evanescent. 3) Painting occupies itself with objects of more universality and variety than music which is based only on sound (an argument so questionable that one is not surprised to find it nowhere else in Leonardo's writings).

The passage on the place of painting and of music among the liberal arts has been commented on in my explanation of Trattato 31.

Other arguments proffered here, such as the comparison between musical scores and letters, are rhetorical rather than serious.

Trattato 31c:

> Se tu dirai le scientie non mecaniche sono le mentali, io ti dirò che la pittura è mentale, e ch'ella, sicome la musica e geometria considera le proportioni delle quantità continue, e l'aritmetica delle discontinue, questa considera tutte le quantità continue e le qualità delle proportioni d'ombre e lumi e distantie nella sua prospettiva.

> If you [the Musician] say that only the non-mechanical [physical, bodily, material] sciences [liberal arts] are concerned with the mind [9] and that, just as Music and Geometry deal with the proportions of the continuous quantities, and Arithmetic with the proportions of the discontinuous quantities, [so] Painting deals with all the continuous quantities and also with the qualities of the proportions [degrees] of [10] shades and lights and distances in their [its?] perspective.

Comments on Trattato 31c:

Trattato 31c introduces a new basis of comparison, the question of whether painting and music are concerned with proportions of "continuous quantities," as is geometry; or with "discontinuous quantities," as is arith-

---

[9] Mistranslated by Irma Richter, *Paragone,* p. 77: "If you say that the sciences are not 'mechanical' but purely of the mind," which implies that *all* sciences are not mechanical, while Leonardo evidently wants to distinguish between scientie meccaniche and scientie mentali.

[10] I. Richter mistranslates as follows: "... with the qualities of proportions, shadows and light ...."

metic. The answer given is that both arts concern themselves with continuous quantities. This statement must be understood in the light of the former explanation that painting is based on perspective ("le cose si toccano l'un l'altra di mano in mano . . ."), (Trattato 31), and of the awareness that music exists as continuous flow. Heretofore its flow, by a poetic rather than scientific argumentation, was proffered as evidence of its transience and mortality, flaws not inherent in the nobler art of painting. Now the flow – that is, the smooth gliding from one tone to the next – elevates music to a "scientia mentale" dealing with continuous quantities, like geometry and painting. Thus, under scientific scrutiny, a sort of equality of rank is established between painting and music.

Leonardo's distinction between continuous and discontinuous quantities comes, of course, from Aristotelian tradition (see especially *Metaphysics,* Book VI 1,2). Its application to the arts of painting and music is Leonardo's own. According to Aristotle, *Logic* 5a, line, space and time belong to the class of continuous quantities "for it is possible to find a common boundary at which their parts join." And it is probably also based on Aristotle when Leonardo regards poetry (or "speech" in Aristotelian terminology) as inferior to music and painting: "speech is a discontinuous quantity, for its parts have no common boundary" (Aristotle, *Logic* 4b32).

As for the distinction between "scientie meccaniche" and "mentali," one should look at Trattato 33, not reprinted here, since it does not deal with music. There, the problem is approached through the consideration of "esperientia," that is, empirical research. The classification of arts into *artes mechanicae* and *artes liberales* is medieval.

Trattato 32:

CONCLUSIONE DEL POETA, PITTORE E MUSICO

Tal diferentia è inquanto alla figuratione delle cose corporee dal pittore e poeta, quanto dalli corpi smembrati a li uniti, perchè il poeta nel descrivere la bellezza o' brutezza di qualonche corpo te lo dimostra a membro a membro et in diversi tempi, et il pittore tel fa vedere tutto in un tempo. el poeta non può porre con le parole la vera figura delle membra di che si compone un tutto, com el pittore, il quale tel pone innanti con quella verità, ch'è possibile in natura; et al poeta accade il medesimo, come al musico, che canta sol' un canto composto di quattro cantori, e canta prima il canto, poi il tenore, e cosi seguita il contr' alto e poi il basso; e di costui non risulta la gratia della proportionalità armonica, la quale si rinchiude in tempi armonici, e fa esso poeta a similitudine d'un bel volto, il quale ti si mostra a membro a membro, che cosi facendo, non remarresti mai satisfatto dalla sua bellezza, la quale solo consiste nella divina proportionalità delle predette membra insieme composte, le quali solo in un tempo compongono essa divina armonia d'esso congionto di membre, che spesso tolgono la libertà posseduta a chi le vede. e la musica ancora fa nel suo tempo armonico le soavi melodie composte delle sue varie voci, delle quali il poeta è privato della loro discretione armonica, e ben che la poesia entri pel senso dell' audito alla sedia del giuditio, sicome la musica, esso poeta non può descrivere l'armonia della musica, perchè non ha potestà in un medesimo tempo di dire diverse cose, come la proportionalità armonica della pittura composta di diverse membra in un medesimo tempo, la dolcezza delle quali sono giudicate in un medesimo tempo, cosi in comune, come in particolare; in comune, inquanto allo intento del composto, in particolare, inquanto allo intento de' componenti, di che si compone esso tutto; e per questo il poeta resta, inquanto alla figuratione delle cose corporee, molto indietro al pittore, e delle cose invisibili rimane indietro al musico. ma s'esso poeta toglie in prestito l'aiuto dell' altre scientie, potrà comparire alle fere come li altri mercanti portatori di diverse cose fatte da più inventori, e fa questo il poeta, quando sinpresta l'altrui scientia, come del oratore, e del filosofo, astrologho, cosmografo e simili, le quali scienze sonno in tutto separate dal poeta.

CONCLUSION OF [THE DISCUSSION BETWEEN] THE POET, THE PAINTER AND THE MUSICIAN

As for the representation of bodily [corporeal] things, there is the same difference between the Painter and the Poet as between dismembered and united things, because when the Poet describes the beauty or ugliness of a body, he shows it to you part by part and at different [successive] times, while the Painter lets you see it in one and the same moment [simultaneously]. The Poet cannot create [establish] with words the real shape of the parts which make up a whole, as does the Painter who can put them before you with the same truth that is possible in nature [in the concrete appearance of nature], and the same thing happens to the Poet [the Poet encounters the same difficulty] as would to the Musician, if the latter would sing by himself some music composed for four singers, by singing first the soprano part, then the tenor part and then following it by the contralto and finally the bass;

from such a performance does not result [ensue] the grace [beauty] of harmony by proportions [musical harmony as produced by the consonance of several voices of different pitch as established by the acoustical proportions], which is confined to moments of harmony (endowed with harmony, i.e., chords) – this is precisely what the Poet does to the likeness of a beautiful face when he describes it feature by feature. You would never be satisfied by such a representation of beauty [of the beauty of the face], because that can only be the result of the divine proportionality of these features taken all together since it is only at the very same moment [simultaneously] that they create this divine harmony of the union of all features which so enslaves the beholder that he loses his liberty.

Music, on the other hand, within its harmonious flow [time], produces the sweet melodies generated by its various voices, while the Poet is deprived of their specific harmonic action, and though Poetry reaches the seat of judgment through the sense of hearing, it cannot describe [render, create] musical harmony because he is not able to say different things at the same time as is achieved in Painting by the harmonious proportionality created by the various [component] parts at the same time, so that their sweetness can be perceived at the same time, as a whole and in its parts, as a whole with regard to the composition, in particular with regard to the [single] component parts.

For these reasons the Poet remains, in the representation of bodily things, far behind the Painter and, in the representation of invisible things, far behind the Musician. But if the Poet borrows from the other arts he can compete at fairs with merchants who carry goods made by various inventors [makers] – in this way he acts when he borrows from other sciences such as those of the orator, philosopher, astronomer, cosmographer and others which are totally separate from his own art.

Comments on Trattato 32:

First, a difference is stated between Painting and Poetry as far as they occupy themselves with the representation of bodily things (figuratione delle cose corporee) – disjointed features are found to be the subject of Poetry, and united features the subject of Painting. In fact, this distinction is only another version of the distinction between arts which present their objects in succession, in the flow, and those arts which present their objects in simultaneity (see Trattato 30). It must, however, be pointed out that Leonardo does not mean to restrict altogether the field of Poetry to figurazione delle *cose corporee,* because later in this chapter 32, he has it compete also with music in the field of the *figuratione delle cose invisibili.*

A very important point is touched upon when Leonardo exalts Painting for being able to put before us features with the truth of nature (con quella verità, che'è possibile in natura), because here a basic aesthetic phenomenon is accounted for – the concreteness of visual appearance – or to say it more precisely, the simultaneous impact of an infinite number of features integrated in their concrete, immediate appearance. This observation of Leonardo goes beyond the famous paragone of the 18th century, Lessing's "Laokoon," which strangely enough, does not analyze this phenomenon of the visual arts. Goethe, we recall, was deeply aware of it – for instance, when he admired Delacroix' illustrations for Faust which, as he remarked (Gespräche mit Eckermann, November 29, 1826) added, or rather, were forced to add by their very medium, details to the scene which were beyond his, the Poet's, medium.

Very striking and almost humorous is Leonardo's argument to prove the inferiority of Poetry to Painting by the absurd picture of the performance of a polyphonic four-voice composition by one single singer, who could sing the four parts of the polyphonic web one after another, thus losing harmony and thereby the whole musical purpose altogether. At the same time, this caricature of Music reveals that Leonardo credits Music, if correctly performed, with *proportionalità armonica,* one of the important advantages inherent, according to him, also in Painting.

The remainder of Trattato 32 returns to the argument about proportions which was taken up before in Trattato 21, 23, 27, 29 and 30. We will briefly examine later in the epilogue whether proportions can really mean the same thing in Painting and in Music.

In a peremptory summary, Leonardo states that in the *figuratione delle cose corporee* the Poet ranks behind the Painter, and in the *figuratione delle cose invisibili,* behind the Musician. What then, we ask, is the comparative rank between Leonardo's most beloved and exalted art, Painting, and Music? He has accorded proportionality and harmony to both of them; he seems also to ignore here the cliché disparagement of music – its evanescence – *la malattia mortale* (see Trattato 29: "la pittura eccelle e signoreggia la musica, perche essa non more immediate dopo la sua creatione"). Nothing then hinders him from regarding Music as equally noble in its own right, in consideration of the peculiarities of this discipline. But this ultimate verdict had already been pronounced in chapter 23, which warns against the confusion of arts for the eye and arts for the ear, concluding: *"lasciavi entrare l'uffitio della musica* (the peculiar business of music): Let music enter by its own merits and do not confuse it with painting, the true imitative science."[11]

EPILOGUE

These chapters of Leonardo's Paragone seem to amount to a mixture of naive, often contradictory statements, commonplaces of his time, rhetorical attempts to bolster the social status of the Painter, and profound original ideas about the nature of the arts, including that of Music.

To be fair, we have to recall that the Trattato was not a book compiled by himself, but composed by Francesco Melzi out of relevant passages – but by no means all the relevant passages – in Leonardo's notebooks and manuscripts.

Furthermore, Leonardo himself was never a consistent organizer of his thoughts, though he frequently reminds himself in his notebooks to write a treatise on this or that – treatises never found and most probably never written in the continuous onslaught of tasks and problems upon him, the artist, scientist, engineer and provider of entertainment for the court.

Leonardo states clearly in Trattato 34 (not included in our selection) that it is only through ignorance that Painting was classed below the "sciences," by which he means the liberal arts. This ignorance is the lack of familiarity with the most recent achievement of Painting, linear perspective – an exact rationalization of sight based on mathematical proportions. This made Painting a quasi-mathematical science of the same nobility as Music, for centuries one of the members of the quadrivium together with geometry, arithmetic and astronomy.[12] This practical purpose colors many, though not all, of Leonardo's comparisons between the arts.

For a summary, it seems practical to list the criteria and arguments proffered by Leonardo in his Paragone for judging the comparative nobility of Music among the arts. Many are notions which were in the air, so to speak; some echo arguments indispensable in the fashionable, intellectual pastime of Leonardo's day, the disputation of the arts and their merits among courtiers and humanists; some are contradicted by deeper thoughts in the Codice

[11] André Chastel, *The Genius of Leonardo da Vinci*, New York, 1961, p. 33, seems to underrate this assessment of music when he says: "Ultimately these [the spatial] arts take a higher position than the temporal arts," perhaps because he does not reprint the critical chapters 23 and 32.

[12] Leonardo was not the only one to fight for the inclusion of Painting among the liberal arts. Half a century earlier, Leon Battista Alberti had taken the same stand. And when Pollaiuolo in 1493 designed the tomb of Sixtus IV, he added the allegorical figure of *Prospettiva* to the figures of the *quadrivium* and *trivium*.

Atlantico and other notebooks of Leonardo, where they are mostly just hinted at and jotted down in Leonardo's typical "self-reminder" fashion. A few, finally, contain new and ingenious ideas.

Cliché Arguments (the numbers indicate the chapters in which they occur):

 a. The eye (Painting) more noble than the ear (Poetry and Music): 16, 20, 21, 24, 27, 28, 29, 31b.
 b. The evanescence of Music; her mortal disease: fading: 23, 29, 30, 31b.[13] Strangely enough, the same blame is not laid on Poetry.
 c. Boredom and disgust caused by repetitiousness: 23.[13]
 d. Poverty of the musical realm; Music concerned only with sound, while Painting is universal, concerning itself with all things that enter the mind: 31b.
 e. Mechanical arts: Music performed with the mouth: 31; see also, 19, 31c; and, deviating from the clichés, 33, not included in our selection.

Serious Criteria:

1. Spatial arts vs. temporal arts

Arts for the eye vs. arts for the ear

The distinction is retained in various versions throughout nearly all of the chapters of the Trattato included in the present essay: 16, 20, 21, 24, 27, 28, 29, 31b – curiously enough, the exaltation of Painting as the foremost visual art is often based on harmony, which is an integral feature of a temporal art: Music. In these contexts, Leonardo stresses harmony as a phenomenon restricted to one single instant, namely the combination of several tones of different pitch in one chord (or as he terms it, *concento*); he never fails to emphasize *in medesimo tempo* – it is perhaps a pity that the compiler of the Trattato did not include also some of the most salient statements of Leonardo on the nature of time as a continuous quantity, for instance BM 173 v, and 190 v, and Arundel Ms. British Museum No. 263 and 132 r.

---

[13] On evanescence and disgusting repetitiousness, see also Codice Atlantico 382 v.a.: "La musica ha due malattie, delle quali l'una è mortale, l'altra e decrepitudinale: la mortale e sempre congiunta allo instante sequente a quel della sua creazione; la decrepitudinale la fa odiosa e vile nella sua replicazione." – ("Music has two ills: one is mortal, the other is related to its decrepitude [feebleness]; the mortal one is always linked to the moment that follows its incipience [each tone of it]; its feebleness causing repetitiousness makes it hateful and vile").

2. *The role of proportions and the continuous quantities: 23, 27, 29, 30,
31, 32:*

A discussion of the various meanings of "proportions" in Leonardo's
writings would go far beyond the limits of this little essay. In the Paragone,
two kinds of "harmonious proportions" are ascribed to Painting: first, the
proportions of the single features of a face or any other object of representation, that create the harmony of the whole; second, the numerical proportions that are implied in mathematical perspective, that as a new method
used by the Painter, made Painting a mathematical art worthy of admission
into the Quadrivium. The first kind of proportions is [seen] paralleled in
musical harmony, that is in the numerical relations between the pitch of
the tones united in one chord. This would restrict proportions to the "vertical" aspect of the flow of music. However, Music admits also the concept
of "lengthwise" or "horizontal" proportions – that is, the relation between
successive sections of a piece of music. There is no clear acknowledgment
of such proportions in the Paragone (see my comment to Trattato 30), but
Leonardo's awareness of the problem appears clearly from statements in
British Museum Arundel 263, 1736. There he discusses, in the Aristotelian
vein, the concept of continuous quantities in geometry (already touched upon
in Trattato 31c), compares point and line with their counterparts in time
and, on this basis, affirms the proportionality of time sections. The passage
is too interesting for its bearing on musical time not to quote it here:

Benchè il tenpo – sia annumerato infra le continue quätità, per essere inuisibile e sanza
corpo, non cade integralmēte sotto la geometrica potentia, la quale lo diuide per figure e
corpi d'infinita varietà, come continuo nelle cose uisibili e corporee far si uede; Ma sol
co' sua primi principi si cōuiene–, cioè col punto e colla linia–; il punto nel tempo è da
essere equiparato al suo instante, e la linia à similitudine colla lūghezza d'una quantità
d'un tempo, e siccome i pūti sō principio e fine della predetta linia–, così li instanti sō
termine e principio di qualūche dato spatio di tempo; E se la linia è diuisibile in ïfinito,
lo spatio d'ū tênpo di tal diuisione non è alieno, e se le parti diuise della linia sono proportionabili infra sé, ancora le parti de tenpo saraño proportionabili infra loro.

"Although time is included among the continuous quantities, it does – since it
is invisible and incorporeal – fall into the realm of geometry, whose divisions
consist of figures and bodies of infinite variety, as a continuum of visible and
corporeal things. But only in their principles do they [geometry and time] agree,
that is with regard to the point and the line; the point is comparable to an instant in time; and just as a line is similar to the length of a section of time, so
the instants are ends and beginnings of each given section of time. And if the
line is infinitely divisible, so is the section of time resulting from such division;
and if the sections of a line are proportionable to each other, so are the [succes-
sive] sections of time proportionable to each other."

Similar statements based on Aristotle's 6th book of Physics, esp. 231b, 7; 232a; 233a; and 233b, 15, are found in Leonardo, British Museum Arundel 263, 176r and 190v; but the reference to proportions between successive sections of time is Leonardo's own, and so is the application of Aristotle's concept of continuous quantities to the field of aesthetics, particularly to music.

If Leonardo thus admits proportions between successive sections of time and therefore also of successive sections of a work of music, it remains strange that he does not explicitly recognize the role of memory in creating forms in the flux. Memory is hardly ever investigated or analyzed by Leonardo as a psychological or philosophical problem, except in connection with Painting, the art that stems the flight of time by eternalizing the presence of a visual image. One of his rare general references to memory is found outside the Paragone, in Codice Atlantico 76a:

A torto si lamētā li omini della fuga del tenpo, incolpando quello di troppa velocità, nō s'accorgiēdo quello essere di bastevole trāsito, ma (la) bona memoria–, di che la natura ci à dotati, ci fa che ogni coas lungamēte passata ci pare essere presente.

Wrongly do men lament the flight of time; they accuse it of being too swift and do not recognize that it is sufficient [sufficiently moderate] in its passage; good memory, with which nature has endowed us, makes everything long past seem present to us.

3. Figuratione delle cose corporee vs. figuratione delle cose invisibili

This distinction may seem at first glance similar to that between arts for the eye and arts for the ear; yet it goes deeper. In chapter 12 Leonardo speaks of the divinity of the science of Painting and, paraphrasing Dante,[14] calls the Painter the lord and creator (padrone, signore, creatore) of all the things which occur in human thought. This concept seems to go far beyond the qualification of painting as an art copying nature.[15] Should not then the idea have occurred to him that Music be still more free and god-like, since it creates "out of nothing"? This seems to be implied in his concept of the figuratione dell invisibile.

Music, in the last analysis is not anymore the "younger and inferior sister of Painting" (Trattato 29), but in every sense "equiparata" (equivalent) to

---

[14] "Arte, nipote di Dio."

[15] When Leonardo speaks of Painting as an art or science "imitating" nature, he means, in line with current theory, by "imitare" recreating nature and not "ritrarre," i.e., redrawing, as for instance in a camera obscura. See to this point also the forcible statements at the end of chapter 27, that Painting can concern itself with creations that have never been created by nature.

Painting (Trattato 30). If Leonardo had never said anything else about Music beyond defining her as a *figuratione dell invisibile,* this definition alone would suffice to convince us of his profound understanding of the nature of Music as a discipline that is not bound to copy nature but with an unparalleled degree of freedom creates forms ("figure") out of a material neither tangible nor visible.

ALFRED SCHUTZ BIBLIOGRAPHY*

I. WORKS BY SCHUTZ (IN ORDER OF PUBLICATION**):

1. Books, Articles, and Reviews:

Der sinnhafte Aufbau der sozialen Welt: eine Einleitung in die verstehende Soziologie, Vienna: Julius Springer, 1932. Pp. vii, 286. Note: A second, unrevised edition (with a brief Foreword by Ilse Schutz) was published by Springer-Verlag in 1960.

Review: *Méditations cartésiennes* by Edmund Husserl, *Deutsche Literaturzeitung,* Vol. LIII, 1932, pp. 2404–2416.

Review: *Formale und transzendentale Logik* by Edmund Husserl, *Deutsche Literaturzeitung,* Vol. LIV, 1933, pp. 773–784.

"Tomoo Otakas Grundlegung der Lehre vom sozialen Verband," *Zeitschrift für öffentliches Recht,* Vol. XVII, 1937, pp. 64–84.

"Phenomenology and the Social Sciences," in *Philosophical Essays in Memory of Edmund Husserl* (edited by Marvin Farber), Cambridge: Harvard University Press, 1940, pp. 164–186 (translated from the German by Richard H. Williams).[1] Reprinted in *Phenomenology* (edited by Joseph J. Kockelmans), Garden City, N.Y.: Doubleday, 1967.

"William James's Concept of the Stream of Thought Phenomenologically Interpreted," *Philosophy and Phenomenological Research.* Vol. I, 1941, pp. 442–452.[3]

---

* In the beginning of his writing career, Alfred Schutz used the Umlaut in his surname (Schütz). Later he dropped the Umlaut and added an "e" (Schuetz). Toward the latter part of his life, he adopted the spelling we follow here: Schutz.

** The order in which they were published is not always, of course, the order in which they were written. For further details about their composition, see the Editors' Notes to the *Collected Papers,* Volume II in particular.

[1] Reprinted in Schutz's Collected Papers, Vol. I
[2] Reprinted in Schutz's Collected Papers, Vol. II
[3] Reprinted in Schutz's Collected Papers, Vol. III

"Scheler's Theory of Intersubjectivity and the General Thesis of the Alter Ego," *Philosophy and Phenomenological Research*, Vol. II, 1942, pp. 323–347.[1]

"The Problem of Rationality in the Social World," *Economica*, New Series, Vol. X, 1943, pp. 130–149.[2] Reprinted in *Sociological Theory and Philosophical Analysis* (edited by Alastair MacIntyre and Dorothy Emmet), New York: Macmillan, 1970. Note: There is some discussion of Schutz in the Editors' Introduction.

Review: *The Foundation of Phenomenology* by Marvin Farber, *Philosophical Abstracts*, Vol. III, 1944, No. 13–14, pp. 8–9.

"The Stranger," *American Journal of Sociology*, Vol. XLIX, 1944, pp. 499–507.[2] Reprinted in *Identity and Anxiety* (edited by Maurice Stein, Arthur J. Vidich, and David Manning White), Glencoe: Free Press, 1960.

"Some Leading Concepts of Phenomenology," *Social Research*, Vol. XII, 1945, pp. 77–97.[1] Reprinted in *Essays in Phenomenology* (edited by Maurice Natanson), The Hague: Martinus Nijhoff, 1966. Also reprinted in part in *Encounter: An Introduction to Philosophy* (edited by Ramona Cormier, Ewing Chinn, and Richard H. Linneback), Glenview, Ill.: Scott, Foresman, 1970.

"On Multiple Realities," *Philosophy and Phenomenological Research*. Vol. V, pp. 1945, pp. 533–575.[1]

"The Homecomer," *American Journal of Sociology*, Vol. L, 1945, pp. 363–376.[2] Reprinted in *The Nature and Scope of Social Science: A Critical Anthology* (edited by Leonard I. Krimerman), New York: Appleton-Century-Crofts, 1969.

"The Well-Informed Citizen: An Essay on the Social Distribution of Knowledge," *Social Research*, Vol. XIII, 1946, pp. 463–478.[2]

"Sartre's Theory of the Alter Ego," *Philosophy and Phenomenological Research*, Vol. IX, 1948, pp. 181–199.[1]

"Felix Kaufmann, 1895–1949," *Social Research*, Vol. XVII, 1950, pp. 1–7.

"Language, Language Disturbances, and the Texture of Consciousness," *Social Research*, Vol. XVII, 1950, pp. 365–394.[1]

"Making Music Together: A Study in Social Relationship," *Social Research*, Vol. XVIII, 1951, pp. 76–97.[2]

"Choosing Among Projects of Action," *Philosophy and Phenomenological Research*, Vol. XII, 1951, pp. 161–184.[1]

"Santayana on Society and Government," *Social Research*, Vol. XIX, 1952, pp. 220–246.[2]

"Common-Sense and Scientific Interpretation of Human Action," *Philosophy and Phenomenological Research*, Vol. XIV, 1953, pp. 1–37.[1] Reprinted in part in *Sociological Theory: A Book of readings* (Edited by Lewis A. Coser and Bernard Rosenberg), New York; Macmillan, 1957 and in full in *Philosophy of the Social Sciences: A Reader* (edited by Maurice Natanson), New York, Random House, 1963. Note: The last work is dedicated to Alfred Schutz.

"Edmund Husserl's Ideas, Volume II," *Philosophy and Phenomenological Research*, Vol. XIII, 1953, pp. 394–413.[3]

"Die Phaenomenologie und die Fundamente der Wissenschaften (Ideas III. By Edmund Husserl)," *Philosophy and Phenomenological Research*, Vol. XIII, 1953, pp. 506–514.[3] Note: Entitled "Phenomenology and the Foundations of the Social Sciences" in Collected Papers, Vol. III.

"Concept and Theory Formation in the Social Sciences," *Journal of Philosophy*. Vol. LI, 1953, pp. 257–273.[1] Reprinted in *Philosophy of the Social Sciences: A Reader* (edited by Maurice Natanson), New York: Random House, 1963, in *Readings in Existential Phenomenology* (edited by Nathaniel Lawrence and Daniel O'Connor), Englewood Cliffs, N.J.: Prentice-Hall, 1967, and in *Sociological Theory and Philosophical Analysis* (edited by Alastair MacIntyre and Dorothy Emmet), New York: Macmillan, 1970.

"Don Quijote y el Problema de la Realidad," *Dianoia*, Vol. I, 1955, pp. 312–330 (translated from the English by Marta Díaz de Léon de Recaséns and Professor Luis Recaséns-Siches). The original English version, "Don Quixote and the Problem of Reality," appears in Collected Papers, Vol. II.

"Symbol, Reality, and Society," in *Symbols and Society* (edited by Lyman Bryson, Louis Finkelstein, Hudson Hoagland, and R. M. MacIver), New York: Harper, 1955, pp. 135–202.[1] Note: A brief comment on this paper by Charles W. Morris and a reply by Alfred Schutz follow on pp. 202–203.

"La Philosophie de Max Scheler," in *Les Philosophes célèbres* (edited by Maurice Merleau-Ponty), Paris: Lucien Mazenod, 1956, pp. 330–335 (translated from the English by Michel Kullman). The original English version is included in Collected Papers, Vol. III.

"Mozart and the Philosophers," *Social Research*, Vol. XXIII, 1956, pp. 219–242.[2]

"Equality and the Meaning Structure of the Social World," in *Aspects of Human Equality* (edited by Lyman Bryson, Clarence H. Faust, Louis Finkelstein, and R. M. MacIver), New York: Harper, 1957, pp. 33–78.[2]

"Kurt Riezler" (a memorial notice, written with Horace M. Kallen), *Proceedings and Addresses of the American Philosophical Association*, Vol. XXX, 1957, pp. 114–115.

"Some Equivocations in the Notion of Responsibility," in *Determinism and Freedom* (edited by Sidney Hook), New York: New York University Press, 1958, pp. 206–208.[2]

"Das Problem der transzendentalen Intersubjektivität bei Husserl," *Philosophische Rundschau*, Vol. V, 1957, pp. 81–107. An English version of this paper, translated by Frederick Kersten in collaboration with Aron Gurwitsch and Thomas Luckmann, is included in Collected Papers, Vol. III. A French version (translated from the German by Maurice de Gandillac) appears in *Husserl* (Cahiers de Royaumont, Philosophie No. III), Paris: Éditions de Minuit, 1959 together with comments by a number of philosophers and a reply by Alfred Schutz.*

"Max Scheler's Epistemology and Ethics," *Review of Metaphysics,* Vol. XI, 1957, pp. 304–314 and 486–501. An enlarged version of this paper appears in Collected Papers, Vol. III.

"Husserl's Importance for the Social Sciences," in *Edmund Husserl: 1859– 1959* (edited by H. L. Van Breda and J. Taminiaux), The Hague: Martinus Nijhoff, 1959, pp. 86–98.[1] Note: The opening section, pp. 86–88, of this paper (a personal remembrance of Edmund Husserl) is not reprinted in the Collected Papers version.

"Tiresias, Or Our Knowledge of Future Events," *Social Research,* Vol. XXVI, 1959, pp. 71–89.[2]

"Type and Eidos in Husserl's Late Philosophy," *Philosophy and Phenomenological Research,* Vol. XX, 1959, pp. 147–165.[3]

"The Social World and the Theory of Social Action," *Social Research,* Vol. XXVII, 1960, pp. 203–221.[2] Reprinted in part in *Philosophical Problems of the Social Sciences* (edited by David Braybrooke), New York: Macmillan, 1965.

Collected Papers, Volume I: *The Problem of Social Reality* (edited and Introduced by Maurice Natanson with a Preface by H. L. Van Breda), Phaenomenologica 11, The Hague: Martinus Nijhoff, 1962 (with a photograph of Alfred Schutz as a frontispiece). Pp. xlvii, 361.

Collected Papers, Volume II: *Studies in Social Theory* (edited and Introduced by Arvid Brodersen), Phaenomenologica 15, The Hague: Martinus Nijhoff, 1964. Pp. xv, 300. Note: This volume contains a chapter on "The Dimensions of the Social World," an English adaptation by Thomas Luckmann of a section or *Der sinnhafte Aufbau der sozialen Welt.* Part of this chapter is reprinted in *Readings in the Philosophy of Man* (edited by William L. Kelly and Andrew Tallon), New York: McGraw-Hill, 1967, with introductory remarks on pp. 184–185.

Collected Papers, Volume III: *Studies in Phenomenological Philosophy* (edited by I. (lse) Schutz with an Introduction by Aron Gurwitsch), Phaenomenologica 22, The Hague: Martinus Nijhoff, 1966. Pp. xxxi, 191. Note: "Some Structures of the Life-World," a previously unpublished essay, appears in this volume (translated from the German by Aron Gurwitsch). Also included are a discussion by Eugen Fink of the chapter on "The Problem of Transcendental

---

* For a different treatment of the problem of intersubjectivity, the reader may wish to see Hermann Zeltner, "Das Ich und die Anderen: Husserls Beitrag zur Grundlegung der Sozialphilosophie," *Zeitschrift für philosophische Forschung,* Vol. XIII, 1959, pp. 288–315 (with a note regarding Alfred Schutz on p. 288).

Intersubjectivity in Husserl" and a rejoinder by Alfred Schutz. A French version (translated from the German by Maurice de Gandillac) can be found in *Husserl* (Cahiers de Royaumont, Philosophie No. III), Paris: Éditions de Minuit, 1959 together with comments by a number of philosophers and a reply by Alfred Schutz.

The Phenomenology of the Social World (a translation of *Der sinnhafte Aufbau der sozialen Welt* by George Walsh and Frederick Lehnert with an Introduction by George Walsh), Evanston: Northwestern University Press (Studies in Phenomenology and Existential Philosophy), 1967. Pp. xxix, 255.

Reflections on the Problem of Relevance (edited, annotated, and with an Introduction by Richard M. Zaner), New Haven: Yale University Press, 1970. Pp. xxiv, 186.
Note: A German translation is planned.

In Preparation:

Die Strukturen der Lebenswelt (edited and adapted by Thomas Luckmann). Note: An English translation is planned.

Helmut R. Wagner (Editor), *Alfred Schutz on Phenomenology and Social Relations*. A book of selections from the writings of Schutz with an introductory essay by the editor. To be published by the University of Chicago Press.

"Fragments on the Phenomenology of Music," in *Lifeworld and Consciousness: Essays in Honor of Aron Gurwitsch on his Seventieth Birthday* (edited by Lester Embree), Evanston: Northwestern University Press – to appear in 1971.

The following translations are planned: The *Collected Papers* into German, *Der sinnhafte Aufbau der sozialen Welt* into Italian, and all of Schutz's works into Spanish.

2. Edited Manuscripts:

Edmund Husserl, "Notizen zur Raumkonstitution," with a Preface by Alfred Schutz, *Philosophy and Phenomenological Research,* Vol. I, 1940, pp. 21–37 and 217–226.

Edmund Husserl, "Die Welt der lebendigen Gegenwart und die Konstitution der ausserleiblichen Umwelt," with a Preface by Alfred Schutz, *Philosophy and Phenomenological Research,* Vol. VI, 1946, pp. 323–343.

3. Unpublished Works:

Among Schutz's unpublished papers, the following are noteworthy: (a) Goethes Wilhelm Meisters Lehrjahre (27 pages) and Wilhelm Meisters Wanderjahre (142 pages); (b) Sinnstruktur der Novelle (Goethe) – about 50 pages; (c) Entwurf für eine Soziologie der Musik – a sketch; (d) Sinnstruktur der Sprache – a sketch; (e) Talcott Parsons' Theory of Social Action (74 pages) with a correspondence of 50 pages with Parsons from February 2, 1941 to March 17, 1941;

(f) Correspondence over many years with Eric Voegelin; (g) An essay on T. S. Eliot's Concept of Culture.

II. WORKS ABOUT SCHUTZ:

Note: Some early allusions to Schutz's *Der sinnhafte Aufbau der sozialen Welt* are to be found in: José Ortega y Gasset, *Man and People,* New York: Norton, 1963 (Spanish ed., 1957); Raymond Aron, *Introduction to the Philosophy of History,* Boston: Beacon Press, 1961 (French ed., 1938); Felix Kaufmann, *Methodology of the Social Sciences,* New York: Oxford University Press, 1944; Ludwig von Mises, *Human Action,* London: William Hodge, 1949. Among more recent works which refer to Schutz are (to cite a representative sample): Aaron V. Cicourel, *Method and Measurement in Sociology,* New York: Free Press, 1964; Amitai Etzioni, *The Active Society,* New York: Free Press, 1968; Richard M. Zaner, *The Problem of Embodiment,* The Hague: Martinus Nijhoff, 1964; Clifford Geertz, *Person, Time, and Conduct in Bali* (Yale University Southeast Asia Studies, 1966); Arnold Brecht, *Political Theory,* Princeton: Princeton University Press, 1959; I. S. Kon, *Der Positivismus in der Soziologie,* Berlin: Akademie-Verlag, 1968; Hans Peter Dreitzel, *Der gesellschaftlichen Leiden und das Leiden an der Gesellschaft,* Stuttgart: Ferdinand Enke Verlag, 1968; Knut Hanneborg, *The Study of Literature,* Oslo: Universitetsforlaget, 1967; Gerard Radnitzky, *Contemporary Schools of Metascience,* Vol. II, Göteborg: Akademiförlaget, 1968. Among the books which are strongly influenced by Schutz's ideas are: Peter L. Berger, *Invitation to Sociology,* Garden City, N.Y.: Doubleday, 1963; Peter L. Berger and Thomas Luckmann, *The Social Construction of Reality,* Garden City, N.Y.: Doubleday, 1966; Harold Garfinkel, *Studies in Ethnomethodology,* Englewood Cliffs, N. J. Prentice-Hall, 1967; Maurice Natanson, *The Journeying Self,* Reading, Mass.: Addison-Wesley, 1970; Gibson Winter, *Elements for A Social Ethic,* New York: Macmillan, 1966; Burkart Holzner, *Reality Construction in Society,* Cambridge, Mass.: Schenkman, 1968. The following list includes works which are either chiefly about or contain noteworthy passages on or especially interesting references to Schutz's thought.

1. Books and Articles

Raymond Aron, "The Philosophy of History," in *Philosophic Thought in France and the United States* (edited by Marvin Farber), 2nd ed., Albany: State University of New York Press, 1968, pp. 301–320.

G. H. Bantock, "Educational Research: A Criticism," *Harvard Educational Review,* Vol. XXXI, 1961, pp. 264–280. Reprinted in *Problems and Issues in Contemporary Education* (compiled by the Editors of the Teachers College Record and the Harvard Educational Review), Glenview, Ill.: Scott, Foresman, 1968.

Bedřich Baumann, "George H. Mead and Luigi Pirandello: Some Parallels between the Theoretical and Artistic Presentation of the Social Role Concept," *Social Research,* Vol. XXXIV, 1967, pp. 563–607.

Lewis White Beck, "Agent, Actor, Spectator, and Critic," *The Monist,* Vol. XLIX, 1965, pp. 167–182.

Robert Bierstedt, "The Common Sense World of Alfred Schutz," *Social Research,* Vol. XXX, 1963, pp. 116–121.

H. Taylor Buckner, "Transformations of Reality in the Legal Process," *Social Research,* Vol. XXXVII, 1970, pp. 88–101. Note: The first five essays of this issue of *Social Research* are published in commemoration of the tenth anniversary of the death of Alfred Schutz.

Robert W. Friedrichs, "Phenomenology as A 'General Theory' of Social Action," *Journal of Value Inquiry,* Vol. II, 1968, pp. 1–8.

Helmut Girndt, *Das soziale Handeln als Grundkategorie erfahrungswissenschaftlicher Soziologie,* Tübingen: Mohr, 1967.

Leon J. Goldstein, "The Phenomenological and Naturalistic Approaches to the Social," *Methodos,* Vol. XIII, 1961, pp. 225–238. Reprinted in *Philosophy of the Social Sciences: A Reader* (edited by Maurice Natanson), New York: Random House, 1963 and *Theory in Anthropology: A Sourcebook* (edited by Robert A. Manners and David Kaplan), Chicago: Aldine, 1968.

Aron Gurwitsch, "The Common-Sense World as Social Reality – A Discourse on Alfred Schutz," *Social Research,* Vol. XXIX, 1962, pp. 50–72. Reprinted as the Introduction to Collected Papers, Vol. III.

Aron Gurwitsch, *The Field of Consciousness,* Pittsburgh: Duquesne University Press, 1964. Note: This book is dedicated to Alfred Schutz.

Aron Gurwitsch, "Social Science and Natural Science," in *Economic Means and Social Ends: Essays in Political Economics* (edited by Robert L. Heilbroner), Englewood Cliffs, N.J.: Prentice-Hall, 1969, pp. 37–55.

Gerald A. Gutenschwager, "Social Reality and Social Change," *Social Research,* Vol. XXXVII, 1970, pp. 48–70.

Jürgen Habermas, *Zur Logik der Sozialwissenschaften,* Tübingen: Mohr, 1967.

Hansfried Kellner, "On the Sociolinguistic Perspective of the Communicative Situation," *Social Research,* Vol. XXXVII, 1970, pp. 71–87.

Fritz Machlup, "If Matter Could Talk," in *Philosophy, Science, and Method: Essays in Honor of Ernest Nagel* (edited by Sidney Morgenbesser, Patrick Suppes, Morton White), New York: St. Martin's Press, 1969, pp. 286–305.

Wilhelm E. Mühlmann, *Max Weber und die rationale Soziologie,* Tübingen: Mohr, 1966

Maurice Natanson, "Alfred Schutz," in *International Encyclopedia of the Social Sciences* (edited by David L. Sills), New York: Macmillan and Free Press, 1968, Vol. XIV, pp. 72–74.

Maurice Natanson, "Alfred Schutz on Social Reality and Social Science," *Social Research,* Vol. XXXV, 1968, pp. 217–244. Note: Reprinted in this volume.

Maurice Natanson, "The Phenomenology of Alfred Schutz," *Inquiry,* Vol. IX, 1966, pp. 147–155.

Maurice Natanson, "Phenomenology, Typification, and the World as Taken for Granted," in *Philomathēs: Studies and Essays in the Humanities in Memory of Philip Merlan* (edited by Robert B. Palmer and Robert Hamerton-Kelly), The Hague: Martinus Nijhoff, 1970, pp. 383–397.

Maurice Natanson, "Phenomenology and Typification: A Study in the Philosophy of Alfred Schutz," *Social Research,* Vol. XXXVII, 1970, pp. 1–22. Note: The Alfred Schutz Memorial Lecture of the American Philosophical Association, presented at the Graduate Faculty of the New School for Social Research, New York City, November 7, 1969.

Maurice Natanson, *The Social Dynamics of George H. Mead,* (with an Introduction by Horace M. Kallen) Washington: D. C.: Public Affairs Press, 1956. Note: This book is a condensed version of a doctoral dissertation directed by Alfred Schutz at the Graduate Faculty of the New School for Social Research, and it is dedicated, in part, to him.

Hans P. Neisser, "The Phenomenological Approach in Social Science," *Philosophy and Phenomenological Research,* Vol. XX, 1959, pp. 198–212.

George Psathas, "Ethnomethods and Phenomenology," *Social Research,* Vol. XXXV, 1968, pp. 500–520.

Albert Salomon, "German Sociology" in *Twentieth Century Sociology* (edited by Georges Gurvitch and Wilbert E. Moore), New York: Philosophical Library, 1945, pp. 586–614.

Larry Shiner, "A Phenomenological Approach to Historical Knowledge," *History and Theory,* Vol. VIII, 1969, pp. 260–274.

Herbert Spiegelberg, *The Phenomenological Movement,* 2 vols., 2nd ed., The Hague: Martinus Nijhoff, 1965. Note: This work is dedicated to Alfred Schutz.

Alfred Stonier and Karl Bode, "A New Approach to the Methodology of the Social Sciences," *Economica,* New Series, Vol. IV, 1937, pp. 406–424.

Michael Theunissen, *Der Andere,* Berlin: Walter de Gruyter, 1965.

Anna-Teresa Tymieniecka, *Phenomenology and Science in Contemporary European Thought* (with a Foreword by I. M. Bochenski), New York: Noonday Press, 1962.

Eric Voegelin, "In Memoriam Alfred Schutz" and "Brief an Alfred Schutz über Edmund Husserl," in *Anamnesis,* Munich: Piper Verlag, 1966, pp. 17–36.

Helmut R. Wagner, "Phenomenology and Contemporary Sociological Theory: The Contribution of Alfred Schutz," *Sociological Focus*, Vol. II, 1969, pp. 73–86. Note: Professor Wagner is also working on a book-length study of the thought of Schutz, tentatively entitled *Phenomenological Sociology*.

Richard M. Zaner, "Dedication Speech: Alfred Schutz Memorial," *New School Bulletin*, Vol. XXVII, No. 3, October 1, 1969, pp. 12–14.

Richard M. Zaner, "Theory of Intersubjectivity: Alfred Schutz," *Social Research*, Vol. XXVIII, 1961, pp. 71–93.

Anton C. Zijderveld, "Rationality and Irrationality in Pluralistic Society," *Social Research*, Vol. XXXVII, 1970, pp. 23–47.

2. Dissertations

Hans Schermann, Phänomenologie und Sozialwissenschaft: Die phänomenologische Fundierung der Wissenschaften bei Alfred Schutz (Mémoire en vue de l'obtention du grade de Licencié en philosophie), University of Louvain, 1965. Pp. 82 (unpublished).

Maurice Collins, Alfred Schutz: Intersubjective Understanding (M.A. thesis in progress, McMaster University).

Thomas Anicetus Aykara, Philosophy of the Social World according to Alfred Schutz (doctoral dissertation in progress, University of Louvain).

H. John Harris, Problems of Intersubjectivity in the Work of Alfred Schutz (Ph. D. dissertation in progress, University of California, San Diego).

W. Dwight Oberholtzer, Alfred Schutz's "Multiple Realities" and Its Implications for Social Ethics (Ph. D. dissertation in progress, The Graduate Theological Union, Berkeley, California).

3. Reviews

A. *Der sinnhafte Aufbau der sozialen Welt:*

Felix Kaufmann, *Deutsche Literaturzeitung*, Vol. LIII, 1932, pp. 1712–1716.

Helen Knight, "Philosophy in Germany," *Philosophy*, Vol. VIII, 1933 (a survey of works by a number of authors, with the review of Schutz on pp. 95–96).

Paul Plaut, *Zeitschrift für angewandte Psychologie*, Vol. XLIV, 1933. A survey of many books, with comments on Schutz on p. 450.

J. Gerhardt, *Jahrbücher für Nationalokonomie und Statistik*, Vol. CXL, 1934, pp. 614–616.

S. Rudolf Steinmetz, "Neuere soziologische Literatur," *Weltwirtschaftliches Archiv*, Vol. XL. 1934 (a review of several books, with comments on Schutz on pp. 4–5).

J. Tonneau, *Revue des sciences philosophiques et théologiques,* Vol. XXIII, 1934, (a survey of works by a number of authors, with comments on Schutz on pp. 300–301).

Eric Voegelin, *Zeitschrift für öffentliches Recht,* Vol. XIV, 1934, pp. 668–672.

B. *Collected Papers,* Volume I: *The Problem of Social Reality:*

Robert M. Barry, *International Philosophical Quarterly,* Vol. III, 1963, pp. 465–473.

Leon J. Goldstein, *Journal of Philosophy,* Vol. LX, 1963, pp. 557–562.

V. J. McGill, *Philosophy and Phenomenological Research,* Vol. XXIV, 1963, pp. 282–283.

James Wilkins, *The American Journal of Sociology,* Vol. LXIX, 1964, pp. 429–430.

C. *Collected Papers,* Volume II: *Studies in Social Theory:*

Llewellyn Gross, *American Journal of Sociology,* Vol. LXXI, 1965, pp. 336–337.

Ernest M. Kuhinka, *Social Forces,* Vol. XLIII, 1965, pp. 584–585.

Leon J. Goldstein, *Journal of Philosophy,* Vol. LXIII, 1966, pp. 190–196.

D. *Collected Papers* (Volumes I and II):

Quentin Lauer, *Erasmus,* Vol. XVII, 1965, pp. 577–579.

E. *Collected Papers,* Volume III, *Studies in Phenomenological Philosophy:*

J. (oseph) J. R. (omano), *The Review of Metaphysics,* Vol. XX, 1967, p. 548.

Quentin Lauer, *Erasmus,* Vol. XX, 1968, pp. 453–454.

F. *Collected Papers* (the 3 volumes)

Jovan Brkić, "Methodological Problems of Sociology – A Review Essay," *Sociologia Internationalis,* Vol. VI, 1968, pp. 105–110.

G. *The Phenomenology of the Social World:*

Egon Bittner, *American Sociological Review,* Vol. XXXIII, 1968, pp. 639–641.

Karsten Harries, *Journal of Value Inquiry,* Vol. IV, 1970, pp. 65–75.

Hwa Yol Jung, *American Political Science Review,* Vol. LXII, 1968, pp. 614–616.

Herbert Lamm, *American Journal of Sociology,* Vol. LXXIII, 1968, (reviewed with another book, the material on Schutz appearing on pp. 779–780).

Choice, Vol. V, 1968, p. 880.

4. Memorial Notices

Aron Gurwitsch, *Philosophy and Phenomenological Research,* Vol. XX, 1959, pp. 141–143.

Hans Jonas, *Social Research,* Vol. XXVI, 1959, pp. 471–474.

Thomas Luckmann, *Kölner Zeitschrift für Soziologie und Sozialpsychologie,* Vol. XIII, 1961, pp. 768–770.

Aron Gurwitsch, *Proceedings and Addresses of the American Philosophical Association,* Vol. XXXVII, 1964, pp. 124–125.